For Virginia W. Callam____
As a sign of gratitude
from her friend & disciple
William Sebastian H.
21st September, 1960

Rembrandt's 'Anatomy of Dr. Nicolaas Tulp'

Rembrandt's ANATOMY OF DR. NICOLAAS TULP

AN ICONOLOGICAL STUDY

WILLIAM S. HECKSCHER

WASHINGTON SQUARE · NEW YORK UNIVERSITY PRESS · 1958

© 1958 by William S. Heckscher

Library of Congress Catalog Card Number: 57-6374

Printed in Switzerland by Buehler Press, Zurich

To Dora and Erwin Panofsky

Contents

Acknowledgments

An art historical study that ranges over a variety of fields and is conducted by a single person must necessarily rely on outside assistance. It was my good fortune to find in a great many disciplines, including my own, specialists willing to come to my aid.

Above all I wish to express gratitude to those among my colleagues who have read the manuscript or parts of it. I am indebted to Erwin Panofsky for the unique blend of encouragement and doubt with which, over the last ten years, he has fortified and chastened me in the pursuit of my investigation. Erwin and Dora Panofsky, in their different ways, have been guiding lights as friends and as scholars. My friend H. W. Janson has invested much of his energy and experience in the production of this book; his time-consuming critical readings of the manuscript have spared me and the reader the embarrassment of many a blunder and awkwardness.

I am grateful to I. E. Drabkin for advice about classical medicine and for criticism of some of my translations from the Latin. Miss I. H. van Eeghen has aided me expertly with regard to archival problems of seventeenth-century Amsterdam. J. G. van Gelder allowed me to benefit by his knowledge of Rembrandt's formative years in particular and of Dutch art and art theory in general. A. B. de Vries allowed me to inspect the research material and data, gathered by him at the Mauritshuis, on which he based the strategy of his excellent plan of restoration; he enabled me to interrogate J. C. Traas, who gave me the fullest report on various data brought to light in the course of his successful cleaning of the "Anatomy."

The following have been generous in assisting and advising me with specific problems: William Brockbank allowed me to inspect his manuscript on anatomical theaters; Julius S. Held supplied material on public anatomies in seventeenth-century Holland; Philip Hofer permitted the long-term loan of rare books; Edward E. Lowinsky supplied information on musicology; A. Hyatt Mayor discussed with me art and anatomy; Curt Proskauer enlightened me on historical anatomical problems; Seymour Slive advised me on problems concerned with Rembrandt's fame; Jhr Six van Wimmenum supplied information on his distinguished ancestor, Nicolaas Tulp; H. van de Waal supplied photographs and information on seventeenth-century scientific illustrations.

For advice on Rembrandt's anatomical blunder (William B. Goddard was the first to explain it to me) I thank the following physicians: Oscar V. Batson, Mrs. M. Emmens-

Vijlbrief, and Myron Hofer II. Philip Cohen drew my attention to signs of *rigor mortis* of het Kint that happily corroborated one of my assumptions.

I gratefully list a number of those who have decisively helped, above all by acquainting me with and by providing bibliographical and other data or photographic and other research material as well as permission to publish such material: Walter Artelt, E. Haverkamp Begemann, Harry Bober, William Burke, Mrs. Anna Maria Cetto, Charles F. Comfort, His Excellency the Canadian Ambassador Pierre Dupuy, Miss Shirley Eliason, J. A. Emmens, Frh. H. M. von Erffa, Giuseppe Fiocco, J. W. Frederiks, The Hon. K. Fremantle, Miss Eleanor Garvey, J.-Y. Grenon, Evert van der Grinten, Mrs. Carl Wallis von Helmolt, Miss J. D. Hintzen, Miss Marie-Germaine Hogan, R. A. d'Hulst, J. H. Jongkees, Enrico Josi, C. H. Kruyskamp, G. I. Lieftinck, Millard Meiss, Ulrich Middeldorf, Lino Moretti, W. H. M. Mutsaers, Charles Parkhurst, E. Pelinck, Howard C. Rice, Miss Judith Sachs, Miss Margaretta M. Salinger, Miss Dorothy M. Schullian, H. Schulte Nordholt, Marc Sieber, Mrs. M. J. H. Singelenberg-van der Meer, G. and F. Staack, Wolfgang Stechow, Mrs. K. Trauman Steinitz, Mrs. Lola L. Szladits, Miss Marianne Vater, Paul W. Ver-Vrais, Miss Leonie von Wilckens, Miss Helen M. Wright.

I wish to express thanks to the Director, to the permanent members, and to the staff of the Institute for Advanced Study at Princeton; repeated membership grants have enabled me to acquire and evaluate my material under the most ideal circumstances any scholar could hope for. Of the many institutes and libraries that at one time or another have assisted me, I should like to name especially: the American Academy in Rome (Laurance P. Roberts, Principessa Rospigliosi), the British Museum, the Kunsthistorisch Instituut at Utrecht (Misses Y. Hoykaas and H. Noë, E. Reznicek, P. Singelenberg), the New York Academy of Medicine (Miss Gertrude L. Annan, Miss Janet Doe), the New York Public Library (division: the Henry W. and Albert A. Berg Collection), the Princeton University Library (Howard C. Rice), and the Wellcome Historical Medical Library, London (F. N. L. Poynter, C. H. Talbot, E. Ashworth Underwood). The Board of Curators of the University of Utrecht have given me every imaginable help for travel. Dean Walter F. Loehwing of the State University of Iowa has granted me secretarial help. Publication of the book has been assisted by a grant from the Bollingen Foundation. Harry N. Abrams, Inc., has generously lent the plates for the frontispiece.

It has been my privilege to lecture on "Rembrandt's 'Anatomy'" at the following institutions: the University of Delaware; the Rijksbureau voor Kunsthistorische Documentatie in The Hague; the University of Lincoln, Nebraska; New York University; the Journal Club, Princeton University; University College, Toronto; the Ikon Club, Utrecht; and the University of Manitoba.

Utrecht, January 1957   William S. Heckscher

Rembrandt's 'Anatomy of Dr. Nicolaas Tulp'

Introduction

And thus through the Art of Painting, the face
of someone—long since dead—may keep on living
(L. B. Alberti, *Della pittura*, II)

Sicut optimi Oratores ac Poetae,
ita Pictores quoque & docent, &
delectant, & permovent

Dus blijckt het . . . dat de gheleghenheyd der Schilders
met de ghelegenheyd van d'Orateuren ende Poeten t'eenemael over een komt;
aenghesien het hun . . . ghelijckelick toestaet t'onderwijsen, te vermaecken, te beweghen

For it goeth heere with painters, as it goeth with orators and Poëts,
they must all teach, delight, and moove
(Franciscus Junius, III, vii, § 2) [262, 263, 264]*

This book offers a great variety of material and documentation, representational as well as literary, in support of the iconological analysis of a single work of art. Yet this amassment appears to me only a small part of what might legitimately have been gathered from an *embarras du choix*. Even where I may seemingly remove myself and my willing reader from the theme indicated by the title, it was my intention to concentrate on material and documentation that would in the end help to deepen our appreciation of this one work of art: Rembrandt's painting of the "Anatomy of Dr. Nicolaas Tulp."

In the first and last chapters I have tried to isolate and interpret social and cultural trends that prevailed in the city of Amsterdam in the early 1630's, to illuminate the time and the place that had witnessed the birth of Rembrandt's first great painting. The rest of my book is devoted to an attempt to place Rembrandt's work in the stream of an artistic and scientific tradition that extends from about 1480 to about 1780.

My study was undertaken in the belief that every great work of art, apart from its forever changing aesthetic appeal to posterity, is an unchanging mirror of its cultural ambient. This is the reason why I have done my best to interpret Rembrandt's painting in terms used by the cultured people in his Amsterdam environment who "talked art" while he realized it. The motto that I have used for this Introduction represents the Latin, Dutch,

* Superior numbers in brackets refer to the Bibliography (p. 193).

3

and English versions of one and the same theoretical dictum about art by Franciscus Junius. These words, as the author makes quite plain, are already found in Cicero and other classical authors treating of rhetoric. Such pronouncements were anything but esoteric in Rembrandt's day; they reflect an attitude that I shall refer to repeatedly by the term "baroque." At the same time I have done my best to steer clear of the professional terms of modern aesthetics and of modern connoisseurship, which I consider one of the most powerful barriers that we have placed between ourselves and historical art. My use of the word "baroque," however, shows that I am neither able nor willing to adhere to my self-imposed rule with absolute rigidity. My book is intended as a study of Rembrandt's contribution to the genesis of the Dutch Baroque. My analysis of the painting is an attempt to show by what means Rembrandt tried to express the chief aims of art as formulated by his distinguished compatriot and contemporary, Franciscus Junius, an archaeologist and philologist whom the Dutch poet Vondel had praised as "the painters' right hand." I believe that many particulars help to show that Rembrandt himself, by means of his "Anatomy of Dr. Tulp," wished nothing more than to "teach, delight, and moove," "t'onderwijsen, te vermaecken, te beweghen."

Rembrandt was at all times deeply involved with tradition. In connection with this particular work we must not forget that a good many representations of formal anatomical sessions had preceded it. Without wishing to question Rembrandt's originality, we must state that his painting belongs to a tradition that is both literary and formal. We cannot expect to do justice to Rembrandt unless we realize that his "Anatomy" is deeply though by no means slavishly indebted to the past and that it is full of meaning to subsequent times. The range of my investigation has been widened on account of the inescapable impression that Rembrandt's sharp on-the-spot observation in the *theatra anatomica* of Leiden and Amsterdam (which were theaters of demonstration as well as musea of oddities) goes hand in hand with his unsurpassed ability to comprehend and to record what I shall show to be the philosophical and psychological overtones of Renaissance anatomies.

We may assume that Rembrandt, once the commission for his painting had been negotiated, began by examining the pictorial prototypes at his disposal, that he looked at the one or two earlier group portraits of anatomists painted in Holland, that he inspected once more the art treasures that were exhibited in the anatomical theaters, and that he turned to the woodcut illustrations of the anatomical atlases. Finally we can be certain that Rembrandt visited the public anatomies and that, like any other intelligent Dutchman, he knew that they, like his pictorial record of one of them, were designed to "instruct, to entertain, and to move."

Rembrandt's "Anatomy of Dr. Tulp" is a group portrait. Like all such paintings it was painted on commission. The terms of this commission would of course stipulate that

Rembrandt should faithfully portray the members (called *overlieden*) who administered the professional corporation known as the Guild of Surgeon-Anatomists of Amsterdam. Yet not more than two of those appearing in Rembrandt's painting were serving as foremen (see Appendix III). This suggests that in spite of its official character the painting was paid not out of guild funds but by members and their new anatomist individually. These people wished to see themselves presented one by one as distinguished individuals and yet as a tightly knit group, sharing high ideals, civic as well as scientific. The painter was to record them at their annual lesson. This kind of gathering was anything but private and secluded. The scene that the picture reveals is in fact a portion out of a larger prospect presented to the people of Amsterdam. The anatomy as enacted by Dr. Tulp and pictorially rendered by Rembrandt was part of a dramatic play that in all its particulars was carefully rehearsed with a view to its public *mise-en-scène*. In a tableau of this kind the guild members, hovering about the guild anatomist and the cadaver, although forming a distinct unit were never secluded from the larger prospect that we must seek beyond the frame of Rembrandt's canvas; the people appearing on the canvas occupy the light-flooded stage that forms the center of the anatomical theater. That Dr. Tulp's theater was makeshift and anything but satisfactory need not concern us at present. The guild members portrayed by Rembrandt occupied the most privileged seats; but as truly as they occupied those seats to observe for themselves, they were also there to be observed. They were privileged, but not to the point of being allowed to obscure procedures to the rest of the audience. An anatomical theater of the seventeenth century was designed to accommodate, under favorable circumstances, from two to three hundred persons. We must therefore try to visualize the presence of a numerous audience in Rembrandt's painting. We cannot doubt its presence as we fasten our attention on Dr. Tulp; he clearly addresses himself to persons outside his inner circle. His eyes roam over that part of the created illusion that we may describe as "our side" of the picture plane. To make that part of the audience come to life we must range in our imagination from the local intelligentsia to the physicians, from the apothecaries to the professors-elect of Amsterdam's new academy of Arts and Sciences, from curious foreign visitors to artists, such as Rembrandt himself, commissioned to record the great event, and from there, finally, to the multitude of Amsterdam's amorphous population. These were people with a vast stomach for all kinds of entertainment, among which the annual public anatomy ranked perhaps highest.

To every one of the two to three hundred individuals who might witness the dissection, the pleasantly morbid actuality of the festive anatomy must have been, year after year, a unique and exciting experience. While naturally the anatomy was a lesson in the first place, it also appealed in Rembrandt's time to those craving dramatic entertainment as well as those in quest of quiet transcendental contemplation.

Rembrandt has made himself the recording eye of this multifarious audience. Focusing on the stage proper, he makes sure that we do not lose sight of the two leads among the *dramatis personae*: first, the maestro with his fine black top hat, forceps in his right hand while he indicates speech with his left—Dr. Nicolaas Pieterszoon Tulpius, the great and respected scientist and physician whose keen eyes range far over the spectators while his hands hover above the corpse; secondly, stressed in terms of light and shade, this corpse itself, the body of a young man who in his lifetime was known as *het Kint* (Aris Kindt), a criminal freshly executed who had constantly been at war with society and whose eyes, closed forever, are now mercifully covered by the shadow of the surgeon who is shown leaning eagerly forward in the direction of the open folio in the far right corner.

From the painting, Rembrandt's first group portrait and at the same time his first major commission, there emerges the image of a young artist eager to establish his reputation. Rembrandt had, as we know, just succeeded in withstanding the lure of the Italian journey that, we may conjecture, he felt threatened to ensnare him with the formalism as well as the themes of Neoclassicism. Yet we should not jump to the conclusion that thereby he had turned his back on the conventions of his day. On the contrary. Much of what distinguishes Rembrandt's "Anatomy" from his earlier work and from that of his less advanced contemporaries is the direct result of his endeavor to express the dictates of the art theory that just at this time was being formulated by his powerful patrons at Amsterdam. Holland's mentors of taste were such men as Constantine Huygens, Barlaeus, Hooft, Gerard Vossius, and Tulp himself; whether they were statesmen, city magistrates, professors, theologians, or members of the professions, they often dabbled, and not without skill, in one or more of the four arts that they felt were subsumed under one valid set of rules: poetry and rhetoric, music and painting. Their ideas first appeared in print toward the end of the decade whose beginning had seen Rembrandt's arrival in Amsterdam. As we know, these rules had been discussed before Rembrandt came to Amsterdam. They were codified as it were in the most important art theoretical treatise of the Dutch Baroque: Franciscus Junius' *De pictura veterum*,[262] published in Amsterdam in 1637.

On account of its title this book has been regarded, much too one-sidedly, as a seventeenth-century forerunner of Johann Joachim Winckelmann's archaeological writings. Junius, as we have seen, stresses the role of the emotions in art. We must realize that other views existed beside his. Precisely in the early 1630's a significant countermovement was about to make itself felt: a rationalistic, antiemotional trend of distinctly Cartesian cast to which Rembrandt in some of his geometrically constructed portraits had paid his tribute. That Rembrandt in his "Anatomy" sided with Junius, who warned the artist not "to trouble his braine with every curious Geometricall demonstration," is evident. It would be hoping for too much if we expected ready documentation to show in what

6

manner Rembrandt might have gained access to the baroque art theory. One literary echo of it occurs indeed in one of his letters. We may, however, speculate on the following broader lines: The man who most likely introduced Rembrandt to Dr. Tulp was Caspar Barlaeus. Barlaeus and Gerard Vossius were the first professors of the newly founded academy of Amsterdam. The philologist Vossius, himself no mean art theoretician, was the brother-in-law of Franciscus Junius. We know that Vossius assisted Junius in the preparation of his book, many years before its actual appearance in print.

These art theoreticians hammered away at one basic theme whose tenor must have been most welcome to any ambitious artist. They preached the equality of painting with rhetoric and poetry. Painting as a mute form of poetry was not perfect unless it was rhetorical. Rembrandt at this critical point of his career must have been eager to place his craft on a solid theoretical foundation and thereby to advance his social status. I am certain that in compliance with the ideas that were rife in Amsterdam Rembrandt strove to enlighten and to move but above all to please others with his art. In the "Anatomy of Dr. Tulp" he made his first significant essay in the field of rhetorical art. His painting offers a fine example of what would be considered *l'art officiel* in the Amsterdam of the 1630's. The "Anatomy" was, after all, intended as a speaking tribute to the *renommée* of the ancient Guild of Surgeon-Anatomists. It was Rembrandt's first attempt to portray someone in the act of addressing a group of attentive listeners.

At the same time his painting was intended, I think, as an acknowledgment of the entry of the city into a new phase of her cultural existence. Early in 1632 Amsterdam had witnessed the founding of the Athenaeum Illustre, the school that was the nucleus of Amsterdam's university. Aris Kindt was executed, portrayed by Rembrandt, and anatomized by Dr. Tulp in the very month in which Caspar Barlaeus pronounced his inaugural oration for the new school: January 1632. In the light of this chronological coincidence we may consider the possibility that Rembrandt's painting had expressly been commissioned as a reminder of the function and merit of the ancient guild whose members and above all whose *praelector,* Dr. Tulp himself, would soon find their prestige enhanced by the presence of the Athenaeum in their midst. With the granting of a charter to the Athenaeum, science and commerce had entered, as was handsomely expressed on the occasion by Barlaeus, into a state of fruitful matrimony. Dr. Tulp was not only Amsterdam's chief anatomist but also a city councilor and a future governor *(curator)* of the city's new university.

Rembrandt's painting was above all a contribution to the fame or, the term more commonly applied in his own time, the *memoria* of those represented in it. We may take it for granted that the success of a painting of this magnitude depended to a large degree on the willing co-operation and collaboration with the painter of those represented in it.

The degree of the intellectual contribution of Dr. Tulp cannot easily be overrated. The part he played in the painting speaks of the advice of an historian of anatomy. The painting serves as an eloquent eulogy of the chief model, to whom it assigns an honored place on the ladder up which anatomical science had progressed. The anatomical detail has here for the first time in an anatomical painting ceased to serve as mere staffage or professional attribute, as we see in the significant role that Rembrandt has assigned to the human hand, dissecting and dissected. This emphasis undoubtedly was meant as a pun, leading from the "hand" to "him that works manually" and from there to the Greek word *cheirourgos* (surgeon), which means just this.

Rembrandt's painting, inherently as well as on account of its theme, stands *sub specie mortis*. The portrait as an art form is from the beginning closely linked with the idea of death. Rembrandt, like all the great postmediaeval portraitists, made himself the recording angel of the haunting dilemma that a new concept of death had imposed on the Renaissance. As has been suggested before, the realistic portrait of the modern age came about as a countermeasure against the threat of ultimate destruction under which each individual spends his days. This fear was the result of the rise of a scientific concept of death that had not existed in the scholastic age. Though no one doubted the immortality of man's soul, one had learned to see the permanence of the individual's personality as an integral part of man's external appearance. This was forever menaced by the forces of death. Sculptors and painters, from the early fifteenth century onward, would be commissioned to record man's perishable appearance in order to safeguard against the grasp of death. The well-known ordinance (1403) comes to mind by which Louis, Duc d'Orléans, commanded "que la remembrance de mon visage et de mes mains soit faicte sur ma tombe en guise de mort" and Alberti's dictum (see Motto).

In a poem called "On the Anatomical Table" (for which see *infra* pp. 113 f.) Barlaeus reflects on how "life's thread is cut by an enemy forever different." Here, as elsewhere in the poem, Barlaeus appears as the true spokesman of the inner circle of surgeons and anatomist occupying Rembrandt's stage. They sought immortality when they commissioned Rembrandt to represent them for all times to come as a group in contemplation of death, of its various causes and effects, of its physiological and its moral aspects. Naturally such reflections would simultaneously lead to a deeper understanding of the phenomenon of life itself.

While considering all this, Rembrandt was certainly also aware of the *communis et vulgaris opinio* that saw in the public anatomy the crowning chapter of the punishment of a pathetic Everyman whose corpse was so callously displayed before the eyes of fascinated spectators, each one of whom felt, dumbly or articulately, that he witnessed a cathartic ritual enacted for his own good.

Rembrandt's painting faithfully records a scientific lesson; in this respect it is above all an artistic landmark in the history of medicine. It is also a homily preached on the theme of the ultimate triumph of science over evil. That that is so we can appreciate when we realize that Rembrandt cast a very rosy-cheeked Dr. Tulp and a very pale cadaver into the form of a type of tomb memorial that was abounding all over Europe. In those memorials the deceased would occur twice: as the realistic portrait bust of a keen-eyed living person, presiding as it were over his own mortal remains, shown as a more or less putrefied or desiccated cadaver.

The Rembrandt of the early 1630's will, I hope, emerge from this study as a veritable Janus, speaking to us through the "Anatomy of Dr. Tulp" with equal authority of the past and of the future, of the present and of the hereafter.

Superior numbers refer to the Notes (p. 123); superior numbers in brackets refer to the Bibliography (p. 193).

The 'Anatomy' and Amsterdam—A.D. 1632

Hier leeft de ziel van Hollant's staet
(Vondel on Amsterdam)

The recent cleaning of Rembrandt's "Anatomy of Dr. Nicolaas Tulp" in the Maurits-huis in The Hague calls for a reconsideration of form and meaning of this much discussed painting.[1] (Pls. I, V–7, and XLVIII–57.) Many particulars hitherto invisible or distorted have been revealed. Two of the portrait busts (the one farthest left and the topmost one) appear not to be by Rembrandt, although they seem to have been added in his lifetime; the face of Tulp himself seems to have been tampered with in the eighteenth century; numerous pentimenti by Rembrandt's own hand are suggestive of his tireless striving for perfection of his composition; the background has become more distinct, although much of the architectonic structure remains a puzzle. Superficially seen, the changes wrought are less spectacular than those that recently transformed the "Night Watch" into a "Day Watch"; yet I believe that from the art historian's point of view they are far more important. The painting is signed and dated: "*Rembrant.* (H[armensz.] L[eijdensis]?) *ft.: 1632.*" The original letters have reappeared in their authentic form underneath repeated refreshings. The inscription is found on a rolling screen suspended from the far wall. Similar screens had occurred frequently as background decorations behind portrait groups of the early sixteenth century. The document bearing Rembrandt's signature looks like an announcement that, under two or three lines constituting a heading, introduction, or title of some kind, consists of three columns of printed matter, each of approximately twenty lines. This may be either a copy of the printed announcement of this specific Anatomy or an ordinance issued by authority of the Guild of Surgeons of Amsterdam. The latter kind of document served to regulate the conduct of those attending anatomical lessons. The texts of such ordinances are known and will be referred to later. As to the former, we know that printed announcements were used for the grand anatomies. Like all ephemeral publications of the Renaissance, such anatomical broadsheets or *affiches* are scarce. For example, only one Elizabethan *affiche* announcing a play (one that, characteristically enough, was never performed) has come down to us. Only one announcement of a public

LECTORI BENEVOLO
OFFICIOSAM SALUTEM.

I quis Abderitarum *forte fit indole & ingenio. qui in differtionibus* Anatomicis *occupatos cum* Democrito *nos peßime agere, non dicam, infanire ftatuat, is vel fe ipfum infanire* Hippocraticum *fibi habeat judicium & fententiam.* Nobis *ad mandatum Sereniffimi* ELECTORIS *Cancellarii & Nutritii hujus* Academiæ *noftræ perpetui, ad opera Naturæ arcana accuratius indaganda, ad* Facultatis *noftræ* Medicæ *commodum, famam & exiftimationem religiose juvandam & tutandam, aliter non incumbit, nifi omne noftrum ftudium omnem que in partibus* Humani Corporis *ritè affecandis, r mandis ac cognofcendis laborem noftrum collocare & impendere. Intuitu enim potius, quod inquit* Medicinæ Parens *nofter* Galenus, *lib. 1. de Ufu partium cp. 17. talia affequi licet, quam verbis doceri; utpote quod* ἐδ᾽ ἱκανῶς δύναται ἐκτυπῶσαι λόγος ἐδεὶς, ὅτως ἀκριβῶς, ὡς ἀ ὄψις; *nulla oratio tàm accuratè defcribere poßit quicquam eorum, quæ fub fenfum cadunt, quàm fenfus ipfe & tactus, fecundum effatum ipfius, libr feq. c 8.*

Hujus officii noftri non potuimus non meminiffe, cum ad operas hafce Anatomicas *tractandas* Corpus *hefterna die decolli* Mafculinum *impetraverimus.*

Ne autem illud pro noftris tantummodò, ad quos quidem primariò fpectat & per inet, privatim invide affervemus, confultum fuit, & omnes alios qui demonftratione & cognitione Suiipfius delectantur, in Theatrum Anatomicum *admittere. Quibus igitur intereffe per aliquot dies placitum fuerit, ii, redemta prius ab* Anatomico *pro more & refundendis fumptibus* Teffera *horâ I ma pomeridiana ad initium demonftrationum futurarum intromittuntur.* Magnifici verò Academiæ RECTOR & ORDINARIUS, *nec non reliqui* PATRES *confcripti* DOCTORES, LICENTIATI *Artifque* Medicæ FAUTORES, *ut fplendidißima fui præfenti ftudiis hifce & laboribus noftris ad illuftriorem multò reddendum confeffum favere velint, maximo rogantur opere. Die X.* Martii, *Anno* M DC XLVI.

Johannes Hoppius, Phil. & Med. Doctor,
Cheirurgiæ & Anatom. Profeffor
Publicus.

LIPSIÆ.
Typis HENNINGI COLERI.

Fig. 1a. "Lectori Benevolo." Affiche[2] inviting to a public anatomy at Leipzig, March 10, 1646 (Städtisches Museum, Zwickau).

MARTINVS BOGDANVS.
DOCTOR MEDICINÆ,
ET
FACVLTATIS HVIVSDEM IN
Almà Bafileenfium Adfeffor.

S. P. P.

C. L.

LLVSTRISSIMI NOSTRI MAGISTRA-
tus beneficio, Tibi, quisquis curiofior fueris intuen-
dum proponam, quæ Natura in nobis omnibus oc-
clufit.   Neutiquam quod Dei opus odio profequi
videor, fed ut Te ipfum noveris, dum luftrabis oculis & auribus utrumque Palatium in fequiori fexu.
Scilicet & id, in quo tuum Spiritum primum concepifti, & id in
quo idem, quamdiu vivis, habitat.   Digito id Tibi monftrabo, juxta
ἐνχείρεσιν mei Præceptoris Cl. Thomæ Bartholini in Danià Medici &
Anatomici fummi.   Imo quid in quovis receffu penitiori agatur,
breviter & folidè oretenus exponam.   Si vis adeffe, ædes habebis liberas Alberti Baurenköningi Chirurgi, cras hora primà pomeridia-
nà, & in pofterum quâvis die.   Cæterum optime Vale, & Fave.
Bernæ Helvetiorum.

Anno Chrifti   M.   DC.   LX.
XIIX. Decembr.

Fig. 1b.   Broadside issued by Martinus B. Bogdanus[58] inviting to an extraordinary "Anatomia publica,"
Berne, December 18, 1660.

anatomy (Leipzig, 1646)[2] has been published: a printed document in the Städtisches Museum at Zwickau, Saxony (Fig. 1a). Another document[58] (Fig. 1b) represents the invitation to an extraordinary public demonstration. Since it is, as far as I know, unrecorded and since it contains allusions to certain aspects of the anatomical lesson that have some bearing on Rembrandt's composition, I shall let a translation follow here:

> Martinus Bogdanus, Doctor of Medicine and Associate of the Faculty of Medicine in the University of Basel, greetings to all who may read this. By the favor of our distinguished magistrates I shall reveal to the sight of any of you who are curious to see what Nature has enshrined in all of us. Not out of a desire to vent malice upon the work of God [the cadaver being that of an evildoer] but so that you may come to know yourself when you examine with eyes and ears [referring to lecture and practical demonstration combined] the two palaces in the inferior sex. To wit the one [i.e. the womb] in which you first received your soul, and the other [i.e. the rest of the body] in which this soul resides as long as you live. I shall point out these things to you with the help of the manual skill [should read: εὐχείρισιν, i.e. the art of anatomy] of my teacher, the famous Thomas Bartolinus [1616–80], foremost anatomist and physician in Denmark. Indeed, what goes on in every inner recess, up to the mouth, I shall explain briefly and thoroughly. If you wish to be present, you will be welcome at the house of the surgeon Albert Baurenköning, tomorrow at 1 p.m. and on any convenient day thereafter. Farewell and be well-disposed. Berne, Switzerland, December 18, 1660.[2]

The recent cleaning has enabled me to make one important discovery: There has appeared an anatomical design underneath the rather crude roll call held by Hartman Hartmansz., one of the attendant surgeons; it is partly covered by the right shoulder of Dr. Tulp. This shows, I believe, a woodcut representing the dissected arm and hand, and the roll call sheet, it turns out, is the left (verso) page of an anatomical atlas of uncertain measurements. This conjecture will be discussed at a suitable point (see pp. 67 f. *infra*).

Finally a few observations are called for as to the anatomical chamber and its accessories. I would mention here that, to me at least, certain structural details in the painting remain oddly and attractively obscure. For example, I fail to see whether the tunnel vault touches the back wall or whether it leaves space, left and right, where the lateral walls (containing shell niches and supporting the tunnel vault) end. Such outlets, though quite possible, are by no means necessary. There exists in the painting one unmistakable outlet to the right. This appeared as a result of the recent cleaning underneath a thick layer of brown paint that had been deliberately applied by a restorer. We see, most prominent of all, an iron ring doing service as a doorknob as well as part of the massively worked door itself. This discovery is not unimportant. It hints strongly that the stage suggested by Rembrandt is anything but purely a child of his fantasy; that it is more likely the faithful representation of the interim theater (1619–39) in which the anatomical lesson of Dr. Tulp took place. History has used every imaginable trick to erase the last vestiges of this particular site, in spite of the fact that the stately building at the New Market in Amsterdam that housed the anatomy is still standing. It is said that this anatomical theater was situated somewhere in the upper floor (of the south tower, still standing) of the St. Anthony Gate (from the seventeenth century onward known as the *Waaggebouw*). This is a fortified place, erected in 1488 and in the course of the sixteenth and especially the seventeenth centuries repeatedly rebuilt and enlarged. The present arrangement of the south tower interior, especially its windows and doors, can in no way be harmonized with the data of the interior shown in Rembrandt's painting. Such features as we can make out, especially the vastness of the far wall, rather point to the ground floor of the building, at least in its present late seventeenth-century state. Quite a different anatomical theater, on the other hand, that of 1690 ff., has left more distinct traces; it occupies gallery and dome of the present Jewish Historical Museum. Except for a copy of the old inscription by Caspar Barlaeus, it has, however, nothing whatever to do with the Rembrandt-Tulp theater of 1632.

The cleaning of the painting has done even more than reveal certain significant particulars hitherto obliterated or obscured. It has given us a new conception of Rembrandt's style of painting. Being the first major work that Rembrandt produced after having settled down in Amsterdam, the "Anatomy" of the Mauritshuis may be called the incarnation of his stylistic achievement of the early 1630's. Genetically speaking, the "Anatomy" is a *novum*. There is in Rembrandt's work preceding it hardly any indication of what we might call preparatory steps. The work itself, as Dr. de Vries will show in his report on the cleaning of the painting, had proceeded laboriously until its more or less ideal form, as we can now partly see it and almost wholly reconstruct it, had emerged. A listing of the newly revealed stylistic elements must begin with a reference to the composition.

In his "Anatomy" Rembrandt has introduced a number of space- and atmosphere-creating devices that his previous work had not known. These represent what Rembrandt himself would, no doubt, consider his "composition"; only the art theory of the time would not speak of either "composition" or "design," but rather of the "ordinance" (Lat. *ordo, ordinatio,* and seventeenth-century Dutch *ordinancy*) of a painting. By this was meant the distribution or deployment of the plastic shapes, and that chiefly of the human figures, in three-dimensional space. This ordinance should not be confused with *scaenographia*, which is the strictly scientific (i.e. mathematical) method of three-dimensional presentation on a two-dimensional surface. As far as I am aware the very thought of the aesthetics of two-dimensional compositional design was quite alien to the imitative arts of the Renaissance. Wherever in the seventeenth century such points as symmetry and the interpretation of plastic shapes in forms of geometrical designs are discussed, such discussions are confined to architecture, in particular to the façades of buildings, or to proportion in the sense of Dürer's *Proportionslehre,* and need not concern us here. As now we turn to the Netherlandish art theoreticians who were active in the first half of the seventeenth century (Carel van Mander, Gerard Joannes Vossius, above all Franciscus Junius) and whose writings could have come to the knowledge of Rembrandt either directly or by word of mouth through communications of his friends, we find this specific use of "ordinance" amply corroborated and defined. Franciscus Junius briefly outlines his theory of painting in the Introduction to Book III under the following five headings:

(1) "Historicall argument" *(inventio sive historia);*

(2) "Proportion, or Symmetrie" *(naturalis membrorum inter se competentia);*

(3) "Colour, and therein Light and Shadow" *(color, et in eo lux & umbra);*

(4) "Motion or Life" [= expression, physiognomy] (consisting of *actio* and *passio);*

(5) "Disposition [i.e. ordinance], or an Oeconomicall placing and ordering of the whole worke" (Dutch *ordinancy* or *schickinghe; collocatio sive oeconomica totius operis dispositio).*

It is with Franciscus Junius' fifth and last heading that we are concerned here.[3] Even the fact that the term "ordinance" stemmed ultimately from the scholastic word *ordo,* by which Aquinas understood "the grouping of the *creaturae* in relation to one another and in turn to God" ("ordo creaturarum ad inuicem, & ordo creaturarum ad Deum"), does in no way contradict its seventeenth-century application. The scholastic concept indeed already points to a kind of hierarchic deployment that the Renaissance could not conceive of otherwise than in terms of three-dimensional space. When, with the postulates of ordinance in mind, we contemplate Rembrandt's original under favorable lighting conditions, the figures seem to assert themselves with a maximum of tangible illusion in the virtual minimum of actual space accorded them. The impression of human beings intensely alive is inescapable. Rembrandt has brought about this illusion through the carefully controlled use of the medium, ranging from the subtlest glazes to noticeable impasto in the high lights and in areas where light and shadow lie as it were in conflict with one another. He has achieved a warm glowing quality even of the cold colors, the many blacks and the *changeant* of the faded violet of the prominent sleeve of Jacob de Witt (surgeon number 5). This warmth of tone is opposed by the coolness of the ivory-colored cadaver (see Frontispiece).

The interplay of light and shadow (the third of Junius' categories) has been assigned a completely novel role in the "Anatomy." Their contrast seems most carefully mapped out and achieved by means of subtle transitions for which we should look in vain in the paintings of Rembrandt's Leiden period. Again we are able to account for this change if we are prepared to assume that Rembrandt had only now become aware of the advice of Franciscus Junius[262] (III, iii, § 10) to avoid the checkerboard effect created by the harsh juxtaposition of colored light and shadow: "The paintings which loosely hitch white and black, one to the other, have the appearance of a white marble floor or a checker-board." Soft transitions are to be preferred. Junius' pronouncement was by no means original with him; yet he had elaborated with greater force and clarity upon advice given by Carel van Mander in his well-known didactic poem. The fundamental change in Rembrandt's style of painting from 1632 onward could, at any rate, not be better characterized.

A further novelty introduced by Rembrandt into the Dutch anatomical scene is the bold diagonal whereby the corpse with particular emphasis serves as a "spatial index."[4] It is obvious that with this Rembrandt has introduced a rather startling variation upon the common scheme, viz. the anatomy in which the corpse, lying flush with the picture plane, is presided over by a chairman in the center who is symmetrically flanked by attending figures. (See, for example, Pl. III–3.) Rembrandt, shunning the solemn approach hitherto favored, leads us as it were from the wings up to such an orderly scene. What urged him to do this we cannot tell; quite possibly he was captivated by the inherent iconographic significance of the prone body placed at an angle to the picture plane, a motif, after all, which, ever since artists used perspective and spatial illusion, had served to indicate "passivity," "defenselessness," "suffering," "death." It was, indeed, not necessary for Rembrandt to go far afield in his search for a suited prototype; this he may well have found and admired in Adriaen Brouwer's "Drunken Peasants in an Inn" (Boymans Museum, Rotterdam; Pl. II-2b). In this painting the main figure is a completely drunken peasant who lies, almost precisely like the corpse in Rembrandt's painting, on a bench just as uncomfortably narrow as the one that accommodates Aris Kindt.

The change of approach has necessitated a general regrouping of figures. The *spiritus rector,* in relation and in subordination to whom all the other figures must be seen, had to be placed to the extreme right from the beholder's point of view. This necessity forced Rembrandt to group the attending surgeons in a tight cluster to one side of Dr. Tulp alone, while the other had, of course, to remain free. For this point compare Rembrandt's "Anatomy" with Pl. IV–5.

Such an approach, which prefers to the head-on view an angle of approximately forty-five degrees, was, it seems, a favorite with Rembrandt just in the 1630's. We encounter it, for example, in the "Raising of the Daughter of Jairus" (Pl. VII-9) and in the early "Ecce homo!" (1635–36). (Pl. XXVII–34.) Curiously enough, where Rembrandt has occasion to repeat those themes at a later time he prefers the head-on view, with the resultant harmonious symmetry. For this difference one might compare the "Ecce homo!" etchings of 1655 (Pls. XXIX-36 and XXX-37) and, of course, the "Anatomy of Dr. Deyman" (Pl. XII-16) of 1656.

The calculated use of what Panofsky has termed "eccentric perspective" we may regard as one of the characteristics of Rembrandt's many-figured compositions of the 1630's. In the "Anatomy" it applies, strictly speaking, only to the *mobilia* (the human beings, living as well as dead, and their furniture), rather than to the somewhat uncertain structural parts, the *immobilia* of the interior. In combination with the strong light coming from above and from our left, this perspective yields two equally significant results: (1) by showing a little more of the shell-niched side wall to the right, Rembrandt creates a handsome foil for Dr. Tulp, the most distinguished person in the picture; (2) psychologically speaking, this approach places the beholder in a position that seems more or less accidentally chosen. This effect, incidentally, the beholder may interpret in the very pleasant sense that he is welcome as an informal witness at a very formal gathering. Other devices too, some of them already referred to, add to our feeling of being drawn into the vortex of the visible segment of a vaster scene. The relatively low tunnel vault, supported by the two side walls, creates an impression of depth, intensive yet difficult to rationalize on account of the intensional silver-gray dimness that prevails outside the tightly knit gathering of the figures. The seemingly casual way in which the undignified feet of the cadaver almost brutally cut the picture plane in the right foreground, the manner in which the axis of the stiffened body points to the rear and creates a recess, serves the same space-suggesting purpose. The *repoussoir* function of the cadaver is underscored by the countermovement of heads and torsos of the living, craning forward with utmost energy. All this strengthens the illusion that the space created by Rembrandt is not confined to his canvas and that this extended space is inhabited by spectators and models alike.

To these general statements I must add a more detailed observation with which I shall elsewhere deal again (see p. 40 *infra*). There are several good reasons to assume that two figures, namely Jacob Koolvelt and Frans Loenen (the surgeon farthest left, number 7, and the one towering above all the others who faces the beholder, number 8) do not belong to the composition as originally conceived by Rembrandt. Koolvelt and Loenen, apart from being both somewhat anaemic, are the only ones seen in a strangely unspatial and unplastic manner. As soon as these two late-comers have been eliminated (Pl. I) the remaining group, including Dr. Tulp and the cadaver, regains a meaningful compactness, whereas the richness of the canvas seems in no way impaired. The generosity with which Rembrandt had originally allowed air pockets between the frame and humanity enhances the impression of concentrated mental energies. Carel van Mander[303] (chap. v, stanza 5) had advised the young artist to proportion his figures to the available space and to avoid making them seem to "carry the frames," or to make them appear like "someone lying in his coffin." — "Dat de Beelden de lijsten niet endraghen / Oft datse benouwt als in Kisten laghen." Rembrandt's presumed reticence in pressing his figures against the frame is thus clearly in keeping with the prescripts of the art theory of his day.

The total effect of all these devices may be summarized as that of secluded dignity amidst attractive intimacy. The isolated and decentralized figure of Tulp becomes the interconnecting link between the seemingly disparate elements in the picture; it is the pivot on which the entire composition hinges. Eccentric perspective, hazed atmosphere, vivid color, the magic plasticity and the calculated distribution of the human shapes—they are about two-thirds life-size—in conjunction with the relative vastness of the canvas, help to stress the lifelike quality of the event represented. This artful ordination of solid shapes whose confusion and profusion can best be described as *venusta plenitudo* may well be considered the artistic manifesto of a new Rembrandt. Junius in fact considered the painter's ability to control a wealth of features the true touchstone of his competence. In the "Anatomy of Dr. Tulp" we witness something that I feel tempted to refer to as the ego-genesis of the artist. At the same time it seems to me that here we witness the genesis of the Dutch Baroque. This, as I see it, is above all expressed in Rembrandt's mastery of seemingly incompatible discords, in the uninhibited assigning of rhetorical functions to a silent *tableau vivant,* in the endeavor to present us with the illusion of a reality as yet far removed from the limiting effects of a newfangled scientific mode of seeing actual snatches of the world in terms of short time exposures in which the range of the human eye was reduced to the vision of the *camera obscura.*[5] This newness of Rembrandt's painting in relation to his past *œuvre* and also in relation to the art of his competitors can perhaps be partly accounted for as we now turn to the impact that the setting he had chosen as his permanent abode must have made on him at the time when he conceived the "Anatomy of Dr. Tulp."

The year 1632 marks a fundamental change in the life of Rembrandt. It was most likely in this year that he decided to stay in Amsterdam permanently. He had moved from Leiden to Amsterdam at some date after June 20, 1631. In Amsterdam he took up residence with Hendrick Uylenburgh, a man well characterized by his motto: "Middelmaet hout staet" (Ovid's "You will go with the greatest safety in a middle path"). Uylenburgh was not only an art dealer but seems to have run a kind of Academy, "la famosa Accademia di Eulenborg" (Baldinucci) for young people of good family who learned to paint by copying pictures. Uylenburgh, it seems, also profited by the sale of their copies. Quite possibly Rembrandt earned his board and lodging in his first months at Amsterdam by acting as a respectable artist in residence.[6]

Rembrandt had been in Amsterdam some six or seven years previously, during a short six months' period when he worked under Pieter Lastman (1583–1633) to conclude his initial training period begun in Leiden. Notwithstanding those earlier moves, the move of the years 1631/32 marks the first great dividing line in Rembrandt's development. The years preceding 1632 were his *Lehr- und Wanderjahre.* The fascination that his juvenilia exercise over the lovers of his art is understandable. But, disrespectful as it may sound, especially to those who believe in the existence of genius *ab utero,* the Rembrandt before 1632, if full of the promise that was as it were ready to crystallize, had been decidedly unformed. He might be compared in these formative years to Shakespeare the mannerist, who created (or rather re-created) *Richard III* and *Romeo and Juliet,* or to young Johann Wolfgang Goethe, the rococo poet, before Sesenheim and Friederike, Strassburg and Herder.

The Amsterdam of the 1630's was itself a new city. It sprang into eminence almost overnight and then grew by leaps and bounds. The beautiful old city as it still stands with its concentrically arranged canals, the *grachten,* was fashioned after the plans of Hendrick Staets (1610). A listing of the changes, additions, and new buildings of eminence that came about in the early 1630's impressively reflects this spirit of rebirth. Two new churches, the "Westerkerk" in which Rembrandt was to be buried and the "New Lutheran Church," date from 1632. Soon after, Amsterdam's first permanent theater followed (1637/38), whose first play was Vondel's "Gysbreght van Aemstel." The hero is comforted at the end by the prophetic words of the Archangel Raphael in which the 1630's are foreseen as a time of miraculous rebirth in which past calamities will be celebrated on a new stage.

Once it had miraculously superseded Antwerp, Amsterdam could claim to be, even before London, Europe's first *megapolis*. Few contemporary illustrations render this particular aspect of Amsterdam (see Pl. II-2a); yet we have moving and eloquent descriptions of the overwhelming impression the city made in those very years on much-traveled persons. Another immigrant from Leiden was Caspar Barlaeus; in his writings introspection, limitless desire to communicate himself to others, and sharp observation are felicitously blended. Barlaeus, who, like Rembrandt, had arrived in 1631 (and who, it is tempting to assume, was the man who introduced young Rembrandt to Dr. Tulp), records the kaleidoscopic wealth of impressions by which the eye is constantly drawn from one spectacle to the next; from the lofty buildings to the vast masses of people, whose cold mercantile faces make him miss the animated physiognomies of the academic inhabitants of his home town, Leiden. It was men like Barlaeus, Rembrandt, and Tulpius who saw to it that the mercantile city became also a center of theology and philosophy, of scholarship and art. At exactly this time another recent arrival, the restless soldier-scientist René Descartes, discovered in Amsterdam an unexpected solitude: "i'y pourrois demeurer toute ma vie sans estre iamais vû de personne." Petrarch, in his *De vita solitaria,* had spoken of the "infoelix habitator urbium." Descartes experienced, and he was perhaps the first person to do so, the exact opposite. Here he was free from the constant menace of what he calls the *petits voisins,* whose courtesy calls had made life in the rustic retreats practically intolerable.[7] Rembrandt's "Anatomy of Dr. Tulp" is a true reflection of the incipient complexity of the city's cosmopolitan atmosphere. Rembrandt, at an early point, has caught something of that intangible element to which Joost van den Vondel refers when he speaks of Amsterdam as the seat of Holland's soul—"Hier leeft de ziel van Hollant's staet." The year 1632, so at least it appears in retrospect, was truly an *annus mirabilis* for Amsterdam and for Rembrandt. For Rembrandt a new phase had begun. Barely beginning to be known as a painter of portraits—only three can with certainty be assigned to 1631 and (by chance to the month of January of) 1632[8]— and renowned above all for the delicate minuteness of his technique, he now turned to ambitious commissions and to subjects in large format. Psychologically, too, the decade beginning with 1632 was a time of great and justified professional and intellectual aspirations and of great social ambitions. In his self-portraits, now mostly life-size, Rembrandt appears, as if experimentally, in the dress of either the elegant gentleman of his day or of the proud humanist. This was a time when he worked, as we know from Constantine Huygens' beautiful report (written at the very end of Rembrandt's Leiden period, *ca.* 1629–31), at a feverish pitch, although his health was delicate.[9]

II

The 'Anatomy' as a Group Portrait

Sic producuntur, quasi in claram lucem,
abditissimae occultorum morborum caussae
(N. Tulp)

Considered merely as a product of craftsmanship, Rembrandt's painting is so radiant, serene, and festive that its subject matter, the dissection of a human body, seems to have lost some of its inescapable horror. The *dignitas humana,* gravely questioned in any anatomy, seems to be restored and if not restored at least balanced as we turn to the self-confident group of surgeons attentively following Dr. Tulp's combined discourse and demonstration. Obviously, however, Dr. Tulp addresses, not the inner circle that we see in the painting, but "us," the beholders, just beyond it. "Here addresses us the eloquence of Tulpius"; these were the words (see pp. 112 f.) in which Barlaeus described the painting as early as 1639.[10] The complete lifelessness of the corpse fails to overwhelm the beholder as he realizes that it is the living function of sinews and muscles that move the fingers which is here being investigated. The almost contrapuntal display in which human intelligences respond with varying degrees of intensity to a number of divergent stimuli—the spoken word, the printed and illustrated pages, the skinned portion of the lower left arm—makes Rembrandt's painting one of the finest artistic tributes to the great scientific endeavors that had only recently begun to mark Holland's independence from the medical schools of the Catholic South generally and of Italy in particular.

The first impression that both fascinates and puzzles the modern beholder of Rembrandt's painting is that of the role played by the human eye. The intensive staring is unparalleled in any other of his portraits. Even if this device was first suggested by Dr. Tulp, we have reason to assume that such a suggestion found Rembrandt ready to use it as a means of expressing "inner emotion." Rembrandt speaks of "innermost emotion" in a letter dated January 12, 1639 and addressed to Constantine Huygens: "The principal reason causing these [two paintings] to have remained under my hands for so long lies herein that I have applied in them innermost emotion to the largest possible extent" *(die meeste ende die naetueree Lste beweechge Lichheijt)*. We must note that J. J. Orlers, Rembrandt's biographer writing in 1641, uses a nearly identical turn of phrase, "natuyrlicke beweghingen," in reference to the "inner motivation" that led Rembrandt away from academic studies and towards art. We may well wonder whether Orlers here repeated Rembrandt's own words. Rembrandt's letter leaves no doubt that he was conversant with the theoretical art language of his time. There is plenty of evidence to show that he was also capable of putting it into practice. Excitation of responses was, in the words of the French theoretician of music Marin Mersenne (d. 1646), "an artifice which through the *Rhetorica Harmonica* (of the composer of songs) elicits from the audience tears, laughter, and other passions." Similarly, of course, the moving of the beholder by means of *Rhetorica Pictorica* was one of the chief ends of baroque painting. Not only did the moving qualities involve the beholder, they must also be exhibited by those represented in the picture; and, last but not least, in order to move, the artist himself must be moved. "A minde rightly affected and passionated is the onely fountaine whereout there doe issue forth such violent streames of passions, that the spectator, not being able to resist, is carried away against his will, whithersoever the force of such an Imperious Art listeth to drive him" (Franciscus Junius, [263] pp. 299f.). The human eye was considered eminently suited for emotion-expressing and emotion-inducing tasks. The eyes have, according to Junius, "supreme power among all other parts of our face, they are the emissaries of our heart, the viewing windows of our soul." From the eyes one can read the emotions "distinctly, as if they were written, nay, that one can comprehend them thus as from all the words in the world." We could wish for no clearer commentary on the specific rhetorical means used by Rembrandt in the "Anatomy."[11] Quite possibly the first encouragement may have come from Dr. Tulp, who, only a few years after the "Anatomy," referred to the anatomist as "the true eye of medicine."[12]

The human eye seems to play an important role also in the one and only classical representation of an anatomy that has come down to us: the "Anatomy" of the Catacomb of the Via Latina outside Rome (Pl. XII-15). When we compare the two "Anatomies" we notice, however, a fundamental difference between the speaking glances in Rembrandt's painting and, on the other hand, the seeing yet not seeing eyes of the classical audience. None of the Roman participants, not even the chairman, bothers to glance at the corpse, in spite of the fact that there too a definite problem—that of the liver, which is being lifted up by means of a cord while the *radius* (the cane of the *demonstrator*) points down at it—is under discussion. Rembrandt alone assigns specific intellectual functions to each pair of human eyes.

It has frequently been stated that with the "Anatomy" Rembrandt made his first contribution, and indeed a distinguished one, to the tradition of the group portrait. The exact place occupied by his "Anatomy" in the development of this genre (which, in the first decades of the sixteenth century, had progressed in two relatively independent streams of development at Haarlem and at Amsterdam) has been outlined by H. E. van Gelder.[13] We are above all concerned with the position of Rembrandt's work in the development of the group portrait as a specifically social phenomenon. Members of Holland's wealthy and intelligent middle class, forever ready to band together corporatively, liked to see themselves represented as they gathered under the pretense of some celebration; whether they were banqueting, deliberating, or parading, they were always dressed in their Sunday best and always at leisure. Motion and emotion ("action" and "passion" in the terminology of Junius) where they occur in the group portrait never seem to speak of transitory stages or moods of the participants; they rather tend to confirm, deepen, and stress some significant static aspect of the theme. On account of this quality the most fluent of group portraits, such as for example Rembrandt's "Night Watch," remain a more or less artificial synthesis of individual portraits. As van de Waal has shown, even where a group portrait aimed at a given event it would never lower its function to that of a mere chronicle. In its hostility to progression and locomotion the group portrait excludes all ephemeral events. We might well ask, therefore, whether Rembrandt in his first group portrait had in fact deviated from this time-honored tradition by showing the members of the Corporation of Surgeons of Amsterdam (the so-called "Chirurgijns Gild," *ca.* 1550ff.) as he had casually observed them on a specific occasion at their work. The answer is reassuringly negative. Rembrandt meticulously kept to the convention as it prevailed in his own day.

In order to understand the curiously festive character that distinguishes the baroque anatomies, we must bring to mind that an anatomy was then a totally different matter from what it is now. Such an anatomy, in contrast to the modern academic ones, was open to the public, and this to such an extent that lecture and demonstration were aimed at the curious layman in the first place, just as the various exhibits of the anatomical theaters served, as we know, moral-didactic rather than scientific-didactic purposes. We are fairly well informed on the specific anatomical lesson that Rembrandt commemorated and, fortunately, dated. We know that the anatomy conducted by Dr. Tulp took place on or immediately after the last day of the month of January 1632, and we may suspect that it went on, in all likelihood, for some four or five subsequent days.[14] Naturally we cannot tell how many days, weeks, months Rembrandt needed to finish his work, but there are indications that he must have sketched the cadaver before the anatomy began and certain details must have resulted from careful advice that would have come from the chief anatomist himself. Undoubtedly much time-consuming planning must have preceded the actual execution of the picture. Here the question arises why Rembrandt should have been commissioned to record a specific anatomical demonstration. Anatomies of this kind were comparatively rare events. The anatomy of the month of January was the one and only public anatomy that took place in Amsterdam in 1632. It was Dr. Tulp's second

Fig. 2. "Anatomy of Dr. Paaw at Leiden." Engraving by Andries Jacobsz. Stoc[kius] (1580–1648), after Jacques de Gheyn II (1616).

annual lesson. All other recorded paintings of anatomies were commissioned, it seems, to record the *praelector's* first lesson. Such anatomies were annual affairs. Festive public anatomies can be traced back to the last decades of the fifteenth century. From then onward we can follow their development far into the eighteenth century, when (in Amsterdam) it was customary to advertise the annual anatomy in the newspapers. The public anatomy as a fete and as a social obligation of either the medical faculty or—as in Amsterdam, which had no medical faculty in 1632—of the surgeons' guild was known all over Europe from the early sixteenth century onward.

Anatomies were from the beginning attended by great crowds. In Rembrandt's Amsterdam they were watched by the guild members and their *knegten,* by the magistrates, and by the domine, *ex officio.*[15] The odd foreign visitor was attracted by them. In Elizabethan England, according to an Ordinance of 1572, even foreign surgeons—"fforeyne, or alian straungers"—who failed to attend the annual anatomy had to pay a fine of *vj d.* The attendance of foreigners seems to be illustrated in an engraving of an anatomy of Tulp's teacher at Leiden, Dr. Pieter Paaw (after a drawing of the year 1616 by Jacques de Gheyn, who intimately knew not only Dr. Paaw but also the academic setting of Leiden), where we see a number of distinctly foreign-looking spectators in the upper rank—among them (to the left) two who, judging by their cassocks and hats, might be a Pole and a Hungarian respectively (Fig. 2). It is possible that Dr. Tulp's anatomy of 1632 attracted Descartes, who, after all, was himself an avid amateur anatomist.[16] Perhaps also a young Englishman was present, one who at that time was enrolled as a medical student at Leiden University: Thomas, later Sir Thomas, Browne.[17] Apart from the distinguished citizens and curious foreigners, we must imagine throngs of ordinary people, women, dogs, and—if they were lucky enough to escape the eye of the overseers—children. (Pl. III-3, 4.)

It seems obvious that an historic frame of reference of this kind—the anatomy as a social "must"—compels us to revise our aesthetic responses to Rembrandt's painting.

III

The 'Anatomy' as Scientific Event and Theatrical Fete

Hic mors juvat vitam
(Inscription of the Anatomical Theater at Heidelberg)

Mentem mortalia tangunt
(Inscription of Amsterdam's projected *Schouwburg* [city theater] 1630)

Undeniably the public anatomies were milestones marking scientific progress. Indeed, it is not an exaggeration to say that, seen scientifically, Rembrandt's painting pinpointed the beginning of a specifically Dutch development in the history of medicine that saw its climax almost precisely one hundred years later, in the accumulated work of Fredericus Ruysch at Amsterdam and of Hermannus Boerhaave at Leiden. But that is only one half

Fig. 3. Jost Amman (1539–91), "Public Anatomy in a Chapel." Woodcut illustrating Paracelsus, *Opus chyrurgicum*,[368] fig. 2 (1565).

of the picture, or even less. I think it has never been properly realized that at the same time the formal anatomies, such as the one conducted by Dr. Tulp and painted by Rembrandt, represented equally important chapters in the historical development of the stage. The success of an anatomy, just like that of any other theatrical performance, depended largely on the size and on the sympathetic response of its audience. The anatomies of this type were expressly designed to attract and to hold large numbers of onlookers. They needed financial success, also, and had therefore to depend on the support and approval of the masses no less than Shakespeare's plays in London or Vondel's in Amsterdam. It is perhaps symptomatic that in the early seventeenth century one local chamber of Rhetoricians shared and then changed quarters (including the stage) with the Amsterdam Guild of Anatomists.[18] The annual anatomies were spectacles open to the public. In this capacity they offered theatrical performances far in advance of those of the Reederijkers' *schouwburgen*.[19] As entertainment the anatomies vied with the sermons of the great preachers, with the arrival of ships with merchandise from the West and East Indies,[20] with the colorful *entrées* of Princes (Pl. II–2a). Above all else, the function of the anatomies might be compared with that of the performances of the organ toccatas and fantasias of Jan Pietersz. Sweelinck and his school. It was the aim of these curious recitals (as stipulated by contract between City and organist) to fill the churches of Amsterdam with their indefatigable sounds at the noon hour and in the evening by candlelight; it was their purpose to attract, to divert, and, where possible, to edify the *burghers*, who, while they listened, sauntered up and down the church aisles, arrested only now and then by the sound of the register stop of the *vox humana*. Thus we still see them in the paintings of Saenredam, Emanuel de Witte, and others.[21] The comparison may at first seem far-fetched, but the anatomies, not unlike the new church music, so perfectly interblended secular and sacred strands that they offered *circenses* to the clapperclaws, while the spiritually inclined might attend them with feelings of devotion.

These two aspects can be illustrated from contemporary evidence. As to the anatomies as *circenses,* we hear over and over again that they were staged with extreme care. In the words of J. J. Orlers, who was a nephew of Leiden's great anatomist Dr. Pieter Paaw, "[waren zij] met groote aensienlickheydt uytgherecht ende ghedaen"—"they were prepared with circumspection and carried out with great decorum" (*Beschrijvinge,*[347] p. 210). Ordinances of the Surgeons of Amsterdam[325] (1605, 1625) stipulated that the audience refrain from laughing and talking and that anyone caught in the act of helping himself to organs such as heart, kidney, liver, gallstones (the so-called *membra naturalia* that were passed around by the amanuenses) was fined the prohibitively high sum of six guilders. Questions from the audience might be submitted, provided they were decent and of a serious kind: "In het Vragen, Antwoorden & alle Onderlinge reden sal alle Smadelijkheyt ende Belacheijt ver-mijdt daer tegen alle Beleeftechijt & Soetighijt, onderlinge beweesen worden (January 14, 1606).[22]

As to the devotion of the intelligentsia to the anatomies, we may turn to a short poem that Caspar Barlaeus wrote in 1639 in praise of Amsterdam's first permanently housed anatomical theater as well as of Dr. Tulp, with a nicely hinted *double entendre* about his occasional actual (but also his permanent painted) presence in that place. In this poem the following lines occur:

> Here addresses us the eloquence of learned Tulpius, while with nimble hands he dissects livid limbs. Listener, learn for thyself, and as thou turnest from one part to another, believe that even in the smallest particle God is enshrined.

> Hic loquitur nobis docti facundia Tulpi,
> Dum secat artifici lurida membra manu.
> Auditor te disce. & dum per singula vadis,
> Crede vel in minima parte latere Deum.

The same idea recurs, with certain variations, in another poem that Barlaeus wrote, *In mensam Anatomicam,* and the stanza quoted was, it seems, actually inscribed in golden letters underneath the highest balcony of the theater of 1639.[23] Lyrical-metaphysical outbursts in the face of anatomy are still encountered in the latter part of the eighteenth century:

> O, wie gross ist doch die Leber, drin des Menschen Zorn gelegen!
> Und wie klein sein Sitz der Liebe, dieses Handvoll Herz dagegen!

> Oh how large is the liver, which enshrines Man's anger!
> And how small in contrast the seat of love, that handful of heart!

This verse by Justinus Kerner graces an anonymous print of an idealized "Anatomical Lesson in a Cave," with a fine view of the Roman Campagna: a strange evocation of the didactic "Anatomy" of the Catacomb of the Via Latina (Pl. XII–15) and a romantic realization of the sixteenth-century postulate that the (idealized) anatomical amphitheater under its tarpaulin should open up into a landscape (see Appendix II).[24]

Anatomical theaters were by tradition amphitheaters. In practice this meant that wooden scaffoldings (oval, semicircular, or circular) were placed inside buildings that already existed. It is quite startling to find that, in Protestant regions and particularly in Holland, most of the buildings accommodating the theaters were chapels. In one or two instances it is even possible to demonstrate that the anatomical table took the place of the altar. I shall refer to a number of examples, almost all found in Holland, and I shall begin with Amsterdam. In about 1550 the first public anatomy took place in that city, in a room of St. Ursula's Convent. In 1578 the anatomical theater was moved from there to St. Margaret's Church ("Sint Margrieten Kercke in de Nes"), which, in a contemporary engraving of

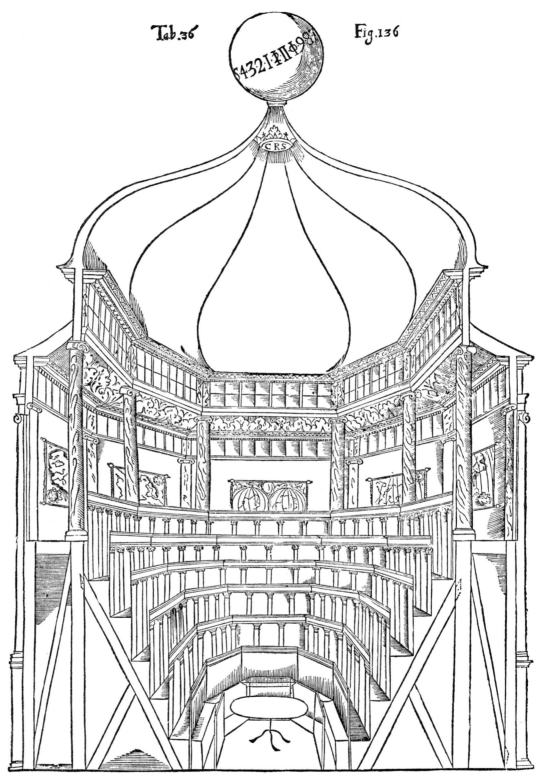

Tab.36   Fig.136

Fig. 4. "Inner View of the Gustavianum." Woodcut illustrating Rudbeck, *Atlantica*,[413] Plate 36, fig. 136 (1679). (After facsimile ed. Nelson.)

which I have been unable to ascertain the exact date, is shown as lying opposite the "Prin-cenhof," at that time known as the "New or Little Meat Hall" ("nieuwe of kleine Vleesch-hal"). A poem underneath the print offers the following amusing observations:

Title: The two Meat Halls. The two meat halls which you see here are well equipped with beautiful "meat" [N.B. Dutch "vleesch," like German "Fleisch," can mean both "flesh" and "meat"], beautiful inside and out, and so much of it that one hardly knows where it all goes. Come on, little ladies, if you feel like investing your money; buy as much as your heart desires—from this kind of "flesh" your spouses won't grow horns.... Do you desire to know what people there are upstairs? Those are the surgeons who make flesh wounds and who are trained in the noble art. At the same time this is the peaceful meeting place of Rhetoricians. While some will bare the wounds of man's body, the others try to cure man's soul.[25]

For twenty fateful years, 1619–39, the surgeon-anatomists and their theater had to occupy makeshift quarters. They had been driven from the Vleeschhal through the dis-turbance of the famous Chamber of Rhetoricians "In Liefde Bloeiende" ("flourishing in love"). They had sought refuge in the vast building known as the St. Anthony Gate. This structure, begun in 1488, had been vastly extended and used as a weighing house in the years after 1617. An inscription, recut and shortened it seems at a later date, is still visible above the entrance of the southeast turret; it reads THEATRUM ANATOMICUM. The inscription and the empty space that had formerly accommodated a bust of Hippocrates (also marked by an inscription) are all that is left of the interim theater, which is of so great concern to us. The (first) permanent theater of 1639 (used 1640–90) was once more in St. Margaret's.[26] And elsewhere in Holland the situation was much the same. The first theater of Utrecht settled down in the Jerusalem Chapel (August 7, 1621), and when—for purely legalistic reasons—the anatomists had to leave it, they moved to another church in the city.[27] Leiden's anatomical theater, the second-oldest permanent theater in existence (1594), was on the raised ground floor of the choir of an old convent chapel (the "Falie" or "Falijde-Bagijnenkerk"). It was here that the anatomical table occupied the place once reserved for the altar. Suspended above the altar, now an anatomical table, we must picture the chandelier with its twelve lights symbolizing the holy Jerusalem. We must keep in mind that this was the first anatomical theater (as well as the first art museum) that Rem-brandt ever visited. This church housed the anatomical theater of Leiden from the late sixteenth century until 1820.[28] Outside Holland we find the first chapel anatomy in a woodcut illustration by Jost Amman[368] of the year 1565 (Fig. 3).

A glance at the moral-didactic commentaries on the public anatomies will help us to understand this curious predilection for chapels and church choirs. I assume that this convention was restricted to countries of the Reformation. Since those anatomies were at the same time a preserve of the humanists, some encouragement might have been found in a tradition that started with Galen. When his *De usu partium* met with criticism, he made, at the urging of his friends, a public demonstration at the Templum Pacis of Rome. This demonstration, his only public one that can be definitely established, he conducted in the presence of distinguished people, among them physicians, in order to affirm the soundness of his position and the error of his opponents; it extended over several days. The Templum Pacis, which sheltered the Roman archives until it was burned in the year 192 A.D., was the customary site of logical disputations. On its ruins was placed the present church of the medical saints *par excellence,* Cosmas and Damian— a fine example of the tenacity of medical tradition.[29]

In one respect the anatomies differed from all the other forms of public entertainment, and this difference too was by no means confined to Amsterdam or to Holland: Public anatomies were celebrated only once a year; everywhere, with clocklike regularity, they marked the height of the winter season.[30] For reasons dictated by the perishable material they worked with, such anatomies could hardly ever last more than five days. It seems that they were preferably conducted after sunset, at least as soon as permanent indoor theaters had come into fashion. In Calvinist Holland, at least, Sundays, no less than any other days in the week, were anatomy days.

The ordinary citizen, in order to be admitted to the anatomy, had to purchase an entrance ticket. This was another international custom. It appears quite likely that the sale of tickets to those wishing to attend public anatomies preceded the sale of ordinary theater tickets by several years and may even have encouraged theatrical confraternities to follow suit. This, incidentally, is only one of a number of aspects suggesting, it seems to me, that studies of the history of the stage should include the anatomical theaters.[31]

In Tulp's Amsterdam such tickets sold for six to seven *stuyvers* apiece. The tradition of entrance ticket sales can be traced back as far as 1497, when we first hear of tickets being sold for an anatomy at Padua. From then on, faculty and guild accounts yield uninter-rupted evidence of the sale of entrance tickets. In Holland this extends deep into the eighteenth century; in Edinburgh we hear of it as late as 1829, when, to the chagrin of the medical students who had to be excluded, a large audience of ticket holders, among them Sir Walter Scott, attended the public and punitive dissection of William Burke.[32]

A closer study of the expense accounts of the Amsterdam Guild is, I think, rewarding. An anatomy fetched on the average two hundred florins. An exceptionally high sum, 315 florins and 8 *stuyvers,* accrued from the dissection of a female. We are reminded of how Thomas Diafoirus, the young physician and mock hero in Molière's *Malade Imaginaire,* tries to woo Angélique by inviting her to attend the dissection of a female corpse at which he will deliver the lecture, "pour vous divertir." (See also Pl. X-13b.)

About fifty per cent of the sums yielded by Amsterdam's anatomies were clear profit. The money was—officially—collected "for defraying the cost." In Basel, for example, the surplus was used for the purchase of fumigators, vessels, calves' eyes, candles, sponges (1571–72). In Amsterdam, however, the money was used to finance a sumptuous banquet of the guild members (the very people we see in Rembrandt's painting), and this was followed by a parade with torches. The Dutch expense accounts, of which we have a good many, include — besides a handsome fee for the hangman — sums up to 100 florins for the hiring of a cook, for the purchase of wine, tobacco (disdained by Dr. Tulp), fish, lanterns, lantern carriers, and sundry items not specified.[33]

We may sum up at this point. Rembrandt's painting is, above all, the representation of a dramatic stage, that of the *theatrum anatomicum*. Barlaeus' words, "here addresses us the eloquence of learned Tulpius," must be taken quite literally, for we, the beholders of the painting, are meant to take the part of the audience. Dr. Tulp's eyes and speaking hand (he makes use of the traditional *allocutio* gesture) range over a vast audience, outside the picture plane, not in thought but in a vividly eloquent address. We, the beholders, are favored with those ringside seats which, according to Amsterdam's *Ordo sedendi pro dignitate,* were reserved for guild members and for physicians over fifty years of age.

The dramatic-rhetorical character of the painting, in spite of or, perhaps, precisely on account of the absolute immobility of the individual members in the picture, emphasizes a possible relationship of the painting to the stage. Indeed, I feel that the anatomy as Rembrandt first depicted it has a good deal in common with presentations of the Dutch stage. Dutch stagecraft of the early seventeenth century made a distinction between two forms in which a scene might be presented on the stage: the dramatic *stuk*, the moving play proper, and the *vertooning* or *toog,* the *tableau vivant,* a form occasionally referred to in Elizabethan England by the term "dumb show." ("Here Prospero discouers Ferdinand and Miranda, playing at Chesse.") Dr. Tulp's anatomy is such an immobile *vertooning,* realistic yet synthetic (by which I mean that a number of reactions not necessarily occurring at one and the same moment are represented in simultaneity), mute yet eloquent, emotional yet without motion. There is in the painting no more drama, if we take the word in its literal sense, than in the movements of a bed of sea anemones.[34]

To Rembrandt's contemporaries it was surely not difficult to link such a *tableau* in their imagination with the "play" as a whole. This dramatic play proceeded in three distinctly separate yet organically interconnected acts: (1) The solemn public execution of the criminal, who in contemporary accounts of this event is referred to as the "patient";[35] (2) The formal public anatomy of the criminal, hanged the day before; and (3) The semi-private guild banquet and torch parade. The curious mixture of this gruesomely impressive and edifying dramatic appeal to both the mind and the soul of the audience makes each of the three acts an ideal expression of the baroque. Rembrandt's celebration of the second act must have suggested many seemingly contradictory things in one. It recorded a first-

33

class public entertainment; it suggested a scientific *tableau vivant;* it offered food for devotional contemplation by demonstrating God's wisdom expressed in the very limbs and organs of the criminal, who, after all, must be considered the *templum animatum,* "the temple of the holy Ghost" (1 Corinthians vi:19).[36] Moreover, the painting helped to show in full light the mastery of the *praelector* and *anatomicus* (to whom his contemporaries referred as "anatomicus gravissimus, felicissimus, facundissimus"), lecturing and demonstrating before a critical audience at a fee of 250 florins;[37] it illustrated the "crisis" between execution and feast; it had a cathartic function as quite possibly it contained echoes of a seasonal ritual for the benefit of society by exhibiting a criminal whose public disgrace and punishment had not ended with the execution.

IV

The 'Anatomy' as a Realistic Record

> For beauty and good fauor is like cleare truth, which
> is not shamed with the light, nor need to be obscured
> (Nicholas Hilliard)

Rembrandt injected into this, his first contribution to the group portrait, elements of realistic, on-the-spot observation that his predecessors in the anatomical corporation portrait had not dreamt of and that, strangely enough, even his followers seemed to be unable to render. This advance can be demonstrated by comparison with anatomical group portraits both before and after Rembrandt. The earliest of these is the well-known "Anatomy of Dr. Sebastian Egbertsz.," by Aert Pietersz., Amsterdam, 1603[38] (Pl. IV-5). It shows the complete contingent of guild members, some thirty portrait busts arranged in three tiers. Statistics of attendance, it appears, are here completely irrelevant. One might reduce or expand the number of portraits without aesthetic or iconographic loss or gain. The centermost bust belongs to the presiding surgeon, Dr. Tulp's predecessor but one. In order to distinguish him from the rest, Dr. Egbertsz. has been provided with a torso. The corpse is pointed out to the beholder by two guild members who have turned their heads so that they face out of the picture. In spite of this exertion the anatomical problem at hand (if any) remains totally illegible. The second corporation piece of this kind, van Miereveld's "Anatomy of Dr. W. van der Meer" in the Hospital at Delft, dates from 1617[39] (Pl. IV–6). It is, as we should expect in so great a master of portraiture, a miracle of concentration. Yet in a short time we discover that the portraits are arranged for the benefit of the beholder, without regard to the anatomy itself. The relatively small area of the torso, displayed with unnecessary distinctness, creates a vacuum in the lower third of the composition. It is curious to observe how the tradition by which the corpse is intentionally concealed perseveres as late as 1727 in Thomas van der Wilt's "Anatomy of Dr. Abraham Cornelis van Bleyswyck," at the Delft Hospital. If we then turn to Rembrandt once more, we are struck by the powerful accent he has placed upon the corpse. What relatively little space could, by tradition, be spared for the corpse has been utilized to the utmost. In its diagonal position the body reaches away from the picture plane into depth and darkness, thereby affording the spectator a distinct gauge of space. The position diagonal to the picture plane is a common and ages-old device by which a prone body can serve to express the suffering, surrender, and passivity in general of the defenseless, the dying, and the dead. We find represented in this way the dying in a deathbed scene, the martyred saint, Christ being nailed to the Cross or being circumcised, the patient under the treatment of a surgeon. Rembrandt may well have been familiar with Adriaen Brouwer's canvas showing "Drunken Peasants in an Inn" (Pl. II-2b). In this painting of the middle 20's the foreground is occupied by the rigid form of a dead-drunk man; not unlike the cadaver in Rembrandt's "Anatomy," he is posed on a narrow bench. Also psychologically Brouwer may have paved the way; more than once he showed members of the lower classes in the incongruous poses of what Aby Warburg has so aptly called "Pathosformeln."[40] Rembrandt, like his predecessors painting anatomical scenes, displays the cadaver in cruel discomfort; he shows it resting on an anatomical table shaped like an ironing board and not much wider, the broken neck unsupported, so that the chest is unnaturally pushed upward. The face—Pietersz. uses a pointing hand to conceal it, while van Miereveld simply blindfolds it—is shown by Rembrandt in complete view, though foreshortened and, what is more important, half veiled by a cast shadow that covers the brow and eyes like a transparent curtain (Pl. V-7). A second area of shadow falls on the feet, so that the chief mass of light is concentrated on the essentials of the cadaver. It is tempting to try to read meanings into the use of those shadows. The Middle Ages had known, besides "night the revealer," *nox revelatrix,* also the "shadow of oblivion," the *umbra mortis.* According to St. Bruno (d. 1101), who is represented as "a Carthusian holding a skull upon which falls a ray of light," "mors dicitur tenebrae." It seems to me not impossible that reflections of such scholastic observations could have survived in Rembrandt's own day. Had not Cesare Ripa[401] put a lantern in the hand of the allegorical figure of "Corpo Humano" with the inscription A LVMINE VITA ("van 't licht komt het leven," Dutch ed. 1644, [402] p. 304) in order to show that the body fails to function without a soul, just as a lantern without its light? We may take it for granted that Rembrandt's Catholic counterpart, Joost van den Vondel, fell short of a just appraisal of Rembrandt's greatness in many respects. But just in his criticism of Rembrandtian gloom, Vondel showed understanding of the iconographic message of Rembrandt's shadows, in which he seemed to express the contrast of light and shadow as that of life and death:

> Dus baert de kunst ook zoons van duisternisse
> Die gaarne in schaduwen verkeeren, als een uil.
> Wie 't leven navolght kan versierde schaduw missen,
> En als een kind van 't licht gaat in geen schemering schuil.

> Thus art also brings forth sons of darkness
> Who like to dwell in shadows, like an owl.
> He who follows life can do without the artifice of shadow,
> And, being a Child of Light, need not hide in gloom.

There is reason to assume that Vondel directed his lucid criticism ultimately to Rembrandt's address. The Old Testament had already interpreted shadow explicitly as evil: "Ego Dominus, et non est alter Deus, formans lucem et creans tenebras, faciens pacem et creans malum" (Isaiah xlv: 6f.). The Renaissance knew the vagrant as "a shadow," as an "Vmbra Vagus" or (in German) "farender man," and defined him as "homo vanus et inutilis sine certa ratione discurrens hinc et inde . . ." However far-fetched this definition, no better one could be claimed—as we shall see later—by the former inhabitant of the dissected body.

A functional, concealing shadow, a moralizing shadow, a typifying shadow—we are free to guess which of these concepts, singly or in conjunction, might have suggested to Rembrandt this novel departure.[41]

We must state the obvious, that by casting a shadow over the face and feet Rembrandt enhanced the concentration of light not only upon the main part of the cadaver, but also upon the living, and above all upon Dr. Tulp himself. The contrast between shadow, symbolizing life in private withdrawal, and light, symbolizing public life, was known to the seventeenth century, and a professor at the University of Amsterdam said in gratitude that Dr. Tulp had launched him in his academic career: "e privata mea vita in publicam, e tenebris in lucem protraxit."[42] Undoubtedly the point of the greatest concentration of light was meant by Rembrandt as the point of greatest emphasis in his later compositions, as was early observed by Joachim von Sandrart, who while he was in Amsterdam (1637–42) knew Rembrandt:

> In seinen Werken liesze unser Künstler wenig Liecht sehen / auszer an dem fürnehmsten Ort seines *Intents,* um welches er Liecht und Schatten künstlich beysammen hielte . . .[43]

Having pointed to the aesthetic and iconographic potentialities and implications of light and shadow in Rembrandt's "Anatomy," we must ask ourselves to what extent reality may have emboldened Rembrandt to use such violent contrasts between light and darkness. We know, as I have mentioned, that it was customary to perform anatomies after nightfall, with the aid of artificial light. I presume that Rembrandt's was such a nocturnal anatomy. Unfortunately little is known about location and arrangement of Amsterdam's anatomical theater *pro tem.* between 1619 and 1639. But if this decidedly temporary theater was equipped with windows of any kind, these can hardly have been better than the ones in Leiden, and those were needed, it seems, only when the theater functioned as a museum, i.e. at all times except during the short-lived anatomical season. When we take all this into account, it does not seem too hazardous to assume that Rembrandt conceived of light and darkness as he actually found them; and what he found, we may conjecture, was a ready-made Rembrandtian effect.[44] Rembrandt, I would suggest, saw the corpse during the actual lesson underneath the usual chandelier, carrying twelve to fourteen tapers or lanterns ("blakers") whose light was naturally concentrated on the corpse, the anatomist, and the guild members, while the rest of the room was plunged into relative darkness.[45] Rembrandt seems to have been the first to give a true impression of the actual lighting of a formal anatomical dissection. We can be even more specific by suggesting that the circle or ellipse of light falling on the scene would in reality not have been likely to reach as far as the feet of the corpse, which would have formed the central axis of the lit-up space. The brow of the corpse is in the shadow of Jacob de Witt, the surgeon who is bending forward to look at the open book at the far right. We may gather at least an impression from other, more or less contemporary theaters that were inspired by the Leiden and Amsterdam traditions; I have in mind the little semiamphitheater of Altorf in Germany (Pl. IX-12). We know, incidentally, that the second permanent theater of Amsterdam (completed August 17, 1691 and now accommodating the Jewish Historical Museum) still operated with a chandelier of eighteen *blakers*.

As we thus contemplate the nocturnal anatomies, a parallel again suggests itself to contemporaneous Dutch stagecraft, which commonly operated with artificial and controlled light effects and whose characters resorted to the use of candles and torches "because one doesn't see too well at night."[46]

Naturally, other corporation pieces that were not exactly anatomical portraits representing a public demonstration may also have exercised some influence on Rembrandt's composition. His triad of heads that forms the center of the group of attendant surgeons may, after a fashion, have been inspired by Nicolaas Eliasz. Pickenoy's "Anatomy of Dr. Joan Fonteyn" of 1625 (Pl. VIII-10). Undoubtedly Rembrandt had made a close study of this painting showing a group of surgeons gathered around a skull, a painting that featured Dr. Tulp's immediate predecessor (poet, and physician to Vondel), master anatomist for the few years from 1621 to 1628. We should, however, note that Eliasz.' painting is a fragment; about four additional figures seem to have been destroyed in the fire at the Waaggebouw of the year 1723.

Such dependences, however, lie in the air, and it is easy to overwork them. More striking are the elements by which Rembrandt's "Anatomy" differs from those of his predecessors —above all, it seems to me, on account of his bold rejection of harmony and in particular of symmetry. Dr. Tulp, in contradistinction to doctors Egbertsz., van der Meer, Fonteyn— in contrast, too, to Dr. Deyman in his own composition of 1656 (Pl. XII-16)—as well as many others painted in Holland at a later date, has been placed off-center. It seems not unlikely that in 1632 Rembrandt, instead of conforming to contemporary taste in corporation group compositions, felt himself aesthetically and intellectually attracted by some of the early anatomical woodcuts that Dr. Tulp or other anatomists may have brought to his attention. Indeed, a type in which the presiding professor is invariably found, in profile or almost in profile, seated to the far right and addressing a group with a cadaver clustered to the left was very common in the first half of the sixteenth century. We find it, a.o., in the "Anatomy" woodcut of Berengario da Carpi's *Isagoge*, Venice, 1535 [51] (Fig. 5).

Fig. 5. "Ceremonial Anatomy." Woodcut illustrating Berengario da Carpi, *Anatomia* [51] (1535).

Dr. Tulp's rank in relation to the members of the Guild of Surgeon-Anatomists might be compared to that of a conductor in relation to the orchestra. As will be shown in Appendix III, not one of the guild members in attendance held a medical degree. A barber-surgeon who, as did actually happen, acquired a degree ceased to be a member of the guild. Rembrandt's task, once he had decided to decentralize Tulp, was therefore not an easy one. Tulp had to be made the center of attention while each individual of a group of persons nearly as important (at least from their point of view) had to be given sufficient prominence to satisfy their claim to permanent *gloria* and *memoria* without thereby detracting from either the corporate character of the gathering or the logical focus of the scene. Rembrandt, had he known Junius, would have found encouragement and guidance in the following passage by which the problem of "ordinance" (disposition) is introduced: "A picture containing many figures refuseth to be . . . dallied with: every scheme or figure must have his proper posture and place according to the present occasion. . . . No wonder then if wee are most taken

39

with pictures of a full and copious argument, seeing such kinde of pictures doth as it were put on a new face almost in every figure, suggesting still unto our greedie eye some fresh matter to feed on. . . . That picture is likely to ravish us, wherein every part is not onely perfect in it selfe, but agreeth with the whole also by a naturall and well-disposed collocation and connexion" (Bibliogr.[263] III, v, § 1, p. 307). A little further (§ 6, p. 311) we read: "It is ever requisite that the very figures which are represented in the worke, should teach us by a speechlesse discourse what connexion there is in them: but because in every historicall relation the things that are a doing are ever most remarkable, so is it that an understanding and warie Artificer doth ever assigne the principall place unto the principall figures which have the chiefest hand in the represented action." Three conventional devices used by Rembrandt to this end are obvious: (1) Dr. Tulp is *cathedraticus*, he is seated in the chair of honor and authority; (2) he is *petasatus*, he wears the broad-rimmed hat, the academic badge of the chairman; (3) his hands, and his hands alone, are prominently shown: his right lifting the *extensores digitorum* (not, as one would expect, the *flexores digitorum* of the palm) with a bloodstained forceps, indicating action; his left raised in the gesture of restrained speech. "In familiar speech it is very gracefull gently to cast forth the arme, slacking the shoulders a little, and spreading the fingers of the hand put forth" (iv, § 2, p. 293).[47]

In spite of the asymmetry (to use a modern term), Rembrandt knew how to relate everything not so much to Dr. Tulp as to what might be called the problem posed by Dr. Tulp. To be able to do justice to Rembrandt's compositional intentions we must, as I have hinted before, eliminate two later intruders: (1) No. 7, Jacob Koolvelt, who is flat and insipid, with blushing ears, whose color is purple, who moreover echoes the pose of the colleague sitting to the right, in front of him (No. 4, Adriaan Slabraen), and who blocks the view of Koolvelt's unseeing eye; and (2) No. 8, Frans Loenen, who forms the apex of a Rigelian pyramid and who has nothing to recommend him in dress, pose, technique, or iconographic *raison d'existence*.[48] If we examine the remaining group (Pl. I) it will be noted that they are so arranged as to form a wedge of psychological energies whose thin end seems to point to the forceps in Dr. Tulp's right hand. Rembrandt must have been aware of an acute compositional danger arising from this: namely, the false suggestion of a dynamic movement beginning in the upper left and, *crescendo,* traveling past Dr. Tulp (following the axis of the corpse) out of the picture into space beyond it in the lower right. This menace Rembrandt controlled by building up a powerful yet discreet roadblock: he planted in the lower right the heavy and well-thumbed tome which, supported by a few smaller books, lies open at the feet of the corpse, facing the surgeons within the picture so that, but for insignificant textual matter (suggesting black letter type if not calligraphy) where the page curls up, its content is hidden from us.

Apart from compositional considerations, the presence of the anatomical atlas in Rembrandt's composition may have been suggested by two interrelated conventions: (1) The book, from the fourteenth century onwards, had appeared in connection with a deceased humanist or churchman, often at his feet, marking his life's achievement. The anatomical atlas has a not dissimilar function in regard to the *corpus vile* of which it seems actually an extension. (2) The book also suggests a very common feature in the anatomical tradition of the Renaissance, which liked to read from the authorities (the *praelector!*) (see Figs. 5, 7). In a sense it is, then, an old-fashioned relic of the days of the late mediaeval disputations; in a sense, however, we may also regard it as an expression of the humanistic spirit, characterizing the age that ushered in the compulsory footnote. I shall come back to this problem at a later point.

Rembrandt, even though anything but a radical, appears in the "Anatomy of Dr. Tulp" as an artist who remained astonishingly free from the *clichés* of the nearer past. He was, as I shall try to show, deeply indebted to the tradition of the anatomy picture, a tradition that will lead us back into the fifteenth and sixteenth centuries; a tradition, moreover, that is international rather than national; a tradition, finally, that leads to the medical historians of his own time (its true connoisseurs)—Tulpius, Paaw, Plempius, and others—and from there back to the great initiators of a new form of art who had taken a creative part in the shaping of the artistic commentaries upon their scientific achievements. The role of the artist as a scientific commentator (in sixteenth-century scientific texts we read frequently that So-and-so "illustravit" a given passage with a gloss or note) and the position of Rembrandt van Rijn in this development will be touched upon repeatedly in the following chapters.

V

The 'Anatomy' and the Two Basic Forms of Renaissance Anatomies

Fiat experimentum in corpore vili

E io ne feci notomia per vedere la causa di si dolce morte
(Leonardo, An. B, fol. 10 *verso*)

Pictorem omnia necesse est scire, quoniam omnia imitatur.
Est philosophus pictor, architectus, & dissectionis artifex.
Argumento est praeclara illa totius humani corporis imitatio,
iam pluribus ante annis inchoata a Leonardo Vincio Florentino,
& pene absoluta: sed deerat operi tantus artifex, ac rerum
naturae indagator, quantus est Vesalius. [86]
(Cardanus, *De subtilitate,* XVII)

The field of didactic anatomy as Rembrandt presents it, and as we now know it as a branch of medicine, is a typical invention of the Renaissance. Although in more than one way antagonistic to the mediaeval autopsies, Renaissance anatomy is a descendant of them. Nevertheless it is something radically new that could not have existed in the Middle Ages. I shall try to explain briefly how this new form, which is presented to us by Dr. Tulp, was the result of thesis (i.e. the mediaeval autopsies), antithesis (i.e. the early Renaissance anatomies), and synthesis (i.e. the modern practical demonstrations, first launched by Vesalius).

Public ceremonial anatomical demonstrations, the so-called *Schulanatomien,* were never performed in the Middle Ages. The learned mediaeval anatomists were content to expound the Greek classics of anatomy in the classroom from their lectern and without the aid of visual material, which might have been bodies, living or dead, or illustrations of them. Those authoritative texts were known to them through the Latin translations of their Arabic renderings, which in turn consisted of paraphrases and commentaries rather than the original texts themselves. Their efforts were, therefore, strictly theoretical; they needed, for reference, an actual cadaver as little as a mediaeval artist needed an actual model for whatever he wished to represent. It took many years for the theorists, the acknowledged teachers and practitioners of medicine—other than the lowly barber-surgeons and chirurgeons—to understand the importance of first-hand knowledge of the structure of the human body, of function and *situs* of the inner organs, let alone of practical public demonstrations of such discoveries. To bring anatomy into the open, powerful taboos had first to be overcome. For even where there existed in the late Middle Ages a desire to dissect for the sake of demonstration, the *communis opinio,* as much as the traditional attitude of the Church, offered tenacious resistance. Not before the thirteenth century do we find any evidence that anatomy in the modern sense was beginning to be envisaged. But even when, as early as 1345, the enlightened Lombard Guido da Vigevano postulated anatomical study as indispensable to the physician and, in fact, issued a practical handbook of anatomy, illustrated (for the benefit of his Parisian colleagues) by a set of fifteen large figures (see Pl. VIII-11) in which he depicted (or had depicted) every important step in the dissection of the human body, we notice that the concomitant text remains, as we examine it more closely, a skillful *montage* of the pronouncements of the authorities, while Guido's figures do not show so much what he had seen as what he knew to exist. It can even be shown that, in some instances, the prototypes that inspired him were works of art rather than human bodies.[49]

I need hardly point out (and this is comparatively irrelevant to our survey) that, especially in the second half of the fifteenth century, we meet transitional forms in which realism and fantasy are curiously intermingled. We have, for example, a curious set of Flemish miniatures, now preserved in the Hunterian Library of Glasgow University,[458] which show two barber-surgeons at work in the out-of-doors under the supervision of a knight of the Golden Fleece who is attended by a great number of ermine-clad colleagues (Pl. X-13b). Setting and garb, it has been pointed out, cannot but be wholly fictitious; yet the public character of the scene as well as the exclusive audience of a group of individuals who undoubtedly aspired after fame through anatomical demonstration bespeaks developments that were decidedly in the air.[50]

As a form of public demonstration anatomy did not gain a firm foothold in the time-honored citadels of medicine, Bologna, Padua, Montpellier, Paris, until the beginning of the sixteenth century. Its subsequent development and spread was so fast that by the end of the century anatomy was practiced in almost every self-respecting medical center of Europe. Where there were no medical faculties (and sometimes even where they existed as, for example, in London) guilds of surgeon-anatomists took over. Yet the ceremonial lesson was in the latter cases in the hands of an outsider not a member of the guild: the anatomist with a medical degree. In either case the part of the presiding anatomist was one of great prestige.

The new anatomy created a completely new nomenclature, Latin rather than Arabic; its findings were rapidly codified in anatomical atlases; the anatomical surgeons were soon wielding instruments specifically adapted to their new art (Fig. 6);[51] special anatomical theaters (older, it seems, than the oldest known Renaissance theaters for purely dramatic

43

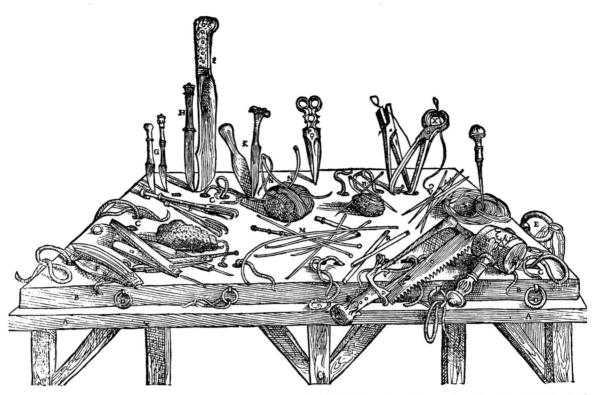

Fig. 6. Joannes Stephan, *van Calcar,* "The Anatomical Table." Woodcut illustrating Vesalius, *Fabrica,*[490] I, xli, p. 200 (1555).

purposes) were systematically perfected (Fig. 4 and Pl. XVI-20); and the corpses were dramatically displayed on rotating wheeled tables.[52]

In order to follow the strands that went into the fabric of Rembrandt's "Anatomy of Dr. Tulp" we must therefore never lose sight of the fact that it represents the synthesis of the two traditions already mentioned, which (since the tradition of the mediaeval autopsies remained very much alive) were to exist side by side for many a decade to come, both doomed to relative sterility until successfully interblended by Vesalius in 1543, less than a century before Rembrandt's picture. The dissecting of bodies meant, at the beginning of the Renaissance, two entirely different pursuits: the autopsies and the formal anatomies. The autopsies or post-mortems derived from the dissections of the Middle Ages. They were, in ordinary circumstances, undertaken out of respect for the person under the knife. An often quoted example is that of the dissection of a queen in the late fourteenth century. The account is, to be sure, completely fictitious. But however fictitious, the first fainting spell of the noble lady, the subsequent disease, her death, and finally the post-mortem undertaken on her nude body were shown in a series of pictures (Pl. X-13a) executed with the optimum of that particular blend of conventional design and partial realism of which only the fourteenth century was capable.[53] In the Renaissance such post-mortems were no longer fictitious. They were purposeful affairs, commonly conducted in the basements of hospitals. As in the Middle Ages, their subjects were, without fail, respected citizens. We can assume that probably the earliest such instance in Renaissance times occurred when the embalming of Pope Alexander V (d. 1410) was combined with a post-mortem.[54] In 1559—and this is only one of innumerable instances encountered in the sixteenth century—there appeared in print a detailed account of the autopsies that Realdo Colombo[102] had undertaken on the corpses of several high dignitaries of the Church, among them that of Ignatius of Loyola (d. 1556). The Popes of the Early Renaissance, above all Sixtus IV, were on the whole sympathetically inclined towards anatomical investigation of this kind. Paul IV sent a corpse from Verona to Rome for the sole purpose of having it dissected.[55] The particulars of autopsies came under the jurisdiction of the Church. For the hospital post-mortems a papal brief was required. There is ample evidence that this document was readily granted to *bona fide* students. Naturally it was also customary for the prospective anatomist to ask the relatives of the loved one for their consent. Cases are, in fact, on record in which the relatives took the initiative by requesting an autopsy, at times out of sheer curiosity. In one or two cases would-be dissectors (e. g. the famous Benivieni) expressed pained astonishment at the refusal of such a common courtesy. It is instructive to see who the people were that did this kind of dissecting. Significantly enough, we find, besides apothecaries and physicians, all kinds of amateur enthusiasts. The most famous of these is, of course, Leonardo da Vinci. Leonardo, aided and advised by the professional anatomist Marc Antonio della Torre, can be credited with having opened, or having caused to be opened, some thirty corpses.[56] A professional man already mentioned, the Florentine Antonio Benivieni, brother of the even more famous Neoplatonic poet Girolamo, wrote a careful account of the observations in nineteen pathological case histories based on the dissection of as many bodies. Published posthumously in 1507, Benivieni's report became the first study of pathological anatomy to appear in print.[57]

While the post-mortems were usually conducted by two, rarely by three or more individuals, in the privacy and seclusion of hospital basements, always with palpable objectives in mind (such as anatomical discoveries from which medicine might profit, or establishing the cause of death, especially where foul play might be suspected), the grand anatomies that I shall now try to characterize were more in the nature of festive and always decidedly public events. Their conduct was in the hands of a strictly circumscribed group of academic teachers. The corpses displayed and dissected were invariably those of criminals. These formal anatomies were enacted to the greater glory of the medical faculties of the universities; a little later, still after the same patterns, to that of the guilds of barber-surgeons, such as the ones of Amsterdam and London. Their character was that of the so-called *quodlibeta,* the sophisticated public disputes that, from the thirteenth century onward, had become as it were the show windows through which the nonacademic outsider could observe and enjoy the goings-on of the universities. The medical faculties of the sixteenth and seventeenth centuries proudly proclaimed their "(venia) legendi, interpretandi, et faciendi medicinam, hic et ubique terrarum, in nomine Patris et Filii, et Spiritus Sancti." The anatomical quodlibets of the medical faculties, like all other academic quodlibets, were spectacles designed to establish and reaffirm such authority; from a strictly scientific point of view they led practically nowhere. It is perhaps permissible to regard them primarily as the academic answer to the miracle plays of the Church, to the *entrées* of Princes, to the *intermedia* of the noblemen, to the religious *tableaux,* and to the carnivals of the guilds and sodalities. They were the fetes of the universities.[58] The crowning feature of the formal anatomy down to 1543 was the verbal disputation, often carried on without reference to the corpse on display. Attention was focused on the anatomical text, which was either read or recited by the presiding *praelector*. The all-over stylization of the show anatomies was also reflected in their outward forms, in the careful distribution of roles among those engaged in the dissecting, demonstrating, reciting, and disputing, and in the elaborate protocol that ruled over the seating of those in attendance—the "distributio," to use the term employed as early as the fifteenth century, "sedendi ordinis pro dignitate."[59]

Although there exist numerous late mediaeval illustrations of anatomical texts, we may take it for granted that no one bothered to attempt a pictorial record of the actual *mise-en-scène* of any of the post-mortems.[60] The grand anatomies, on the other hand, at once demanded and received pictorial commemoration. In Johannes de Ketham's well-known collection of medical texts, the *Fasciculo di medicina*[269] (1493), we see, for example (and it does not matter that professedly this is an illustration of a Mundinus text), in a compressed form, the representation of a typical anatomical quodlibet as it actually took place in Padua from the 1480's onward.[61] (Fig. 7.) This woodcut represents a legitimate antecedent, formally as well as spiritually, of certain aspects of Rembrandt's "Anatomy of Dr. Tulp"; it is more closely linked with it than with any other Dutch anatomy of the seventeenth century. In the chair, distinct from all others in the picture, we find the professor of medicine, whose rank is emphasized by his academic garb. As if to enhance the tradition-bound appearance, the Paduan teacher makes use of the scholastic *comput digitale,*[62] enumerating, we may conjecture, the general schedule by which the anatomy will be conducted; in this particular case in accordance with Mundinus' *Anothomia* of the year 1316.

Other anatomists, in the last decades of the fifteenth century, might follow Galen's *De anatomicis administrationibus,* which had by then become generally available. Although Dr. Tulp does not read from one of the books near him, but rather, as we have seen, addresses his audience at large, we may nevertheless assume that in his case, too, some

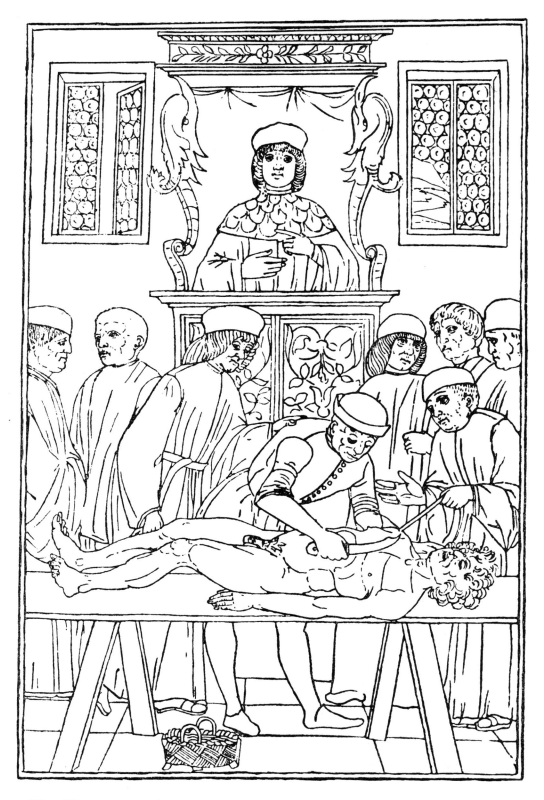

Fig. 7. "Quodlibetum anatomicum." Woodcut illustrating Joannes Ketham, *Fasciculo*,[269] Part Six [= Mundinus], sign. f ii *verso* (1493).

authority is cited from the open page of the folio in the painting's lower right, whereby, quite likely, comparison is made with text or illustration, or both, found on the open *verso* of another anatomical atlas (the *quondam* roll call sheet). But here the agreement ends. In the baroque anatomy the books, which stand for textual authority, are important; yet, since there are at least two that are being consulted, we are left in doubt as to whether one is more important than the other. In any event the authoritative texts are treated as equivalent to the actual anatomical evidence. In sharp contrast to Dr. Tulp, the Paduan professor is completely out of reach of the corpse. The shrinking of available space, the resultant intimate crowding that brings the anatomist into close contact with the spectators and the spectators with the cadaver as well as with him, becomes the symbol of a new scientific attitude.

But further observations are called for in the woodcut scene. The actual dissecting, which is about to begin, is in the hands of a menial. He is the *chirurgus* of the mediaeval post-mortems, also known as the *incisor, prosector* (or *resector*); in sixteenth-century England as the *steward*. In the *Fasciculo* woodcut he is the only person present who does not wear academic garb. The appellation *prosector* for the menial is not without historical significance, because at some Continental universities (such as Hamburg) *Prosektor* is, or was until recently, the title of the *Ordinarius* of Anatomy himself. This implies, at some point in the past, the fusion of two functions, the "professing" and the "prosecting," whose emphatic segregation had been the hallmark of late mediaeval school medicine.

Finally there is the busy little man who, to judge by his gesture, directs the manual labors of the *prosector*. The cane—originally the *radius* of the classical astronomer (and, therefore, among others, also the attribute of Urania)[63]—may, at a later stage of the anatomy, be used to illustrate for the benefit of the spectators an argument that has occurred in the recitation of the professor. The *demonstrator* or *ostensor,* to give him his official title, here has, as it were, the function of the high priest, mediating between the infallible godhead and the common mortals. The division of functions into theoretical, practical, and demonstrative must be ultimately derived from classical antiquity. What until recently was nothing but surmise, encouraged by the purely negative assumption that the Renaissance would not create such intricate hierarchies *ex nihilo,* has quite unexpectedly been moved into the range of the probable: on April 5, 1956 the world learned that among the fifty-odd wall paintings discovered in a hitherto unknown private cemetery off the Via Latina Antica in Rome, there had come to light the representation of a public anatomical demonstration that can be dated in the fourth century A.D. This painting (Pl. XII-15), the only known classical representation of a public anatomy, shows, in a central position, an aged philosopher of a type not unlike that used to represent Galen or medical authorities in the Vienna *Dioscurides* illustrations. He is flanked on either side by a number of younger men wearing the toga who appear to be listening intently while, with a rhetorical gesture of his right hand, he lectures on the dissected cadaver of a small person who appears in the left foreground. The darker than flesh-colored body is pointed at by the *radius* that is wielded by a *demonstrator* (second from right). The theme under discussion seems to be the liver, which (being of an even darker color than the complexion of the rest of the body),[64] is lifted from the corpse by a second assistant by means of a cord. This man may be compared to the menial of the Ketham anatomy. The Roman fresco opens up all kinds of speculative possibilities and makes it very enticing to assume that the illustrators of early Renaissance anatomies must have had access to some classical representation of an anatomy, long since lost, that would, in many points, agree with the one of the Via Latina. How else could we explain the sudden appearance of the classical *radius* and of the menial, both so far removed from the lecturing philosopher?

We know that the most important part of the academic *quodlibeta* consisted of the professor's reading or reciting from an acknowledged text, which then became the basis of the subsequent *disputatio*. Such texts were found in the works of the authorities: either Avicenna's *Canon*, Book I (being the Arabic summary of Galen) or, from the fourteenth century onward, Mundinus' *Anothomia,* whose authority was actually not superseded until 1543, when Vesalius' *Fabrica* appeared in print.[65]

We can date the true rebirth of the classical anatomy from the last decade of the fifteenth century. It was of the greatest importance in this connection that in 1490 Galen's original Greek text, and with it at least a portion of his anatomical writings, had appeared for the first time in a direct Latin translation. Galen, known and praised throughout the Middle Ages—it was pointed out that, anagrammatically, GALENVS reads ANGELVS—if invariably in some disguise and often under the name of an Arabic authority, was from 1490 onward considered the *dernier cri* in matters anatomical.[66] The gain to medicine was, on the whole, undeniable; however, as far as anatomy is concerned Galen's influence was in more than one sense retarding.

When we try to evaluate Renaissance anatomies in the light of the advance of learning we come to the curious conclusion that in the late fifteenth and early sixteenth centuries it was that typically mediaeval procedure, the post-mortem, that truly helped further scientific investigation and progress. At the same time the undisputedly novel public dissections of the universities, with no possible antecedents in the Middle Ages, carried on by the humanistically trained *avant garde* (some of the greatest anatomy teachers at Paris University in the first half of the sixteenth century were originally Graecists), got bogged down in the mire of a typically late mediaeval formalism. Galen's ascendancy may perhaps in part account for the fact that for a considerable span of time it was the unspectacular post-mortems conducted by such curious amateurs and nonconformists as

Leonardo da Vinci—that is, by practitioners to whom Galen meant little or nothing—that helped advance the knowledge of human anatomy. As regards progress, Galen suffered from one decided weakness: he saw on the whole no particular gain in dissecting the human body. To be sure, his pronouncements in the matter are at variance with one another. But he maintained that no one with access to monkeys had ever dissected a human corpse with profit, not even, in his own words, "that of a German killed in the war."[67] Consequently, Galen had dissected pigs galore, a fact that to the Galenists of the Renaissance was a matter of great pride, while the anti-Galenists did their best to hold it up to ridicule. I believe that this point of view is taken by the titlepage of the first volume of *Galeni Opera Omnia* (Venice, 1541)[166] as well as subsequent editions, which show among other scenes Galen dissecting a pig while, to the right in an anteroom, further animals, such as pigs and sheep, are readied for dissection. Andreas Vesalius' *Fabrica*, Basel, 1555,[490] known for its outspoken criticism of Galen, uses repeatedly, among other historiated initials, a large initial *Q* which shows putti adroitly dissecting a pig strapped to one of the new-fangled dissection tables (Fig. 8). The degree to which this may have been meant as an anti-Galen picture is naturally difficult to ascertain. The difficulty is less, however, with the monkeys so highly advertised by Galen.

This emphasis on monkeys as an equivalent for human beings was, as we know, vastly exploited by the Vesalians. They argued, it has been suggested, that if ancient man with

Fig. 8. Joannes Stephan, *van Calcar*, "Q." Woodcut initial used in Vesalius, *Fabrica*,[490] (1555), *passim*.

his much vaunted beauty did not, anatomically speaking, differ from apes, then the most famous of all ancient statuary groups, the one showing Laocoön with his unfortunate but handsome sons, might just as well be represented by apes. Naturally the Laocoön group was, apart from all other considerations, Antiquity's great contribution to the problem of muscles and sinews. If we believe in the appearance of classical remains at the right psychological moment—an admittedly "transcendental speculation," to use Schopenhauer's term for this phenomenon—we may find food for thought on reflecting that the Laocoön group was discovered in Rome early in 1506, and that within twelve months, Benivieni's book on pathological anatomy, the first of its kind, had appeared in print. The synchronicity offers a powerful testimonial to the intensified interest of the Renaissance in problems of human anatomy.[68] How natural it was for the humanists of the sixteenth century to see the Laocoön group in terms of anatomy has been demonstrated by H. W. Janson, who suggested and, I believe, proved that the Titian-inspired woodcut of the Laocoön group *en singes* was executed by Boldrini for Vesalius to serve as a belligerent broadsheet in the great anatomical dispute that had begun to gather momentum around the middle of the century.[69]

VI

Vesalius' *Fabrica* as an Antecedent to the 'Anatomy'

> *[Et contra:]* The ape is a ridiculous imitation of man
> (Galen, [163a] *De anatomicis administrationibus,* IV, i)
>
> Deus stupendi artificii artifex, mundalis regiae
> admirabilem speciem fabricavit
> (Alanus ab Insulis)

Anatomy became a scientific discipline with the publication in 1543 of Andreas Vesalius' *Fabrica*. Vesalius, throughout his book, was moved by a sincere desire to rectify Galen's errors. Nowhere did he deny Galen's greatness. Yet the radical Galenists took exception to the supposed anti-Galenist tenor of Vesalius' book, so that in a sense the book itself was the point at issue of the great controversy. For a considerable time this controversy beclouded the simple fact that the *Fabrica* was the first wholesale demonstration of correct surface and internal anatomy, the first wholly satisfactory mapping out of all or nearly

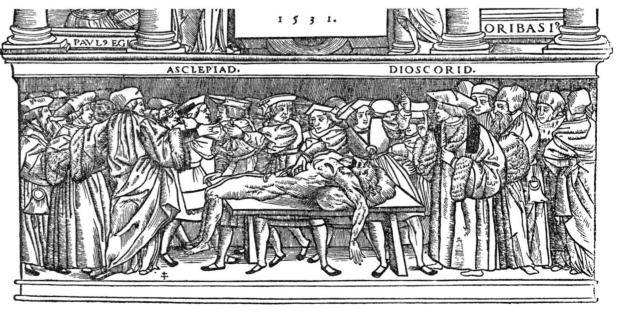

Fig. 9.   "Quodlibetum anatomicum at the University of Paris." Woodcut border (bottom) of the frontispiece of Galen [163] (1531).

all the secrets of the fabric of the human body, in both word and picture prior to the discovery of the circulation of the blood and the invention of the microscope. The book was, from the beginning, designed to appeal to the cultivated reader, not necessarily a physician. Charles V and Melanchthon owned copies of it;[70] Vasari expressed the greatest admiration for both illustrations and text; and artists, habitually greedy for authoritative pictures, were to profit by its beautiful illustrations for generations to come.[71] Final and undisputed acknowledgment of its greatness came late, in the early seventeenth century, and not, as one might expect, at one of the Catholic universities but, perhaps more effectively than anywhere else, at Leiden (see p. 76).

Andreas Vesalius' *opus magnum*, the *De Humani corporis fabrica libri septem*, its popularizing "compendium" (to use Vesalius' own word), known as the *Epitome*, and a translation into High German, all appeared in Basel in the summer of 1543.[72] This, it has often been pointed out, was also the year when Copernicus published his long-overdue *De revolutionibus orbium coelestium*.[106] This and the *Fabrica* constitute two powerful blows at two of the greatest encyclopaedists of late classical antiquity, Galen with his simian anatomy and Ptolemy with his geocentric astronomy. To these we may add, for the same year, Petrus Ramus' attack against the authority of Aristotle's dialectic and the first Latin translation of the *Koran* (by Robert Retensis and Herman Dalmata), a book whose *praemonitio* has been ascribed to Martin Luther, and whose introductory epistle as well as the editing was in the hands of P. Maurice de Montboissier, abbot of Cluny. These publications, launched by self-confessed humanists, were a wholesale declaration of scientific independence; strangely enough, it occurred soon after the final recognition of the Jesuit Order by the Vatican, in the year in which Juan Luis Vives' *De veritate Fidei Christianae contra Ethnicos, Judaeos, Agarenos sive Mohametanos, ac perverse Christianos, libri quinque* appeared in Basel, and at the very moment when the Council of Trent gathered to reaffirm some of the most unscientific concepts of the Middle Ages, which the Renaissance had successfully managed to discard or at least to suppress.

In a positive sense Copernicus and Vesalius helped to establish entirely new sets of gauges and devices by which macrocosm and microcosm respectively could be defined and charted in terms of objective calculations, an achievement of which both authors were themselves keenly aware.[73]

The frontispiece (Fig. 10) shared by *Fabrica* and *Epitome* and recut for later editions was to prove enormously influential, both as a work of art and as a scientific manifesto. It shows the anatomy of a female. The *theatrum* is the customary wooden scaffolding put up in what seems to be a palatial cortile. We may assume that the anatomy takes place under the open sky. The dissection has just started, with all the fanfare of the public demonstrations. The *venter inferior* has already been opened—the customary *incipit* of Renaissance

ANDREAE VESALII
BRVXELLENSIS, INVIctiſsimi CAROLI V. Imperatoris
medici, de Humani corporis
fabrica Libri ſeptem.

GVM CAESAREAE
Maieſt. Galliarum Regis, ac Senatus Veneti gratia &
priuilegio, ut in diplomatis eorundem continetur.

BASILEAE, PER IOANNEM OPORINVM.

Fig. 10. Joannes Stephan, *van Calcar,* "Vesalius Publicly Demonstrating and Lecturing." Woodcut frontispiece, *Fabrica* [490] (1555).

demonstrations. This was done because in the *venter inferior* are situated the *membra naturalia* which are "citius putrabilia." A breathless crowd of students and observers drawn from all classes of society (with what seems to be a fair sprinkling of protagonists and antagonists of the new method) has gathered to watch as the master himself, a young man not yet twenty-nine, places his bare right hand with a pointing *stylus* or *tentaculum* in the abdominal cavity, while his left hand is raised in a gesture of speech. His handsome face is turned proudly to the beholder as if to repeat his famous *dictum:* "Galen never saw a uterus—not even in a dream."[74]

Of course, much of this anti-Galenism was exaggerated. Vesalius was the last to deny that he was deeply indebted to Galen; and he was more so than he would admit himself. This debt extended even to his own errors, as when, for example, he stated that the appendix is not found in adults (which holds true of apes); when he described and depicted the branching of the aortic arch in terms of simian rather than human anatomy; or when he described the purely fictitious *rete mirabile,* a kind of alchemical furnace where, according to Galen and his mediaeval disciples, "vital spirit" issuing from the heart was transmuted into "animal spirit."[75]

Vesalius was a well-rounded scholar. As a youth he had moved in swift succession through three fundamentally different stages of formal education. Beginning as a student of Scholasticism, he was next trained as a *homo trilinguis* in keeping with the finest Erasmian tradition,[76] and he ended a fervent Ciceronian. Vesalius' death and the circumstances accompanying it might lead to some more "transcendental speculations." According to a sixteenth-century report Vesalius was buried in the Church of Santa Maria delle Grazie on the island of Zante (at Zacynthos), October 15, 1564. This was the very place where Cicero's remains had just been discovered and reinterred for a final rest. A happy ending indeed, at least in the eyes of Vesalius' contemporaries![77]

Medicine and in particular the literature of medicine had been cultivated in Vesalius' own family for four generations. When he wrote his *Fabrica* he was firmly entrenched in the camp of the Ciceronians,[78] but I believe that we should be closing our eyes to some very important elements in his make-up as a practical anatomist and a writer on "Natural Philosophy" (thus he refers to himself) if we were to disregard the continuing influence of his earlier, strictly scholastic training.

In view of his humanistic attitude it was of the greatest consequence to the advance of science in the second half of the sixteenth century and beyond that Vesalius himself took such inordinate pride in his manual skill.[79] As early as 1536, when only twenty-one, Vesalius was a student in Paris; his teacher, the eminent Guenther of Andernach, officially thanked his young assistant for having, with his great dexterity in dissecting, aided him in the discovery of the *vasa seminaria.*[80] Vesalius' claim to have been the first to succeed in putting together a functional skeleton (when, in 1536, he had managed to snatch the body of a young man from the gallows at Louvain) has never been contradicted.[81] That Vesalius' title to outstanding manual skill was "in the stars" had even been announced in print by his famous contemporary and colleague Gerolamo Cardano, one of the subtlest observers of his day. Cardano declared that everything in Vesalius' birth date and hour (according to him 5:45 a.m. December 31, 1514) was "up to measure, inasmuch as Mars in the square of Luna affords cleverness and agility of hands"—"studium et agilitatem manuum praestat."[82] Vesalius' contemporaries were plainly fascinated by his combination of scholarship and dexterity. When, after his stay in Paris, he returned to Louvain he startled everybody there by lecturing and anatomizing simultaneously. He did, however, conform on that occasion (1537) to tradition in one point: a professor presided over his anatomy, but had the good sense to refrain from lecturing.[83]

The rather puzzling word *fabrica* in the title of Vesalius' book should, I think, be interpreted in the light of this dichotomy in his make-up. In scholastic tradition the *demiourgos* of antiquity who creates the world had become the divine *faber* who in his creative act combined the manual dexterity of the worker in stubborn materials with intuitive possession of the ideas suggesting the forms of tangible matter. Vesalius, by using his senses to trace the secret design of the *faber mundi*,[84] emulated as it were the *faber* who had contrived the "fabrica humani corporis," spiritually as well as physically. It was in this sense, I believe, that Vesalius would have wished us to understand the word *fabrica,* both in the title of his book and in the many instances within the text.

It should, however, be stated that the specific use of the word *fabrica* to denote the human body was not original with Vesalius. It occurs in patristic writings and is approximated in such titles as that of Lactantius' anatomical work *De opificio Dei (ca.* 303 A.D.). The words "fabrica corporis" appear in the title of an unpublished medical manuscript in the Bodleian Library that dates from the fifteenth century, a circumstance clearly indicating that Vesalius' choice of the term *fabrica* was within the range also of late mediaeval writers.[85]

Vesalius' quick mind suffered from the roundabout way in which anatomy was taught at the University of Paris as elsewhere. He was therefore proudly aware of having brought to an end once and for all the tradition-bound aspect of the anatomical quodlibets, those "detestable rites," as he calls them, with the professors perched "like jackdaws in their pulpits" (Fig. 7), with their verbal fireworks, their time-wasting digressions and question periods ("ridiculis quaestionibus dies aliquot abeunt," *Fabrica* preface), and he was conscious of having abolished the ignorant carving and butchering (these are again Vesalius' words) of the extramural prosectors, who were unable to name what they saw and touched.[86]

Naturally, such a change must have been in the air. That so it was can best be illustrated by means of a woodcut at the bottom of the titlepage of the accepted school text by which anatomical dissections were being conducted at Paris University: Galen's *De anatomicis administrationibus*[163] (1531) (Fig. 9). The editor and translator of this text was Johannes Guenther of Andernach, Vesalius' teacher, already mentioned.[87] The picture is confusing. This fact in itself is significant. The stylized and carefully preconceived arrangement of the formal anatomies has gone, and yet there can be no doubt that the woodcut is intended to show an anatomical demonstration. It is impossible to tell who is who in this representation. The conventional concept of the presiding professor and of the disciplined quodlibet has vanished into thin air. Instead we get a free-for-all, engaged in by some twenty-five persons. All are in academic gown. The class distinction between those teaching, those demonstrating, and those menially handling the corpse—the tripartition of the formal anatomy that, as we saw, the Renaissance had inherited from classical antiquity—has been eliminated. The abdomen of the corpse has been opened, and not just one discussion but a number of lively discussions are under way. An enthusiastic youth, one hand immersed in the viscera, beckons with his free hand to the group of elders to his right. The professor to the beholder's right is engaged in an argument rather than simply holding forth. Another student has assumed an exaggerated contrapposto pose, indicative of divided attention, as he offers a handful of entrails to the elderly man on the beholder's left. Here then a whole world order collapses as what not so long ago had been a stylized ceremony, with carefully assigned roles, becomes the very incarnation of the new spirit of direct investigation, skeptical, democratic, and Protestant.

The Galen woodcut was a first symptom.[88] Vesalius' *Tabulae sex* [493] was a first resolute step in the direction of a new scientific attitude, and his *Fabrica* was a dramatic turning point. We must ask ourselves why those special efforts were needed and why the resistance that had to be broken down was so great.

The reluctance on the part of the academic teachers of anatomy to relinquish their beloved cathedra so that they might do their own observing and dissecting, and their concomitant readiness to accept a statement even though its only claim to credence might be its age or the language in which it had originally been composed, reflects the curious dichotomy between Theory and Practice that had prevailed throughout the Middle Ages —a dichotomy to which the Renaissance had fallen heir.[89]

In order to appreciate the harmonized duality in the "Anatomy of Dr. Tulp," it will be necessary to sketch the stages that led up to Vesalius' and Tulp's synthesis of thinking and acting. Mediaeval man could envisage himself as being beset by three basic shortcomings: Cupidity, Ignorance, Debility. Cupidity might be overcome by exercising the Virtues in a life regulated by the Seven Sacraments; such a path, if all went well, would lead to Charity and to the hope of ultimate Salvation. It was the education of Christ, "quod sola ducat ad beatitudinem et non aliqua Ars alia."[90] Both the physician and the *chirurgus* of the Middle Ages were professionally unconcerned with Salvation; this they wisely left to the Church and her servants. We may therefore leave Cupidity and the Virtues aside, turn to the other two shortcomings, Ignorance and Debility—which called for Theory and Practice, man's rational and terrestrial weapons in his fight against these threats—and see how these were related to anatomy as a craft and as a science. Ignorance had to be countered by the Seven Sciences, which in the Middle Ages were grouped into *trivium* and *quadrivium*, the logical and the mathematical disciplines. Their aggregate, the Seven Liberal Arts, the sum total of the theoretical knowledge accessible to the human mind (not counting that bestowed on man through divine revelation), would ultimately lead to divine wisdom. Finally, there was Debility, man's mortal weakness, the legacy of Adam's trespass. It could be countered, as Adam and Eve had shown when they delved and spun, by neither prayer nor the weapons of the mind but by practical manual labor alone; that is, by exertions designed to ward off the hazards, to diminish the discomforts, to control the thorns and thistles that beset human nature at every step in its postparadisian phase. The motivation was *dura necessitas;* the frame of mind in which those who battled Debility went about their task was that of the *Cura* of the Romans, who turns up, personified as Frau Sorge, at the end of Goethe's *Faust II.*[91] In order to know and to serve God, man must live, and, although not by bread alone, bread is a prerequisite. In contradistinction to the relatively stable canon of the Liberal Arts—which, however, occasionally contained Medicine (Varro) in its speculative-theoretical aspects—the listing of the mechanical ones remained comparatively vague and arbitrary.[92] Originally the Mechanical Arts were characterized by the common trait that all of them aimed at objectives that had to be attained if man was to survive in his fight with the elements of nature. They ranged from the carpenter's skill in furnishing adequate shelter to the sailor's ability to make port, from the farmer's success in raising grain to the barber's experience in dressing wounds, and so on.

As a result of the division of nonpolitical and nonpriestly society into those that overcame Ignorance (which was anchored in the human mind) and those that fought Debility (as it was daily revealed by external factors) we encounter, on the one hand, the noble devotees of the liberal arts and, on the other, the ignoble practitioners of the mechanical arts. Throughout the Middle Ages these two groups, perpetuating a tradition that goes back to classical antiquity—the freedmen versus the *banausoi*—remained strictly separated by a barrier reinforced by the all-powerful injunction of 1 Corinthians vii: 20: "Let every man abide in the same calling in which he was called." For those among the scientists of the Christian Middle Ages that craved tangible proof of their theories, the Doubting

Thomas was a warning example as effective as that of the cobbler who criticized Apelles had been to the Ancients.[93] He who in mediaeval times found it necessary to follow the counsel of the senses rather than that of the *auctoritates* was deemed a victim of *Curiositas*. The *Curieu* of the Renaissance, in contrast, was a collector of objects that might serve as tangible evidence of the divine plan.

It is not to be wondered at, then, that in the realm of mediaeval anatomy none of the great theorists was ever known to have tried to verify—for example, by actually poking a knife into a corpse—the theories that authority had handed down to him. Mundinus, in the first decade of the fourteenth century, initiated the practice of having a menial perform a post-mortem according to his directions—an epochal event. And yet there existed in the thirteenth century, and probably much earlier, men skilled in the use of anatomical knives, scalpels, saws, and similar tools. They were the menials who did the post-mortems, the legal autopsies, penal amputations, and judicial dissections of dead criminals, besides surgical operations and bloodletting—all of which, on one occasion or another, must have given them some insight into the *situs* of internal organs, veins, nerves, tendons, muscles, etc. However, the professions from which these men were recruited were definitely ignoble ones, and the practitioners, being *idiotae,* had no way of formulating or recording, let alone pooling, their experiences. Since it was such villainous persons as barber-surgeons, bath keepers, professional tormentors, and public executioners (sometimes unwilling Jews pressed into service) that did the occasional dissecting of human bodies, no one was likely to object to their pursuits, but, on the other hand, no one paid much attention to their experiences and possible discoveries.[94]

A comparison between the *Fasciculo* anatomy (Fig. 7) and that of the Paris Galen of 1531 (Fig. 9) affords a nice commentary on the contrast between the surviving mediaeval duality and the modern synthesis of theory and practice *in statu nascendi*. Before anatomy-as-a-fete could make its influence felt on Dr. Tulp and on Rembrandt it had to disinte-grate into the *chaos formativum* of anatomy-as-a-free-for-all. Rembrandt's "Anatomy of Dr. Tulp" seen against this background is a truthful reflection of the modern scientific world, firmly established by 1632, in which it is taken for granted that empirical research will be summoned to support theoretical speculation—an ideal illustration of what Francis Bacon had in mind when he used the image of a *"double scale* or *ladder,* ascendent and descendent—ascending from experiments to the invention of causes, and descending from causes to the invention of new experiments" (1605).

VII

The 'Anatomy' as Ideal Synthesis of Theory and Practice

Coegi me ad declarandum anothomiam per figuras
(Guido da Vigevano, 1345)

The barriers between Theory and Practice persisted deep into the Renaissance. In the sixteenth century for the first time the realm of the liberal arts was successfully invaded on a broad front by the practitioners of the mechanical ones, while occasional representatives of the liberal arts prided themselves, as Vesalius did, on their "mechanical" skill.[95] On the whole the scientific future lay with the underdogs,[96] i.e. mechanics who prided themselves on their competence in a clearly defined and delimited field of operation.[97] But however enterprising they might be as individual craftsmen, their practical experience and professional competence were doomed to remain useless to others unless they knew how to distill them into theories; and theories, in turn, were doomed to remain ineffectual unless they could be broadcast through the printed word. On some subjects—and anatomy was one of them—even printed texts would be of little avail unless supported by intelligible diagrams and by illustrations showing the human frame in correct proportions. Here the artists came in; for almost inevitably, by choice, by tradition, and by necessity, they were at home in more than one of the mechanical fields outside their own craft, and in the sixteenth century they had succeeded, above and beyond any of the other mechanics, in placing their own work on the pedestal of mathematics (i.e. perspective and proportion), thus making painting and sculpture part of the liberal arts. Fields such as anatomy, now halfway between the mechanical and the liberal arts, they cultivated by practicing anatomy themselves, by illustrating anatomical atlases, or by representing the surface anatomy of the human body so admirably in their free creations that a work of art could at times inspire the medical scholars as much as nature itself. "Small wonder, then, that painters rushed in where doctors feared to tread" (Panofsky). Leonardo da Vinci could proudly refer to himself as "pittore anatomista."

The finest tribute to the "pittore anatomista" came from Gerolamo Cardano in his *De subtilitate*[86] of 1553. (See also our Motto to Chapter V *supra*.) Having ranked *pictura* ("mechanicarum omnium subtilissima") higher than *sculptura*, because the former uses shadows and colors and commands perspective, Cardano goes on to say: "The painter inasmuch as he must imitate everything must know everything, including some of the latest inventions. The painter must be a philosopher, an architect, and himself versed in dissection ("dissectionis artifex"). An illustration of which consists in that most distinguished imitation of the entire human body which several years ago Leonardo da Vinci had begun and nearly brought to perfection: yet the master of the entire work was yet wanting and the investigator of the nature of things, and this is Vesalius." That this *dictum* was current in the circle of Rembrandt's art-minded friends becomes evident through Vossius' quotation of it *in extenso* in his "De graphice" of 1650.[98]

It was unavoidable in all mechanical fields that, for lack of modern texts, a hiatus should occur where there arose this sudden desire for codification of a new kind of knowledge in printed books. This hiatus was temporarily bridged by a sudden revival in print of practical handbooks composed in the late thirteenth and early fourteenth centuries. A few examples will suffice to illuminate this situation. Modern scientific agriculture was brought into being by fifteenth-century readers of Petrus de Crescentius' thirteenth-century treatise on rustic matters, the *Liber ruralium commodorum,* whose illustrated *editio princeps* appeared in 1471.[111] Pierre de Maricourt's (Petrus Peregrinus') *De magnete* of 1269,[370] published in its *editio princeps* in 1558 and illustrated with several woodcut diagrams,[99] lent its name to and became the prototype of William Gilbert's study,[183] which can claim to be one of the earliest scientific works whose theoretical findings were based entirely on rigorous observation and experimentation. Gilbert's *De magnete* appeared in London as late as 1600. The mediaeval *Portolani,* practical handbooks indispensable to navigators, especially in precompass days, were printed in Dutch editions from 1490 onward and, in the hands of English sea captains, contributed decisively to Admiral Howard's victory over the Spanish Armada. Copernicus owned and used a copy of the thirteenth-century *Astronomical Tables* of Alfonso X. The publication of Mundinus' *Anothomia* of 1316[331] —its *editio princeps,* issued at Bologna as well as Pavia, dates from 1478, with subsequent editions in quick succession—helped to pave the way toward modern anatomy.[100] Thus, as has often been pointed out, tongues that had been tied for hundreds of years were suddenly loosed in a revolution—spiritual, material, social, all in one—perhaps as radical and certainly as far-reaching as that of the contemporaneous Reformation.

Naturally the protagonists of the new order were wary of all codified authority.[101] They were instinctively skeptical of the two great spiritual powers of their day, Scholasticism and Humanism: Scholasticism because it tended to prevent anyone from leaving his preordained sphere of activity; Humanism because it operated with the time-honored authorities of the classical past.

The progressive anatomists in particular had to overcome the deep-rooted aversion of the Humanists, who strenuously objected to pictures illustrating "their" texts. A frontispiece that gave *cachet* to a publication and decorative borders, especially if they also served practical functions (such as the division into books and chapters), might be tolerated.

The Humanists' deep-seated aversion to book illumination has, as we have learned recently, its striking parallel in classical times. Classical manuscripts were, as Carl Nordenfalk puts it, "instruments for declamation," just as, to us, scores and phonograph records are tools for musical performances. Texts, in classical antiquity, were meant to be recited, and where there are adornments they served primarily as reading aids; they marked the divisions of the text, rather than helped embellish the book, to say nothing of elucidating the ideas expressed by the author.[102]

The terms "illustrare" and "elucidare" were originally used to denote verbal commentaries on authoritative texts. Illustration of books by pictures that aspired to the glories of a scholarly commentary or glossary were, for a long time to come, anathema to the devotees of the word. Book illumination in all fields claimed by the Humanists was extremely slow to assert itself as an independent form of scientific communication. Its unavoidable association with the illuminated manuscript page of the mediaeval codex militated against its employment for classical and related texts. Any subject matter hallowed by ancient authority, such as anatomy, had to be kept from being contaminated by illustrative images. Inroads could be made at first only from the periphery, as it were. The process was astonishingly slow. Significantly enough it was a German, Conrad Peutinger, rather than a Southern European, who published the first illustrated book on Roman epigraphy, reproducing specimens found not in Rome but in Augsburg, for which a "special fount of lapidary capitals was cast."[103] Certain fields, such as geometry (Euclid, 1482),[145] architecture (Vitruvius, 1511[495] —"cum figuris et Tabula ut jam legi et intellegi possit"), numismatics (1517),[161] the Roman column (Diego de Sagredo, 1526), medicinal botany (Brunfels, 1530),[72]104 succumbed more easily because here the texts were almost useless without accompanying images. One might, of course, point to Francesco Colonna's *Hypnerotomachia,* which appeared in 1499[103] in a sumptuous edition, as a seeming exception to the rule. After all, in its woodcuts we find a treasure house of classical imagery, architecture, statuary, epigraphy, hieroglyphics, ground plans, fashions, armor, sacrifices, artificial gardens, *trionfi,* and, threading their intricate course through all this, a pair of fictitious lovers worshiping pagan divinities and straying among real ruins. But much as we cherish these illustrations as an Early Renaissance paradigm in the reception of classical antiquity, there is enough evidence to show that the book-buying public of Colonna's own day—and that is to say the Humanists—took little note of the *Hypnerotomachia,* which, financially speaking, was an outright failure. In the words of E. P. Goldschmidt, who devoted an important study to *The Printed Book of the Renaissance*,[193] the reason is that Francesco Colonna's work was a "romance" rather than an "archaeological disquisition."[105] Dante's *Divine Comedy* (a work as central to the Humanists of the Early Renaissance as Horace's *Odes* and *Satires* or Cicero's *Letters* or the *Hermetics*) tempted Botticelli to enter into competition as it were with Cristoforo Landino's commentary when he essayed his first set of illustrations for the Florentine edition of August 30, 1481.[118] His illustrations never went beyond the nineteenth of the thirty-three cantos of the *Inferno*. If we may trust Vasari, the project made Botticelli a laughingstock among his contemporaries, for, "senza aver lettere o appena saper leggere, commenta [sic] Dante!"[106] In spite of Erasmus' interest in art and his love of conceits that lent themselves equally to *pictura* and *poesis*, Holbein's marginal illustrations for the *Praise of Folly*[139] were not published before the last quarter of the seventeenth century.[107] Typically enough, the first illustrated Ovid (*Metamorphoses*, Bruges, May 1484)[348] offered a set of images illustrating what turns out to be a French translation of Pierre Bersuire's *Ouidius moralizatus* of *ca.* 1340—crude and beautifully literal woodcuts fashioned after the pictures of an illuminated manuscript of *ca.* 1480;[349] and when Bersuire's Latin original was published, early in the sixteenth century, it at once incurred the wrath and ridicule of such opposites in the camp of Humanism as Martin Luther, Erasmus of Rotterdam, and François Rabelais.[108]

As we now turn to the field of anatomical illustration, we find that the idea of the anatomical atlas in the modern sense had not been realized before the year 1538, when young Vesalius issued the so-called *Tabulae sex*[493] by way of a trial balloon.[109] Six years later, in the introductory paragraph entitled *Lectori* (found on the titlepage of his *Epitome*),[491] Vesalius addressed the reader with the astonishing statement that it did not matter one way or the other whether one started a problem with text or with *tabulae* (i.e. illustrations).[110] How does such radical disregard of the time-honored pre-eminence of the word harmonize with the fact that Vesalius was a Humanist first and foremost? Quite obviously the revolt against the humanist disdain for pictorial commentaries had no hope of success unless it started in the humanist camp itself. In Vesalius the singular combination of uncompromising Ciceronianism[111] with an implicit belief in the truthfulness and trustworthiness of the senses (especially those of touch and sight) accounts for the success of his anatomical picture atlases. These problems were, however, far from easily settled. Only one year had elapsed after the publication of the *Tabulae sex* when Jacobus Sylvius, Vesalius' powerful and eloquent opponent in the controversy-to-come, declared that Galen would never have wished to resort to pictorial aids. Even the most learned zeal could add nothing to his anatomical descriptions; for proof, one ought to compare Galen's Greek text with what Sylvius calls the book of Nature. Pictures, Sylvius stated, were detrimental to the physician and, at best, suited to arouse the imagination of women.[112] Vesalius undoubtedly took up this challenge when, in his *Fabrica*, he scoffingly spoke of the "seeming contradictions that could be gleaned from the anything but mendacious book of the human body"—"paradoxa ex hominis haud mendaci libro deprompta."[113] In 1551 Sylvius gave vent to particular horror at the frivolous use of shadows in the *Fabrica* woodcuts, which he branded as "decidedly superstitious and obscure, and thoroughly useless . . ."[114] No wonder that to the adherents of the new observances authority for authority's sake was a great black cloud. Leonardo expressed this notion beautifully when he said: "Anyone who in discussion relies upon authority uses not his understanding but rather his memory."[115]

VIII

Rembrandt's Appreciation of Dr. Tulp,
the 'Vesalius Redivivus' of the Seventeenth Century

Manus (inquiunt) est organum organorum
Manus [Dei] est, quae eligit, & reprobat,
quae laudat, & vituperat, quae absolvit, & condemnat
(O. Scarlatini,[422] pt. 1, p. 197)

(i) Manus vero, . . . vix dici potest quot motus habeant
(ii) As for the hands, . . . it is hard to set downe how many motions they have
(iii) Wat de handen belangt . . . het is onuytdruckelick hoe veele en
gantsch verscheydene beweghinghen
daerin te vinden sijn
(F. Junius,[262, 263, 264] III, iv, § 2)

Rembrandt made his debut with the "Anatomy of Dr. Tulp." The mere statistics of his commissions in the next years give clear evidence that he had succeeded in pleasing the members of the anatomical guild. This pleasure must have been derived, in part, from factors outside the purely aesthetic realm. In the eyes of those who commissioned the painting its chief merit, I venture to suggest, must have been the complete balance between lifelike realism and its manner of idealizing the models individually and corporatively. This public success could not have come about had Rembrandt not shown deep interest in the scientific side of his theme. We might, however, well ask at this point whether, by crediting Rembrandt with a strong interest in medical science and medical illustrated works, an interest transcending the call of duty as it were, we are not simultaneously questioning his integrity as an artist; an artist who here for the first time unfolds the full force of his creative energies in the posing and solving of problems of composition and design, in the ordinance of masses and the distribution of light—phenomena utilized to the full in the creation of a secluded and yet inviting interior space and in the study of psychological relationships expressed by the careful interweaving of glances.

That the "Anatomy" is a miracle of organization is true enough. But the seventeenth century was not as yet responsive to purely aesthetic considerations, so that we must not rely on them too heavily. Moreover, a few details in the painting seem to cast doubt on a one-sidedly aesthetic view of Rembrandt's inner motivations. Dr. Tulp is shown explaining the function of the *musculi digitos moventes* of the lower left arm and hand. We have had occasion before to point out that Renaissance anatomies began with the *venter inferior*. This was, a. o., true of Rembrandt's second anatomy, which dates as late as 1656 (Pl. XII-16). An anatomy that, like the one of 1632, begins with the hand is therefore most likely a deviation from actual reality, yet not, as one might expect today, by poetic license but for reasons of thematic emphasis. Coincidence will have it that there exists one earlier dissection of the left arm (and right leg) in what has been characterized, rightly I think, as "the earliest example of an 'artistic' anatomy in pictorial form." This is the wholly fictitious dissection of a female, undertaken by members of the Order of the Golden Fleece, found in manuscript 9 of the Hunterian Library at Glasgow [305f] (fol. 22 *recto*) (Pl. X-13b), a Flemish work of the second half of the fifteenth century.[116] The fact, then, that Rembrandt's representation of Tulp beginning with the dissection of the arm is, to put it mildly, highly improbable as a statement of the actual procedure allows us to hazard a guess about his preparatory steps in designing the anatomy proper. I think that the painted cadaver is based on most careful sketches and observations before the actual body, after the execution and before the beginning of the dissection. I also think that Dr. Tulp, for reasons of his own, suggested that Rembrandt should portray him, against all convention, at work on the functional aspects of the hand and that for this purpose he, Tulp, furnished Rembrandt with a scientific representation (most likely a Vesalian woodcut that might have been taken from any number of anatomical atlases). (Cf. Pl. X-13b and Fig. 11 a and b with details of the dissected arm and hand.) Needless to say, Rembrandt's copy of a woodcut appearing on the roll call sheet points in that direction. That Rembrandt painted or sketched the anatomical particulars "from life," that is to say while Dr. Tulp's anatomical lesson was in progress, can be ruled out. To say it once more: a seventeenth-century anatomy would never begin with arm or hand. The dissected parts Rembrandt has clearly superimposed on a cadaver drawn after nature. Once this observation has been made, especially in front of the original painting, the pasticcio quality of the painted cadaver becomes inescapably evident. The dichotomy between realistically observed corpse on the one hand and mechanically copied anatomical detail on the other is stressed by the fact that the dissected parts are totally out of proportion with the rest of the body. We need only compare the dissected arm with the considerably shorter and well-proportioned right arm. Besides, the anatomy as designed by Rembrandt is faulty. Since there does not seem to exist the possibility that the dissected part was painted or even altered by a later hand, this faultiness points to the probability that Rembrandt used an anatomical illustration and, undetected by Dr. Tulp, failed to interpret it correctly. The tendons that correctly appear on the back of the right hand (the *extensores digitorum*) have been transposed by Rembrandt to the palm of the left. The fingertips are curled up, clearly indicating that the palm of the left was meant to be shown after all (see Pl. XLVIII–58). My "Hier irrt Rembrandt" is uttered not in a spirit of carping but in order to clarify the probable steps that he took in the development of this painting.[117]

Rembrandt shows the corpse surrounded by books, one of which is undoubtedly illustrated with woodcuts of the dissected lower arm and hand. In connection with the problems of composition and design I had occasion to refer to the folio at the feet of the corpse. This tome, placed on a separate table or lectern against three or four other books piled one on top of another in still-life fashion, with the spine of one separate upright volume visible farther back, is what we might call "the portrait of a book." The effect intended is perhaps not completely intelligible, because the canvas at right and left (about two centimeters of it on either end) is folded back over the inner support. The unbecoming nineteenth-century frame, even after having been reduced by about four centimeters in 1950, still covers too much of what ought to be visible.

Rembrandt may have needed the open folio as an anchor to provide compositional stability. Undoubtedly the book was also there to be noticed for its own sake. It is open at a passage that deals, as has been suggested, with the muscles moving the fingers of the human hand. It would be indeed attractive if we could categorically state that the folio is the 1555 edition of Vesalius' *Fabrica* [490] as was suggested by Jantzen in 1926. If it were so, the open pages would be 258 and 259 (Fig. 11). Unfortunately the typographical matter on the open left page has in its grouping of letters, to say nothing of the type face, no resemblance to those pages in Vesalius' book. They rather seem to be written in Rembrandt's characteristic semigothic script, of which, however, only initial B can be ascertained. We know too little, I think, of the liberties Rembrandt might take with lettering to tell whether he would ever deviate so far from the original form. The calligraphy of the letter in the hand of the portrait of "Martin Looten" (1632) is partly decipherable. The "Scholar" of 1631 (in the Ermitage) is, on the other hand, clearly excerpting a tome written in an undecipherable hand of which, again, only initial R can be seen. We must therefore state that the open folio in Rembrandt's "Anatomy" is not a Vesalius, but at best a Dutch work. Since, however, the average Dutch anatomical publication of the early seventeenth century prefers quarto size, the folio size could possibly point to a manuscript.

Only after an opportunity to re-examine the original did I discover that there is a second anatomical atlas in the painting. Its open pages appear more distinctly after the recent cleaning, but still covered by the roll call sheet, in the hand of Hartman Hartmansz. (Pl. I-1a). At first I thought, as is generally assumed, that we had discovered an anatomical drawing by Rembrandt himself; but closer inspection shows—and this new evidence is partly a disappointment—that what a later artist turned into the roll call sheet is not a single sheet but a verso page belonging to the left half of an open book whose right

quod in ᶠcubito &ᶠ tibia habetur,etiam primi ufus ligamentum exiftit,quum   *f* 7 *tab.* V.
& ad ofsium connexū egregiè auxilietur. quamuis etiā hçc omnia & ad quinti   *g* 4. & 11 *tabulæ* 2
ufus ligamentorū claffem reijci poffent,quòd non obfcurè mufculis etiã prin-   *fig.* 4.
cipium porrigant. Qui enim internā & externā pubis ofsis foraminis fedé ob-
tegūt mufculi,ab illius quoq; foraminis membrana partim enafci dicentur:uti
etiam ab eiufmodi ligamēto in tibia nōnulli mufculi originis portionem affu-

Ligamētorum differentia. munt.. Porrò ut ligamentorū non idem ufus eft, & plures inter ligamēta eius
Ab ufu. gratia confurgunt differentiæ: ita quoq; in ortu,infertioneq̃,& partibus quas
Ab ortu. cōmittunt,uariant: quum alia ad folas fpectent cartilagines,ut laryngis,& nafi
alarū ligamēta: alia ad fola offa,ut genu,cubiti,humeri,& alia permulta corporis ligamēta: alia ad cartilaginē & os pertineant,ut ea quę pectoris ofsi,coftarū
nectunt cartilagines. Alia uerò aliã partem quampiã ofsi aut cartilagini cōmit
A partibus, quas conne-ctunt. tunt, ut corporis mēbranæ ad unā ferè omnes: atq; hæc femper duabus partibus funt cōmunia. Alia uerò uni dūtaxat ofsi priuata cēfentur, ut fex cubiti ex-
A partibus, quibus com-mittuntur. teriorum ligamentorū,quæ tranfuerfim ducuntur quinq;. nam primū, quod
ulnæ radioq; cōmune eft,non ad unicum tantum os referetur.Infuper & quæ
pubis ofsiū foramina opplent mēbranę,huc quoq; fpectāt,fi modò illę (quum
A fubftantia. non ligent) in ligamentorū numero habeātur. Subftantia demū alia conftant
molliori,magisq; membranea,ut omnia ferè quæ in orbem articulos ambiūt:
quanquam in illis rurfus quædam fit differentia.Digitorum enim internodia
mollius ambit ligamentū,quàm humeri articulum:& huius denuò duritiem,
coxendicis articuli ligamentū longè fuperat.Alia autem dura funt, mediamq;
inter ligamenta quæ articulos ambire dixi,& cartilagines, naturam fortiūtur.
unde etiam Græci hæc νευροχονδρώδη σύνδεσμα,quafi ligamenta cartilaginea di-
cas,appellant. Huius generis omnia propemodum funt, quæ extrinfecus arti-
culis non obtenduntur,fed inter offa ipfa latitant: quale illud eft,ʰ quod ex me-   *h* o.
dio capitis femoris in coxendicis acetabulum fertur, &ⁱ ea quæ uertebrarum   *i* *fig. cap.*
corpora intercedunt,&ᵏ id quod ex media tibiæ fede,quà hæc femur refpicit,   14 *lib.* 1 R.
inter femoris capita ducitur,&ˡ quædam malleolos talo nectentia, & quod fa   *k* X.
crum os iliumq; offa interuenit,& generatim omnia quæ inter offa fedem ha-   *l fig.*
A fitu. bent.Vnde etiam & fitu ligamenta inter fe pugnant,quum alia extrinfecus of-
fibus obducantur,ut molliora illa: alia autem inter ipfa offa,ubi fe inuicem re-
fpiciunt,cōtinguntq;, fituentur,quemadmodum cartilaginea propemodum
A forma. uniuerfa.A forma quoq; ligamenta differentiam mutuantur: funt enim quę-
dam prorfus lata, membranea & tenuia:uti illud, quod fecundùm cubiti lon-
gitudinem inter ulnam radiumq; cōfpicimus: & illud,quod pari modo inter
fibulam & tibiæ os, ubi hæc mutuò dehifcunt, obferuatur,& etiam pleraq; in
orbem articulos circundātia: eaq; tandem omnia, quæ tendinibus mufculisq;
obuoluuntur.Alia autem craffa funt,& ex his quædā teretia: utᵐ ligamentum   *m fig.*30
ex dente fecundæ ceruicis uertebræ, in occipitis os procedens:&ⁿ id pariter,   *cap.*1.
quod tranfuerfim denti obducitur,primæq; uertebræ eft peculiare: deinde   *n eiufdem*
&ᵒ ligamentum, femoris caput coxēdicis ofsi in articuli medio committens,   *fig.* H.
teres etiam uifitur.Alia ampla lataq; funt,utᵖ tertium peculiarium humeri ar-   *o* 3 *f. cap.*
ticuli ligamentorū: præter membraneū quoddā, in orbem articulū ambiens.   49 P.
Infuper genu articuli peculiaria omnia, craffa quidem funt, non tamē prorfus   *p* 13 *tab.* V.
teretia: ut & cartilaginea,talū tibiæ & fibulæ colligātia.Rurfum quædam con
tinua,& nullo foramine peruia cernūtur,ut ligamentorum maxima multitu-
do,quædā uerò aliquid tranfmiffura perforantur,ut ligamēta anuli modo ten
dines tranfmittentia: & membrana pubis ofsis foraminis, neruo cum uena &
arteria

Fig. 11a.   Vesalius, *Fabrica*,[490] p. 258 (1555).

arteria uiam præbens: ut & membraneum ligamentum, inter tibiæ os & fibu
lam consistens. Commune autem omnibus ligamétis est, quòd obtuso admo- *Ligamentis*
dum sensu (nollem enim dicere nullo) participent: ne propter crebrum fre- *communia.*
quentemꝗ; motum, & cótinuum affrictum, dolore uexentur. Qua etiam ferè
ratione (quum scilicet natura sicca sunt) ne ocyus exsiccétur, ligaméta muco- *Viscidus liga*
so quodam lentoꝗ; humore, ut etiam articulorum cartilagines, oblinuntur. *mentorum*
humor.

QVID MVSCVLVS. CAPVT II.

PRIMA huius Capitis figura, musculi structuræ ratio, qua
omnes dissectionis professores musculum formari hactenus tradi-
Φ,Ω. *derunt, utcunꝗ exprimitur. Quod enim inter* Φ *&* Ω *contine-*
tur, nerui cuiusᵈa est portio suprà infráꝗ abtruncata. uerùm hæc
characterum indice opportuniùs explicabuntur.

A Nerui in plures soboles distribuendi portio.

B Nerui A notati soboles, musculi constitutionem subiens.

C Ligamentum, quod ab osse ad musculum constituendum prona-
scitur, cui æqua ferè cum nerui sobole debebat esse proportio.

D Ligamenti & nerui ad musculum efformandum congressus, ac
prima in fibras distributio, musculiꝗ caput.

E Sedes, qua fibrarum maxima est diuisio, & qua musculi uenter
consistit.

F Diuisionis fibrarum concursus, commixtióꝗ, & tendinis seu cau-
dæ musculi initium.

G Tendinis pars, quæ mouendo ossi inseritur.

PRIMA SE-
CVNDI CA-
pitis figura.

SECVNDAE FIGV-
ræ, eiusdemꝗ characte-
rum Index.

SECVNDA figura, musculorum
humeri, seu brachij os, & cubiti ossa, &
extremam manus sedem ambientium fi-
bras, à carne quodammodo liberas, com-
monstrat, unà cum quarto brachiū adeun-
tium neruo: ut hic, quàm fieri posset com-
modissimè, musculi fabricæ natura oculis
subijceretur.

H Humeri caput, quod scapulæ articulatur.

I Quartus brachium petens neruus.

K Principium musculi cubitum extenden-
tis, qui ab humeri capitis radice exoritur.

L Principium alterius cubitum extenden-
tis musculi, qui ab humiliori scapulæ costa
pronascitur.

M Sedes, qua quartus brachiū accedens ner-
uus, duobus cubitum extendentibus mu-
sculis propagines offert.

N Cubitum extendentium musculorum fi-
nis, seu eorundē in posteriorem ulnæ pro-
cessum insertio.

O Posterioris ulnæ processus pars, quæ excar-
nis perpetuò cernitur.

P Quartus brachium petens neruus, inibi
conspicuus, quà posteriori sedi exterioris tu-
beris humeri innititur, ac musculis hinc
ab hu

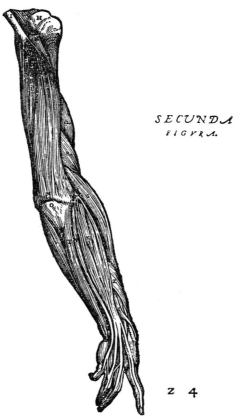

SECVNDA
FIGVRA.

Z 4

Fig. 11b.   Vesalius, *Fabrica*,[490] p. 259 (1555).

half remains concealed under the right shoulder of Dr. Tulp. Dr. de Vries, the director of the Mauritshuis, showed great wisdom, it seems to me, in refraining from an all too radical cleaning and in resisting the temptation to remove the roll call sheet. It is, however, difficult in the circumstances to make out the details by Rembrandt's hand that certainly lie underneath it. Two words suggesting a heading ("Anathomia…"[?]) can be seen on the original page. They do not seem to suggest printed letters, but that too cannot be stated with absolute certainty. The possibility remains that the "book" that Hartmansz. firmly clasps with his left hand may also have been intended to represent an illustrated manuscript. The illustration, which thus might be the representation of either a drawing or a print, looks not unlike the large woodcut that we see on the right-hand page (p. 259) of Vesalius' *Fabrica* of 1555 [490] (Fig. 11b). I suspect, then, until further evidence pro or contra can be brought to light, that this sketch is fashioned after the *Secunda Figura* of the Second Book (chap. ii, sig. z 4). The Lord giveth and the Lord taketh away. Walter Artelt has clearly demonstrated that Jantzen's argument for Rembrandt's ownership of the *Fabrica* of 1555 is not tenable, because the anatomical atlas (adduced by Jantzen as proof of his contention) is Laurentius' *Historia anatomica*,[281] one of the many works in the wake of Vesalius' opus. Yet I believe that Rembrandt may after all have owned the Vesalius (at least as late as 1656), because he seems to have made use of it for his second anatomy, the "Anatomy of Dr. Deyman" in Amsterdam; for here the head of the corpse is undoubtedly derived from Vesalius' *Tertia septimi libri figura*,[490] which is found on p. 758 and which, in a large series of cranial figures presented by Vesalius, is the only one that shows an unbearded face[118] (Fig. 12).

There are at least three main traditions that I believe to be iconographically responsible for the rich array of books in Rembrandt's "Anatomy." They by no means exclude one another. Of course, above all, the book was an integral part of every traditional anatomy picture; from the beginning it was the text under discussion of the anatomical quodlibet. Apart from the Ketham anatomy already discussed (Fig. 7), I would draw the reader's attention to the elaborate representation of *Real. Col*[ombo] *Crem. de Viscer. Lib. XI,* which indicates the actual topic of the "Didactic Anatomy of Barber-Surgeon Master John Banister" of the year 1581[26] (Pl. XI-14). Secondly, the book may claim a time-honored tradition as an attribute of the humanist's portrayal. These representations begin with tomb memorials and ultimately go back, in part at least, to representations of the Evangelists and, in imitation of them, Church fathers as well as inspired theologians. The earliest known tomb memorial of this type, showing a learned author with his books, dates from about 1475; it represents a professor of canonical law, Johannes Mainberger (Ingolstadt, Frauenkirche). It is here that convention begins to place a book or books at the feet of the reclining figure of the deceased. But this may also be, consciously or un-

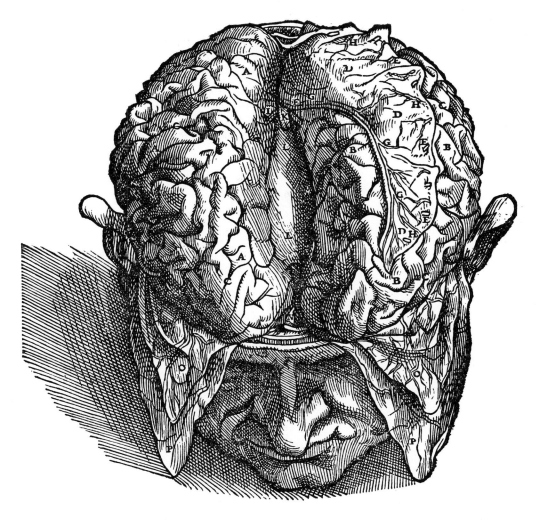

Fig. 12. Joannes Stephan, *van Calcar,* "Figura tertia septimi libri." Woodcut illustrating Vesalius, *Fabrica,*[490] p. 758 (1555).

consciously, the revival of a third and much older tradition that links the book with the effigy of a person deceased. I have in mind the *pugillares* of the classical deathbed scenes, the tablets on which the last will and testament of the dead was recorded. The second and third categories, too, may have found an echo in Rembrandt's "Anatomy." The rich array of books seems to justify the prominence of Aris Kindt; they were the works of the great anatomists that referred to his frame as the ideal Microcosm reflecting the divine plan[119] (Fig. 13). And finally we must realize that in Rembrandt's work in the 1630's certain books (such as the fat folio bound in soft leather at the feet of the corpse) played a prominent part and undoubtedly belonged to the *requisita* of his workshop.

Fig. 13. "Homo sev Microcosmvs . . ." Woodcut frontispiece of Robert Fludd, *Anatomiae amphitheatrum* [155] (1623).

Notwithstanding the difficulties in identifying the books in the painting, it is probable that they are "the authorities." Rembrandt, as much as the persons in his painting, quotes, as it were, from these authorities. Furthermore, there can be no doubt that the painting was commissioned as an apotheosis of Dr. Nicolaas Tulp. The fact that Dr. Tulp is shown busying himself with the anatomy of the human hand allows us to be even more specific. Rembrandt's contemporary Barlaeus summed up the "Anatomy" as he saw it in 1639 by stressing, besides the "eloquence of learned Tulpius," the nimbleness of his dissecting hands (see p. 22 above). These, as we have seen, were the combined characteristics of the modern anatomist that Vesalius had been the first to propagate. But apart from such general agreement Rembrandt managed to implant in his representation a reference that established an even more immediate link with Tulp's great predecessor of the sixteenth century. Taking into account the preceding considerations, we must ask ourselves why Dr. Tulp should have wished to see himself portrayed as the master of the anatomy of the hand, the *organum organorum* as St. Albertus Magnus and others called it.[120] This question brings to mind the large woodcut portrait representing Vesalius (Pl. XIV-18) which, dated 1542, is found in the *editio princeps* of the *Fabrica* publications of the subsequent year and in the Basel edition of 1555, as well as in many others thereafter. Vesalius is shown in half figure, displaying a specimen of a dissected lower arm. On an adjacent table, as if a *titulus* were needed, we notice on a curling piece of paper a casual longhand notation that begins: "De muscolis digitos / mouentibus (etc.)."[121] Vesalius, as the reader of his Introduction to the *Fabrica* knows, was a veritable cultist of the human hand. He could point to the etymology of the word *chirurgia*, which may be translated "manual intervention" and which Hieronymus Brunschwig, in 1497,[74] rendered with "Hantwirckung der Wundartzney," and he might consequently speak in rhapsodic terms and at length of the hand as the "primarium medicinae instrumentum." Vesalius was proudly conscious of having paved the way for his revolution in anatomy when, as an undergraduate, he performed a feat hitherto unattempted: the dissection of the muscles of the human hand.

Small wonder that as a result of the *imitatio Vesalii* it became a fashion even to cast anatomists in their portraits in the Vesalian character. I shall mention a few examples. There is in the first place an engraved portrait of Giulio Casserio (1561–1616), Vesalius' successor's successor at Padua, who, although most famous for his anatomy of the ear, nevertheless had himself represented dissecting the human hand—in content though not in form a descendant of the Vesalius portrait[122] (Pl. XVII-21). Most curious is the portrait of "Bontius Leo" (whom I have been unable to identify) painted by Leandro da Ponte, Bassano (d. 1622) (Pl. XV-19). Since the name of the sitter as well as the coat of arms may well be a later addition, it seems to me not impossible that this is an instance of the appropriation of an idealized portrait of Vesalius. The painted portrait of Volcher Coiter (1534–*ca.*1600) of 1575 shows the anatomist-embryologist in a gesture of speech while his left hand holds a dissected arm and hand.[123] In a sense Rembrandt's "Anatomy," if we regard it as a eulogy of Dr. Tulp, stands in the tradition of those portraits of anatomists who had cast themselves in the Vesalian pose or who were in some fashion associated with the dissected human arm and hand. We may presume that Dr. Tulp intentionally appeared as the Vesalius redivivus of his age, and we must ask to what extent he was worthy of the epithet.

Nicolaas Tulp was born in Amsterdam on October 11, 1593. He died in The Hague on September 12, 1674. He signed his name and in private life referred to himself by his proper name "Claes Pieterszoon"; in its Latinized form, Nicolaus Petreus. The name Tulp was, indeed, not a family name. It was an appellation derived from Claes Pietersz.' parental house, which, it is said, may earlier have served as an auction place for tulips. Ample evidence shows that the inner identification of Tulp with the "tulp," the Dutch word for the flower, increased as the years went by. After the exciting years 1636–37 no one could doubt the magic of the staggering value that the *tulipomania* had bestowed on the tulip. In an age so ready to resort to metaphor one was naturally inclined to pun on names. In this sense we must understand the significance of the exquisite "Tulip Beaker" (Pl. XLVI-55) that was made for Nicolaas Tulp by Amsterdam's most outstanding silversmith, Janus (Joannes) Lutma, in 1652 when Tulp was almost sixty years of age. Lutma had chosen as a prototype a specimen of the renowned "Admirael" species, of which some fifty members were known that on the average fetched prices as high as Dr. Tulp's annual salary as an anatomist. The highly prized flame-colored markings, which are carefully recorded in the contemporary catalogues (Pl. XLVI-55), Lutma suggested by means of an alternation of smooth, shining patches on the gilt surface of the flower petals, and minutely punched areas by their silver-gray matness were meant to indicate the flaming red markings of the "Admirael de France" (cf. Pls. XLVI-55 and XLVII-56). A contemporary French writer praised in those tulips "la tendre chair blanche marquée de sang." Lutma's silver tulip rises from a small mound of earth that only slightly covers the bulb and is adorned with minute replicas in shallow relief of various plants, roots, and what seems to be an indication of rippling water. The flower petals are, on the other hand, disproportionately large in order to accommodate the beaker. A tiny but true-to-life lizard has crawled up the flower stem and is about to inflict a ferocious bite upon the petals. This motif, ultimately derived from the dragons crawling up Romanesque candelabra and croziers, may have been encouraged by the tulip paintings and sketches of Jacobus Marrel (1614–81), who frequently enlivened his still lives with crawling things. If however we regard the beaker as a personal tribute to Tulp, the lizard's role may well have been designed as a memento of the forever menacing attack of Death. The beaker nicely sums up the personality of Tulp as that of a great man whose justified pride was tempered by constant awareness of life's fleeting quality.

Tulp was indeed a distinguished scholar. He was the first to describe the *vasa lactea* as well as the *valvula ileo-coecalis,* discovered in 1632 and known as the *valvula Tulpii.* These discoveries at once became internationally known, and distinguished men in the medical field credited them—with how much right I cannot say—to Tulp.[124] He was, besides, an important figure in the civic affairs of his home town, Amsterdam. He served, among other posts, as magistrate, i.e. city councilor (1629–53) and four times as Burgomaster (1654ff.); he was city treasurer on eight different occasions (1645–72), Orphan Master (1649 and 1660), curator of the Latin school; and Curator of the University (1666ff.). He inspired the reform of 1636 that for the first time unified the Dutch Pharmacopoeia (the so-called *Winkelboek*), a tribute to his great talents as an organizer and as a competent botanist.[125] While Tulp flourished, Jacob van Campen, inspired by Palladio, Scamozzi, and Ripa, designed (1648ff.) Holland's most remarkable neoclassic baroque building, the Town Hall, now the Royal Palace in Amsterdam. Miss K. Fremantle has published contemporary evidence that by implication makes it more than unlikely that Tulp would have approved of the great prominence of the heathen gods in its iconological program. But although Tulp may have been somewhat narrow in his cultural appetites and bigoted in his religious outlook, he belonged to the very exclusive *Muiderkring,* the informal assembly of Holland's most distinguished neo-Latin poets and thinkers. He was moreover a connoisseur of scientific illustrations,[126] the first to publish reliable portraits of two animals of mythical repute: the narwhal *(unicornu marinum)* and the anthropoid ape *(satyrus indicus),* the latter a live orangutan sent to Prince Frederik Hendrik of Nassau from the East Indies.[127] Tulp was the first to give a delightful description of the Chinese tea ritual.[128] He served as *praelector* and *anatomicus* of Amsterdam's venerable Guild of *Chirurgijns,* 1628–53.[129] At a very early date he taught special courses to Amsterdam's midwives,[130] and he entertained his sophisticated colleagues in the city government with private anatomical demonstrations in the City Hall. All these were extracurricular activities. Dr. Tulp, finally and principally, was a general practitioner. He was *primus* among the fifty-eight doctors and accredited apothecaries; of the latter Amsterdam, a city of about 150,000 inhabitants, counted sixty-six in the year 1640, thanks largely to the efforts of Dr. Tulp. He was the first to go out to his patients in a one-horse coach (which he kept in the basement of his house on the Keizersgracht),[131] and he did so as long as the use of coaches in the city was permitted (1663). As a physician he was wise in his conservative use of drugs, and he was full of warm human interest in the individual fortunes and backgrounds of his patients, many of them artists and their relatives,[132] whom he approached with an impressive mixture of gravity, perspicuity, and humor, as he showed over and over again in his *Observationum libri* (1641 ff.).[477-80]133

Dr. Tulp, then, was a great and good man and a first-rate scientist in all possible branches of medicine, including anatomy. There are, however, more specific reasons, I believe, for linking him with the Vesalius tradition. Tulp was a product of the University of Leiden. The medical faculty of Leiden had not only witnessed but actively engendered a Vesalius renaissance, in testimony of which Dr. Pieter Paaw (Tulp's teacher as well as the founder of Leiden's anatomical theater) had published in 1616, two years after Tulp's promotion, a reissue of Vesalius' *Epitome* of the *Fabrica*. Paaw thereby implicitly laid claim for Leiden to the legacy of one of the proudest products of her great sixteenth-century counterpart: the Catholic school of Louvain, Vesalius' *alma mater*. In his "Lectori Benevolo" (Leiden, 1616)[492] Paaw says that all the world had conferred upon Vesalius the title of "Prince of Anatomists"—except for Italy, which would not admit defeat at the hand of a *homo Transalpinus:* "Principis imo Anatomicorum titulum ipsi conferente totius humani generis consensu. Solis exceptis Italis, qui se ab homine Transalpino superatos in studio quo ipsi prae ceteris mortalibus perdiu excellere credebantur indignati," and so forth (fol. 2 *recto*). Dr. Tulp, who in 1614 had returned to Amsterdam, may have felt that it was incumbent upon himself, a very conscious *homo Transalpinus,* to transfer to his home town of Amsterdam the glory that shone upon Leiden from both Padua (Pieter Paaw's *alma mater*) and Louvain.134

Rembrandt dated his painting 1632. Since we know this to be the date of the actual anatomy, we may assume that he finished it not long after January of that year. But whatever the exact date of completion, January 1632 was the month of the painting's birth and, quite likely, also of the commission. January 1632, at the same time, had brought final recognition to Amsterdam's "illustre school." There was ample reason, then, to wish to commemorate at the very center of mercantile activity what amounted to the dawn of a new era of scientific endeavor. That such expectations and hopes were amply fulfilled will be shown in our last chapter.

IX

Dr. Tulp's Attitude Toward Rembrandt:
'Arte sua vix ulli secundus'

Vitam et virtutem a parentibus accepit, caetera sibi ac virtuti suae debuit

That Dr. Tulp and Rembrandt were sympathetically inclined toward each other, we may conclude from what I have said. Dr. Tulp was the kind of man with whom Rembrandt could talk and from whom he could learn a great deal, while feeling himself respected as a craftsman in his own right. It has been suggested that Rembrandt's decision to settle in Amsterdam in 1632 (the exact date of his arrival, sometime late in 1631, cannot be ascertained) was partly caused by this most flattering commission. Undoubtedly it promised relations with a great scientist who was also a socially prominent man, a leading figure in the affairs of a city whose affluence and rising reputation had just begun to attract numerous outsiders from the more tradition-bound parts of the seven United Provinces, as well as from other countries.[135] Whether this contact was maintained after 1632 we have no way of telling; at least, none from explicit documents. Rembrandt and Tulp were, after all, exceedingly busy men. There is, however, some roundabout evidence suggesting that their paths crossed once more in after years. In the first place, Rembrandt was intimate with Jan Six (1618–1700), whose mother, Anna Wijmer, he supposedly portrayed in 1641 and who had become (June 28, 1655) the son-in-law of Nicolaas Tulp by marrying his daughter Margaretha.

It is also possible that Rembrandt was Dr. Tulp's patient and that he consulted him at some point in the nine-year period following the "Anatomy." An unnamed painter was a patient of Dr. Tulp's in or before 1641. Dr. Tulp, in common with many other anatomist-surgeons in the seventeenth century, was also a general practitioner specializing in pathology and neuropathology, as we know from his *Observationes* (i. e. case histories) published in its *editio princeps* in Amsterdam, 1641. Moreover, he treated several Amsterdam artists and their relatives.[136] One of the artists (mentioned in Book One, chap. xviii) remained unnamed, for obvious reasons of professional discretion. He was referred to in terms hardly applicable, at least from the point of view of the seventeenth century, to anyone but Rembrandt: "arte sua vix ulli secundus." This "Insignis Pictor"—in Tulp's phrase—

suffered from the somatic delusion that his bones were melting away like wax, so that his limbs seemed to him in constant grave danger of buckling under his weight. Pain and anxiety compelled the *malade imaginaire* to spend an entire winter in bed, until, by humoring him while at the same time secretly treating what he had diagnosed as his true complaint, an atrabilious condition, Dr. Tulp managed to guide him away from melancholy and permanently back to health and work:

> This patient perceived the restoration of strength to his bones, the return of normal functioning to his joints, the freeing of his stride, and some other matters; but how that foolish delusion of one whole winter had been cunningly extirpated — that he neither perceived nor suspected, though he was a man in other respects anything but dull-witted, and in his own art accomplished and second to hardly any.

The complete text of this chapter will be found in Appendix I. It is a remarkable piece of psychological interpretation, whoever the victim of the delusion, and deserves to be read next to Vasari's *vita* of Piero di Cosimo and to the famous report on the treatment of the suicidal impulses of Hugo van der Goes ("tam famosus in arte pictoria, ut citra montes sibi similis . . . temporibus illis non inveniebatur"), a report in which Caspar Offhuys had immortalized the great skill and foresight of *pater* Thomas Wyssem, prior of the Red Cloister near Brussels.[137]

We know as yet much too little about the interrelation of diseases to their time. Fashions in illness undoubtedly existed in the past as they do in our own day. It is curious to hear that Caspar Barlaeus, one of the most exquisite neurotics of his day, did not dare sit down because he suffered from the delusion that his behind was made of glass. Since such delusions were considered (and treated) as melancholy afflictions, we can even envisage the possibility that Rembrandt, in his temporary delusions, may have thought he had found legitimate access to the finest attribute of genius, *melancholia*.[138]

X

Rembrandt and 'Original Composition'

Poeta nascitur, non fit

Ars pingendi initia sua habet a natura. Nam insitum est nobis imitari:
ac magnam ex imitatione capimus voluptatem; cui ars incrementa sua debet
(G. I. Vossius,[502] § 3, p. 62)

Two hitherto neglected facets of Rembrandt's personality and character seem to me to come, however vaguely, to the fore. Though a constitutionally insane Rembrandt is a *contradictio in adjecto,* a Rembrandt *melancholicus*—though for the time being he must remain hypothetical—is an engaging speculation, especially from the point of view of the seventeenth century, which could hardly pay an artist a higher compliment. The unnamed suffering artist of Tulp's lucid account perfectly embodied the traditional classical-mediaeval definition of medical melancholia, a condition which, according to Constantinus Africanus, was primarily physical, involving mental *accidentia* aptly described by Constantinus, in truly Aristotelian terms, as "timor de re non timenda, cogitatio de re non cogitanda, certificatio rei terribilis et timorosae et tamen non timendae, et sensus rei quae non est."[139] Tulpius' therapy, we may guess, aimed at re-establishing a balanced *commixtio* of temperamental juices. A person whose black bile was neither too hot nor too cold might rate as the noblest of beings: as a "melancholicus harmonicus." The second neglected facet of the artist is the circumstance that he was deeply involved with problems pertaining to anatomy as a science two years before the first independent publication presenting surface anatomy for artists appeared in print.[140] This aspect may be as difficult to accept as that of a Rembrandt suffering from neurotic delusions.

We prefer to think of Rembrandt as a sensitive artist, blind to extra-aesthetic factors such as his model's particular professional aptitude and the ephemeral prestige of the Institution or Corporation to which he was attached. It is here that we tend to forget three considerations: First, great men rarely oblige by conforming to our ideal image of them, however closely this image may be based on historical sources. In consequence we are bound to detect occasionally in their biographies some form of *penchant,* hobby, idiosyncrasy, or fetish that, however insignificant in the great man's *vita* as a whole, will seem painfully at variance with one's common sense or *cliché* notions. Secondly, we tend to forget that even the most stable of personalities is subject to unpredictable vacillations. Rembrandt, however, was not only not stable, but in 1632 he was about to embark upon a phase during which he demonstrated an amazing receptivity to all kinds of external and hitherto alien influences, above all those that were coming to him from the humanistic camp. It has lately been shown that Rembrandt should not only be counted among the great baroque commentators upon the Bible, but also that in his planning of the "Claudius Civilis" (Stockholm)—that is to say in his intellectual interpretation of the customs and mores of the early Dutch and Teutons, the *fratres Romani Imperii*—he showed himself to an astonishing degree independent of the views held by his painter colleagues, who in contrast to Rembrandt based their knowledge on Grotius' treatise of 1610 and dressed the Batavians in Burgundian costume.[141] Thirdly, we tend to forget that our concept of the artist as a genius did not by any means have general currency, even among the artists themselves, in the first half of the seventeenth century. The idea of heaven-inspired gifts that can raise an individual beyond the limits of rank, sex, nationality, and birth had existed again, after the hiatus of the Middle Ages, since the beginning of the Renaissance. Vasari, in fact, had applied it to Leonardo, Michelangelo, and other artists, although, characteristically enough, for their acumen as imitators of Nature. When we turn to the Holland of the 1640's it is interesting to note how elated were Rembrandt's learned friends and well-wishers at the *ingenium* of a fellow artist, that of a multitalented lady of high social standing: the poet Roemers Visscher's younger daughter, Tesselschade (1594–1649; widowed 1634). This young lady, apart from being a member of the leisure class of her day, can best be described as an art amateur in the best sense of the word. In Barlaeus' rhapsodic words:

> The entire lady is a miracle to me . . . as regards *ingenium* there exists nothing more divine and sublime. She conceives of things belonging to realms where vulgar minds do not penetrate. Whatever lowly and humble thing SHE treads underfoot is yet higher than the clouds to THEIR contemplative faculties. She does not contrive apophthegms, she founds them. In sententious sayings and in repartee she is pointed and full of wit. She writes verses not in one language but in Dutch, French, Italian, and she makes them elaborate so as to keep the midnight oil burning and full of concealed meanings so that a second, nay a third reading leaves you all the more learned. She paints with the brush, and challenges Apelles. She sculpts, and challenges Praxiteles. She weaves and spins in competition with Arachne. She sings to the envy of Sappho. She beats the lyre after the manner of Orpheus or Amphion. She composes and arranges bows and wreaths of fruit, leaves, flowers, shells with such art as to leave doubt whether nature yields to art or art to nature. She imitates flowers in lace so that you would swear them to be live ones. She writes with such accurateness and elegance that the printing presses have long lost their praise. Her speech is persuasive as well as of rare beauty. She expresses with her eyes truthfulness, with her gait modesty, with her gestures condescending gravity. The *virtus* of her soul is a single quality but one which comprises all others. The Greeks [Aristotle] call such a quality "Justice, all Virtue in sum."

It is possible that an allusion to this eulogy, with distinct satirical undertones, occurred on the Amsterdam stage in 1648 when it was said of an embroideress that she obscured even the paintings of Rembrandt with her needle—"dat zy de schilderyen / Van Rembrant zellever, verduistert met de naald, &c."[142] Rembrandt, as Seymour Slive has shown in *Rembrandt and His Critics,* did not have to worry about the acclaim of his contemporaries. Yet, however hard Rembrandt may have tried in the 1630's to cast himself in the role of Apelles and to disguise his sister or Saskia mythologically, we sense at once that he, a painter who painted for a living, had relatively little to offer to the arbiters of *ingenium* among his contemporaries.[143] As Slive sums it up: "His name came easily to the lips of his peers when they thought of painters; but none of them suggests he was an unparalleled genius or an uncompromising rebel." The Roman *dictum:* "Poeta nascitur, non fit," although revived as a Renaissance aphorism, was not taken as an injunction until much later—that is, not before the second half of the eighteenth century, nearly a hundred years after Rembrandt's death.[144]

One of the most eloquent and at the same time most effective pleas advancing the novel concept of the creative artist as the chief and only exponent of untutored genius, and with it the concept of plagiarism (which, of course, had existed before), is found in an anonymous pamphlet that appeared in London in 1759 and was such a success that a second edition became necessary the same year. This work was the *Conjectures on Original Composition,*[524] whose author, Edward Young, then seventy-five, was and still is best known as the poet of the *Night Thoughts.*[145] A few phrases taken more or less at random from the *Conjectures* read as follows:

> Genius comes out of Nature's hand, as *Pallas* out of Jove's head, at full growth, and mature: *Shakespeare*'s Genius was of this ["adult," as opposed to "infantine"] kind (p. 31) . . . Genius may be compared to the Body's natural Strength; Learning to the superinduced Accoutrements of Arms . . . (p. 30). An *Original* [viz. work of art] may be said to be of a *vegetable* nature; it rises spontaneously from the vital root of Genius; it *grows,* it is not *made* . . . (p. 12). *Shakespeare* mingled no water with his wine, lower'd his Genius by no vapid Imitation. *Shakespeare* gave us a *Shakespeare* . . . (p. 78).

From this eighteenth-century point of view, which scorns imitations, Shakespeare in his writings and Rembrandt in his etchings and paintings might be cited again and again as the outstanding examples of untutored genius; that is, genius that produced, to quote Vincent van Gogh (on Rembrandt), "without the aid of intellectual intervention," genius privileged to bring forth the highest and noblest of which the human spirit is capable. The first reference to Rembrandt as "vrai génie" comes from an Englishman some fifty years after his death, and the first comparison between the genius of Rembrandt and Shakespeare occurs in the writings of Johann Kaspar Füessli at the end of the eighteenth century.[146]

In the wake of this all-powerful concept of "Rembrandt giving us a Rembrandt" there has been an understandable tendency to forget that both Shakespeare and Rembrandt grew up at a time when artists were as yet far from creating for the sake of creation and when they learned by copying and imitating other artists whom their masters considered exemplary—a habit that neither Shakespeare nor Rembrandt ever found necessary to discard in after years.

The social status of painters in the Lowlands and elsewhere was anything but uniformly stable and assured in the early Baroque. The first half of the seventeenth century everywhere was a period of transition. Rembrandt's own career offers a good illustration: he moved from commissions and from sales aided by art dealers towards increasing independence until in the end he painted for his own satisfaction. The advent of the intervening art agent helped to loosen the patronage relationship between the artist and the Maecenas. Italy sees the beginnings of a new social class, difficult to place: the independent artist-*bohémien*, of whom the Dutch *Bentvueghels* offer an example. The artist does everything in his power to differentiate himself from his fellow citizens in dress and mores. France sees the advent of the dictatorial academician. In Velasquez' and Murillo's Spain we hear of a lawsuit, symptomatic of this uneasiness as to the artist's place in society, brought to establish whether or not the ten-per-cent tax on products of manual labor should be levied on painters. This happened in 1633, one year after Rembrandt's "Anatomy of Dr. Tulp," and again on a later occasion.[147] Rubens—the diametrical opposite to Rembrandt, who rubbed his paint into his clothes and inflicted his pet monkey on an unwilling *clientèle*[148] —was an *eques* as well as a scholar. At the height of his fame he would dictate letters while painting, and, more subtly still, he would actually "dictate" compositions to his assistants. Such radical transfer of the trappings of the ivory tower to the artist's *bottega,* the delegation of the brushwork to a staff of menials, as well as the employment of engravers to help spread artistic ideas, was perhaps chargeable not so much to Rubens's desire to commercialize his art as to a desire to withdraw from its ungentlemanly aspects. We should look in vain for such newfangled aspirations in Rembrandt.

At this point I shall ask the reader to assume for the time being that Rembrandt, in his design of the "Anatomy of Dr. Tulp," was formally and by content indebted to a number of sixteenth-century prototypes that were not necessarily representations of anatomies. If that is true (and I hope to demonstrate it in detail), how are we to understand his mentality when (in the words of Edward Young) he "superinduces Accoutrements of Arms," when he quotes as it were from sixteenth-century scientific literature (see p. 70), when he "lowers his genius by vapid Imitation," and when he follows patterns created by others, down to details such as his stage setting or the arrangement and function of his *dramatis personae* or the accessories such as the authoritative books?

82

Rembrandt, a son of his epoch, stood under the sway of the theory of imitation, both as a carry-over from scholasticism and in its new formulation by the humanists. *Imitatio* turned to nature or the exemplary work of art, forever avoiding what the Italian theorists called *ritrarre*. The classical *artes poeticae* and, in the field of rhetoric, Cicero and Quintilian took over in the writings of Franciscus Junius, Gerard Joannes Vossius, and others, where the Fathers and St. Thomas Aquinas had left off.[149] To the Middle Ages and to the Renaissance artistic creativity was at best a shadow of the creative act of God; a divinely inspired gift. This interchangeability of terms referring to either artistic or cosmic creation was natural to the Fathers of the Church: "You are painted, Man, painted by the Lord your God. You have a good artist and painter; do not wantonly destroy that picture."[150] According to St. Thomas Aquinas it is "necessary to assume that in the divine mind there be a *forma* [we should speak of a 'model'] in whose similitude the world was made." This statement follows upon a discussion of the possible forms of creation: (1) "natural," as for example, "fire breeds fire," "man breeds man"; (2) "intelligible," that is, "divine." To illustrate the latter form of creation Thomas cites the architect "in whose mind there pre-exists the house [which he is planning to build]; and this may be called the idea of the house. . . . Only that house can be called true which accommodates the similitude of the *forma* that is found in the artist's mind." And, as Thomas readily admits, in practice this usually means that, rather than resort to the mental *forma,* the artist will turn to the exemplary realization of the idea or *forma* in someone else's work; "for thus a given artist will conceive the *forma* from some art-work [*artificio*] [which he has seen] from the pattern of which he intends to work."[151] The artist's willing dependence on the inner *forma* and his untiring quest for valid external *exempla* (that is, the crystallizations of such *formae* in the exemplary works of others) represent the very counterpole to free artistic creativity as it began to flourish in the course of the eighteenth century. This dependence alone makes it possible to speak of style in art. Such reliance on authoritative patterns, taken for granted in the Middle Ages, was far from having spent its normative force in Renaissance and Baroque. Franciscus Junius sees the ideal of *imitatio* in the seeking of an "unequal equality" of the modern work with its *exemplum:* "Our Imitation is then onely to be commended, when it doth after a most lively manner set forth in every particular the true force of the work imitated."[152]

As in every great work of art of the time, we may expect to find also in Rembrandt's "Anatomy" the liberal use of *exempla* gathered from the most divergent quarters, which through the alchemy of Rembrandt's art have been united into one incomparable *forma* that may be called all his own. To do justice to this *forma* that Rembrandt carried in his mind we must try to trace the *exempla* in patterns already in existence and demonstrably known to Rembrandt, because he used them in others of his compositions, too. We must

83

also look out for the archetypes behind the *exempla*. This quest will lead us to scenes of lamentation and of martyrdom and to justice pictures than can claim to be the legitimate ancestors of Rembrandt's "Anatomy of Dr. Tulp." Those forms were, in turn, carriers of certain meanings. Consequently there will be found in the "Anatomy" a variety of nuances of meaning that will help explain why it is in part a sacrificial scene, in part a ritual scene, and in part a scene of justice.

Fig. 14. "Public Anatomy." Woodcut illustrating Bartholomaeus Anglicus, *De proprietatibus rerum*,[38] V, chap. i, sign. f. vj *verso* (1495?).

XI

The Origin of Anatomy Pictures:
A Study of Antecedents in Form and Content

Nihil innovetur nisi quod traditum est

Our attempt to interpret Rembrandt's "Anatomy of Dr. Tulp" will be greatly aided, I think, by a study of the origins of the earliest anatomy pictures. The earliest true representations of public anatomies are found in illustrations of late mediaeval anatomical texts. But even before the earliest *quodlibeta anatomica* there were transitional forms, that is to say didactic autopsies conducted for the benefit of a broader public. The first of these lead us back to the year 1345. In that year we find a series of interrelated illustrations produced by Guido da Vigevano. They present us with a curious hybrid form, half postmortem, half public demonstration, that makes them important to this survey. The pictures designed by or for Guido were expressly made to serve as a substitute for the benefit of physicians unable to attend an anatomy. As we turn to the *Secunda figura anothomie*, first of a subsequent series of representations of the various steps of dissection (Pl. VIII-11), we see the author himself: Guido da Vigevano, physician to King Philip VII of France. Dressed in academic habit, he is shown wielding a knife in an effort to open the *venter* lengthwise. This was the traditional *incipit* of a dissection as prescribed by Mundinus, reputedly Guido's teacher. The anatomist is standing beside the upright cadaver. The art historian will notice at once that the corpse is curiously related to representations of nude corpses on tombs. Although we know of the latter no examples before the last decades of the fourteenth century, I believe that we should count here, as in other pictures of his series, on Guido's dependence on *exempla* rather than on first-hand observation of nature. The fact that the earliest known *gisants* occur in France and Western Switzerland respectively indicates a close relationship in which at present it seems impossible to give precedence to either *gisants* or the early anatomical representations as found in Guido's *Anothomia*. Our suspicion of Guido's dependence on art works is strengthened when we discover that the first figure in the actual series, the representation of a living nude on whose torso the names of some of the interior organs have been inscribed for purposes of demonstration, was inspired by some piece of sculpture rather than having been drawn from life. The *exemplum* Guido used in this case may have been a church portal figure, or he may possibly have been inspired by a minor work of art, such as an ivory, attached to a shrine; witness the tiny canopy above the head, which the artist did not think it necessary to eliminate[153] (Pl. VIII-11). Needless to say, Guido da Vigevano's interesting and in many ways highly original series did not and could not lead to the creation of a representational type of general validity for later artists. This could, in fact, not happen until formal anatomies had become performances open to and leveled at a general public. It was only then that the need was felt for the creation of an acceptable standard of representation.

Once anatomies had begun to be performed in the open, as public events and according to certain generally agreed rules, artists must have cast about for useful prototypes showing them how to go about the grouping of their figures and the designing of some kind of stage setting. Figure composition and stage setting had necessarily to be found outside the field of anatomical illustration. A picture of one of the earliest formal anatomies may be that encountered in a woodcut illustration of Bartholomaeus Anglicus' *De proprietatibus rerum*. This mediaeval encyclopaedia, of which Book Five was devoted to the anatomy of the human body, had been translated into French in the course of the fourteenth century, *s.t. Proprietaire des choses*,[37] the *editio princeps* of which appeared in Lyon in 1482. The woodcut is found at the head of Book Five, chap. i (sign. e. iiij *verso*). (Fig. 14.) Later editions, such as the English rendering (Westminster, 1495[38]), repeated this picture with slight variations. Most likely the artist who designed the woodcut had at his disposal no picture that would show him in graphic rendering the conduct of a formal public anatomy.[154] Nevertheless the picture was not intended as an illustration of the mediaeval text, but was plainly aimed at representation of a new kind of event. How, we must ask, did the design come about? A clear-cut *invenzione* we can rule out as being just as unlikely as the idea of this artist's attending a formal anatomy, sketch pad and silverpoint in hand. We had after all seen that even Rembrandt's realism applied only to certain parts of a composition that was on the whole anything but the faithful rendering of a *camera obscura* view.

If, as is more likely, the fifteenth-century artist turned to "some art work which he had seen and from whose pattern *[forma]* he intended to work," I believe that a seemingly unrelated type of religious representation may well have been of service to him: the conventional type of the "Lamentation of Christ" ideally answered all or almost all the requirements of form. If we compare the Bartholomaeus Anglicus woodcut with almost any "Lamentation" or "Entombment of Christ" done in the latter part of the fifteenth century[155] (Pls. XVIII-22, 23 and XIX-24, 25), formal resemblances appear undeniable.

This is surely not by accident. Whether anatomy or lamentation, the task was essentially the same: a number of people had to be grouped about a corpse in such a manner that the corpse was not obscured; consequently they were arranged behind it and distributed in a pattern of symmetrical balance, with one person at the head and one at the foot end. A second prerequisite shared by both themes was a display of intense emotion focusing on the prone body. The "Lamentations" supplied an initial pattern, and if in the long run this type proved inadequate, we must seek the reason not so much in the realm of forms as in that of psychological association.

The emotional substrata of the formal anatomies demanded and found their true and lasting inspiration in a different sphere. The "Lamentation" type served its purpose only so long as the emphasis remained on the didactic aspect of the formal anatomy. It was, in fact, adaptable to a few basic variations. Where, for example, a presiding chairman was called for, all the artist had to do was to insert into the conventional "Lamentation-anatomy" the image of the inspired teacher seated upon his cathedra.[156] This type we have seen in the off-center anatomist in the woodcut of Berengario da Carpi's "Anatomical Lesson" of 1535 (Fig. 5). The artist has even stretched the type far enough to equip one of the "mourning bystanders" with a knife so as to provide for the anatomizing menial of the formal anatomies.

This was, however, the point at which the Lamentation type had to be abandoned. Justified demands for action upon the corpse must have compelled artists to turn to totally different categories of *exempla*. Such patterns of violent interference with a passive body were ideally provided by scenes of martyrdom. We can even speak here of effect and countereffect. It is no mere accident that at the time when formal anatomies came into the open the cruelties inflicted upon defenseless but willing victims experienced a remarkable efflorescence in the arts. These cruelties ordained by heartless pagan rulers or cruel Jews for the stolid adherents to the Christian faith, the flayings and dismemberments narrated in saints' legends and chronicles, and in addition the tortures described by the myths of the ancients (e.g. the Flaying of Marsyas), must have exercised a strong influence on anatomical representations, and these were doubtless inspired in turn by the public dissections. While those concerned with curing the diseases of the human body had discovered step by step how much could be gained for their craft by painstaking observations of the dead or defenseless body, the artists depicting martyrdoms came to realize that they in turn could intensify their emotional message by mastering such scientific data of surface and functional anatomy as the public dissections were liberally placing at the disposal of everyone willing to buy the official entrance ticket.

To preceding centuries the flaying of a saint had been primarily a literary event, a *legendum*. If from the relatively innocuous text of the *Legenda Aurea* we turn to the "Martyr-

87

dom of St. Bartholomew" as depicted by Stefan Lochner (Pl. XXI-27), the sufferings of the missionary to India who was skinned alive become horrible and impressive reality. Even if we turn from here to a clumsy broadsheet, an Italian engraving of the late 1470's recording the ritual murder of the hapless little St. Simon of Trent, whose adroit dismemberment by his Jewish tormentors is shown in careful detail,[157] we understand how much the representation of cruelty could, and in fact did, learn from surgery and vice versa. In short, the artist's careful study of cruelties inflicted and received, his explicit desire to make the beholder shudder, whether through a saint's martyrdom or through a ritual murder, must be considered an important factor in the advance of scientific investigation of the human body. Anatomists could turn, as we know they actually did, to works of art to study muscles and sinews. The adjustment from one to the other was comparatively easy: all that had to be provided to turn a martyrdom into an anatomy was a change in emotional climate.

There was still another important group of immediate prototypes that, to harmonize with dispassionate scientific investigation, required little or no psychological adjustment. The emotions of compassion and horror ordinarily evoked by the contemplation of the suffering saint could be transformed with a minimum of change into feelings of agreeable satisfaction if the victim were tortured in the name of Justice. This effect came to pass in the so-called Justice Pictures produced in the Netherlands in the second half of the fifteenth century. On the surface these were secular paintings, a kind of democratic art that applied all the persuasive realism of the North to telling moral tales of crime punished and steadfast virtue rewarded. We should not forget, however, that the Justice Pictures as a cultural phenomenon belonged to the realm of late mediaeval theological literature as much as to that of secular writing. The sphere of art that produced the Justice Pictures, beginning with Rogier van der Weyden, had adapted as far as content is concerned a literary form long extant. For the Justice Pictures depended for their themes on stories from late mediaeval anthologies that had stored a great wealth of colorful tales from all corners of the world. These stories had never been told or, we may be certain, enjoyed for their entertainment value alone. Invariably they were subjected to the discipline of their *moralizationes*. Compilations such as the thirteenth-century *Tabula exemplorum* [465] or the fourteenth-century *Gesta Romanorum* [179–80] were among the most popular source books of late mediaeval preachers; they were as indispensable to them as the *Gloss* to the two Testaments, [185] the *Golden Legend* [249] and Jacopo de Voragine's *Sermones aurei*, [250] Nicolaus de Lyra's *Postilla*, [338] or the alphabetically arranged allegorical dictionaries of Alanus ab Insulis [4] and Petrus Berchorius. [50] Although the *exempla* provided *novelle*, their homiletic essence was still fully appreciated in the fifteenth century and the early sixteenth when artists became interested in them as an inexhaustible store of iconographic matter.

88

The northern Justice Pictures, as the legitimate descendants of *exempla* literature, were actually popular sermons painted. Taken as narrative pictures, as no doubt they should be, they are nevertheless only half understood unless we experience them at the same time in the light of their *moralizationes*. One of the best-known Justice Pictures is Gerard David's representing the flaying of Sisamnes on orders from Cambyses. This picture (dated 1498) is, I think, of particular significance for Rembrandt's composition. The artist's source of inspiration was certainly not the classical story as told by Herodotus (which, at the time the painting was planned, was not available); we can also rule out the version of Valerius Maximus, simply because it was not likely to have come to the attention of David or of David's iconographic advisers. The story could be found nearer at hand, in the *Gesta Romanorum* (XXIX), where it was not only properly moralized but also related (as Dr. Panofsky pointed out to me) to a part of the liturgy called *Missa in injustos judices*.[158] This double association with liturgy and with theological moralization is stressed by the title under which the story is found in the *Gesta*: "Notabile de judicibus malis," wherein we should note that *judex* might mean both "judge" and "magistrate." The title in the Dutch version of 1484[180] (sign. iii *verso*) reads: "Van den quaden rechteren een merkelic stuck."[159] Although the *Gesta Romanorum* was not the only popular anthology that carried this story, I should consider Gerard David's knowledge and use of the *Gesta* the most likely, for it was not only the most widely read of the *exempla* anthologies but also the most popular of them in the Lowlands. The *Gesta*, between *ca.* 1470 and 1481, had gone through more than sixteen printed editions, almost all of them issued in the Lower Rhine region.[160] The Dutch version of 1484 that appeared in Zwolle is, moreover, remarkable because it is, as far as I have been able to ascertain, the one and only illustrated *Gesta* incunabulum —unfortunately, however, without an illustration of the punishment scene of Chapter XXIX.[161]

Gerard David's "Notabile de judicibus malis," as the pictures should therefore really be called, consists of two panels: "Arrest" and "Punishment." We are concerned with the latter (Pl. XXII-28), for in it the flaying of the Unjust Judge who had accepted a bribe is depicted in relentless and realistic detail. This panel renders two events that follow one another in time. In the foreground the vivisection takes place, and in the background the Judge's son is shown being inaugurated in a chair draped with his father's skin, "so that [in the words of the Emperor, who in the *Gesta* version remains unnamed] should anyone offer him a gift, in order to make him forsake the right path, he should contemplate his father's skin, lest the same punishment overtake him." The *moralizatio*, significantly enough, transforms this story into a kind of symbol of the Last Judgment: the Emperor, no longer a prince of this earth, signifies Jesus Christ, while the Unjust Judge stands for Everyman, who is stripped of his evil *humores*.[162]

I have dwelt on the form and content of this particular Justice Picture because it seems to me that significant affiliations link it with Rembrandt's "Anatomy." David's panel anticipates, generally speaking, the position of the corpse and the distribution of the attendant persons. Even the figure of Dr. Tulp himself, at once presiding and dissecting, can be traced in the flaying scene if upon the torturing menial who busies himself with the victim's arm we superimpose the image of the divinely inspired Emperor standing to his right.

The reader may find it possible to admit the menial among the formal and functional ancestry of Dr. Tulp; when we trace the evolution of the late mediaeval *prosector*, whose function had been merged with that of the *praelector* ever since the publication of Vesalius' *Fabrica* in 1543, we can envisage this kind of lowly mechanic among the ancestry of the noble anatomist of the post-Vesalian era. The godlike Emperor and Judge may be less easy to accept. I hope, however, to be able to show in the last chapter of this book that Dr. Tulp was, in a very palpable sense, also the moral judge and even the *triumphator* over the subjugated corpse of the executed criminal under his jurisdiction—a most real subject of his triumph.

I consider it not impossible that Rembrandt may have had some knowledge (through copies, paraphrases, or variants) of the composition of Gerard David. If so, it would certainly not have been hard for him to view it in the light of an association with the concepts of anatomy. I am encouraged in this assumption because Rembrandt might well have had occasion to see in Leiden's anatomical theater a representation of the "Judgment of Cambyses." The inventory of 1628 fails to disclose whether this was a mounted print in an oak frame or, perhaps, an actual painting. But the difference matters little for the kind of impression Rembrandt would have received. The works of art hung in the *theatrum* were almost all distinctly related to certain conventional aspects of the anatomy. We shall see later on that one of them, a copy of Michelangelo's "Last Judgment," will help offer a key to another iconographic aspect that in turn will provide a further link between the flaying scene and Rembrandt's "Anatomy."[163]

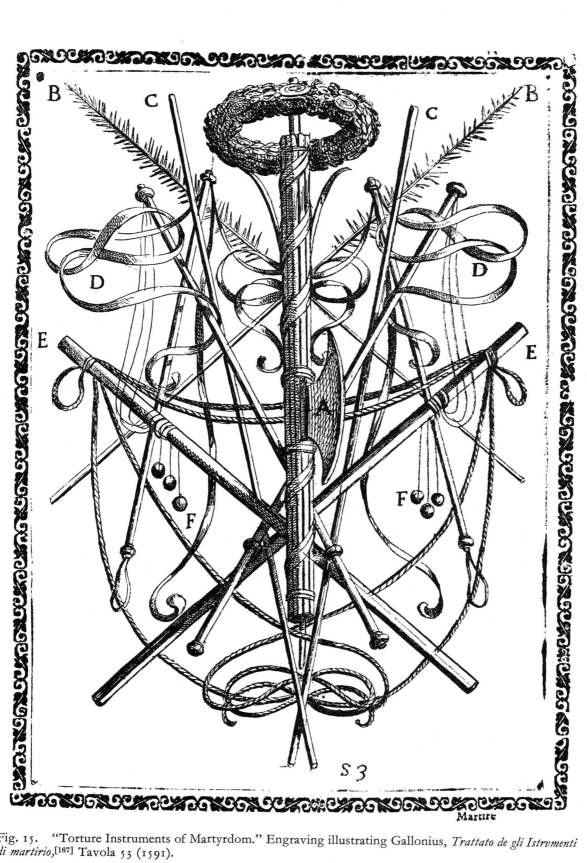

Fig. 15. "Torture Instruments of Martyrdom." Engraving illustrating Gallonius, *Trattato de gli Istrvmenti di martirio*,[167] Tavola 53 (1591).

XII

Rembrandt as Heir to the Northern Renaissance
of the Sixteenth Century

Turpe est contentum esse id consequi, quod imiteris

Formally, Rembrandt's painting should be seen as a composite of two completely different sources of inspiration. His "Anatomy of Dr. Tulp" in its festive aspect is heir to the spirit and form of the woodcut in the Ketham *Fasciculo* (Fig. 7); what I should like to call its dynamics ultimately derive from a demonstration of competent cruelty such as the one offered in Gerard David's panel discussed in the preceding chapter.

The assumption of such a carry-over from David's "Notabile" to Rembrandt's "Anatomy of Dr. Tulp" is, it seems to me, contingent on the affirmative answer to two questions: (1) Would Rembrandt actually go so far as to borrow the compositional scheme of his first group portrait from a Flemish Primitive? (2) Even if we were to admit the possibility of Rembrandt's using such a compositional scheme of the Northern Renaissance, would it be possible for him, the contemporary of Huygens and Grotius, to accept the gross cruelty exhibited in David's Justice panel and sublimate it to the heights of the detached scientific interest displayed by Dr. Tulp and his fellow surgeons?

As to the first question: The early decades of the seventeenth century witnessed a powerful revival in Holland of appreciative interest in the art of "the renowned Netherlanders and Germans," "der vermaerde Nederlanders ende Hoogduytschen," as Carel van Mander called them in the subtitle of Part II of his *Schilder-Boeck (editio princeps* [302] 1603 ff.).[164] In 1618 there appeared in Amsterdam the *Theatrum Honoris,*[13] a book of nearly 70 portraits of famous artists of the fifteenth and sixteenth centuries, ranging from Hubert van Eyck to Dürer and Holbein, Goltzius and de Gheyn. Hans Holbein the Younger's "Madonna of Jacob Meyer" was acquired by the Amsterdam art dealer Michel Le Blon (1587–1656) about 1632. By intervening stages the panel reached the ducal Court at Darmstadt, where it is to this day. But someone—most likely Bartholomeus Sarburgh, a German painter who had worked in Switzerland and had come to Amsterdam in 1632— copied the painting between 1632 and 1638, the result being the Dresden "Madonna of Jacob Meyer." This replica, however obvious its deviation from the style of a preceding century, was conceived and perfected with consummate skill and understanding of the sixteenth-century original.[165] The Dutch emblem writer and printer D. P. Pers added to his very literal translation of Cesare Ripa's *Iconologia* [402] on p. 500 *s.v.* "Malinconia" an extra heading: "Melancholy as portrayed by Albert Durer," "soo die van *Albert Durer* is afgemaelt."

That this newly awakened interest was far from merely antiquarian is borne out by the lively echoes of it in Rembrandt's *œuvre*. He not only owned a copy of Dürer's *Vier Bücher von menschlicher Proportion* in the first Dutch edition,[128] Arnhem, 1622 (a copy of which is found in the Rembrandt House at Amsterdam), but he paraphrased from it the famous figure inscribed in a circle. Rembrandt's interest in Northern Renaissance art was second only to the influence that the compositions of the Italian High Renaissance exerted on him.[166] It ranges from literal quotations to light paraphrases, from faithful structural imitations to meaningful variations on Northern Renaissance themes.[167] Thus we find, for example, Rembrandt copying a Rogieresque "Pietà" in one of his drawings, a swift, fragmentary sketch[168] (Pls. XXIV-30 and XXV-31). In his famous "Family Group" of *ca.* 1668 (Pl. XXV-32), some twenty years after the "Night Watch" and some thirty-six after the "Anatomy of Dr. Tulp," Rembrandt did not hesitate to follow Maerten van Heemskerck's "Family Group" of before 1532, now preserved in the Staatliche Kunstsammlungen at Cassel (Pl. XXVI-33). Heemskerck's painting not only inspired Rembrandt's remarkably tectonic way of treating and arranging the human figures like so many terraced steps, but it also influenced such seemingly insignificant details as the berets, the basket motif, the hand of the little one reaching out for the mother's bosom, and, last but not least, the all-pervading mood of irrepressible gaiety that, as if by contagion, seems to fill every member of the family. Characteristically enough, Rembrandt's debt came to light only accidentally, when the two paintings were exhibited together in the Museum Boymans at Rotterdam in 1947–48.[169] Perhaps the deepest insights can be gained if we follow the development of the theme of the "Ecce homo!" in Rembrandt's etchings.[170] As a young man he, or someone in his entourage, made an etching after one of his own (painted) compositions dated 1635–36 (Pl. XXVII-34). In his advanced years he repeated the theme. Where previously he had placed the stage—that is, the stairs leading up to Pilate's praetorium—in a diagonal in depth, suggesting by his calculated use of eccentric perspective an accidental and true-to-life approach (not unlike that of the "Anatomy" of 1632), in 1655 he presented (Pl. XXIX-36) a tremendous and detached tableau of studied calm, tectonic grandeur, and classical proportion—one that by its oblong spread, complete frontality, and clarity of disposition helped to discipline and objectivate the beholder's emotions and, within the picture itself, to shrink humanity (including that of Christ) down to a minimum. In this late instance Rembrandt followed quite obviously an engraving by Lucas van Leyden dated 1510. (Pl. XXVIII-35.) However, this word-for-word dependence on the earlier Northern master did not last for very long. In a subsequent state of his etching Rembrandt dismantled the architecture by vigorously trimming the upper and lower margins of his plate (cf. Müntz, *A Critical Catalogue,*[328] No. 235 / V) and, finally, in a still later state, he completed the process by eliminating the mass of the people who, in imitation of Lucas van Leyden's "Ecce homo," had at first gathered in the foreground underneath the parapet on which Christ is displayed (Pl. XXX-37). As a result of these afterthoughts Rembrandt's debt to Lucas van Leyden was virtually wiped out. The whole is, I think, a clear-cut lesson that will help to throw light on the degree of Rembrandt's willingness to follow tradition once it was authoritatively established, and on his equally strong unwillingness to be bound by his chosen prototype once he discovered that it might hamper rather than aid his own spiritual vision.

Purpurea quid opus ueste? heu: num cernis ur illi
Omnia purpureo membra cruore rubent?

Fig. 16.   Jacques Callot, "Ecce homo!" Etching (Lieure 285).

The Roman rhetoricians had known the fateful difference between creative imitation and the slavish following of a given prototype: "Turpe est contentum esse id consequi, quod imiteris"; in the paraphrase of Franciscus Junius: "the true following of a rare Masters Art, doth not consist in an apish Imitation of the outward ornaments, but rather in the expressing of the inward force."[171]

This brings us to our second question, whether Rembrandt could accept the gross cruelty in Gerard David's "Justice Panel" and lift it to the heights of scientific detachment that we find in his "Dr. Tulp." One of the best examples of how Rembrandt managed to sublimate and spiritualize the crudities of others is found in the case history of his "Danae" in the Hermitage at Leningrad (Pl. XXXI-38). When we turn to any of his antecedents—such as Titian's "Danae" in the Prado (Pl. XXXII-39)—we find that Danae, daughter of King Acrisius, surreptitiously visited by Zeus in the guise of a golden shower, had commonly been depicted as the paradigm of meretricious love. The Roman poets and, in their wake, the Fathers of the Church had seen Zeus' shower as a shower of golden coins, and the painters of the Renaissance had followed their lead. Rembrandt, and he alone (as Panofsky demonstrated) among the many who represented the subject in the sixteenth and seventeenth centuries, turned the golden shower into flashes of mysterious light, announcing the overshadowing of the divinity and possibly thereby alluding to the mystical concept, favored in religious writings of the late fourteenth century, that saw in the myth of Danae and the Golden Shower a prefiguration of the immaculate conception of Jesus.

Whether Rembrandt could have been aware of this scholastic idea of a noble Danae we cannot tell. There exists, however, a significant parallel to it in Dutch baroque writing. In 1632 Joost van den Vondel alluded to the ruse by which Marie van Reigersbergh aided her famous husband, Hugo de Groot, in his escape (1621) from Castle Loevestein. In his poem "Hvigh de Groots Verlossing," Vondel described Loevestein in intentional imitation of Horace's description of Danae's tower while implicitly he celebrated Marie's deed (he also compared her to the Virgin Mary) in terms of Danae's liberation.[172]

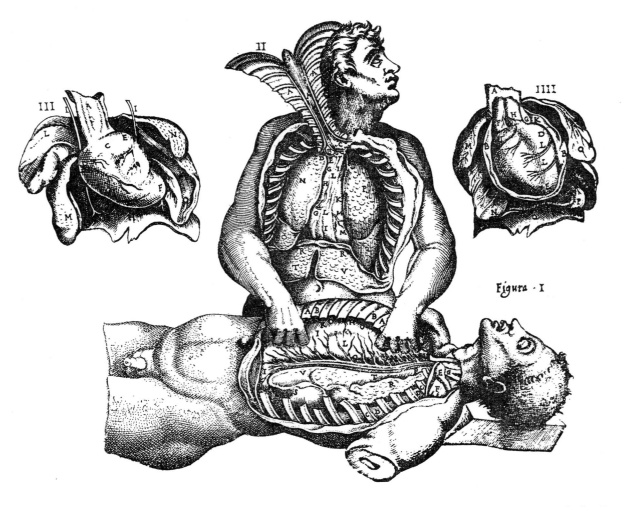

Fig. 17.   Gasparo Becerra, "Cadaver Anatomizing." Engraving illustrating Valverde, *Historia*,[485] IV, detail of Tavola 1 and 2, p. 108 (1560).

XIII

The 'Anatomy' as Record of a Penal Anatomy

. . . quia dictum est: Oculum pro oculo, et dentem pro dente

The few instances offered in the preceding chapter may suffice to point to a Rembrandt bent on "conceiving," as St. Thomas Aquinas put it, "the *forma* from some art-work which he has seen, from the pattern of which he intends to work," yet a Rembrandt who is at the same time inclined to depict terrestrial things only after he has revolved them in his mind and agitated them in his fantasy (to paraphrase Barlaeus). Rembrandt, in other words, felt amazingly free to metamorphose the chosen *exemplum* or pattern in accordance with his inner conscience—forever ready to fill old bottles with new wine. He understood that "a good Imitator must by all meanes be a concealer of his Art" (Franciscus Junius). Later ages have at best admired the metamorphoses undertaken by Rembrandt while shutting their eyes to his imitations. And Rembrandt does indeed, by virtue of his power of sublimation, appear as an isolated phenomenon in the North. Danae, in the course of the seventeenth and eighteenth centuries, would become a *meretrix* once more, and anatomies would once more reveal, as they had done before, their preponderant indebtedness to those penetralia of the human mind that account for martyrdoms and their inversions in the Justice Pictures.

Our incomplete knowledge of the actual appearance and location of the anatomical theater in Amsterdam around 1632 leaves insufficient clues for a reconstruction, let alone a critique, of the setting as Rembrandt represented it.[173] All we know is that from 1639 onward Dr. Tulp conducted his famous anatomies once more in the *anatomie kamer* on the Old Meat Market, "boven de Vleeschhal." Only then could the theater claim to be permanent. I have pointed out in Chapters I and III that Rembrandt's "Anatomy" fell in the twenty-year interregnum (1619–39) when the public dissections were probably conducted somewhere in the upper story of the St. Antonie-Waag (the Weighing-house), then conceivably spacious enough to accommodate *theatrum* as well as guild chambers.[174]

In examining Rembrandt's insights into the cultural background of the public anatomies we need not confine ourselves to guesses about the interim theater of Amsterdam. We may assume that he was intimately familiar with Dr. Paaw's anatomical theater in Leiden, about which we are much better informed (Pl. XXXIII-40). This theater would have appealed to more than anatomical appetites, for it was in the full sense of the term a *Kunst-und Wunderkabinett* and most likely the nearest to a public art museum that Rembrandt could have visited in his formative years.[175] We have no proof from primary sources of Rembrandt's acquaintanceship with the theater. Julius Held suggested that the skeleton of a horse that appears in the engraving of the Leiden theater, dated 1616, might have served Rembrandt for his "Polish Rider," but Van Regteren Altena pointed out that Amsterdam too boasted a "sceleton hominis in Sceleto equi." Quite possibly Rembrandt was acquainted with both, and anyway Dr. Tulp, Rembrandt's iconographic adviser, was a product of Leiden and of its anatomical theater.[176] One glance at the beautifully detailed print representing the Leiden theater, engraved after all by Rembrandt's teacher's brother, Willem van Swanenburgh (1581–1622) (after a drawing by Jan Cornelisz. van 't Woudt), suggests something of the atmosphere that young Rembrandt must have imbibed. Here were skeletons of man and beast, human skins, and an occasional corpse, displayed in an atmosphere calculated to remind the visitors of St. Paul's ominous words that "Death is the Wages of Sin."[177] In looking at this print we must keep in mind the dual function of anatomical theaters: While in use for public demonstrations, they were, however short-lived, *theatra* in the literal sense. For the rest of the year they were (as Jacobus Balde, S. J., Caspar Barlaeus, and many others among Rembrandt's close contemporaries keep stressing) devotional and moralizing museums and for that reason an important branch of the *Kunst- und Wunderkammern* of their day. It is the Leiden theater in the latter sense that we are examining at present.[178] (Pls. III-3 and XXXIII-40.) Everywhere there are mementos illustrating the moral lesson of Death, reminding physicians and visitors alike that life is transitory and that death came into the world through Man's Fall. Prominently we see Adam and Eve, two animated skeletons, flanking the Tree of Knowledge in the center foreground. Other skeletons hold banners proclaiming traditional death warnings: PVLVIS ET VMBRA SUMUS. NOSCE TE IPSUM. MORS ULTIMA LINEA RERUM, etc. A reclining putto with skull and hourglass presides over the whole, and even the human skin, the "praeparata pellis humana," is there. It is undoubtedly the skin of a criminal, such as Gielis Caelewart of Haarlem and Suster Luijt, whose skins, as we know, were preserved at Amsterdam. We see how the skin is being admired by a gentleman and a lady to whom it is displayed by one of the *custodes*. Their interest is most likely not scientific. The emotions evoked are, I am convinced, those of edified and moralizing contemplation. One saw here, in the words of Rembrandt's first biographer, J. J. Orlers, "a human skin which is shown and held in readiness for didactic purposes." There is evidence that the displays in the *theatra anatomica* when these were used as museums were not intended for medical instruction; serious osteology was taught in Leiden in the *auditorium medicum* in the University Building.[179]

We have encountered the skin interpreted in a moral sense before, in Gerard David's "Notabile de judicibus malis," where, according to the *moralizatio*, it stood for man's evil *humores;* i.e. the very frailty incurred by man at the *lignum scientiae boni et mali* that in Leiden marked, as it were, the access to the anatomical table, which in turn stood in the place formerly occupied by the altar. The moral interpretation of the human skin as we find it at the end of the story of the Unjust Judge in the *Gesta Romanorum* was anything but arbitrary. That the skin might quite generally be considered a *memento mori* or, more specifically, as *memoriae peccatorum,* we can ascertain by consulting Petrus Berchorius' *Dictionarium* of about 1340, a book that saw a steady stream of reissues through the sixteenth, seventeenth, and even eighteenth centuries,[50] *s.v.* "pellis." In the conventional sense of *memoriae peccatorum* Michelangelo made use of the human skin in his "Last Judgment" in the Sistine Chapel (Pl. XXXIV-41). A heroic St. Bartholomew, fashioned after the Torso Belvedere, rising with the Elect, is shown dropping his skin—no longer needed—to the lower spheres. The skin is so shaped as to form the mouth of a hound holding the dejected features of Michelangelo himself between his teeth. The self-imposed punishment becomes in fact formidable if we reflect that the skin will drop into Hades. Such associations had not been forgotten in seventeenth-century Holland. In fact, a copy of Michelangelo's "Last Judgment," framed in oak (whether painting or print cannot be ascertained), was listed in the inventory of the Leiden anatomical theater compiled in the 1620's—the very years when the young painter Rembrandt had every opportunity to see the "Last Judgment"—next to the "Judgment of Cambyses."[180] We are at liberty to picture Rembrandt being led from the one to the other and, soon after, approaching Dr. Tulp's commission at Amsterdam with those memories in his mind. Rembrandt, incidentally, was not the only one who appears to have given expression to the moral-didactic function of the criminal's anatomy. When in 1639, some seven years after his "Anatomy," Amsterdam's anatomical theater received its first permanent quarters, the following lines composed by Caspar Barlaeus appeared in golden letters under the highest balcony:

Evildoers who, while living, have done damage, are of benefit after their death. Their skins teach this, even though they have no voices . . .

Qui vivi nocuere, mali, post funera prosunt . . . Exuviae sine voce docent . . .

It will be useful to keep in mind the close connection between the advance of science and the punishment of crime as this connection was here expressed by the Dutch poet-philosopher, who was close, we may believe, to both Rembrandt and Dr. Tulp.

From here we may turn to the realm of folklore, where we find that the criminal's skin was an accepted part of seventeenth-century thinking. A "true story" (of the year 1688), attested by a "highly learned *medicus*," tells how an anatomized criminal appeared as a ghost—"all muscles and no skin"—about the noon hour to the tanner and his wife to

99

reclaim his skin. The tanner wisely refrained from any commitments, thereby foiling the ghost. Erasmus Francisci, the nearest thing to a journalist in the seventeenth century, leaves little doubt in the reader's mind that every word of this story must be believed.[181]

The concept of retribution, the Old Testament idea of "an eye for an eye," the selective punishment of the limb that has sinned—this must be considered one of the constituent elements of the public anatomies. In the Middle Ages this concept finds expression not only in poetry and fiction but also in law. Punitive dismemberments are documented from the Middle Ages down to the seventeenth century. Public dissections of criminals were decidedly based on the idea of retribution.[182] In this regard it is not unimportant to note that most sixteenth-century anatomists have been accused, at one time or another, of vivisection—a moral error that was at least mitigated if the victim was a malefactor. It should be added, however, that those accusations have been disproved in almost every known case.[183] And yet it cannot be denied that provocation existed. Any unprejudiced beholder of Joannes Stephan van Calcar's beautifully posed corpses—some in the well-known poses of classical statues—cannot fail to notice among them that of an executed criminal, hanging yet not quite hanged *(Septima Musculorum Tabula* of the Second Book of Andreas Vesalius' *Fabrica).* [489, 490, 491] Juan de Valverde's *Historia de la composicion* of 1556 [485] even went one step farther when in his illustrations (on the whole thinly disguised borrowings from Vesalius-Calcar) he showed one corpse anatomizing another, an amusing inversion of the idea of vivisection[184] (Fig. 17). We know, finally, that the dissection of living organisms as a scientific ideal, not necessarily realizable, existed in Vesalius's mind. To this, in fact, he devoted the final chapter of his *Fabrica.* He was strengthened in this by the common and justified assumption that the ancients had favored it also.[185] Nor, as H. W. Janson has shown, was Vesalius above toying with the idea of a vindictive use of anatomy. In the woodcut initial *V* (Fig. 18) in the *Fabrica* edition of 1555 Vesalius had himself represented as a triumphant Apollo flaying a vanquished Marsyas, who in reality was Sylvius-*sylvanus,* once his teacher in Paris but now his denigrator and opponent.[186]

Again it will be rewarding to descend to the reaches of folklore, where imagination has freer play. If the medical profession was comparatively safe, it was tempting to fasten such accusations on more or less defenseless minorities. Above all the Jews, already suspect of ritual murder, became prime targets once more, especially since some of the most successful surgeons and anatomists of the sixteenth century were Jews or of Jewish extraction.[187] For an illustration we may turn to Elizabethan England. London audiences had been stirred by the revival of one of the ineradicable mediaeval slanders: Shylock's demand for Antonio's pound of flesh. Shakespeare had kept close to his mediaeval prototype or prototypes. In the fourteenth-century *Cursor mundi,* for example, precisely this motif had been worked into the well-known legend of the "Invention of the True Cross."

It is here that the Jew who finally divulges the whereabouts of the Crosses to Emperor Constantine's mother, Helena, anticipates Shylock in every respect, while Helena takes the part of Shakespeare's Portia.[188]

Fig. 18.   Joannes Stephan, *van Calcar,* "V." Woodcut initial used in Vesalius, *Fabrica,*[490] (1555), *passim.*

But this seems only one element in the Elizabethan play. It is hard to believe that Shakespeare or, for that matter, his audience was totally unaware of a curious parallel in the notorious case of Dr. Lopez, a Jewish physician and anatomist executed in 1594, i.e. four years before the *Merchant of Venice* was entered in the Stationer's Register (July 22, 1598). Roderigo Lopez (1525–94) had been a physician to Queen Elizabeth from 1586 onward. For a while he had been associated with the Earl of Essex. He was the first doctor chosen for St. Bartholomew's in London, where he presided over the annual anatomy in 1569, undoubtedly a great distinction. Accused of clandestine relations with the Spanish Crown (an Elizabethan denigrator described him as a "perjur'd and murdering villain —worse than Judas himself"), Dr. Lopez had been found guilty and executed, more or less against the wishes of the Queen, at Tyburn June 7, 1594.[189] The Lopez case had taken time to gather momentum. In the year of the execution there occurred what we may take to have been the first literary reference to it, a violently anti-Semitic exposure of the Jewish anatomist and his lust for vivisection: Thomas Nashe, in his picaresque novel *The Vnfortvnate Traueller,* tells how his hero, Jack Wilton, gets into the clutches of a vindictive

Jew. This Jew, Zadoch by name, having gained power over poor Jack, sells him to another Jew, a Dr. Zacharias, who is the Pope's physician. Since the plague is rampant in Rome, Zacharie is at a loss how to procure a healthy specimen for his "yearlie Anatomie." Jack Wilton is a heaven-sent gift, and Nashe describes to the smallest detail how in his imagination the captive hero anticipates the impending anatomy. Jack is saved at the eleventh hour by the intervention of one of the Pope's concubines, a kind of caricatured Portia, who brings about the just punishment of the guilty Zadoch, which, needless to say, consists in a most colorful vivisection.[190]

This is, of course, only one side of the picture. In order to obtain a more balanced view we might turn to Rembrandt's great contemporary, the Alsatian poet Jacobus Balde, S.J. (1604–68). Balde devoted the twelfth of his *Medical Satires* (Munich, 1643)[22, 23] to the praise of the most accomplished Vesalius—"Vesalii anatomici praestantissimi laus." In this poem Balde compares two kinds of "theaters," viz. the common *Kunst- und Wunderkammern* of his day (with their Sirens, Centaurs, and Chimaeras, their rhinoceros horn and scaly dragon's belly, their shell-decorated recesses, their pickled serpents, and monstrous storks, clutching an egg with a calf's foot) and Vesalius' exhibit of cadavers and skeletons, in which utility and delight (St. Augustine's categories!) compete with each other. To Balde, Vesalius' exhibits are works of art of the highest order; they are more beautiful even than the famous sights of Rome—"omnia Vesalii statuae [sic] spectacula vincunt" (line 41). And if asked why, Balde will answer that man can learn to appreciate his own diminution in size and stature only in the presence of what he calls "non homo"—the cadaver. While thus the anatomies of Vesalius help to cut man down to size, they are yet the best aids for theodicy, since no one can deny that what has been built so subtly requires an architect—"aedificatus homo est. Aedilem habuisse negabis?"

Balde, like Rembrandt, acknowledges the horror of the anatomies, but in his own way he arrives at a spiritualized vision of the ultimate purpose that both Vesalius and Tulp had clearly acknowledged.[191]

We should be mistaken if we were to conclude that with Balde and Rembrandt, Tulp and Barlaeus, an era of anatomical enlightenment had begun. Their attitude—scientific, devotional, legalistic, metaphysical—represents an exception rather than a rule. For as we turn from the Baroque to the Age of Enlightenment we shall encounter, not enlightened resolutions of inherent conflicts, not a turn toward a purely scientific attitude, but satire of the most brutal kind, commenting on the punishment fitting the crime.

William Hogarth's well-known series entitled "The Four Stages of Cruelty" presents in its last climactic print a straight revival of the mediaeval concept of penal dismemberment. Under the cloak of a public anatomy we witness the winding-out of the victim's intestines in illustration of the retributive punishment of crime. The gruesome picture

(Fig. 19) holds the middle as it were between anatomy and vivisection, as in circumstantial detail it acquaints us with the villain's "dire disgrace."[192] The purpose of the "Four Stages of Cruelty" is to describe in picture and in verse the Progress of one Thomas Nero, who—*nomen est omen*—had advanced from maltreating dogs and torturing horses to rape and, finally, murder. This was a case history that apparently lent itself ideally to a timely and intentionally crude adhortation of the lower classes.[193] Picture and verse in this series are in complete agreement. The poems, it has been suggested, were composed by the Rev. James Townley. Townley was an enlightened, witty, scholarly, and at times somewhat cynical schoolmaster and playwright.[194]

The punitive anatomy, represented on the fourth sheet, shows Thomas Nero writhing on the dissecting table. The theater is that of the Surgeons' Company, Barber's Hall, London. The chief anatomist, who was also the first curator of the pathological museum at St. Bartholomew's Hospital and a friend of Hogarth, is Dr. John Freke (1688–1756).[195] Dr. Freke is shown presiding in his ornate chair. He appears as a close relative of the professor in Ketham's *Fasciculo* woodcut (Fig. 7). The arrangement of the anatomical theater impresses us as a summing-up of the tradition that began with the frontispiece of Vesalius' *Fabrica* (Fig. 10), with additional echoes derived from Leiden (Fig. 2, Pls. III-3, XXXIII-40). Illustrations of the Dutch medical comedy may have had a share of influence as well.[196] The whole, however, I should like to think, was purposely designed in what Hogarth in that very year, in a different context, had referred to as "the ridiculous manner of Rembrant."

Townley's three stanzas run:

Barber's Hall 1751

Behold the Villain's dire disgrace!
    Not Death itself can end.
He finds no peaceful Burial-Place;
    His breathless Corse, no friend.

Torn from the Root, that wicked Tongue,
    Which daily swore and curst!
Those Eyeballs from the Sockets wrung,
    That glow'd with lawless Lust!

His Heart, exposed to prying Eyes,
    To Pity has no Claim:
But, dreadful! from his Bones shall rise,
    His Monument of Shame.

I believe that, in the end, this astonishing product of human minds is much more than it professes to be: i.e. a moral and abhorrent warning to the plebeians of London and, as such, doomed to be ineffectual. Formally Hogarth may have aimed at a revival of the

Behold the Villain's dire disgrace!
Not Death itself can end.
He finds no peaceful Burial Place:
His breathless Corse, no friend.

Torn from the Root, that wicked Tongue,
Which daily swore and curst!
Those Eyeballs from their Sockets wrung,
That glow'd with lawless Lust!

His Heart, exposed to prying Eyes,
To Pity has no Claim:
But, dreadful! from his Bones shall rise.
His Monument of Shame.

Fig. 19.   William Hogarth, "The Penal Anatomy of Nero Wolfe." Fourth etching illustrating the "Four Stages of Cruelty"[230] (1751).

cruelties found in the Northern martyrdom and Justice Picture scenes. The motif of the evisceration may, as a matter of fact, have been suggested to him by a painting such as Dirk Bouts' "Martyrdom of St. Erasmus" (Pl. XXXVI-43 a). It is just this kind of punishment, however, that leads us into the sphere of the anthropologists who have recorded Germanic punishment rituals in which evisceration is the reward of the criminal who has damaged the bark of a sacred tree. His atonement becomes effective as a form of vicarious suffering; it is beneficial—in a way that we may suspect to be at the bottom of all such ceremonies—to a guilt-ridden society.[197] In folk thinking the criminal, even though quite dead, is still capable of sensations. A seventeenth-century criminal might fear the anatomy even more than the execution. Thus we hear that a condemned peasant asked not to be "rollfincked" ("man solle ihn doch nur nicht lassen rollfincken"); he would be ready to die without much ado. Dr. Werner Rolfink, a contemporary of Tulp and Rembrandt, was the well-known founder of the anatomical theater at Jena who performed annual dissections at the archducal court at Weimar. Even when a rare voice of protest was raised against the public dissections, it was principally directed against their penal character. Hugo de Groot argued: "Antiquity knew not these torture chambers of the dead, where these unnecessary cruelties are practised by the living upon the dead."

But in a deeper sense public anatomies were magic precautions taken in order to protect society against the criminal's power to do evil, which the execution alone had by no means managed to annihilate. In primitive societies the evildoer must be vivisected or dissected so that the king, or the medicine man who does the dissecting, may discover the diseased organ, seat of the demoniacal power—the *evu* or *likundu*—which can then be properly destroyed.[198]

When I referred to the "Stages of Cruelty" as a mediaeval relapse I had in mind the possibility of Hogarth's more or less conscious appreciation of a view particularly prevalent in the late Middle Ages. This view saw and described Death as a force that holds sway over all and applies its merciless eye-for-an-eye, tooth-for-a-tooth threat to all who have forsaken the narrow path of virtue. We encounter it perhaps most impressively in the death poetry of a group of *flagellanti* who referred to themselves as "disciplinati di Gesù Cristo." They flourished in the second half of the thirteenth century, and their emotions were crystallized in spiritual songs in the vernacular that became known as *laude*. Easily the most impressive of these death hymns is Jacopone da Todi's well known *Lauda* Twenty-Five.[199] It begins with the common death warning: "Quando t'allegri, omo de altura, / va', pone mente a la sepultura." Then follows a discourse that, *mutatis mutandis,* we have already encountered in the three stanzas of Townley's fourth Thomas Nero poem. The living here taunts the dead with stereotyped questions touching the fate of his limbs and organs. Sadly Jacopone's dead replies:

These eyes I have lost through my sin of looking with them desirously / I never thought that I would forfeit my nose when I followed the world's false vanities / I have lost my tongue with which I spoke and sowed so much strife / etc., etc., etc.

It is hard to tell whether the Hogarth-Townley team might have known a late mediaeval poem such as the twenty-fifth *Lauda* of Jacopone da Todi. I know, however, at least one instance of the *Dies Irae,* another Franciscan hymn of the thirteenth century, read by an animated skeleton of the eighteenth century who, in deep emotion, has sunk to his knees.[200]

We can also foresee how this kind of painstaking scrutiny of the moral power called Death, which directs destruction and disease in their relentless attack on Man's sinful limbs and organs, will turn out to be an important factor in the genesis of the new scientific vision of death and disease as soon as man's new understanding sees natural causes in operation in their place and as soon as its moral springs have run dry. And yet we have noticed how the opposite is also true, and how scientific anatomy will again and again become the starting point of didactic-moralizing intentions.

XIV

The 'Anatomy' and the Changing Aspect of Death

Corpus uero magis magisque corrumpitur, uel aetate uel morbo uel uariis
afflictionibus; donec ueniat ad ultimam, quae ab hominibus Mors uocatur
(Eugippius, after 533 A.D.)

Zerstörung feiret keinen Augenblick (Paracelsus)

Anatomies before and after Rembrandt (not omitting Dr. Tulp's) appear related, as I
hope I have shown, to a much broader pattern than that which considers them merely as
a contribution to the history of medicine. This pattern we may declare to be, in general
terms, man's attitude toward death.

Death, at the end of the Middle Ages, had begun to play an entirely novel role in
religious and philosophical thought. It is perhaps not too much to say that the Renaissance
was stirred more deeply by the *arcana* of death and life, generation and degeneration,
birth and rebirth, than any era before or after. Petrarch in the fourteenth century had
dramatically introduced the problem by exclaiming: "humanis autem in rebus, quid mihi
majus mortis monstraveris, quid par morti"—"in human affairs what thing greater than
Death could you show me, what even that would equal it?"[201]

I believe that the preoccupation with anatomy as an art and as a science can be taken
as one of the most impressive symbols that the Renaissance had been able to create in
token of this new interest in man and in his fate under the sway of death. Of course, the
Fathers of the Church had shown understanding of the aims of the anatomist, and they had
also appreciated the beauty of the human body, as a phenomenon apart from its functional
utility. For example, St. Augustine in a discussion in his *De civitate Dei* [19] (XXII, xxiv)
—in which he refers to the anatomists and their aims with remarkable understanding, if on
the whole rather critical of them—had expressed such views most succinctly. To St. Augustine and his followers the human body and its beauty posed problems rooted first of all
in moral considerations. Man's body existed as a structure solely *in majorem Dei gloriam.*
Its beauty, particularly in the male, could be divined where specific appurtenances are
plainly useless, such as man's beard and the symmetrically arranged nipples of his breast.
Claritas and *consonantia,* thus ruling over the human body and its beautiful appearance,
are subsumed under the concept of the Good—"tam claritas quam consonantia sub ratione

boni contenentur" (St. Thomas Aquinas).[202] Vesalius may be credited as being the first to have uttered the postulate that "the proper study of mankind is man," the first to have referred to the investigation of the *coaptatio* between body and mind—in sum to ourselves—as the worthiest subject of human inquiry.[203] We should realize, I think, that this truly modern postulate was ultimately rooted in scholastic thought. However, only with the Renaissance had Death and Life become close correlatives. Only then had they been recognized as two different aspects of one and the same phenomenon, the uniqueness of the Ego. As a modern critic has put it: "Das Ichbewusstsein ist nichts als ein Korrelat des Todesbewusstseins" (Panofsky). The Renaissance practitioners of anatomy assure us again and again that the chief objective of their inquiries is life and its secrets, which can only be gained at the price of death. In the words of what we may take to be one of Leonardo's soliloquies:

> You who investigate this our machine, let it not sadden you that you impart knowledge of it at the expense of another man's death; but rejoice that our Creator has equipped the intellect to such an excellence of discernment.[204]

Vesalius devoted an inordinately large amount of space of his *Fabrica*[490] (V, chap. xiiff.) to a discussion of the mysteries of procreation.[205] Gabriele de Zerbis' *Liber anathomie*[527] of 1502 already had contained an extensive appendix (28 pp. on 14 fols.) entitled: "De generatione embrionis."

In regard to death we find that two fundamentally different views could be held at one and the same time, at least from the fourteenth century onward. The older one, dating back to St. Paul, accepted throughout the Middle Ages and reaffirmed by the *decreta* of the Council of Trent[473] (June 17, 1546, within three years of the appearance of Vesalius' *Fabrica*), saw in Death the Wages of Sin (the "stipendia enim peccati, mors," of Epist. ad Rom. vi:23; Hebr. ii:14, and elsewhere in the Bible).[206] The second view, which originated in the Early Renaissance and was not formulated in so succinct a phrase until later, implied that death (just as much as life) was nothing but the result of the operation of the laws of nature—a certain "virtus insita rebus," a potentiality implanted in things, as Giordano Bruno calls it.[207] Even where, in Renaissance times, we find death viewed in terms of Hermetic philosophy, the new organic message is clearly set off against the mediaeval moralistic insights: "Dissolutio mors non est, sed mistionis resolutio quaedam, soluitur autem vnio non vt ea quae sunt intereant, sed vt uetera iuuenescant."[208]

Needless to say, it is only where the second view prevailed that a serious and fruitful scientific interest in anatomies became possible at all. And yet, as I have tried to show, there was forever present at the back of even the most enlightened Renaissance anatomist's mind the other view that saw in death (and especially in that of the criminal under the dissecting knife) a just reward for mortal shortcomings of the old Adam.

The words "anatomy" and "corpse" could be, in certain contexts in Renaissance and Baroque writings, virtually interchangeable. We need only turn to Cesare Ripa's *Iconologia* [401] to find that "an 'anatomy' like those which are painted and which show death in a white shroud" are fitting reminders of *Giustitia rigorosa*.[209] "L'Anatomie Vivante" was the nickname that the eighteenth century reserved for Voltaire.[210]

XV

The 'Anatomy' and Amsterdam's *Athenaeum*

Moraliza sicut placet

. . . dat gij . . . niet en sult soeken noch ansien uwes selffs
off uwer vrienden bate off schade, dan alleen den gemeenen
oirber van der stede, bij uwer bester wetentheit ende verstande

[that you shall strive neither after your own aggrandizement nor
after advantage or disadvantage of your friends but solely
after the general welfare of the city,
to the best of your knowledge and ability]
(from the Oath of the Amsterdam Guild of Staalmeesters,
quoted after H. van de Waal,[504] p. 100)

I believe, as I have tried to indicate by the heading of this chapter, that Rembrandt's painting should be understood as an artistic reflection of some profoundly stirring social and cultural developments that occurred at the very time and place of its creation. The year 1632 was, in more than one respect, an *annus mirabilis* in the history of Amsterdam. Let us once more turn to Caspar Barlaeus, who felicitously formulated what others must have felt when in an inaugural address he celebrated the official opening of Amsterdam's "Illustre School," a transitional form that preceded the actual founding of Amsterdam's University but in retrospect was quite rightly considered the beginning of a true academy. This event took place in January 1632. Barlaeus was the acknowledged spokesman not only of the new Academy but also of the distinguished group of Dutch writers and scholars, socialites, and *beaux esprits* who belonged to the exclusive Muider Castle circle *(Muiderkring)*; Dr. Tulp, one of them, had referred to Barlaeus in his *Observationum liber I,* chap. xxxii[477 ff.] 211 as "the greatest orator and poet of our age."

Caspar Barlaeus, originally a Remonstrant theologian, had spent rather trying years, from 1619 until 1631, as a private tutor at Leiden. In 1631 he hopefully arrived in Amsterdam to become a professor of philosophy and medicine at the university whose charter had yet to be granted. His eager, unsettled, melancholy, and yet profoundly humorous letters and poems, written during the months of waiting and suspense, should be read in order to get an impression of what Rembrandt may have felt himself at this time and in rather similar circumstances. On January 9, Barlaeus celebrated the opening of the *Schola, Hooge* or *Illustre School* or *Gymnasium* (not to be confused with Amsterdam's Latin school) or *Academia* or *Athenaeum Illustre*—to mention just some of the names by which this new academic venture was known—with an oration that bore the challenging title "MERCATOR SAPIENS—over den verstandingen koopman" (i. e. concerning the cultured merchant).[212] His speech was a plea for co-operation between Amsterdam's "sons of Mercury" and the newly arrived teachers who were devotees of science and philosophy.

In spite of or perhaps on account of its truly professorial flavor the oration was a popular success and had to be translated into Dutch. Barlaeus wittily alluded to Martianus Capella's *Wedding of Mercury and Philology* (early fifth century) when he spoke of the envisaged co-operation between scientists and businessmen as the Wedding between Wisdom and Commerce. This turned out to be a truly prophetic assessment of the prerequisites of Holland's greatness in both science and commerce. Barlaeus' formula stuck. We encounter it years later in an address of some of Amsterdam's foremost physicians, the *Collegium Medicorum,* to the burgomasters, who speak of the *familiaritas* that prevails at Amsterdam between Mercury and the Muses—"illa familiaritas, quae hic Musis cum Mercurio."[213] The future, moreover, showed that no better setting could be found than that offered by Amsterdam. Scientists and thinkers as well as artists were quick to respond to the novel atmosphere in which, under the leadership of a particularly enlightened city government, the representatives of spheres of interest that seemed mutually exclusive showed ready sympathy and, if not always understanding, at least respect for the pursuits of their counterparts. Dr. Tulp, as we know, promoted the School and its growth with all his might, and it is only just that on the occasion of its fortieth lustrum he was celebrated as one of its founding fathers.[214] One of his so-called *monita medica* (primarily intended as advice for a healthy regimen) says: "Man's best manner of living is for each one to live according to his own nature" ("De beste manier van leven is elck sijn Eijgen natuer"). It seems as if many of Amsterdam's communal leaders had been guided by it.

We must turn from here to what I should like to call the psychological and the magic-folkloristic undertones of the anatomies in general and of Dr. Tulp's of January 1632 in particular. The annual anatomies were, from the beginning, seasonal fetes. The annual anatomy in both Italy and the Northern countries was celebrated in and around the Christmas season and occasionally in the season of Carnival. The anatomical theaters were at first put up in the open. Undoubtedly the cold winter air was welcome at a time when means of preserving the cadaver for the necessary three to five days were still in the experimental stage.[215] But this purely utilitarian explanation does not wholly account for the persistence of the public anatomies as a seasonal ritual. Christmas, after all, marks not only the height of the cold season: it also ushers in the new unfolding of nature. The anatomists were deeply concerned with the *arcana* of life, creation, death, and regeneration; I have referred to this concern in the preceding chapter. At the same time the objects of their public demonstration were invariably the *corpora vilia* of criminals. We must try to see these two components as a key to the inner motivation of these fetes.

An inner conflict had to arise where the enlightened anatomist's quest for a devout study of the *coaptatio membrorum* was countered by the rather pertinent question why one should even try to elicit answers from the corpses of the morally inferior.[216] The only possible explanation why this obvious dilemma had practically no unfavorable repercussions is that the toleration of criminals in this seemingly miscast role, viz. as tools of theodicy and teachers of God-ordained beauty, can be understood only when we accept the operation of powerful magic-folkloristic associations between anatomy and punishment, punishment and atonement, criminal and God. To the Renaissance thinkers, ultimately, all was in harmony—πάντα συμπαθέα. More specifically, in Rembrandt's day it was understood that physiological data had nothing to do with social stratification. There was, physiologically speaking, no difference between "noble blood" and "ordinary blood."[217]

The persons immediately concerned with the creation of the painting, Dr. Tulp and the guild members (as well as Rembrandt himself), were undoubtedly conscious of the element of atonement in the public anatomy and of its ultimate metaphysical aim, the "Know Thyself."[218] They were acting high priests in a drama whose cathartic function, even for the uninitiates, was taken for granted. To hear their voices we need only listen to the utterances of Caspar Barlaeus. I shall cite at length some of his most significant commentaries on the anatomical scene, because I think they provide a key to even the hidden recesses of the onlookers' souls.

Barlaeus celebrated the opening of the Amsterdam Anatomical Theater—an important event in the annals of the City—in a poem that, short as it is, has never to my knowledge been published *in toto*. I referred to it in Chapter III, and I pointed out that I regard the allusion to Dr. Tulp as an explicit reference to Rembrandt's painting, which, as we know, graced the walls of the new permanent structure (1639 *et seq.*):

On the Anatomical Place Recently Erected in Amsterdam

Evildoers who while living have done damage are of benefit after their death. The art of healing reaps advantages even from their death. Skins teach without voices. Mortal remains though in shreds warn us not to die for crimes. Here addresses us the Eloquence of learned Tulpius while with nimble hand he dissects livid limbs. Listener, learn for thyself, and as thou proceedest from one to another, believe that even in the smallest part God is enshrined.

In locum Anatomicum recens AMSTELODAMI exstructum.

QVi vivi nocuere, mali, post funera prosunt,
 Et petit ex ipsa commoda morte Salus.
Exuviae sine voce docent. & mortua quamvis
 Frusta, vetant ista nos ratione mori.
Hic loquitur nobis docti facundia Tulpi:
 Dum secat artifici lurida membra manu.
Auditor te disce. & dum per singula vadis,
 Crede vel in minima parte latere Deum.

With slight variations these verses were inscribed in gold letters under the uppermost balcony of the new theater (1639).[219]

Not later than 1646 Barlaeus wrote a poem on the Anatomical Table that carries the message of sin and atonement one step farther:

On the Anatomical Table

Here lies spread out Man and offers to all the World spectacles of his pitiful state. To miserable mortals he exposes his naked limbs, and since this happens on account of the Fall of Sin, he lacks shame. Here stands the table, bloody like that of Thyestes, and it turns round and round bodies which are restless because of their shame. Brow, finger, kidney, tongue, heart, lung, brain, bones, hand, afford a lesson to you, the Living. You may examine here publicly that which is healthy and that which is diseased, and you have here the evils where Nature has been deficient. You learn to understand through what specific flaw each single part succumbs, under which rule it may rise again, as well as the astonishing accidents of the human forum. To this one greed was detrimental or mad lust. This one was destroyed by furor, that one by the pernicious admixture of the water he had drunk. Just as we die in a thousand different ways, we are wounded not just by one cause alone. Now it will be the sea, then the land, finally the pernicious air that does the damage. The elements, which are favorable on the whole, are detrimental to the cure. And life's thread is cut by an enemy forever different. While this you contemplate in the remains of the defunct, learn that it is through God that you live hale, teach this to yourself.

In mensam Anatomicam.

Sternitur & toti praebet spectacula mundo,
 Qui jacet afflictae conditionis Homo.
Exponit nudos miseris mortalibus artus,
 Et quia peccati labe, pudore vacat.
Mensa Thyestaeae similis stat cruda, rotatque
 Corpora, flagitiis, irrequieta suis.
Frons, digitus, ren, lingua, caput, cor, pulmo, cerebrum,
 Ossa, manus, vivo dant documenta tibi.
Adspicis hic coram sanum quodcunque vel aegrum est,
 Et mala naturae deficientis habes.
Quo vitio pars quaeque ruat, qua lege resurgat,
 Discis & humani fata stupenda fori.
Huic gula, vel funesta fuit malesana libido.
 Hunc furor, hunc potae perdidit humor aquae.

113

Mille modis morimur, nec causa laedimur una.
    Nunc mare, nunc tellus, nunc gravis aura nocet.
Quae nos cuncta fovent, obsunt elementa saluti.
    Et vario vitae rumpitur hoste tenor.
Haec cum defunctis lustras spectator in extis,
    Disce Deo sopes vivere, disce Tibi.[220]

A third poem in the same edition of Barlaeus' *Poemata* (Amsterdam, 1646),[32] which must have originated some time before 1639, is entitled

On the Anatomical House Which Can be Visited in Amsterdam

Father Amstel saw rise lofty towers against his banks, and Churches dedicated to God Almighty. He saw sails disperse all over the immense Globe, and as many harbors open up to his ships as there are warehouses which swell through the products of Nature—goods which either the rich Orient or the rich Occident bring forth. He saw here also houses established for the tragic buskins, and new pulpits speak with different seers. He saw goods of all sorts being weighed and structures specifically adapted to such task. And weapons of war being stored in vast arsenals; weapons by which the wrath of fierce Tagus is broken. Being thus preserved, he said: What I provided for the City is insufficient, nor does that adornment suffice to my praise. Erect, valiant Republic, funerary theaters, erect accommodation which cruel Venus Libitina shall inhabit. Elsewhere we live unencumbered. This house we found for Death, this hall is rigid with skins forcibly removed. Here, keenly intent, we behold whatever we are inside, and that which is hidden in the midst of our bodies' *fabrica* is brought to light. This structure is the seat of the soul, this is the venerable tabernacle of the mind, this insignificant receptacle contains divinity concealed. Whatever we were we are no longer. Behold, a life's span has withered. And once the light has been extinguished, man disintegrates in putrefaction. Behold this, O citizens, and tell your Magistrates that here you can learn the ways of death and a desire to shun death.

In Domum ANATOMICAM, quae Amstelodami visitur.

VIderat excelsas in se pater Amstela turres
    Surgere & ingenti templa dicata Deo.
Viderat immensum dispargi vela per orbem,
    Et portus ratibus tot patuisse suis.
Tot pandos naturae opibus turgere penates,
    Quas Oriens vel quas Vespera dives alit.
Viderat hic tragicis aptari tecta cothurnis,
    Et nova diverso pulpita vate loqui.
Viderat omnigenas librari pondere merces,
    Officiisque aptas talibus esse domos.
Armaque disponi spaciis Mavortia magnis.
    Arma, quibus duri frangitur ira Tagi.
Cum sic sospes ait: minus est, quod fecimus urbi,
    Nec decor ad laudem sufficit iste meam.
Erige funereos praestans Respublica circos,
    Erige, quos habitet trux Libitina, lares.

Vivimus incolumes alibi. haec penetralia morti
    Condimus, haec raptis pellibus aula riget.
Cernimus hic avidi, quicquid sumus intus, & illa
    Quae latet, in media fabrica luce patet.
Haec animae locus, haec mentis veneranda taberna est,
    Haec minor occultum capsula numen habet.
Quod fuimus, non jam sumus. En, defloruit aevum.
    Et lacer extincto lumine sordet homo.
Adspicite haec cives & dicite Fascibus: hic vos
    Posse modos mortis discere, nolle mori.[221]

The quintessence of Barlaeus' pronouncements seems to lie in the lessons learned and the benefit reaped from the lesson taught by the anatomies to the individual and to the community. The leitmotif is the idea that the dissection of the cadaver of the criminal is also a punishment for crimes of which society, nay man individually, is capable. The concept that gives the punishment of the criminal cathartic significance for the people as a whole lurks, as a matter of fact, behind the penal codes of even the most highly civilized peoples. In connection with the punitive anatomy as a fete for which tickets are sold to the public, there comes to mind the scapegoat criminal who is sacrificed at the annual spring festival for the benefit of the people. I cannot think of a more cogent explanation of the seasonal recurrence of the academic *quodlibeta anatomica* and their successors, the public anatomical fetes.[222]

As now we turn again to January 1632, are we not tempted to ask ourselves whether this kind of magic association played its part also in Amsterdam? We have seen that the cadaver under Dr. Tulp's jurisdiction was that of a criminal. Fortunately we are well informed about his identity. The *Anatomij-Boek*[305a] of the Amsterdam Guild registers the hanging and the subsequent dissection on January 31 *et seq.*, 1632, of the quiver maker Adriaan Adriaansz., a native of Leiden. This man, also known as Aris Kindt, was a pathetic criminal with profoundly antisocial impulses; he had tried to end an insufferable prison term in the *tuchthuis* of Utrecht by attempting to murder one of the guards. On the day preceding the anatomy, he had been hanged for a grave assault and battery that endangered the life of a man whose cloak he had tried to take with the aid of another criminal (see Appendix III).[223]

Amsterdam had got her school not without strenuous resistance on the part of the University of Leiden. Was it not, then, a happy coincidence and, perhaps, even more than that—at least, if we believe in the associative power of magic-folkloristic undertones in the public anatomies—that Aris Kindt happened to be a citizen of Leiden? The triumph of the Guild of Surgeon-Anatomists of Amsterdam, in the light of such considerations, was the punishment *in effigie* of a foe of long standing and a good omen for the city.[224]

Fig. 20. "The Large Crucifixion." Drawing after illumination of Herrad of Landsperg, *Hortus delicia-rum*,[219] fol. 150 *recto* (twelfth century).

XVI

The 'Anatomy': a *Trionfo* of Dr. Nicolaas Tulp

Deus autem miscendo bonitatem suam huius fabricae malitiam temperavit
(Eugippius)
Sapientia vincit malitiam

Out of the conflicting tendencies that sought expression in the public anatomies Rembrandt managed to form an ideally rounded image that does equal justice to the strictly scientific investigation of the human hand (an approach grown out of the late mediaeval post-mortems) and to the strictly formal fete perpetuating the *quodlibeta* of the Renaissance. Besides those triumphs of theory and practice, happily controlling each other, Rembrandt succeeded in expressing in his painting the idea of an atonement ritual in general (by contrasting with the coarse and lifeless appearance of the criminal the vital energies of the guild members) and a *trionfo* over death and sin in particular through the skillful use of iconographic devices that I shall now discuss.

It has already been suggested that the anatomy of the woodcut in the Ketham *Fasciculo* of 1493 can rightfully rank in form and content as one of Dr. Tulp's early ancestors. The kinship rests primarily in the idea of the presiding surgeon. How conventionally Rembrandt conceived Dr. Tulp, we appreciate when we notice that his hand, raised in an *allocutio* gesture, suggests at the same time that Tulp is also engaged, like the professor in the Paduan anatomy (Fig. 7), in some kind of dialectic enumeration of points. This detail may be accidental, but it is not accidental that both are seated in the traditional chair of authority. We have had occasion to observe that Dr. Tulp's peculiar position, off-center toward the right and at the feet, as it were, of the cadaver, is found in Berengario da Carpi's *Isagogae* of 1535 (Fig. 5). The (nonmedical) philosopher lecturing on death was, curiously enough, cast in a very similar pattern even earlier—a pattern that, I think, more distinctly reveals the *trionfo* idea in the representations in which a magister is shown confronting a corpse. We find it, for example, in Guyot Marchant's *Danse Macabre*[307] (1492). (Fig. 21.) The *magister cathedraticus,* seated at a desk stacked with books one of which lies open, is shown facing the prone figure of Death, who has lost his crown; it lies beside him in the grass. The *magister,* with the aid of an angel, holds a vast bannerlike scroll on which there is inscribed a detailed prescription for the triumph of the *sapientes* over the *infernum* ("Sic igitur cuncti sapientes viuere certent: Ut nichil inferni sit metuenda palus").[225]

Dr. Tulp, distinguished from the others as behooves the *cathedraticus* by keeping his head covered (a tradition still observed at Dutch universities)[226] is not only seated in a prominent chair: what architecture can be discerned about him shows that he is intentionally so placed that a recess topped by a handsome shell niche is placed behind and above his head. Pentimenti, visible even in a good photograph, show clearly how Rembrandt has gone out of his way to bring out the shell by lowering the crown of Tulp's top hat. As elsewhere in the painting, meaning and form seem to balance each other ideally. The conch niche (less pronouncedly echoed in a second recess to the beholder's left) forms a beautiful foil for the chairman and at the same time designates him, by alluding to a time-honored tradition, as the fountainhead of inspired wisdom. The *concha* (in this case a pecten shell whose lip is pointed downward) goes back to classical antiquity, and it was one of the pagan symbols liberally accepted by the Church at a very early point. It is found, for example, in Early Christian art above the empty cathedra as an inspiring emblem of heavenly indoctrination, alternating with the table of the four Gospels; so we see it in the Baptistery of the Orthodox in Ravenna, *ca.* 450 A.D. Similarly it occurs in an Asiatic sarcophagus as a suitable foil for the figures of standing philosophers (Pl. XXXVIII-45). In Carolingian art the classical shell niche might even merge with the concept of the halo.[227] The *concha* was consciously revived as a motif of supreme importance in the Early Renaissance, where we find it abundantly used behind saintly figures of explicit authority—above all John the Baptist and the Madonna. We may suspect that in those instances the authority of mediaeval usage fortified the revival of a classical tradition. To point to any particular prototype that might have influenced Rembrandt is naturally next to impossible. He may have seen in a Reederijkers play a "Lady Rhetoric" under her pecten shell as she triumphed over "Contempt of Reason" and over "Scorn of the Arts" personified. He may also have seen Holbein's "Madonna of the Burgomaster Meyer," whose original panel, in 1632 in the hands of an art dealer in Amsterdam and copied in that year or soon after (the Dresden version), showed one of the finest pecten shell niches of the Northern Renaissance.

Rembrandt himself made use of the shell niche and its iconographic message in another work signed and dated 1632. This painting, in the National Gallery of Canada, Ottawa, represents, I suggest, "Esther Putting on Her Royal Apparel." Queen Esther appears here, I believe, as the great interceding figure in the Old Testament, a role in which she serves in, for example, chap. xxxix of the *Speculum humanae salvationis:*[452] "Hester orat regem Assuerum pro populo" (Esther v). "Maria ostendit filio pectus et ubera." She is, in other words, divinely inspired, and she must be understood as a prefiguration of Mary interceding with the Lord on behalf of mankind. If my conjecture is right, Rembrandt would have placed the Queen before the shell niche to indicate her high mission.[228]

The *concha* in Rembrandt's "Anatomy" has, however, a still more specific meaning. If (as I have tried to do in Pl. XXXIX-47), we isolate Dr. Tulp and Aris Kindt from the spectators in the picture, the result is that anatomist and cadaver appear in striking similarity to a not uncommon type of Renaissance tomb memorial. I have in mind the commemorative portrait busts of great men (often hyperrealistically conceived) who, set against a shell niche, are shown triumphing as it were over the *gisant,* which may be either the image of the deceased himself (as in Antonio Pollajuolo's "Tomb of Innocent VIII" in St. Peter's in Rome) or a corpse or skeleton suggesting death in general (as in the "Tomb of Dr. John Colet," to be discussed forthwith). These shell-foiled portrait busts derive, as I believe, ultimately from a classical prototype closely associated with the idea of death and immortality; that is, the portrait busts of Roman citizens as they appear singly or in pairs on the faces of sarcophagi, set against a pecten shell to suggest the journey into the Hereafter (Pl. XL-48). I suggest, therefore, that in the two figures of Tulpius and the corpse we may see some kind of triumph configuration. In order to interpret its structure in general terms, I shall now present three works of art apparently containing, each in its own way, elements that in their totality constitute the triumph idea in Rembrandt's configuration. At the same time I shall trace what seems to be the development of these elements and their migration from Italy to the North. The three examples are the triumph of a saint, the portrait bust of a humanist, and an Elizabethan tomb memorial.

(1) Filippino Lippi, in his "Triumph of St. Thomas Aquinas" (1489), shows the saint enthroned and flanked by personifications of the *Quadrivium*. His throne is underneath a *baldachino*[229] that consists of a tunnel vault framing a huge pecten shell (Pl. XL-49). At St. Thomas' feet we see Heresy cringing in defeat, personified—we may assume—by Averroes, who is shown holding a scroll with the inscription: SAPIENTIA VINCIT MALITIAM.

(2) The inspired humanist, shown as a bust in front of a shell, appears in Andrea da Fiesole's idealized portrait of Marsilio Ficino, which offers one of the earliest Renaissance examples of the ecstatic head inclination and heavenward glance indicative of divine inspiration (Pl. XLI-50).

(3) It has been pointed out that this type of portrait migrated to and was paralleled in England, where we find what might be called a synthesis of the "Triumph of St. Thomas" and the idealized portrait of Marsilio Ficino. I am referring to the once famous shell niche portrait bust commemorating John Colet, Dean of St. Paul's. The bust itself, lost like the rest of the tomb in the Great Fire of 1666, seems to have been one of those hyper-lifelike representations that ultimately derived from the late mediaeval *imagines* of the

119

deceased placed on catafalques. Colet's bust was shown as presiding over an "artificiall Askeliton." The tomb in its entirety (Pl. XLII-51) suggests an ultimate stage in the development of the Italian Quattrocento wall tomb. Originally (as for example in the Donatello-Michelozzo tomb of Pope John XXIII) the bust was that of the Virgin Mary. As soon as the place of Mary was taken by the bust of the deceased the *gisant* became even more emphatically the image of the portrayed's mortal and putrefied flesh. The idea of the death and resurrection of the flesh was expressed in the tablet originally affixed to Colet's sarcophagus: "ISTUC RECEDIT GLORIA CARNIS / MORERE MVNDO VT VIVAS DEO / LOUE AND LYUE."[230]

Dr. Tulp, seated against his shell niche, presiding over the cadaver of Adriaan Adriaansz., is celebrating a triumph: that of communal science over the egotistical ignorance of sin. The inevitable and deserved eradication of the criminal, which repeats itself year after year, makes it possible for the chief anatomist to rise vicariously, like a Phoenix, from another man's ashes as it were, to lasting fame. Here too, then, we witness the triumph of SAPIENTIA over MALITIA. By making Dr. Tulp's death-transcending *gloria* ultimately not a personal one but that of the Guild of Surgeons of Amsterdam, Rembrandt avoids committing himself to either alternative: that which saw in death an annihilation of personality and that which saw in it a first step toward vainglorious perpetuation of the individual. The personages portrayed, including Adriaan Adriaansz., have been immortalized, to be sure, but only so far as they have become part of the immortal idea of scientific investigation undertaken for the common good.

We are reminded of Dr. Tulp's proud personal motto, one that the emblem books prescribe for teachers and magistrates: CONSVMOR ALIIS INSERVIENDO—"I consume myself by serving others."[231] Indubitably an association was felt with the last words of Christ: "Consummatum est (et inclinato capite tradidit spiritum)" (Joh. xix: 30). The thought can be expressed emblematically by an apt image: that of the candle, which, by giving light to others, consumes itself. Appropriately enough, Dr. Tulp had himself represented in 1634 pointing to a candle half consumed by its flame, with the motto carved on a stone parapet (itself reminiscent of Roman tomb memorials as they are found in the North) underneath a human skull.[232] (Pls. XLIV-53 and XLV-54.) The magic of what we may call the emblem of Dr. Tulp is by no means diminished when we call to mind that he accepted this portrait in lieu of a doctor's fee for having treated the artist's sick child.

Of all his contemporaries in the arts and in literature, Rembrandt was possibly the least affected by the emblematic vogue that liked to exercise the reader's and beholder's mind by posing witty riddles and pointing up heroic morals in ever new forms.[233] Traces of it in Rembrandt's work are the exception rather than the rule. The "Anatomy" may be said to approximate an emblematic attitude, inasmuch as a motto may serve to unlock its enigma. Above all we should, I think, see Rembrandt as a poet who externalizes poetic ideas.

He celebrated Dr. Tulp and the surgeons with rare insight in his painting by subordinating individual aspirations to permanent ideals. His creation amounts to an apotheosis of the scientific spirit as it could flourish with such vigor only in a Commonwealth whose members felt it natural to think of themselves as constituting parts of a corporation.

Mnemosyne of forms and spiritual contents of the past blends in with the forceful realism with which Rembrandt had rendered the actuality of his day. With the "Anatomy" of 1632 he had become—to transfer to him words with which James Joyce characterized the poet—"a mediator between the world of reality and the world of dreams."

Fig. 21.   "Death Loses His Crown." Woodcut used in Guyot Marchant, *Mirroer tressalutaire*[307] (1492).

Notes

The superior numbers in square brackets, following names of authors alone or of authors accompanied by short titles, refer to correspondingly numbered entries in the Bibliography.

[1] The composition of the "Anatomy of Dr. Tulp" has frequently been analyzed; above all by Alois Riegl,[398] Textband, pp. 181–89; Riegl was preceded by Josef Strzygowski.[461] An early attempt was made to see Rembrandt's anatomies as part of a specifically Dutch development; cf. Paul Triaire,[474] esp. pp. 32–41, and *passim*. A fine survey, although marred by great inaccuracies, is found in J. G. de Lint's *Rembrandt*,[288] chaps. ii and iii. A recent study that contains a number of suggestive observations to which the present study is under obligation is Hubert Schrade's.[432] However, as the reader of Schrade's article will see for himself, I am in opposition to the essential arguments of his genealogy of Rembrandt's composition. For an excellent treatment of the Dutch group portrait, cf. H. van de Waal,[504] *passim*.

Most compositional analyses are, I believe, vulnerable. One figure, if not two, is a decidedly post-Rembrandtian addition. Both may have been sanctioned by Rembrandt, but they seem to form no part of the original compositional intentions. Albrecht Jordan[260] (preceded by Wagenaar,[508] p. 58) held that surgeon number eight, van Loenen, was not listed as a guild member. Van Loenen is the apex of a (nonexistent) pyramid; he gazes sheepishly out of the picture. He is shoddily painted and does not fit into the very consistent color scheme that rules most of the remainder of Rembrandt's painting. Jordan's three pages contain extremely sharp and worth-while observations that

have been, on the whole, disregarded. H. W. Janson suggested to me some time ago that the person farthest left, Jacob Jacobsz. Koolvelt, might also be a later addition. He is the last but one (i.e. number eight) on the roll call list held by Hartman Hartmansz. Psychologically and aesthetically he has no place in the composition. See also Note 48 below.

I am grateful to Dr. A. B. de Vries, director of the Mauritshuis, who has liberally allowed me to examine some of the detailed X rays and infrared photos (Pl. I-1b) made under his guidance. I am also under obligation for his permission to use some of the unpublished information as well as conclusions drawn by himself in the course of the recent cleaning (winter and spring 1951).

The great number of pentimenti in the "Anatomy" might easily be attributed to the lack of assurance of a young painter faced with a new theme as well as a new format. It has been shown that Rembrandt's late work is equally marked by trial passages that have been repainted; cf. A. van Schendel.[422a]

[2] For the *Affiche*[2] of a public anatomy (Fig. 12), see Otto Clemen,[99] *passim*. The unrecorded Invitation[58] (the original of which was kindly presented to me by Dr. H. W. Janson) is probably unique in that it invites to a nonacademic public anatomy in a private house. "Die von Doctor Bogdan in Burenküngs hus verrichtete Anatomey" is expressly mentioned in the *Ratsmanual* of Berne, May 6, 1661; cf. Yvonne Thurnheer,[480a] pp. 68ff.

³ It seems to me that more even than Carel van Mander's so-called *Leergedicht*,[303] Franciscus Junius' treatise voices the art theory that influenced Rembrandt's "Anatomy." The fact that Junius wrote his book while he was in England as librarian and art curator of Thomas Howard, Earl of Arundel, and that it was not published in its *editio princeps* until 1637,[262] the author's own Dutch translation appearing at Middelburg in 1641,[264] should not militate against this assumption. It has been shown that G. J. Vossius, Barlaeus' first and only colleague at the new Academy, who was intimate with Rembrandt's Amsterdam circle of friends and sponsors, helped his younger brother-in-law Junius through many years preceding the actual publication of his work. We encounter Vossius' first reference to Junius' intention to treat of the "pictura veterum" in a letter dated 1629. Vossius draws Junius' attention to Molanus' well-known *De picturis et imaginibus sacris* (ed. Leiden, 1619) and to the most recent publication in the field, Boulenger's *De pictvra, plastice, statvaria libri dvo* (1627);[62a] see Vossius, Epistola CXLIII, *Opera*,[502b] IV, pp. 84f. Boulenger, not Junius, was the Winckelmann of the seventeenth century. See also A. M. F. B. Geerts,[173] pp. 58 ff. I at first hesitated to try to explain certain aspects of Rembrandt's work by means of a treatise devoted to the "pictura veterum." Junius' merits as an archaeologist have quite rightly been stressed (see for example Luigi Salerno,[415a] especially pp. 238f.), but unjustly to the exclusion of all others. The attentive reader, expecially of Books I and III, will note again and again that Junius endeavors to formulate a humanistic yet unacademic art theory for the benefit of the artist of his own day.

For the scholastic definition of "ordo" see St. Thomas Aquinas,[470] especially pars Ima, quae. xxi, 2, 3mo. Curiously enough van Mander,[303] fol. 15, stanza 1, hints that the original meaning of "ordinancy" describes a regulated and well-ordered social group, as in a kingdom or family.

⁴ J. G. van Gelder[176] has beautifully traced Rembrandt's development before 1632; he has shown that a drawing in the British Museum, the "Stoning of St. Stephen," already uses the motif of the passively enduring body placed in a diagonal to the picture plane; see Plate V, fig. 8.

⁵ Franciscus Junius advises the use of discords, "even as a discord in musicke maketh now and then a comely concordance: and it falleth out very often, that the most curious spectators finde themselves, I know not how, singularly delighted with such a disorderly order of a counterfeited rudenesse"; III,[263] v, § 10, p. 317.

For the earliest demonstrable use of the *camera obscura* (well before 1632) by artists, I must refer the reader to a forthcoming study by Charles Parkhurst.

⁶ New material on the relationship between Rembrandt and Uylenburgh will be found in H. F. Wijnman,[515] p. 94 and *passim;* also see Nikolaus Pevsner,[376] p. 130, note 1. For the seventeenth-century belief in the artist's prenatal destination according to van Mander, cf. Ernst Kris and Otto Kurz,[277] p. 57. The *terminus post quem* of Rembrandt's move from Leiden to Amsterdam in 1631 is discussed by Jan Veth,[494] p. 9.

⁷ Cf. Caspar Barlaeus' poem "Amstelodamum,"[29] ed. Leiden, 1631, p. 459. In his private letters Barlaeus, less guardedly, speaks of his difficulty in getting accustomed to Amsterdam's two rivers, het Y and the Amstel, and how he misses the learned faces and the pleasant walks of Leiden; see his letter to Constantine Huygens, Amsterdam, May 10, 1631, ed. *Epistolarum Liber, pars prior*,[35] No. 176, pp. 394ff.; also see Note 212 below. Biographical material on Barlaeus (van Baerle) will be found in Note 219 below.

I cannot pass over René Descartes' beautiful letter from Amsterdam to his friend Balzac, who lived in the retreat of his Chartreuse. In this letter Descartes sings the praise of Amsterdam in tones that at times seem almost to parallel and elsewhere to corroborate and amplify the impressions recorded by Barlaeus. Descartes recommends the big city for its lack of

> petits voisins, qui vous vont quelquefois importuner, & de qui les visites sont encore plus incommodes que celles que vous receuez à Paris; au lieu qu'en cette grande ville où ie suis, n'y ayant aucun homme, excepté moy, qui n'excerce la marchandise, chacun y est tellement attentif à son profit, que i'y pourrois demeurer toute ma vie sans estre iamais vû de personne. Ie me vais promener tous les iours parmy la confusion d'vn grand peuple, auec autant de liberté & de repos que vous sçauriez faire dans vos allées, & ie n'y considere pas autrement les hommes que i'y voy, que ie ferois les arbres qui se rencontrent en vos forests, ... Le bruit mesme de leur tracas n'interromt pas plus mes reveries, que feroit celuy de quelque ruisseau ... ie voy que tout leur trauail sert à embellir le lieu de ma demeure, & à faire que ie n'y aye manque d'aucune chose. Que s'il y a du plaisir à voir croître les fruits en vos vergers, & à y estre dans l'abondance iusques aux yeux, pensez-vous qu'il n'y en ait pas bien autant, à voir venir icy des vaisseaux, qui nous apportent abondamment tout ce que produisent les Indes, & tout ce qu'il y a de rare en l'Europe. Quel autre lieu pouroit-on choisir au reste du monde, où toutes les commoditez de la vie, & toutes les curiositez qui peuuent estre souhaitées, soient si faciles à trouuer qu'en cettuy-cy? [*Lettre* xxxiii, Amsterdam, May 5, 1631,[123] pp. 202–4.]

The importance of Descartes' letters for the discovery not only of Amsterdam, but also of the concept of the baroque metropolis, was brought to my attention back in my student days at Hamburg by Dr. Panofsky. See also H. de la Fontaine Verwey.[156] Barlaeus and Descartes were acquainted; cf. Cohen,[100] p. 551. Rembrandt himself may have known

Descartes; cf. J. Q. van Regteren Altena,[391] p. 6.

8 (i) The portrait of the so-called "Lieven Willemsz. van Coppenol," at the Cassel Gemäldegallerie, and (ii) the one of "Maerten Looten XI Januari 1632" (thus Rembrandt's inscription), being the portrait of an Amsterdam merchant of Flemish descent. Cf. A. Bredius,[65] Nos. 164 and 166; (iii) the so-called "van Coppenol," Leningrad, Hermitage, Cat. 1901, no. 808, Bredius, No. 146, dated 1631.

9 For the relevant passages of Huygens' autobiography see C. Hofstede de Groot,[228] "Urkunde" No. 18; also see *Rembrandt Tentoonstelling*,[393] "Archiefstukken," No. II. Particulars concerning Rembrandt's state of health in and about 1632 will be found in Note 137 below and Appendix I.

10 W. Thoré-Burger in his *Musées de la Hollande*,[77] pp. 196f., was the first modern critic to express this: "Peut-être y a-t-il encore d'autres auditeurs dans la salle, car le professeur regarde devant lui, comme s'adressant à une assemblée qu'on ne voit pas, et Slabbraan, Harmansz. [sic] et van Loenen jettent aussi là un coup d'œil."

11 For the three chief aims of rhetorical painting see the Motto to my Introduction. That the *permovere* which Cicero demanded could also be applied to baroque music has recently been shown by J. G. van Gelder,[177] p. 406 and *passim*.

J. J. Orlers,[347] p. 375, speaks as follows of Rembrandt's "inborn inclinations" which, literally, moved him toward the art of Painting and Drawing, away from the studies at the university of Leiden: " ... en heeft daer toe gants geen lust ofte genegentheyt gehadt / dewijle zijne natuyrlicke bewinghen streckten alleen tot de Schilder ende Teycken Conste."

Marin Mersenne's [317] passage (II, propositio vii, p. 290) deserves to be quoted in full: " ... priusquam de cantu componendo apud te cogites, explorandum qua voce, quo tono, quibus interuallis ea verba pronuntiaret egregius Orator, vel actor, vt pro viribus auditores verbis, postea canendis, excitaret, atque commoueret: Optimus si quidem musicus qui Rhetoricam Harmonicam adeo foeliciter exercuerit, vt ab auditoribus suis lachrymas, risum, & alia passionum . . . testimonia elicuerit." For Mersenne see also E. Panofsky,[363] p. 5.

G. J. Vossius ("De musice,"[502] chap. iv, pp. 40–43) writes: "Musices finis est honesta aurium, atque animi, voluptas," and "Honesta haec Musices voluptas etiam valetudini confert . . . Quin morbis etiam certis mederi, traditum est." Finally: "Etiam Musice magnam obtinet vim in animos humanos. Quod & poetarum fabulae testatum facient."

12 The anatomist is the " . . . verus medicinae oculus. Cujus lumine, ut irradiantur intima corporis penetralia: sic producuntur ejusdem beneficio, quasi in claram lucem, abditissimae, occultorum morborum, caussae . . .," Nicolaas Tulp, *Observationes,*[477] "Epistola dedicatoria" addressed to Pieter Tulp, his son, on his graduation from Leiden University. Such a dedication to a son is, as far as I know, a unique event in that age. Pieter died on December 7 of that very year at the age of twenty-two.

13 H. E. van Gelder,[174] pp. 241–50, who summarizes the analyses of Riegl and Weissbach.

14 C. Hofstede de Groot,[228] p. 24. The painting was the property of Amsterdam's Guild of Surgeons. It was moved in 1639 (from where?) to the first permanent Anatomical Theater in the former St. Margaret's Chapel and from there, in 1691, to the second permanent structure, the St. Anthony Weighing House, where it was kept (after a fashion) until 1828, when it was purchased by the Crown. An excellent survey of some of the basic data on the Guild, its Deans, its theaters, etc. will be found in B.W.Th. Nuyen's book.[343] See also Note 59 below.

That the Dutch group portrait was neither true history nor true genre was first pointed out by H. van de Waal,[504] pp. 75 f.

The locations and migrations of Amsterdam's anatomical theater can be summed up as follows: (i) *ca.* 1550–78 at St. Ursula's Convent; (ii) 1578–1619 at St. Margaret's Convent (= Little Meat Hall); here the anatomists had to share their quarters with members of the Rhetoricians Chamber "In Liefde Bloeiende" ("Prospering in Love"), which arrangement more or less forced their next move; (iii) 1619–39 somewhere in the St. Anthony Gate (= Weighing House), where a (modernized?) architrave still marks the entrance to the south tower: THEATRUM ANATOMICUM; this was the location of Rembrandt's anatomy; see also Notes 25 and 26 below; (iv) 1639–90 back at St. Margaret's Convent (=Little Meat Hall); (v) 1691–nineteenth century once more at the St. Anthony Gate, but in a newly constructed part that is still standing, although heavily restored in the eighteenth and nineteenth centuries (at present = the Jewish Historical Museum of Amsterdam); cf. T. den Herder,[218] pp. 13–27, and E. H. M. Thijssen,[468] p. 18.

15 Galen's demonstrations also, it seems, were attended by magistrates and by cultured Romans in general; cf. Max Simon,[445] p. xlvii, note a. See also Note 29 below, and Pl. XII-15.

16 For East European students at Dutch universities, see Hans Kauffmann,[267] pp. 59ff. For the Elizabethan ordinance see D'Arcy Power,[382] p. 27. We know that Descartes was an avid anatomist who with his own hands dissected the heads of sundry animals in order to explain in which part to find imagination, memory, etc. ("I'anatomise maintenant les testes de diuers animaux, pour expliquer en quoy consistent l'imagination, la memoire, &c.")—*Lettre*[123] xlvi, addressed to Mersenne from Deventer, November or December 1632, p. 263; cf. the letter to the same from Amsterdam, April 15, 1630 (= No. xxi, p. 137): "I'estudie maintenant en chymie & en anatomie tout ensemble, & apprens tous les iours quelque chose que ie ne trouue pas dedans les liures," etc., etc. See also C. L. Thijssen-Schoute,[469] *passim.* For Jacques de Geyn's great popularity and intimate knowledge of the academic situa-

tion at Leiden, see van Regteren Altena,[390] p. 7 and note 5.

[17] On December 21, 1633 Thos. Browne was promoted to the "supremus in Medicina gradus" by Vorstius of Leiden University; cf. R.W. James Smith,[451] *s. h. v.*, p. 34.

[18] Cf. Julius Held's article.[215]

[19] Amsterdam did not have a permanent stage before the *Schouwburg* (Holland's first theater) opened on Jan. 3, 1638; cf. C. N. Wijbrands,[514] p. 7, and also Jan Wagenaar,[507] II, p. 398. Before this date plays of a quite different sort were shown privately and under the sponsorship of the various *Reederijkerskamers*. See Note 14 above.

[20] See Barlaeus' poem quoted in full, pp. 114f.; Note 220 below.

[21] We are fairly well informed on the duties of the Dutch organists, and in particular those of Amsterdam, at the beginning of the seventeenth century. The situation as witnessed by a somewhat baffled foreigner is nicely summed up in the De Bòvios journal entry [68] describing an organ recital in the Groote Kerk at Amsterdam on December 11, 1677:

> ... e poi la sera venne similmente il signor Bleau, che ci condusse a vedere una cosa assai ridicolosa: ogni sera ... nella chiesa Maggiore vi è un gran concorso di popolo di ogni sorta, che passaggiando per quel gran tempio di tanto in tanto come stupido sta a sentire la melodia dell' organo, che è toccato da uno che non cessa di suonarlo, se non allora che tutta le gente è uscita. Suonansi diverse arie, e si come l'organo è ottimo, così il suonatore non era de' mediocri. In quest' organo vi è un registro, che toccato imita la voce umana, in maniera che pare agli orecchii di chi sente, che canti un bel concertato coro di diverse voci. Al suono di quest' aria tutti cessarono di passeggiare, et ognuno attentissimo stava rivolto all' organo. Veduta questa curiosità, ci ritirassimo all' albergo.

Nothing could better illustrate the psychological and aesthetic appeal of the "vox humana," whether it occurred in an organ fantasia or in a painting like Rembrandt's "Anatomy."

Calvinistic service music was severely restricted. But we hear of church recitals outside the service as a standard feature in the organists' contracts between 1593 and 1634. It was customary in Amsterdam, especially during the inclement seasons, for the burghers to walk up and down the churches, very much in the way in which the Italians use their glass-covered galleries. The favorite hour, it seems, was from eleven to noon, but evenings were not excluded; cf. Sir John Reresby,[395] p. 145, who speaks of "evenings, when candles being lighted, company walk in the churches to hear them." The inordinate length of many of Sweelinck's fantasias (and this was pointed out to me by E. E. Lowinsky) becomes understandable only if we see their function, to tempt people into the Church and away from public houses and taverns: "tot recreatie ende verlustinge vande gemeente ende omme dezelve duer middel van dien te meer uyt herbergen ende tavernen te houden" (contract of the organist Cornelis Schuyt, 1593 *et seq.*). Philip Jansz. van Velsen (1601) was to exercise his playing "om de gemeente tot zyn gehoor willich te maecken te trecken ende aen te locken"; cf. B. van den Sigtenhorst Meyer,[443] p. 95 and tables on pp. 96f. and 98. Not every one approved of the organ music; Constantine Huygens' treatise [245a] shows better than many a favorable report how deeply stirring those recitals must have been. An hour of organ music is compared to a voluptuous banquet; it leads to love-making in the dark corners of the church (pp. 21ff.).

[22] I have followed the wording of this ordinance as it appears in manuscript Amsterdam, [305aaa] pp. 28f., § 9 (written in the hand of 1645). See Joh. Monnikhoff[325] and E. H. M. Thijssen,[468] pp. 33 ff. For the earliest mention of a "sedendi ordo pro dignitate" and other aspects of administration concerned with public

anatomies, see the account of Alexander Benedictus (1497)[44] cited *in extenso* in Appendix II.

23 In general I might refer to Zedler's article "Anatomia"[526] (written 100 years after Rembrandt's "Anatomy"), in which (col. 89) the following passage occurs: "Den herrlichen und grossen Nutzen, welchen die Anatomie in der Theologie, Iurisprudenz, Medizin und Philosophie hat . . ." It is interesting that Medicine is number three out of four. For the most sumptuous allegorical, emblematic, hieroglyphical, etc., treatment of every part and aspect of the human frame, cf. Octavio Scarlatini,[422] in which even the exact steps in the course of an anatomical dissection are described; cf. pt. 2, pp. 161–64. For Barlaeus' poem see Note 24 below.

24 See Barlaeus' poem cited in full in Chapter XV, p. 113. One can still see the poem with its Dutch translation under the cupola of Amsterdam's anatomical theater of 1691ff., which now houses the Jewish Historical Museum; see Notes 14 above and 219 below. Hitherto it was assumed that the first reference to the "Anatomy of Dr. Tulp" occurred in 1711 on the occasion of von Uffenbach's[481] visit of February 20. For the poem by Justinus Kerner and the anonymous engraving see Adolf Kronfeld,[278] p. 14 and fig. 8.

25 Cf. B.W.Th. Nuyens,[343] fig. 1 on p. 9, from which I quote *in extenso* the original Dutch text found on the (undated) print:

Vleys-hallen tvvee, siet ghy hier vvel
          voorsien,
Van veel schoon vleysch, soo buyten als
          van binnen,
In overvloedt, dat men nau can ver-
          sinnen,
Waer het al blijft, 't geen brengen hier de
          Lien.
Comt Vrouvvkens vry, vvilt hier u gheldt
          besteden,
Coopt vvat u lust, en vvat u vvel
          behaeght:

vvant van dit vleysch de Man gheen'
          hoornen draeght:
Die reyn in comt, die sal oock reyn uyt
          treden.
Vraeght ghy, vvat volck dat daer om
          hooghe is?
'Tzijn Chirurgijns, die vvonden maken
          fris,
In d' Edel Const sy vvorden ondervvesen
Red'rijckers soet hier comen oock by
          een:
D' een doet de vvond' van 's Menschen
          lichaem scheen,
De and're pooght de Ziele te ghenezen.

26 Cf. Note 14 above. The old entrance to the south turret that leads up to what was once the anatomy chambers is still standing. Apart from the fact, however, that the lettering, THEATRUM ANATOMICUM, strikes one as relatively modern, the inscription is incomplete, at least if we can trust Jan Wagenaar's careful account,[508] p. 56, § 3.

27 For Amsterdam, *ca.* 1550, see Nuyens,[343] p. 7; for Utrecht, S. Muller Fz.,[330] pp. 104f.

28 For the "Falijde-Begijnen" chapel used at Leiden, cf. Appendix II B, and for an excellent reconstruction that distinctly shows the anatomical table where the altar would have been, see fig. 4 in J.A.J. Barge.[28] See also, for the outer appearance of the Faliede-Begijnenkerk, fig. 3, *ibidem*. Jost Amman represents an anatomy as taking place in a chapel in 1565 (Fig. 3); see also Note 40 below. After the French Revolution the Hôtel de Cluny at Paris (now Musée de Cluny) was bought by a surgeon who used the chapel of the abbots (erected, on the second floor, 1485–89) (Salle XX) as "une salle de dissection."

29 For this observation, see, for example, Baier,[21] p. 101, Max Simon, II,[445] p. xlvii, note a, and George Sarton, *Galen*,[418] p. 23, note 31 bis. I have gratefully followed, in the passage dealing with Galen's demonstration, some suggestions contained in a letter of June 1956 from my friend Prof. E. Drabkin.

[30] For the extremes to which, at least in Renaissance fiction, the anatomist might go in order to procure a suitable corpse, see Note 37 below; for nineteenth-century reality, see Note 180 below.

[31] Professor George Kernodle of the University of Arkansas points out to me, in a letter dated May 17, 1953, that entrance tickets were not sold for *Reederijkers* performances or for their contests, the so-called *landjuweelen*. It seems, from what Dr. Kernodle writes, that entrance tickets for professional theatrical shows cannot be traced back farther than 1500. This would make the sale of anatomical entrance tickets somewhat the earlier. I have failed to trace a single public entrance ticket. The Archives of Amsterdam have a folder containing miscellaneous material pertaining to the Surgeons' Guild; there I came across an annual pass for surgeon-apprentices that (duly filled in) reads: "KNEGT. Overluiden van het Chirurgyns Gild permitteeren [*Jacobus Hoolboon*] van [*Deventer*] knegt van [*Mr. Martinus Berkman*] vryheid Jaarlyx alle chirurgicale Lessen en Anatomische Demonstraties by te woonen . . . [*23 Feb. 1761 Pieter Jas. Overman*]." See also Note 33 below.

[32] See Note 180 below.

[33] Molière, appropriately, was known in the seventeenth century by the nickname "l'anatomiste de l'humanité." Young Thomas Diafoirus tries to win Angélique's affections: "Avec la permission aussi de Monsieur, je vous invite à venir voir, l'un de ces jours, pour vous divertir, la dissection d'une femme, sur quoi je dois raisonner . . ." *Le Malade Imaginaire*,[324] II, vi. For the general setting see Docteur Cabanès, *Mœurs Intimes du Passé*,[80] chap. "La Vie d'Étudiant aux Temps de Molière," pp. 189ff.

The anatomy of Levie Abrahamsz., October 19, 1647, was conducted by Dr. Tulp. It yielded, in five lessons, 229 florins and 8 stuyvers. For these accounts, especially under Dr. Frederik Ruysch (1666–1731), cf. Thijssen,[468] pp. 40ff. The sale of entrance tickets is first mentioned in 1497 when Alexander Benedictus[44]

makes reference to the manner in which the *collectae pecuniae* should be administered by two trustworthy men; see Appendix II. For sale of "Ticketts for the Demonstrations" and for their form in Elizabethan England, see d'Arcy Power's article,[382] pp. 28f. Thijssen,[468] p. 33, mentions that as late as 1720 anatomies were being advertised in the Dutch newspapers.[9a] Entrance tickets were sold as late as 1829 for the public dissection of William Burke; cf. Note 180 below. The anatomical banquet and parade can hardly be called a Dutch invention. Its form was also quite customary in Shakespeare's England; see d'Arcy Power,[382] p. 26. In Basel the surplus was actually used for the purchase of fumigators, vessels, calves' eyes, candles, and sponges (1571/72); see Gottfried Richter,[396] p. 25, note 32.

I am not aware that there exists a general study of such convivial expenses as are listed, among others, in the Dutch and English anatomical expense accounts. Such bills, as far as I know, can be traced back at least to the fourteenth century; see, for example, MS. on vellum of a banquet of the Confraternity of St. John the Baptist at Beauvais for the year 1330, recently offered for sale. For a good survey of Dutch guild banquets in their more or less outrageous forms, for edicts by which one tried to regulate them and for the role played by the consumption of tobacco, drink, card games (10 different ones were known), and music on these occasions, see A. J. M. Brouwer Ancher,[69] pp. 93–100.

[34] See G. Kalff,[266] p. 27. In English emblem books pictures without their mottoes were called "dumb figures" or "dumb shows"; see George Wither,[517] p. 90. For the *togen*, sing. *toog*, as a form of *tableau vivant*, which had its place in the so-called "Spelen van sinne," cf. J. J. Mak,[301] pp. 66–68. J. G. van Gelder,[176] p. 26 (298), using a completely different approach to the problem, has remarked upon the "moment of complete immobility which has seized the group [of surgeons] here gathered."

35 For a detailed description of the form of execution that we have to imagine as preceding Dr. Tulp's anatomy of January 1632, see Hans Bontemantel,[59] pp. 58–68.

36 For a discussion of the criminal's body as a means of theodicy, see Note 191 below and p. 102.

37 For Dr. Tulp as guild anatomist, see Note 38 below. Completely separate from the formal and public anatomies, true medical research was carried on in the city hospital, the *gasthuis* of the Dutch towns. Such anatomical research, which consisted of autopsies on patients who had died of natural causes, was at times impeded by short-sighted magistrates. Not so in Amsterdam, where it flourished during Dr. Tulp's extended terms of office. His medical research ranged from demonstrative to truly scientific dissections. Where bodies could not be easily procured the black market must have offered a lucrative business. Body and bone snatchers were severely punished; a husband and wife accused of this crime were publicly exhibited with the stolen skulls under their arms; cf. E. H. M. Thijssen,[468] pp. 26–29.

The significance of Dr. Tulp's *allocutio* gesture as the beginning of a tradition in Rembrandt's work (leading from there to the "speaking" Mennonite Cornelis Claesz. Anslo, 1641) has been dealt with by J. A. Emmens,[138] *passim;* also see Note 47 below.

38 Dr. Sebastian Egbertsz. was a product of the medical faculty of the University of Padua and, like Dr. Tulp in the subsequent generation, a burgomaster of Amsterdam as well as Dean of the Guild of Chirurgs. He died in 1621, a victim of the same plague epidemic that killed Jan Pietersz. Sweelinck. He was succeeded by Dr. Joan Fonteyn (d. 1628) (Pl. VIII–10), whose successor was Dr. Tulp. Tulp held the office of *anatomicus* and *praelector* of the Guild until 1652, when he was in turn succeeded by Dr. Deyman. Tulp, elected November 24, 1628, began his term of office at the Guild January 2, 1629 with an oration in Latin. His invited audience consisted of magistrates and physicians. Tulp's first anatomy dates from January 31, 1631; in the words of the *Anatomij-Boek*[305a]: "Doctor Tulp . . . is [aangewezen] als prelector 1628 . . . en heeft sijn aanvang genomen 1629 . . . en heeft syn oratie gedaan aan gilt en genode magistraten en doctoren int Latijn ende hij heeft naa het afsterven van Doctor fontijn sijn eerste ontleedinge gedaan als volgt / Den laatsten Januarij 1631 . . ." We may assume that Rembrandt familiarized himself with the painting by Aert Pietersz. before he set to work on his own. Pietersz.' "Anatomiestuck" was completed December 9, 1603, after two years of labor; cf. A. Bredius,[64] p. 3. Also see Appendix III.

39 Miereveld's "Anatomy" was done for the Delft Guild, whose permanent anatomical theater had been founded in 1624. According to the inscription as well as contemporary documentation kindly placed at my disposal by the Oude- en Nieuwe Gasthuis at Delft, the painting was executed by Pieter Michielsz. van Miereveld, aged 21, after the designs of his father. Pieter's portrait appears in profile to the right: a youth in grave contemplation of the anatomist. Several workshop assistants can be seen behind the skeletons. Jacobus Vallensis (foreground left) rests his hand on a small volume which is inscribed GALENVS.

40 Although Adriaen Brouwer was no longer in Amsterdam when Rembrandt arrived, his influence on Rembrandt was undoubtedly great; cf. J. Veth,[494] p. 8 and W. von Bode,[57] p. 50.

The diagonal position of the passively enduring body occurs in post-classical times a.o. in the Vienna Genesis ("Death of Jacob") of about 500 A.D. and, perhaps for the last time before the onset of the actual Middle Ages, in a miniature showing the "Martyrdom of St. Lawrence," a work of the tradition-bound Ottonian *scriptorium* of Fulda, which dates from about 1000 A.D. (MS. Bamberg, Cod. lit. I [A. II, 52] fol. 144 *recto*). For the Renaissance revival of the motif cf., for example, Albrecht Dürer's "Death of the Virgin" (engraving), echoed in Rembrandt's etching of the same theme and first rendered in the 1630's in his drawing "Raising of the Daughter of Jairus," (Pl. VII–9); Jean Fouquet's "Torture of St. Apollonia," at Chantilly; Gerard David (school), "Christ Nailed to the Cross," London, National Gallery; Gerard David, "Flaying of the Unjust Judge" (see Pl. XXII–28 and Chapter XI below); Georg Bartisch, "Medical Demonstration," 1575 (see E. Holländer,[234] fig. 20). The earliest representation of an anatomy in which the corpse appears in a diagonal position goes back to at least the fifteenth century. It is found in a badly damaged illumination (in which only part of the reading surgeon is visible), dating from the beginning of the century. The scene illustrated is that of the *incipit* of the *Anatomy* of Guy de Chauliac, Paris, Bibl. Nat., MS. français 396,[101] fol. 6 *verso*. See Karl Sudhoff,[462] fig. 17 on p. 376 and text p. 377. The first diagonal position of a public anatomy to appear in print seems to be a woodcut by Jost Amman illustrating Paracelsus' *Opus Chyrurgicum*,[368] fig. 2 (Fig. 3). Cf. Robert Herrlinger,[220] fig. 1 on p. 25. For a mythological representation, "Apollo and Marsyas" by Master MF (an engraving of 1535), cf. Holländer,[234] fig. 7. A classical prototype: the "Death of Meleager," Roman sarcophagus (Pl. XIX–25); its echo in the Renaissance: a marble relief attributed to Andrea del Verrocchio, representing the "Death of the Wife of Giovanni Tornabuoni" (Pl. XIX–24).

41 See G. J. Bleeker,[56] *passim*. Professor H. van de Waal, Leiden University, in a lecture entitled "Rembrandt and Chiaroscuro" delivered at Princeton University, October 1952, drew attention to the iconographic function of chiaroscuro in the work of the mature Rembrandt. My attempt at interpreting the effect of the cast shadow on the face of the corpse was greatly stimulated by van de Waal's remarks. For the concept of the shadow of death in mediaeval writing, cf. St. Gregory, *Moralia* as quoted by D.W. Robertson, Jr.,[403] p. 299: "Per umbram mortis oblivio debet intellegi; quia sicut mors interimit vitam, ita oblivio exstinguit memoriam." The most significant night passage in the New Testament, Nicodemus' secret visit to Jesus, receives the following commentary in the *Glossa ordinaria*: "*Nox*. significat litteram legis, vel ignorantiam cordis, vel timorem." In Paul's Epistle to the Romans (xiii, 12) we read: "Let us therefore cast off the works of darkness, and put on the armour of light." These were the words that led to the Conversion of St. Augustine in 386.—For St. Bruno, see ed. Migne, *P.L.*,[321] CLII, col. 879, and Helen Roeder,[405] *s.v.* "Ray of Light." For the vagrant as "Vmbra" see the *Vocabularium rerum*,[497] one of the earliest printed vocabularies (1473/74).—Vondel's poem is quoted in translation after F. Schmidt-Degener,[428] p. 25. These observations occur in Vondel's poem on Philips de Koninck's "Sleeping Venus" [or Danae?]; it was first linked with Rembrandt by Arnold Houbraken,[240] pp. 53ff.; for this complex question cf. also Seymour Slive,[449] pp. 70 (note 3)f., and 184, note 3.

42 The scholar was Professor Petrus Francius, whom Tulp had invited to speak in the auditorium of the Athenaeum in 1672; this led to his professorship two years after; see H. C. Rogge,[406] p. 114 and note 4.

43 *Teutsche Academie*, 1675, II, 3, xxii, p. 327.

44 The following observation is necessarily conjectural: Rembrandt composed his "Anatomy" out of the usual series of sketches done prior to the actual anatomy. In this connection Dr. Philip Cohen of New York has pointed out to me in a letter of October 1957 that the bulging muscles of the dead man are indicative of *rigor mortis*: "Since rigor mortis sets in a few hours after death and lasts only about 24 hours, Rembrandt must have made his portrait [of the dead] between 6–36 hours after the . . . execution." It is almost certain that at this time the corpse had already been transferred to the anatomical theater; that this was so is suggested by the manner in which the cadaver is awkwardly placed (with broken neck and exaggeratedly raised chest) upon the characteristic anatomical

table; it is further suggested by the lighting conditions (which, however, might have been entered at a later point just as well). Again, the assumption that Rembrandt would have attended the anatomy in order to work out the anatomical details shown in his finished painting (i.e. the anatomy of lower arm and hand) is highly improbable. The dissected portion is faulty from an anatomical and also from a proportional and perspective point of view; the right arm, although flush with the torso, barely reaches the loincloth with the fingertips, whereas the dissected left hand reaches beyond it. The strongest argument, however, lies in the fact that no ordinary public Renaissance anatomy would ever start with the hand or, in fact, with anything but the *venter inferior;* cf., for example, Rembrandt's "Anatomy of Dr. Deyman" (Pl. XII–16). I shall resume my discussion of these problems in another context.

45 A "blaecker" = "Lychnuchus pensilis vel pendens. candelabrum laquearibus, aut parietibus affixum" ("a light-source that can be suspended or one that is hung up. A chandelier held by ropes, or attached to the wall"); see *s. h. v.* tomus I of Cornelius Kilianus Dufflaeus'[129] *Etymologicum.*

The earliest anatomical theater erected is the one at Padua (1594), still extant but disused in 1872. (Pl. XVI–20.) It was originally lit by fourteen candles. The theater, unsurpassed in its spatial economy, presents as it were the inside of a wooden funnel which is so narrow that it affords standing room only, except for cadaver and anatomist. It had no windows prior to 1844. Dr. Pieter Paaw was a product of Padua; he fashioned the anatomical theater in Leiden (the second permanent theater being the first in the North) also in its details after the one erected by Hieronymus Fabricius ab Aquapendente, his great teacher. Leiden (founded 1597) shows certain improvements over Padua: e.g. liberal window space, the result of its theater's having been erected in a former chapel. It became the *ur*-pattern of all

subsequent theaters in the Northern countries. Although we have no detailed information on Amsterdam's temporary theater in the time of the Rembrandtian "Anatomy," it is striking that as late as 1732, exactly a hundred years later, Amsterdam used not more than twelve *blakers;* see E. H. M. Thijssen,[468] p. 19, note 1. For a representation of the interior of the second permanent theater see B. W. Th. Nuyens,[343] fig. 15 on p. 34.

I have been unable to establish a *raison d'être* for the solitary candlestick that appears in the open-air anatomy in the frontispiece of Vesalius' *Fabrica.* The Barber-Surgeons Guild of London stipulated in 1555 that the anatomist should be provided with a "waxe candell to loke into the bodye." Anatomies in London at that time were conducted in the forenoon and afternoon; see d'Arcy Power,[382] p. 27. Such solitary candles are found in numerous anatomical representations. (Fig. 11 and Pl. IV-6.)

Whether and to what extent Rembrandt's judicious contemporaries would be able or willing to observe the corpse aesthetically, we cannot tell; the earliest reference to "een . . . schoon lichaam" dates from 1645, when Dr. Tulp dissected, characteristically enough, a young man who, though a criminal, was of good family, Govert van Haerlem by name; see Thijssen,[468] p. 40.

46 See G. Kalff,[266] pp. 16 and 17. We may perhaps conjecture that the stage both imitated and influenced painting; for the role and origin of Gerard van Honthorst's candlelit scenes cf. J. R. Judson,[261] *passim.*

47 The passage in Franciscus Junius' Dutch version[264] (p. 284) reads as follows: "Het heeft oock sijne bysondere welstandigheyd datmen in een ghemeynsaeme sachte aenspraeke sijnen arm maetighlick uytstrecke, mids de schouders een weynigh ontlaetende, ende vinghers van d'uytgestreckte hand bequaemlick uytspreydende."

J. A. Emmens in his recent article "'Ay Rembrant, maal *Cornelis* stem'"[138] (*passim* and esp. figs. 7 and 8) has beautifully shown that the first instance of the use of the extended left hand in the *allocutio* gesture occurs in Rembrandt's *œuvre* in the figure of Dr. Tulp. We could wish for no better evidence of the intentionally rhetorical character of Rembrandt's "Anatomy." Rembrandt selects the same device once more in 1641 for the explicit purpose of displaying his ability to portray the voice of the preacher Anslo, a *tour de force* to which he had been challenged by Vondel in a much-disputed verse.

[48] Frans van Loenen, traditionally reputed to be the only one in the picture not a Guild member, was probably added by the same hand that listed the names; the list is now displayed on what purports to be a single piece of paper in the hand of Hartman Hartmansz. (1639?). Originally this surgeon was holding with his left hand the left-hand pages of an illustrated anatomical atlas of which the recent cleaning has revealed traces. Digits appearing near each individual portrayed correspond to those on the roll call palimpsest. Under favorable lighting conditions the two portraits that I think have been added (No. 7 = Jacob Koolvelt, seated farthest to the left, and No. 8 = Frans van Loenen) appear grayish and flat as against the plastic and animated types of the remaining five attendant surgeon-anatomists. To this evidence it must be added that van Loenen, as Dr. de Vries informs me, originally wore a hat (see Pl. I–1b)—an affront to Dr. Tulp and an additional iconological *testimonium paupertatis*. For van Loenen's disputed Guild membership see Note 1 above, p. 18, and Appendix III A.

[49] See Notes 112 and 153 below.

[50] See E. C. Streeter and C. Singer,[458] *passim*, with five illustrations.

[51] Twenty-three different instruments are displayed on the anatomical table in the *Fabrica*,[490] I, chap. xli, p. 200 (Fig. 6). This *tabula* is reprinted and pirated endlessly and deep into the seventeenth century; it was intended also for animal vivisection, as the rings to fasten securing ropes seem to indicate (Fig. 8). The best historical survey of the development of the anatomical instrumentarium is found in A. Faller's richly illustrated study,[149a] pp. 3–23 and *passim*.

For a survey of the development of anatomical nomenclature before and (in spite of the author's title) after Vesalius, see Johannes Steudel.[457]

[52] For the two *primordia*, the *tabula versatilis* (1545), and the *mensae anatomicae rotis instructae* see M. Roth,[410] note 3 on p. 22. Mobile furniture was, it seems, a novelty to the sixteenth century (1505ff.); see S. Giedion,[182] p. 290. The table at the bottom of the frontispiece of the *Fabrica*,[490] which bears the privilege, is made to resemble an anatomical table. For an example of mobile furniture earlier than instances given by Giedion, see Percy Macquoid and Ralph Edwards,[299] II, p. 290, fig. 1 (1485).

[53] See Note 60 below. The first recorded autopsy that can be dated was one conducted at Bologna by three menials under the supervision of two physicians in the year 1302; see M. Roth,[410] p. 5 and note 4.

[54] The Bolognese surgeon-anatomist-embalmer Petrus de Argellata gives a minute description of the preparatory steps, which, if not through intention certainly *de facto,* amount to a careful autopsy of the Pope; the relevant passages are reprinted by Ernst von Rudloff,[414] pp. 37f. See also Charles Singer,[446] p. 88.

[55] For Erasmus' letter referring to the anatomy of Dean John Colet (d. 1521) see Note 230 below. The reference to Ignatius of Loyola occurs in the last book of Realdo Colombo's *De re anatomica*,[102] p. 266. The fifteenth book seems by its wording to have been originally a letter or a tract (addressed to "Iacobe Bone") which either Colombo himself, or his sons, soon after their father's death (which must have taken place shortly after the consecration of Pope Pius IV, elected 1559, crowned January 6, 1560), decided to append to the work. After an extensive account of *monstra* (as part of Realdo's discussion of "Rare Things that are found in Anatomies") he begins a description of stones

that he has encountered in post-mortems. Whether Ignatius suffered from all the stones listed or only from the last one, located as "in vena portae," remains uncertain. In any event he is the first of the nonmonstrous patients to be listed. He heads a catalogue of various dignitaries of the Church whom Colombo prides himself on having investigated (p. 267) to please the relatives ("in affinium gratiam") on account of the high station of the subject ("ob subjecti dignitatem") or "on account of the rarity of the disease" ("ob morbis raritatem"); to all of which he added that *honoris gratia* he would call attention to the fact that the *excellentissimus* Antonius Musa Brasaulous from Ferrara had attended one of his dissections. We also learn here that the corpse of one Francesco Capella was sent to Realdo from Verona to Rome through the good services of Pope Paul IV and that the addressee of Book XV was present to witness a thorax filled with water and an ulcerated heart with tumors that were hard *praeter naturam,* esp. in the left ventricle. Another of his corpses was that of one of his own "much lamented" students, which "miser iuvenis" lacked, it seems, the pericardium. After the high clergy comes, as Realdo's prize case, that of a hermaphrodite, the account of whose dissection occupies the last page and a half (268f.). The Ignatius passage reads as follows: "Lapides autem innumerabiles pene hisce manibus extraxi inuentos in renibus [kidney] colore vario, in pulmonibus [lung], in iecore [liver], in vena portae [fissure of the liver], vt tuis oculis vidisti Iacobe Bone in venerabili Egnatio Generalis congregationis IESV" (p. 266).

See also Leonardo Olschki,[344] p. 103, note 2, C. Singer and C. Rabin, pp. xxiv and xxixf., and C. Singer,[446] p. 88.

56 For the importance of the contribution of amateurs who were artists to the progress of anatomy as a science see Erwin Panofsky, *The Codex Huygens,*[355] p. 91, and "Artist, Scientist, Genius,"[360] *passim.*

57 See Ralph H. Major.[300]

58 For the academic *disputationes de quolibet,* see Erwin Panofsky,[358] p. 23 and note 8. The *disputationes de quolibet* as a thrilling public ceremony still exist in the Lowlands and especially in the Dutch universities: the doctoral promotions are often attended by a hundred or more curious citizens who breathlessly follow how the "most learned" *opponentes* question thesis and theses ("stellingen") which the "highly esteemed" *promovendus* (on his way to becoming "very learned") must defend against the objections ("bedenkingen") of his faculty, until the "pedel" with his seventeenth-century scepter announces "hora est!" Characteristically enough, at art historical promotions art works under discussion are only orally referred to. The popularity and the importance attached to the *quodlibeta anatomica* is attested by the fact that, with certain modifications, they were being conducted in Italy and in France from the end of the fifteenth century deep into the sixteenth and seventeenth; in the British Isles, as we know, a. o., from Holinshed's *Chronicle* [233] and from Thomas Nashe's *Vnfortunate Traveller,*[336] as well as from comparatively rare representations in art (Pl. XI–14), from the Elizabethan Age onward into the nineteenth century; in Holland (beginning in Amsterdam) from *ca.* 1550 down to the eighteenth century.

There exists at least one representation (miniature in oils on paper) of an English anatomy of the year 1581 (Pl. XI–14). This shows the President of the Guild of Chirurgs acting as chairman while John Banister, Master Surgeon, attended by stewards, is in charge of the anatomy proper. The chirurgs, except for the president, wear white sleeve guards. Banister and the President are distinguished by wearing hats (cf. *doctores* Tulp, van der Meer, Fonteyn, and others). (Pls. I-1, IV-6, VIII-11, Fig. 19.) Dr. Pieter Paaw, in Buytewech's drawing of an anatomy at Leiden, is the only one not to wear a hat—in itself a distinction and, like many distinctions, possibly a hardship on account of the chill. The tome carefully depicted in the John Banister "Anatomy" (cf. the folio(s) in Rembrandt's painting, which will be discussed further below) opens at the chapter beginning: "Intestine [igitur] a ventriculo exoriuntur"; it is Colombo's *De re anatomica (ed. princeps)* mentioned in Note 55. See also d'Arcy Power,[382] *passim,* and Eugen Holländer,[234] fig. 52 and pp. 78 ff. The first public anatomy of a person not a criminal occurred at Amsterdam February 19, 1684 when Frederick Ruysch dissected a female of Italian origin. According to manuscript Amsterdam [305a] *(sub hoc dato)* : "... is door de E[dele] heer professor Anatomiae fredericus Ruijsch begonnen te ontleden een vroue persoon, gebooren in italie." On November 2 of the same year Dr. Ruysch dissected a female who had been received from the hospital: "Anathomie gedaan door de E. Heer Professor & prelector fredericus ruijsch over een vrouwe persoon uijt gast huijs: daar van ontfangen." It is perhaps significant that Ruysch (1666–1731), the successor of Dr. Deyman, was the first anatomist of Amsterdam who was at the same time professor at the university.

⁵⁹ See M. Roth,[410] note 2, p. 18, and note 4, p. 17.

When the new anatomical theater was put up in Amsterdam in 1691, the three inner rings were reserved for magistrates, *inspectores collegii medici,* and physicians over fifty years of age; the next ring (standing room only) served for ordinary surgeons, and numbers seven and eight for the theater attendants and for the paying audience; for further details of arrangement and subtleties of precedence, see E. H. M. Thijssen,[468] p. 17. This new theater was still fashioned "na de wijze eener Roomsche schouwburg" ("in the manner of a Roman theater") *(ibidem)*. The earliest ideal plan of an anatomical theater (seating five hundred!) dates from 1493; it is here, as far as is known, that the word *theatrum* is first used in connection with a specific, though temporary, structure for formal anatomical demonstrations; it is here also that the Roman circuses, the amphitheaters of Rome and Verona, are first suggested as a fitting prototype; see Alexander Benedictus,[44] cited *in ex-*

tenso in Appendix II. The crucial words are: "... loco praeterea amplo perflatili, temporarium theatrum constituendum est circumcauatis sedilibus, quale Romae ac Veronae cernitur ..." The first nonanatomical theater, a wooden amphitheater of short duration, was built at immense papal expense on the Capitol in the year 1513. Cf. W.S. Heckscher,[210] note 88. According to George Kernodle,[268] p. 76, the first amphitheater backdrop used on a Renaissance stage dates from 1533. Another, purely ideal *theatrum anatomicum,* that of Carolus Stephanus [456] (III, chap. xl, Paris, 1545; see Appendix II), was semicircular in ground plan, covered with a tarpaulin, and designed in such a way that it afforded a beautiful vista into the surrounding countryside—an impressive and, quite possibly, intended synopsis of macrocosm and microcosm. Vesalius may well have had this idea in mind when he inspired van Calcar to design a continuous landscape for the figures—skeletons and musclemen alike—of his *Fabrica.* See Note 191 below. For the first permanent theater at Padua, erected by the teacher of *doctores* Paaw and Egbertsz., the anatomist Hieronymus Fabricius ab Aquapendente (*ca.* 1533–1619), cf. Richter,[396] pp. 37ff., and figs. 5 and 6 (our Pl. XVI-20), and K. J. Franklin,[149] ed. of H.F. ab A.'s *De venarum ostiolis,* figs. 4 and 5 and p. 28. Also see Notes 33 and 45 above. In essence, it seems that the Paduan theater was little more than the wooden skeleton that the anatomical professors set up in the open throughout the sixteenth century, which was here turned into a permanent indoor structure.

For the ambivalence of the various terms denoting scientific theaters see Note 191 below.

⁶⁰ Karl Sudhoff published two important representations of post-mortems dating from the thirteenth and fourteenth centuries respectively: (i) the *chirurgus,* following the physician's instructions, has removed the liver of a female corpse; the picture, in spite of its epic character, is entirely lacking in suggestion of an actual event in a credible setting. It is part of the series

mentioned in the text to Note 22 above. Late thirteenth-century MS. Oxford, Ashmole 399, fol. 34 *recto*; cf. *Archiv*,[462] VII, 6, fig. 15 (2) (Pl. X-13a); (ii) in the *World Chronicle* of Rudolf von Ems (*ca.* 1400) an illumination shows how Nero has his mother cut open in order to see "where he had lain"; the admittedly fictitious account (most likely a mediaeval contamination with reports of the evil deeds of Maximianus Herculius, who, for purposes of divination, cut open pregnant women), however, leads to a realistic and rather credible representation of an early fifteenth-century autopsy; Sudhoff,[462] fig. 16.

The results of fictitious post-mortems in the Middle Ages (which, far from being intended as hoaxes, must have been accepted by contemporaries as wholly within the realm of credibility) were at times very gratifying. The *Tabula exemplorum* of *ca.* 1277[465] tells of a certain knight who, out of love for the Lord, visited the holy sites so that he might weep copiously there. At the Mount of Olives his prayer ("that he might join the Lord") was granted: his soul escaped from his body. His distraught friends and servants turned to a *medicus* for information about the cause of his unexpected death. The physician inquired of what complexion the deceased had been, and when he learned that he had been serene in the love of the Lord he pronounced as the cause of death that his heart had burst from overabundance of joy. "And when they [sic] opened his side, they found indeed that his heart had burst and that it bore the inscription AMOR MEVS IHESVS" (ed. J. Th. Welter,[465] § 311, p. 84).

[61] Ed. and tr. Charles Singer, *s.t. The Fasciculo*.[270] A useful summary of the formal anatomies of the fifteenth century is offered by J. Playfair McMurrich,[297] pp. 18 and 20. All such accounts ultimately derive from Vesalius' Preface to the *Fabrica*,[151] for which see Note 86 below. For the Ketham authorship see some observations by Otto Kurz,[279] pp. 138ff. For the tenacity of representations of the formal *cathedra* anatomies see the woodcut in Berenga-

rio da Carpi's *Isagogae*,[51] Venice, 1535 (Fig. 5), which is reproduced by C. Singer and C. Rabin,[447] Plate II, fig. 2 (where it is conveniently placed opposite the Ketham woodcut).

[62] The origin is undoubtedly classical and scientific (geometry, astronomy); cf. Friedrich Marx.[310] For the later tradition see O. Chomentovskaja.[96]

[63] For the use of the *radius* (pointer) in classical science and for its representation in art and literature, cf. Otto Brendel,[66] on pp. 11ff. and esp. note 1 on p. 13. I owe my knowledge of this article to my colleague J. H. Jongkees.

[64] I am most grateful to Professor Enrico Josi, Ispettore dei Musei Lateranensi, who has most generously allowed me to make use of his intimate knowledge of the new catacomb. For the classical type of physician-philosopher, cf. manuscript Vatican,[305n] Med. graec. I (Dioscurides), fol. 4 *verso*, ed.,[273] Plate 65, fig. 77. For the very common type of "Apostle Collegium," cf. J. N. Bakhuizen van den Brink,[21a] fig. 63.

[65] For Mundinus as a sixteenth-century guide in the conduct of anatomies see M. Roth,[410] pp. 23f. See also Note 156 below.

[66] In the great late mediaeval history of medicine composed by Guy de Chauliac, Galen represents the apex of all classical medicine; see Edith Heischkel,[213] pp. 30ff. From Carolingian times onward Galen and Hippocrates were named next to Cosmas and Damian as "clari magistri quos medicina celebrat." Galen's works had begun to appear in print in Latin translations made from the Greek original from ed. Venice, 1490 on. The next important landmark was the edition of 1525, in which Galen's two bibliographies of his own writings (*s.tt.* "De libris propriis liber" and "De ordine librorum suorum liber") appeared in print for the first time; see Theodore Besterman,[52] pp. 3 and 59.

[67] *De anatomicis administrationibus*,[163b] III, chap. v, ed. Galeni . . ., *Omnia quae extant*, I, Basel, 1562, p. 153:

Has itaque uniuersas uenas, quas in hominibus ante concisionem conspicis, in simia dissecta uideris. Quare penitiores etiam particulas haec animantia, perinde ut homines, obtinere constat. Quod cum ita sit, consuluerim prius te in simia ipsa subinde exercitari, ut si humani corporis consecandi quandoque copiam nactus fueris, prompte singulas partes detegas: quod non uulgaris opere est, neque quisquam in ipsa parum exercitatus repente potest assequi. Etenim medicorum in anatomis exercitatissimi, qui multa diligentia corporis particulas inspexerint, in multis errorem commisisse uidentur. Quamobrem nihil, qui corpus hostis germani in bello mortui, quod aduersus Marcum Antonium gerebatur, incidebant, amplius praeter uiscerum situm addiscere potuerunt. At qui in alijs animantibus, & potissimum in simia prius se exercuerit, promptissime singulas, quae inciduntur, partes detegit: & procliuius est uiro laboris cupido prae exercitatioque in anatomis, antea conspecta quaedam, in humano cadauere subito condiscere, quot alteri non exercitato manifesta multo ocio ad amussim inuenire.

You shall therefore see the entire system of veins which you behold in humans before cutting them in the monkey when he is dissected. For this reason it is a fact that this creature has inner veins (organs) just as human beings do. Since this is so, concern yourself above all with the monkey himself, next let yourself be trained so that if at some time you may have an opportunity of dissecting a human body, you may open it for the sake of single parts. Normally there is no opportunity for this, nor can anyone who is only moderately versed understand this quickly. And even those among the physicians who are the most experienced in anatomy, who with great diligence have inspected the particulars of the body, have, so it appears, committed errors in many ways. For this reason, those who cut into the body of the enemy, a German who died in the war that was waged against Mark Antony, could learn nothing beyond the situs of the viscera. . . . [Whereupon he continues to advocate the study of apes and describes the hazards of chance dissections of men killed in the *venationes* of the arena, of highwaymen found lying unburied in deserted spots, or of children exposed to die: Qui uero pueros expositos complures incidunt, persuasum habent corpora hominum simiarumque persimili structura constare.]

Now see also C. Singer's tr.,[163a] pp. 76f. Galen may have dissected the human body after all; cf. p. 358 of H.W. Janson's study;[253] we are here, of course, concerned only with Vesalius' views and not with their degree of historical verisimilitude. In Vesalius' well-tempered estimate "Galen himself dissected never a human body lately dead"—"nobis modo ex renata dissectionis arte, diligentique Galeni librorum praelectione, & in plerisque locis eorundem non poenitenda restitutione constet, nunquam ipsum, nuper mortuum corpus humanum resecuisse," *Fabrica,*[490] fol. a 4 *recto*; tr. Benjamin Farrington,[151] p. 1362. In III, chap. viii, p. 470, Vesalius[490] (discussing an instance of Galen's erroneous description of veins) is more outspoken when he states:

Quas quum simijs conuenire uidit, quam illarum corpus humano simile sit, longa oratione inducere conatus est, nullam, nisi ante dissectionem omnibus obuiam, sibi perspectum habens differentiam; quum interim tam uarias & innumeras hactenus in ossibus, musculis, & uenis quoque proposuerim, mihique inde non uulgariter persuadeam, humanum corpus nunquam a Galeno fuisse aggressum.

Galen did, however, inspect the bones of mummies, "licet ipsi arida, ac ueluti ad ossium inspectionem parata hominum cadauera occurrerint," *loc. cit.*

[68] The Laocoön group had come to light at a time when anatomical and proportion studies had reached a considerable height; in those years Leonardo did the bulk of his anatomical work together with Marc Antonio della Torre, who died in 1512. See Margarete Bieber, *Laocoon,*[54] pp. 1f., note 2, and, for a painstaking investigation of the exact place of discovery, C. C. van Essen,[143] *passim.* For Antonio Benivieni[48] see Arturo Castiglione,[90] p. 370. I have lost my excerpts of an out-of-the-way article that deals with the first papal brief authorizing archaeological excavations in 1506, near S. Nicola in Carcere.

Schopenhauer has discussed the "appearance of classical remains at the right psychological moment" as follows:

> Hierauf nun [referring to his discussion of the noncausality in events, which yet may assume the power of necessity] beruht das zufällige Zusammentreffen aller Bedingungen einer in höherem Sinne nothwendigen Begebenheit; das Geschehn Dessen, was das Schicksal gewollt hat. [N.b. The following is a note in Schopenhauer's *Handexemplar.*] Hierauf z.B. beruht es dass, als in Folge der Völkerwanderung die Fluth der Barbarei sich über Europa ergoss, alsbald die schönsten Meisterwerke Griechischer Skulptur, der Laokoon, der Vatikanische Apoll u.a.m. wie durch theatralische Versenkung verschwanden, indem sie ihren Weg hinabfanden in den Schooss der Erde, um nunmehr daselbst, unversehrt ein Jahrtausend hindurch, auf eine mildere, edlere, die Künste verstehende und schätzende Zeit zu harren, beim endlichen Eintritt dieser aber, gegen Ende des 15. Jahrhunderts unter Papst Julius II., wieder hervorzutreten ans Licht, als die wohlerhaltenen Muster der Kunst und des wahren Typus der menschlichen Gestalt. [*Transcendente Spekulation über die anscheinende Absichtlichkeit im Schicksale des Einzelnen,* ed. Paul Deussen,[429] p. 241.]

[69] See H.W. Janson,[253] *Titian's Laocoon Caricature and the Vesalian-Galenist Controversy,* Appendix, pp. 355–68 and Plate LVI.

[70] For an English rendering of a long poem that Melanchthon inscribed on the two blank pages preceding the titlepage of the *Fabrica* in his possession (copy in the Armed Forces Medical Library, Cleveland, Ohio) see Harvey W. Cushing,[115] pp. 80f. For a facsimile of the original, cf. Elmer Belt, *Philipp Melanchthon's Observations,*[314] with a tr. by Dorothy M. Schullian,[433] p. 440. I am greatly indebted to Kate T. Steinitz of the Elmer Belt Library of Vinciana, to Dr. Schullian, and to Miss Estelle Brodman, the latter two of the Armed Forces Medical Library, for making these data available to me.

[71] Vasari, in spite of a slight error of fact in his statement, must have seen and read the *Fabrica* with van Calcar's illustrations, "which," in his words, "the most admirable Andrea Vesalius caused to be engraved on copper [sic] and published in his works." Speaking of the *fiamminghi,* whom he praises as careful observers of the Italian manner, Vasari writes as follows: "Conobbi ancora in Napoli, e fu mio amicissimo, l'anno 1545, Giovanni di Calker, pittore fiammingo molto raro, e tanto pratico nella maniera d'Italia, che le sue opere non erano conosciute per mano di fiammingo; ma costui morì giovane in Napoli, mentre si sperava gran cose di lui: il quale disegnò la sua notomia al Vessalio"; ed. VII,[487] p. 582.

[72] All the bibliographical data will be found in Harvey W. Cushing,[115] pp. 73ff., 109ff., 114f. But see also F. M. G. de Feyfer's extensive article[154] and especially the folding table (preceding p. 17), which gives an excellent idea of the immense spread of the Vesalian illustrations. A thorough exposé of the seven months that Vesalius spent in Basel supervising the printing of the *Fabrica* and of the translation into German will be found in Henry E. Sigerist's[442] article.

The three works published in 1543 are so closely interrelated that they may be regarded as an organic unit. How closely their unity was felt at the time becomes clear from a copy in the possession of Mr. Philip Hofer in the Harvard College Library, whose sixteenth-century owner had *Epitome* and German translation bound together. Mr. Hofer generously placed his copy of the Basel ed. of the *Fabrica*[490] (1555) at my disposal, and it is from this that I have taken the Latin quotations.

In choosing the term "fabrica" for his atlas of anatomy Vesalius had, in all likelihood, no actual precedent. For one exception see Notes 85 (and text) and 97 below. *Anatomia* and, where the manual aspects were stressed, *Chirurgia* were the terms commonly in vogue. "Fabrica" became fashionable after 1543; how fashionable is shown in the posthumous edition of Battista Gelli's *La Circe* which in 1596 appeared in Vienna *s. t. De naturae humanae fabrica dialogi decem* . . .

73 For the Council of Trent see Note 206 below. For Copernicus see Edward E. Lowinsky's paper on "The Concept of Physical and Musical Space in the Renaissance,"[291] pp. 57ff. For the links between Vesalius and Ignatius of Loyola see M. Roth,[410] pp. 77f.

Of the *ca.* forty-two books published in Basel in 1543 I have mentioned the important *editiones principes*. For the *editio princeps* of the *Koran* in Latin[275] see also Harvey W. Cushing,[115] pp. 154f.

Several events of 1543 might be mentioned here *curiositatis causa*: (i) At approximately this time Giovanni Battista da Monte (*ca.* 1489–1551), Vesalius' friend and colleague at Padua, introduced for the first time the clinical method didactically; see Charles Donald O'Malley and J. B. de C. M. Saunders,[346] p. 595. (ii) The first botanical garden is said to have been established at Padua (in about 1543); see Charles Pickering,[378] *sub hoc anno.* (iii) In 1542 (reissue: 1543) appeared Leonhard Fuchs'[160] important work on herbs, *s. t. De historia stirpium;* see Harvey W. Cushing, "Vesaliana," No. 149. (iv) The program of the Academia della Virtù was formulated, the objective being to assure a pure

text of Vitruvius; its promotion in a letter by Claudio Tolomei dated November 14, 1542. (v) In this year Ralph Hogge of Buxted and Peter Baude, his French assistant, succeeded in casting a cannon of iron in one piece (which they bored afterwards); see L. F. Salzman,[416] p. 165. (vi) At approximately this time the Dutchman Philippus Gallaeus composed his *Imagines,* in which he celebrates, among other novelties (such as the discovery of America, the advent of syphilis, the invention of stirrups), the nautical compass, the art of printing, distilling, silk manufacture, clockmaking, gunpowder; see Edgar Zilsel,[529] p. 133 and note. (vii) Cardano published Vesalius' horoscope[85] about 1543; see Note 82 below.

74 *Fabrica*[490] V, chap. xv, pp. 664ff., *s. t.* "Galenum muliebrem uterum neque dissecuisse, neque descripsisse . . ."; also II, chap. xxxiii, p. 341: "[Galenus] uteri descriptione eleganter delusus, qui non muliebrem, sed uaccinum carpinumue describit uterum . . ."

For an interesting attempt to explain the symbolical Who's Who in Vesalius' frontispiece I refer the reader to M. H. Spielmann's discussion,[453] pp. 132–35.

75 C. Singer and C. Rabin give a brilliant account of the sixteenth-century anatomist's persistent inability not to see something whose existence their authorities had postulated on philosophical and theological grounds; see Bibliogr.,[447] pp. xliii–xlv.

In his Preface to the *Fabrica* Vesalius acts in keeping with the best scholarly tradition. On historical grounds he sings the praise of Galen ("the author of all good things" is one of many like expressions throughout the book). At the same time he refuses to bow to Galen's authority where he finds clear evidence that Galen erred—by his own estimate in more than two hundred instances, "multo saepius quam ducentiis." It is, as Vesalius makes plain, "the sectaries of Galen" whom he wishes to censure, not Galen himself; see Preface, tr. Benjamin Farrington,[151] p. 1364.

It is perhaps no exaggeration to suggest that Vesalius wrote his *Fabrica* as a running commentary on Galen's anatomical writings. The entry "Galenus" occurs, in the most admirable *Index* of the edition of 1555,[490] 330 times; in the vast majority Galen is being contradicted, corrected, or modified.

That at least some of Vesalius' most highly qualified contemporaries felt his case to be a just one becomes clear when we turn, for example, to the frequent references to "Vessalius" in Realdo Colombo's *De re anatomica* (1559)[102]—Colombo, by no means uncritical in details, beginning with his address to the candid reader, bestows ample praise on his master (who survived him by about four years) —or when we read Conrad Gesner's remarks in the entry "ANDREAS Vesalius Bruxellensis" of his superb Galen bibliography:

> In his autem suis doctissimis & accura-tissimis libris, innumera Galeni loca expli-cat, illustrat, emendat: et multa eius errata arguit, plurima a se primum inuenta pro-dit, uir propter summam in re anatomica peritiam diligentiamque incomparabilis nec unquam satis laudatus.

This is found in the 1562 ed. of Galen's *Omnia, quae extant,*[163b] fol. B 3 *recto*. It is prob-ably not saying too much if we point to this entry, its form and character, as the true proving ground of "critical bibliography" based on "systematic bibliography." Methodologically this seems to be the birthplace of modern philo-logy as a discipline. The fact, mentioned in Note 66 above, that it was Galen himself, above all other classical authorities, who had shown the path with the two bibliographies of his own works, may well be regarded as the prime incentive. For Conrad Gesner's role as the first "universal bibliographer" of the Renaissance see Theodore Besterman,[52] chap. v. For the true anti-Galenists of the sixteenth and follow-ing centuries see Note 101 below.

76 A survey is found in C. Singer and C. Ra-bin,[447] p. xiv. Vesalius' studies as a child, in his most impressible years of education, had been scholastic. Next, when he was seventeen, he entered upon the "Erasmian" course of study at Jerome de Busleyden's *Collegium trilingue* (a school that I think has never been surpassed), where Juan Luis Vives had been a student under Erasmus. It has been shown that later on Vesa-lius entered upon a third course, disdained by the Erasmians (the disdain was mutual), by becoming a fervent Ciceronian (cf. Note 78). Obviously much of the two earlier stages re-mained with him as indelible *Wissensgut*. As ob-viously Vesalius, conscious of his radically novel contribution to science, would show little rev-erence for the scholastic authorities, especially where they spoke as anatomical authorities. In this sense we must appreciate his reference to "Alberti illius magni indictissimo *de Virorum mulierumque secretis libro*" and his reference to Scotus as "ineptissimus quidam Michael Sco-tus"; *Fabrica,*[490] V, chap. xv, p. 667. For a pos-sible indebtedness of Vesalius to St. Augustine cf. Note 202 below. New light on Vesalius may be expected from C. D. O'Malley's forthcoming biography. For some preliminary observation see this author in *Isis,*[345] *passim*. For the *Colle-gium trilingue,* cf. Henry de Vocht's monumental study,[497a] and for Vesalius' part in its curricu-lum, II, esp. pp. 324f.

77 For the documents of this case cf. George Sarton's beautiful account, 1954,[419] esp. pp. 132f.

78 Cf. the most important study, *Andreas Vesalius, The Humanist,* by L. Edelstein.[132] The two anatomists who, as teachers, in-fluenced Vesalius the most strongly, Guenther and Sylvius, had both been classical scholars before turning to medicine; see Harvey W. Cushing,[115] pp. xxivf.

79 Vesalius, in pleading for recognition of the role of the hand in the art of healing (= *cheirour-gia*), speaks of it as "primarium [medici, *scil.*] instrumentum"; he complained that medicine had neglected its primary instrument "ut ad plebeios, ac disciplinis medicae arti subseruien-tibus neutiquam instructos, id quasi uideatur

esse demandatum"; *Fabrica,*[490] Preface, fol. a 2. Shrewdly, yet with perfect honesty, Vesalius counters any possible suspicion of his speaking as a mere mechanic by pointing out that it was the decadent Romans who allowed their slaves to do what among Greeks had been the prerogative of the physician: "Galen frequently impresses upon us his joy in manual dexterity," "Galenus . . . crebro inculcat, quantum manus artificio oblectatus sit," *loc. cit.*

Vesalius was by no means the first theorist who had turned practical. As early as 1269 Pierre de Maricourt (Peregrinus)[370] postulated that the scientist must at the same time be "industriosus in opere manuum"; see Edgar Zilsel,[531] p. 30. This notion was definitely at home in the second half of the thirteenth century: "Master-masons, with a rod and gloves in their hands, say to others 'cut it for me this way,' and labor not themselves, yet take higher pay; that is what many modern prelates will do"; from a Sermon of 1260, quoted by G. G. Coulton,[108] pp. 173f. Also see V. Mortet and P. Deschamps,[326] p. 290, and G. P. in *Romania* (XVIII, 1889, p. 288), as cited by E. Panofsky, *Gothic Architecture,*[358] note 9. As always, exceptions existed also to the rule of strict division between theory and practice; Zilsel observed, quite rightly, that alchemy was a case in point, inasmuch as it was a discipline that for obvious reasons made it obligatory for the adept to do his own weighing, measuring, heating, pouring, and testing; Bibliogr.,[531] p. 26. There were, however, other fields too, perhaps less spectacular, e. g. mechanics, that by their very nature demanded a combination of "Theory and Practice Useful in the Craft of Ingenious Contrivances"; for al-Jazari's treatise *sub hoc titulo* cf. Kurt Weitzmann,[510] p. 249.

80 See Harvey W. Cushing,[115] pp. 44f., where the earlier literature is listed. Johannes Guenther recalled, after Vesalius' death, an instance in which under his own chairmanship Vesalius "did work for me"; see Singer and Rabin,[447] p. xxi, last note. Through Vesalius himself we know of two possible anatomies at the time when he was a student under Guenther in Paris; see Note 121 below.

81 One of Vesalius' functional skeletons survives fairly intact; he dissected at Basel a criminal executed May 1543 and left his skeleton —"artificiose a se paratum, artis & industriae suae specimen"—to the University; cf. G. Wolf-Heidegger,[520] *passim* and illus. p. 211.

82 Cardanus based his horoscope, as he admits readily, on personal knowledge of the life and circumstances of his friend and colleague Vesalius as much as on the constellation of the stars; for tr. and facsimile of the horoscope, cf. Harvey W. Cushing,[115] p. xxxviii and fig. 5. Appropriately, the horoscope appeared in its *editio princeps* in the year 1543 *s.t.* "De Geniturae LXVII. insignes casibus & fortuna,"[85] fol. 178 *recto*. Vesalius was in good company, for Cardanus cast Christ's horoscope also—the first, I believe, since Cecco d'Ascoli's (1257–1327) fateful attempt, to do so with relative impunity.

83 See C. Singer and C. Rabin,[447] p. xxi.

84 Characteristically, Vesalius claimed the ability to recognize bones blindfolded; see C. Singer and C. Rabin, [447] p. xxi.

85 MS. Oxford, Bodleian Library, Douce 45 (21619),[305k] fol. 52–63. Lactantius' treatise was often copied in the late Middle Ages and is found in anatomical writings at that time. Such excerpts from patristic authorities were still being compiled in the seventeenth century; cf., for example, "Sententiae ex S. S. Patrum scriptis collectae, et humani corporis partibus aptatae," MS. Oxford, Corpus Christi College, CXXXII (III),[305l] fol. 63 *verso*–69 *verso*.

86 See M. Roth,[410] p. 25, note 1. I shall cite part of Vesalius' passage on *quodlibeta* in the tr. of Benjamin Farrington,[151] p. 1361, followed by the original Latin,[490] found on fol. a 3:

This deplorable dismemberment of the art of healing has introduced into our schools the detestable procedure now in vogue, that one man should carry out the dissection of the human body and another give the description of the parts. These latter are perched aloft in a pulpit like jackdaws, and with a notable air of disdain they drone out information about facts they have never approached at first hand, but which they merely commit to memory from the books of others, or of which they have descriptions before their eyes; the former (viz. the menials) are so ignorant of languages that they are unable to explain their dissections to the onlookers and botch what ought to be exhibited in accordance with the instruction of the physician, who never applies his hand to the dissection, and contemptuously "steers the ship out of the sailor's handbook," as the saying goes. . . .

Ad haec, quum uniuersa administratio tonsoribus committebatur, non solum uera uiscerum cognitio medicis perijt, uerum etiam dissecandi industria prorsus intercidit: eo quod scilicet hi resectionem non aggrederentur: illi uero, quibus manus artificium delegebatur, indoctiores essent, quam ut dissectionis professorum scripta intelligerent: tantum abest, ut difficillimam artem, manu ipsis traditam, id hominum genus nobis asseruaret, utque haec deploranda curatiuae partis dispersio, detestabilem ritum in Gymnasijs non inueheret, quo alij humani corporis sectionem administrare, alij partium historiam enarrare consueuerunt. His quidem graculorum modo, quae nunquam aggressi sunt, sed tantum ex aliorum libris memoriae commendant, discriptaue ob oculos ponunt, alte in cathedra egregio fastu occinentibus: illis autem adeo linguarum imperitis, ut dissecta spectatoribus explicare nequeant, atque ex physici praescripto ostendenda lacerent, qui manu sectioni nunquam adhibita, tantum ex commentario nautam non sine supercilio agit. Atque ut sic omnia perperam docentur, ac ridiculis quaestionibus dies aliquot abeunt: ita quoque spectatoribus in illo tumultu pauciora propo-

nuntur, quam lanius [the butcher] in macello medicum docere posset.

See also J. Playfair McMurrich,[297] p. 20.

87 Frequently reproduced; e.g., C. Singer and C. Rabin,[447] fig. 8. The text was revised by Vesalius in the reissue of the giant ed. of Galen's *opera omnia*;[166] see Harvey W. Cushing,[115] pp. 66ff. The book was, however, superseded in August 1536 by Guenther's handy compendium for students of medicine, *s. t. Institvtionvm Anatomicarvm secundum Galeni sententiam ad candidatos medicinae libri quatuor . . .*, Basel,[200] which appeared in an ed. revised by Vesalius, Venice, 1538;[201] cf. Cushing,[115] pp. 47f. See now the ed. and tr. by Charles Singer.[163a] The Wellcome Historical Medical Library in London has a copy of Galen[163] with Vesalius' ownership entry.

88 In the eyes of Vesalius it must have seemed belated, for he scorned those Parisian anatomists, and he criticized them (i) for neglecting to combine with the study of the viscera that of the blood vessels and (ii) for concerning themselves exclusively or principally with the viscera, to the neglect of all other observation; see for this criticism Preface to the *Fabrica*,[490] fol. a 3ff. At the same time it would be conceivable that the woodcut might reflect young Vesalius' beginning influence; see C. Singer and C. Rabin,[447] p. xxi, and the Introduction to C. Singer's ed. and tr. of Galen's work,[163a] *passim*.

89 In general, see E. Panofsky,[360] *passim*. The art historian needs no reference to two surveys of the special problem of the relationship of the *artes*, both *liberales* and *mechanicae*, to the fine arts: (i) Julius von Schlosser,[424] pp. 46ff., and (ii) Rudolf Wittkower,[518] *passim*.

For the inevitable dilemma resulting from the social change, I can do no better than quote E. Panofsky's observations on Dürer's marital problems: "Agnes Frey thought that the man she had married was a painter in the late mediaeval sense, an honest craftsman who produced pictures as a tailor made coats and suits; but to her misfortune her husband discovered that art was both a divine gift and an intellectual achievement requiring humanistic learning, a knowledge of mathematics and the general attainments of a 'liberal culture.'" *Albrecht Dürer,*[356] I, p. 7.

90 See A. L. Gabriel,[162] p. 39.

91 For a beautiful discussion of Frau Sorge and of Goethe's classical sources (esp. Hyginus Hispalensis), see Konrad Burdach,[76] pp. 1–60, esp. 37ff. The modern world, in which psychoanalysis can claim "die Not des Lebens" as the spring of all mental development is far removed from this kind of reasoning; see Ernest Jones,[259] p. 438.

92 Varro (116–27 B.C.), in his *Disciplinarum libri,*[486] enumerates the nine liberal arts, which, besides architecture (No. 9), include medicine (as No. 8). Isidore of Seville, though for reasons of symmetry he feels obliged to banish *medicinae ars* from the canon of the seven liberal arts, stresses that the *medicus* is very much in need of each single one of them; see Bibliogr.,[241] IV, xiii. To Petrarch, however, the *medicus* is a *mercennarius et infamis artifex* who ranks, in relation to the *artes,* with the peasant; see his *Invectiva,*[374] esp. pp. 25ff. and 31f. As late as 1614 Francis Bacon could speak of people "so lowe" as "Barbers-surgeons and Butchers, and such base mechanicall persons," Bibliogr.,[20] p. 6. In a Dutch medical comedy of 1686 we hear that physicians must be counted among the trades: "De Doctors worden maer bij Ambachts-luij gereekend"; cf. J.B.F. van Gils,[184] p. 55.

93 In illustrating I Corinthians vii:20 Joost van den Vondel tells the story of the cobbler in picture and in verse; see his *Den gulden winckel,* LXXIII (1613);[499] also Note 94.

94 For the tenacity of this prejudice see Note 92 above, Edgar Zilsel,[530] pp. 23ff., and Note 147 below.

95 For a discussion of the thirteenth-century antecedents see Note 79 above.

96 See Edgar Zilsel's classic, "The Origins of William Gilbert's Scientific Method,"[531] p. 26 and *passim.*

97 To illustrate the astonishing specialization of the crafts and trades in the sixteenth century I have drawn up a list of some of the professions with bearing on both anatomy (and medicine) and the fine arts, leaving unchanged the terms current at the time:

I. Medical Trades
  1. *balnearii* (bath attendants; bleeders)
  2. *chirurgi* (incisores, prosectores, stewards) (these are the barber-surgeons of the anatomies)
  3. *edentarii* (exodontists)
  4. *lanarii* (butchers; cf. Leonardo's experiments with pigs to observe the heartbeat, *Quaderni d'Anatomia,*[284] Windsor Castle, I, p. 171; see also Note 86 above)
  5. *tonsores* (the barbers proper; this is Vesalius' term for the menials of the anatomies; see Note 86 above).

II. Artistic* and Related Trades
  1. *acupictores* (embroiderers)
  2. *adumbratores* (draftsmen)
  3. *arcularii* (cabinetmakers)
  4. *aricularii* (needlemakers)
  5. *aurifabres* (goldsmiths)
  6. *balistarii* (crossbowmakers)
  7. *bombardii* (gunsmiths)
  8. *caelatores gemmarum* (intaglio workers)
  9. *calcarii* (spurmakers)
  10. *campanularii* (tinkle bell makers; German: Schellenmacher)
  11. *carpentarii* (wheelwrights)
  12. *circinarii* (compass makers)
  13. *clauicularii* (nailmakers)
  14. *confectores horologij* (watchmakers)
  15. *conflatores orichalcei* (workers in brass)
  16. *conspicillarii* (spectacle makers)
  17. *digitaliarii* (thimble makers)
  18. *fabres* (smiths)
  19. *falcarii* (scythemakers)
  20. *illuminatores imaginum* (book illuminators; German: Brieffmaler)

21. *laminarii* (those who beat armor plates)
22. *lapicidiae* (stone masons)
23. *laterarii* (brickmakers)
24. *loricarii* (chainmail makers)
25. **pictores* (panel painters)
26. **sculptores* (woodblock cutters; German: Formschneider)
27. *siguli* (potters)
28. **statuarii* (sculptors)
29. *tornarii* (makers of spindles, etc.)
30. **vitripictores* (stained-glass window painters)

The list represents a selection from one of the most useful compendia of estates, crafts, and trades, by Hartmann Schopperus, entitled *ΠΑΝΟΠΛΙΑ,*[430] 1568. Two gifted Dutchmen, Jan and Kaspar Luiken, transformed the book into an emblem book, *s. t. Het Menselyk Bedryf*[294] (1694); followed by several re-issues, a.o. Amsterdam, 1725, 1730; Leiden, 1888; see Mario Praz,[384] II, 1947, p. 100, and John B. Knipping and P. J. Meertens,[272a] pp. 119f., according to whom the book (illustr. and text) is by the father, Jan, alone. The illustrations are close to those of Jost Amman, although brought up to date. The Printing Press represents God, who impresses a soul upon the paper, the frail Potter's ware represents the perishable part of Man's existence, etc. It is obviously impossible always to draw clear lines of demarcation between the various crafts. Schopperus' catalogue begins with Pope and Clergy, followed by Emperor and Princes, and it closes with Musicians, Jews, Beggars, Fools, and the Militia. Within these rather arbitrary groups the crafts and trades proper, a total of eighty-eight, are listed without any apparent order. In its relative disorganization we may compare this wealth, which amounts to all but complete recall, to the Paris "Anatomy" in illustration of Galen. (Fig. 9.) The individual entries themselves are systematic: each craft or trade is headed by its Latin and German name or names, followed by Amman's capable and descriptive woodcut, under which there appears a laudatory poem in Latin. The type of estate

book is not new; its emphasis on *Stände* is revolutionary.

The typical attitude of the fifteenth century toward the pre-established place of the members of the various estates ("Beggar Servingman Artisan," etc. ranging to "King Emperor Pope"), their relative position in regard to the divinity, is well illustrated, e. g., by Mantegna's "Tarocchi"; see Jean Seznec,[435] p. 157. A first serious attempt to describe the estates and, among them, the trades and crafts, their appellations, their particular tools, *sine ira et studio,* is found in the *Vocabularium rerum* [Latin-German];[497] next to butchers, hunters, tailors, ploughmen, merchants, musicians, criminals, ecclesiastics, we find [no pag. or fol. or sign.] "De medicis et eorum qui pertinent ad medicas artes." It is curious how this love of enumeration applied to professions is still alive in children's counting-out games: "tinker tailor / soldier sailor," etc., etc. The earliest serious and at the same time systematic listing of estates occurs in the first half of the sixteenth century. This is Barthelemy de Chasseneu's *Catalogus Gloriae Mundi*[95] (1529), which, on 390 leaves, shows the important members of society and lists, among others, architects, farmers, goldsmiths, surgeons. De Chasseneu's opus is a grandiose attempt to arrange the estates, professions, crafts, etc. in a descending scale—the very opposite of Schopperus' ill-organized but democratic line-up and, of course, rather similar to the intricate *ordines sedendi* of the early *quodlibeta anatomica* as we see them illustrated in the de Ketham *Fasciculo* woodcut (Fig. 7). Sigismund Feyrabend's "Epistola dedicatoria" to Schopperus' *ΠΑΝΟΠΛΙΑ*[430] offers an interesting apologia for the lowly estates, which he bases on St. Paul's "sicut enim in uno corpore multa membra habemus omnia autem membra non eundem actum habeunt" (Epist. ad Rom. xii: 4ff.). Jost Amman's woodcuts were used as late as 1659 in Thomas Garzoni's *Piazza universale;*[171] cf. also Bibliogr.[172] The earliest illustrated set of guild pictures known to me, found in the Codex Behaim (Cracow, Jagellonian Library, fol. 237–307), dates from 1505; see Friedrich Winkler.[516a]

Specialization, as we have already seen, was pre-eminently a sixteenth-century phenomenon. How far it might go is curiously illustrated by a most popular treatise on the craftsmanlike and mechanical aspects of the martyrdoms of the Early Christians; cf. A. Gallonius, *Trattato*[167,168] (1591 and later editions and tr.). (Fig. 15.)

Vesalius in his programmatic Preface dedicated the *Fabrica* to Emperor Charles V. Legitimately enough, he appealed in it to the Emperor's interest in the mathematical sciences. Undoubtedly he was also aware of the Emperor's penchant for mechanical contrivances such as the automata that he himself produced after his retirement from the world of politics. The importance of the princes' interest in handicrafts cannot be easily overrated: Maximilian I, Albrecht Dürer's sponsor, perhaps largely in wishful self-reflection, had himself appear in his epic the *Weiss Kunig* (last redaction,[311] 1514) as a practitioner of painting, building (in stone and wood), minting, armor plate beating, etc. In some of the woodcuts he appears dressed in his regalia, yet wielding the tools of those crafts (cf. ed. Vienna, 1775,[311] pt. II, chap. xxixff.). In real life Maximilian operated a wood-turning bench that may still be in existence (coll. Count H. Wilczek, Kreuzenstein Castle); see Julius Schlosser,[424] fig. 81. Francis I was an amateur painter. This princely preoccupation with the crafts must have influenced the steady ennoblement that took place in the course of the sixteenth century. Other contributing factors were, it seems, the *Kunst- und Wunderkammern;* they consisted, on the one hand, of *naturalia* (hence the German *Naturalienkabinette*) such as unicorn horns, ostrich eggs, roses of Jericho, shells, mummies, foetuses, etc. and, on the other, of *artificialia,* products of manual skill that were not, as one might expect, primarily works of art, but rather works of art-ful contrivance *(ingenium)* such as automata, clocks, locks, astronomical and nautical apparatus, tools, and

musical instruments; see Schlosser,[424] esp. pp. 98ff. François Rabelais (1533) and Juan Luis Vives (1531) followed Maximilian's lead and preceded Schopperus in stressing the significance of the illiberal arts and advocating them as a *sine qua non* in the princely curriculum; see W. E. Houghton, Jr., *The History of Trades,*[241] pp. 31f. As early as 1536 Paracelsus inserted in his *Wundartzney*[366] (Augsburg) special chapters on the diagnosis and treatment of diseases contracted and wounds sustained by workers in the new chemical and mechanical industries (I, iii, chap. 7, and II, ii, 9f.).

The ennoblement of the artisans begins in the late Middle Ages. In the fifteenth century we may find it in the Dances of Death, in the vulgarizations of the *entrées* and *trionfi dell' antichità,* such as Lorenzo de' Medici's *Canti Carnascialeschi* (section xvi), and in the ever widening scope of the Labors of the Months and of the "Planetenkinderbilder." The roots of these new tendencies, it has been suggested, may possibly be traced in the social and intellectual aspirations of the more ambitious craftsmen. Though this is true, I believe that we should not overlook the *moralizationes* of the fourteenth century, which systematically subjected the entire earthly scene, including the occupations of the manual workers, to their interpretations *in malo aut in bono*. Petrus Berchorius, for example, transfers the Platonic idea of the *deus artifex* to the *in bono* interpretation of the word "Faber" (see his *Dictionarium*[50] of the 1340's, ed. Venice, 1583, pt. II, p. 89, *sub hac voce*). To Bersuire God becomes the "Faber Gloriosus, qui fabricat opus mirabile ... id est mundi creator ... id est Deus, qui sine malleo vel secure fabricauit, & fabricat uniuersa ..." This description of the toolless super-*faber* follows upon the description, graphic and succinct as always, of the word "fabricare" as pertaining "ad illos artifices mechanicos, qui cum manualibus laboribus percussionibusque et ictibus solent aliquid construere, vel formare." It is not impossible that here there is some awareness on the part of this author of the role that the *faber* played in ancient and in primitive society, where he is the musician, the magician, and the initiate. Jesus also, as Bersuire points out, is a *faber*: "fabri filius, ergo faber" (cf. Matthew xiii:55). The *Glossa ordinaria* to this passage reads: "*Fabri filius.* Non sine re voluit dici fabri filius, non illius quem putant (they, being the *Judaei*), sed fabricatoris omnium"; ed. Migne,[185] col. 134. As soon as later generations turned Bersuire's allegorical interpretations into equations, the earthly *faber* became a creator in his own right.

But the link between the mechanics and the creative godhead is not exclusively biblical. For the *locus classicus* in antiquity, cf. Cicero's *Tusculan Disputations*[98] (I, xxv): "Omnes magni: etiam superiores, qui vestitum, qui tecta, qui cultum vitae, qui praesidia contra feras invenerunt; a quibus mansuefacti et exculti, a necessariis artificiis ad elegantiora defluximus ..." An impressive note indeed. Echoes of the tenor of this passage have been traced in late mediaeval cycles such as that of the lowest zone of the well-known bas-reliefs of the Campanile in Florence; see Jean Seznec,[435] pp. 30f., and, especially, note 47 *ibidem*. Both a link-up with this kind of classical thinking and a wholly new impulse came in the last decade of the fifteenth century from writings such as Polydore Virgil's *De rerum inventoribus* (1499), in which manual and mechanical inventors are listed.

Finally see E. R. Curtius,[114] pp. 529ff., "Gott als Bildner," with numerous scholastic quotations which use "fabrica," "fabricare," "fabricator," where at present we should use "create" and its derivatives.

98 For the reference to Leonardo see E. Panofsky,[360] pp. 86f. The passage from Cardano,[86] pp. 573f. (XVII, *s. t.* "De artibus, artificiosisque rebus") reads as follows: "Est enim pictura mechanicarum omnium subtilissima, eadem vero & nobilissima. Nam quicquid plastices aut sculptura conatur, mirabilius pictura fingit, addit vmbras & colores, & opticen sibi iungit, nouis etiam additis quibusdam inuentionibus: nam pictorem omnia necesse est scire, quoniam omnia imitatur. Est philosophus pictor, archi-

tectus, & dissectionis artifex. Argumento est praeclara illa totius humani corporis imitatio, iam pluribus ante annis inchoata a Leonardo Vincio Florentino, & pene absoluta: sed deerat operi tantus artifex, ac rerum naturae indagator, quantus est Vesalius." G. I. Vossius'[502] quotation of this passage occurs §21, pp. 7of.

99 How seriously the book was treated in the sixteenth century we can gather from the copy in the British Museum (C. 54.bb.6.),[370] which belonged to John Dee (1562). Dee added marginal notes and diagrams of his own in profusion, and its editor, A. P. Gassari, supplied an interesting bibliography, chronologically arranged, that lists ten ancient authors, fourteen patristic and scholastic ones, and fifteen of his own time.

100 See W. S. Heckscher,[207] pp. 55f. For Mundinus see J. Playfair McMurrich,[297] pp. 23f., and George Sarton,[417] pp. 846f.

101 This negative attitude did not always lead to rewarding results, especially in the field of anatomy. Paracelsus, the self-confessed *Lutherus medicorum,* held anything not springing from Nature to be like a labyrinth without a proper entrance or exit. He contrasted the *codices scribentium* with the *lumen naturae,* and he scorned the masses that clung to the letters in the books ("der grösste Haufe hält sich allein an die Buchstaben der Bücher ..."). Cf. also his observation: "darumb das deine bücher also plerren (drone away), darumb sol es also sein. darum auch das ires leren auf den hohen schulen, also darumb sol es gleich sein. o we, nicht sol das sein, etc."; *Der ander Theil,* treatise I, Introduction (1536), ed. Karl Sudhoff,[366] X, i, p. 233. Consequently Paracelsus turns to Nature for his knowledge and for his remedies: "also werden all dinge, so di natur volbringen sol, aus der erfarenheit der natur erfunden werden und aus eigener fantasei lassent sich die ding nicht erfinden"; treatise II, chap. i, ed. Sudhoff,[366] p. 286. From here, then, springs Paracelsus' denial of the very basis of anatomy: that is, the belief, common in the sixteenth century, that Man as the microcosm is the

reflection of the macrocosmic order of all things; *ibid.*, chap. ii, Sudhoff,[366] p. 288. Paracelsus therefore inevitably became the first great anti-Galenist. The line of anti-Galenists that he began by-passed Vesalius uncompromisingly; it led rather to van Helmont (1577–1644) and to Robert Fludd (1574–1637), although the latter worked anatomy into his curious system of interconnections (Fig. 13); see Heinrich Heinrichs,[212] *passim*.

Another testimonial can perhaps be found in Leonardo's anatomical writings, which were, as I believe, unpublishable (at least in the sixteenth century) principally because they lacked the backbone of a bibliography, which even in, for example, so practical-minded a man as Vesalius is still very fundamental; see Note 75 above. Leonardo expressed his antagonism repeatedly; he saw in "bookworms the step-sons of Nature."

102 Carl Nordenfalk,[342] pp. 9ff. For the decidedly unaesthetic, unperspective, and generally unartistic character of explanatory diagrams and designs accompanying Hellenistic scientific texts and their mediaeval copies, see the brilliant reconstruction of Kurt Weitzmann,[510] pp. 244–66, esp. 246f., and the summary, pp. 264 to end. A need for the systematic articulation of written texts, beyond the division into books, was not felt in classical times; division and subdivision by chapter and paragraph came about as part of the general systematization of the High Scholastic *summae*; see E. Panofsky,[358] pp. 32ff.

103 See E. Panofsky,[362] note 138 on p. 289 and fig. 73, and E. P. Goldschmidt,[193] p. 19 and fig. on p. 21. Also see Note 105 below and W. S. Heckscher,[208] pp. 57f. and note 7. Andrea Alciati's *Emblematum liber* (the illustrated work of an Italian humanist) appeared in its first edition in Augsburg (1531) with a dedication to Conrad Peutinger; see Praz, II,[384] *s.v.* "Alciati."

104 See Note 113 below. Andrea Fulvio[161] based his 204 portrait medallions (engraved white on black by Ugo da Carpi, d. 1525) on

the collection of the printer Mazocchi, the printer and publisher of his work.

105 E. P. Goldschmidt,[193] pp. 51f. and in general chap. ii, "Illustrations."

106 *Le Vite,*[487] III, p. 321.

107 Ed. Basel.[139]

108 See M. D. Henkel,[217] pp. 7ff. E. P. Goldschmidt made the important observation that "not a single classical Latin text printed before 1493 [i.e. Terence] contains any woodcut or engraved illustration"; *The Printed Book,*[193] p. 37. For Rabelais' attack see the Prologue to *Gargantua.*[387] I am convinced that Erasmus wished to castigate and travesty Bersuire's method when he translated: "Jesus Christ, the Word and the Son of the eternal Father, came into the world according to the profets," as follows: "Optimi maximique Jovis interpres ac filius, servator, rex juxta vatum responsa, ex Olympo devolavit in terras"; quoted after J. Huizinga,[244] p. 172. For Luther's attitude see E. Panofsky and F. Saxl,[365] p. 277 and note 63. Luther could plainly be a humanist on occasion; when, for example, he referred to the old languages as "the sheaths which contain the blade of the Spirit" (i.e. the Gospels), or when, in his lecture on Isaiah (lxv:24), he compared man's situation with that of Atlas—"vere sicut Atlas soli sustinemus pondus coeli" (ed. *Kritische Gesamtausgabe,*[296] p. 390).

109 Only two years earlier (1536) Paracelsus' most important medical handbook, *Der grossenn Wundartzney das Erst Buoch,*[366] had appeared at Augsburg with nineteen full-page woodcuts, which the printer, Heynrich Steyner, had calmly appropriated from Hieronymus Brunschwig's *Cirurgia*[74] of 1497; see K. Sudhoff,[366] X, i, p. XV. Paracelsus became, on the other hand, a kind of Northern Alciati (denied by Praz)[384] when he accompanied his remarkable *Prognostication*[367] (1536) with thirty-two emblematic-mantic woodcuts that form, with his prophecies of a politico-religious nature, an organic whole.

110 The frontispiece, including the text, is conveniently reproduced in L.R. Lind, *The Epitome of Andreas Vesalius,*[491] Plates.

111 See Ludwig Edelstein,[132] pp. 548ff.

112 Conveniently summarized by M. Roth,[410] p. 125 and note 3. For the following *Vaesani depulsio* of 1551[463] see H.W. Janson,[253] p. 359. Among the progressive scholars who sided with Vesalius were Conrad Gesner, Realdo Colombo, and Hieronymus Cardanus; see Notes 15 and 82 above. But the negative attitude prevailed, at least numerically. Undoubtedly this negative attitude is reflected, for example, in the fact that the *Tabulae anatomicae* of Bartholomaeus Eustachius (d. 1574) saw their *editio princeps* as late as 1714[148]—"quas a tenebris tandem vindicatus, praefatione notisque illustravit Jo. Maria Lancisius"; see L. Choulant (M. Frank),[97] p. 201. It should, however, be stated that another of Eustachius' writings, his *opuscula anatomica*[147] of 1564, equipped with a fair number of (curiously enough) etched illustrations prefixed to his tripartite work (on nine plates of indifferent quality), appeared during their author's lifetime. But another illustration is afforded by Giovanni Battista Canano's projected illustrated anatomical *opus,* of which only Vol. I (on muscles) appeared in print at Ferrara;[82] a work of the utmost rarity with illustrations engraved after Giovanni Grani da Carpi in 1543 or earlier. Here too a revival was planned in the eighteenth century, judging by an unpublished manuscript facsimile copy with an Introduction that (apart from palaeographical evidence) allows us to place it in the latter part of the century; the manuscript is preserved in the Wellcome Historical Medical Library; see Bibliogr. *s.v.* Canano.[83] The earliest successful attempt to launch an illustrated anatomical atlas was Jacobus Berengario da Carpi's *Isagogae breves* of 1522,[51] presenting the results of autopsies for the benefit of medical students; see C. Singer and C. Rabin,[447] pp. xxxif. and figs. 16 and 17 on p. xxxii.

In 1345, roughly two hundred years before the *Fabrica,* Guido da Vigevano composed the first "Schulanatomie,"[199] which has come down to us in an early manuscript fully equipped with illustrations that, *expressis verbis,* were intended as didactic aids (see p. 43). Guido advised his colleagues to look at these pictures often so that they might commit them to memory; see the Motto to this Chapter. But whereas Vesalius raised scientific illustrations to the rank of emancipated scientific commentaries (as Botticelli had aimed at making his early set of Dante illustrations serve as independent commentaries on the *Commedia*), Guido regarded his pictures as mere emergency solutions dictated by the particular situation in Paris, at this time apparently much different from that in Northern Italy, which (viz. Lombardy) was Guido's home. His argument runs as follows: "Quia prohibitum est ab Ecclesia facere anothomiam in corpore humano [that is, anatomical demonstrations as well as autopsies were forbidden] . . . coegi me ad declarandum anothomiam per figuras, et credatur mihi experto, cum pluribus et pluribus vicibus ipsam feci in corpore humano [that is, profiting by autopsies]"; MS. Chantilly, Musée Condé 334, fol. 257; ed. and illus. Wickersheim,[199a] p. 5.

113 The "Book of Nature" is a time-honored topos; cf. E.R. Curtius,[114] pp. 323ff., to be complemented by E. Panofsky,[363] p. 6, note 1[b]. See Ludwig Edelstein,[132] p. 556 and note 25. Vesalius,[490] in his Preface to the *Fabrica* (fol. a 4 *verso*), lashes out at "certain men who vehemently condemn the practice of setting before the eyes of students, as we do with parts of plants, delineations . . ." "Verum hic quorundam iudicium mihi succurrit, qui non duntaxat herbarum, sed & humani coporis partium quantumuis etiam exquisitissimas delineationes rerum naturalium studiosis proponi, acriter damnant: quod has non picturis, uerum sedula resectione, rerumque ipsarum intuitu disci oporteat."

The botanical work that Vesalius had in mind may have been Otto Brunfels,[72] *Herbarum vivae Eicones,* Strassburg, 1532. Next Vesalius appeals, by way of *argumentum ad hominem*—the Preface being addressed to the great amateur mathematician and astronomer Charles V (cf. Note 97 above)—to related problems in mathematics:

Pictures greatly aid the understanding of these [i.e. anatomical] things, and how much more accurately they put the things before the eyes than even the clearest language, nobody can have failed to experience in geometry and the other mathematical disciplines.

Quantum uero picturae illis intelligendis opitulentur, ipsoque etiam uel explicatissimo sermone rem exactius ob oculos collocent, nemo est qui non in geometria, alijsque mathematum disciplinis experiatur. [Tr. Benj. Farrington,[151] p. 1364.]

Finally (Farrington, *loc. cit.*) Vesalius refers to two specific anatomical works that, as he knows, have appealed to the Emperor's grandfather and to the Emperor himself. That the second publication (which was illustrated) was undoubtedly Vesalius' own, viz. the *Tabulae anatomicae sex,*[493] of April 1538, has been pointed out to me by Dr. F.N.L. Poynter. As for the other, I know of only one medical treatise—supposedly one of the first books to postulate that the professor of anatomy should do his own dissecting—dedicated to Maximilian I, a work by Alexander Benedictus; cf. Arturo Castiglione,[91] p. 831.

114 Adding: "Galen did not allow even plants to be depicted"; see Harvey W. Cushing,[115] pp. xxxff.

115 To which belongs a second paragraph that reads: "... you should give greater praise to a man of probity unskilled in letters than to one skilled in letters but devoid of probity." *Codice Atlantico,* fol. 76 *recto,* ed. and tr. Edward McCurdy,[284] I, p. 95.

116 Cf. E. C. Streeter and C. Singer,[458] fig. 2 and text pp. 208f.

117 See Note 118 below.

118 Hans Jantzen,[255] pp. 313f. The *Fabrica*[490] copy—(that it is one is made more than dubious by evidence to be given below)—that appears, as Jantzen suggests, in Rembrandt's painting cannot be open at page 159; what the author had in mind was probably pp. 258 and 259, the partly visible verso and invisible recto of the tome at the feet of the cadaver. (Figs. 11a and b). The difficulty begins with the very small amount of typography, if typography it be, visible in Rembrandt's painting. Although Rembrandt does no more than simulate the appearance of letters, the letters he suggests are most likely not roman—not printed but handwritten letters. If the book should therefore suggest a sumptuously bound manuscript, the question (unanswerable, it seems to me) would arise whose opus it is. Unfortunately we know very little about the role of script, writing, typography in Rembrandt's work. Just in 1632, he can be most accurate; cf. his meticulous imitation of calligraphy in the portrait of the writing master Lieven Willemsz. van Coppenol at Cassel; A. Bredius,[65] No. 164. Another, wholly conjectural possibility would be an opening somewhere between pp. 365 and 378 (being chap. xliii of Book II, entitled "De musculis manus digitos moventibus"). None of the pages suggested, however, can be compared to Rembrandt's partly visible verso in the typographical grouping of characters. Jantzen could not know that there is a second open atlas, which, although only partly visible, is unmistakably open at a page that shows both illustrations and text; as I have suggested, it is the quondam roll call sheet in the left hand of Hartman Hartmansz., which, at closer inspection before the original, turns out to be the open verso of a book whose recto pages are covered by the bust of Dr. Tulp. None of the relevant *Fabrica* pages has on its left-hand side illustrations (of the human lower arm and hand) that compare with those in Rembrandt's roll call atlas. It might be stated, however, that the appearance of the newly discovered book page

in the painting shows similarity to p. 259 of the *Fabrica* (Fig. 11b).

Finally, as to Jantzen's suggestion that Rembrandt owned a copy of the *Fabrica*[490] of 1555, it has been pointed out that the anatomical atlas in Gerard Dou's "Still-life" is a copy of a Vesalius-inspired work, Andreas Laurentius' *Historia anatomica,* Frankfort, 1600;[281] see Walter Artelt,[18] Plate IV, figs. 5 and 6. For further arguments, see pp. 70 f. Surely quite independently of Rembrandt, Alexander Read made use in his anatomical *Manvall* (London, 1638)[389] of the Vesalian unbearded head that, as I believe, inspired the head of the cadaver in Rembrandt's "Anatomy of Dr. Deyman." For the rest of the body Rembrandt, as has been pointed out by others, seems to have been inspired by one of the many later paraphrases of Andrea Mantegna's representation of the "Dead Christ" in the Brera at Milan. The most likely work of art to have communicated the prone body in extreme foreshortening to Rembrandt was the etching after the "Pietà" of Orazio Borgianni (*ca.* 1578–*ca.* 1616), a painting of about 1615; see F. Zeri,[528] Cat. No. 286, p. 44, and J. L. A. A. M. van Rijckevorsel,[399] figs. 266, 268.

For Rembrandt's so-called anatomical drawing in the "Anatomy of Dr. Tulp" see *New York Times,*[337] Section 1, p. 6, for the only (preliminary) report on the recent cleaning that I know.

I am inclined to believe that at least one other woodcut had some influence on Rembrandt's painting—specifically on the dissected parts themselves, which, as I have stated, have the appearance of a woodcut imitation rather than of a study from nature by Rembrandt himself. See Note 117 and p. 66 for my arguments. The fundamental flaw in the structure of the dissected parts seems to be that the *flexor sublimis digitorum* originates from the outer instead of the inner side of the arm. This anomaly has led me to the consideration that possibly Rembrandt used the anatomical representation of a right hand seen from above. It is strange indeed

that Dr. Tulp and his confreres should have failed to detect this flaw. Yet Dr. de Vries, the Director of the Mauritshuis, assures me that there is no indication that the dissected portion has suffered through overpainting or changes at a later date. Dr. Oscar V. Batson, Chairman of the Department of Anatomy at the University of Pennsylvania, in a letter (June 18, 1954) from which he generously allowed me to quote, writes:

> I have been told that museum guides in 1905 were pointing out to anyone whom they supposed to be a physician that there was an anatomical error in the Rembrandt painting. This error is mentioned specifically by F. Wood Jones in his *Principles of Anatomy as Seen in the Hand.* I am familiar with the appearance of the forearm in unembalmed cadavera. The anatomic specimen would not account for the ungraceful appearance of the muscles in the dissection. . . . The dissected area seems wholly out of drawing with the rest of the picture. [Follow several suggestions as to causes of so blatant an error.]

119 Cf. Kurt Gerstenberg,[178] esp. pp. 137f. and figs. on pp. 133 and 136. For the classical tradition, if the anatomy table is seen as the *lectus funebris,* see Note 155 below. For the *pugillares,* see *ibidem.*

120 This is, as was naturally known in the Renaissance, a classical topos; see, for example, Realdo Colombo,[102] V, chap. xxxiii, 156, where the author begins his discussion of the muscles of the human hand with the words: "MANVS (vt Aristo. & Gal. inquiunt) organum est organorum."

Still in Rembrandt's circle the surgeon could be called "handmaster" ("handmeester of chirurgijn"); cf. *Woordenboek,*[520a] *s.h.v.,* and Franciscus Junius,[264a] *s.v.* "Sirgeon."

121 For this woodcut see M. H. Spielmann,[453] chaps. i (esp. 1–5) and iv (pp. 121–24).

It may be more than accident that the man who made himself the protagonist of the hand, with uncommon insistence and deep under-standing of what his plea implied, considered himself (and was considered by his contempo-raries) a Northerner. Vesalius' family came from Wesel *(Vesalia)* in Westphalia *(teste* the weasels in the armorial escutcheon in the frontis-piece of the *Fabrica).* (Fig. 10.) The putti sup-porting the Vesalian escutcheon stand on a *cartellino* that bears author's name and title in which Vesalius is described as "BRVXELLEN-SIS." This, I think, should be sufficient to dis-courage those that try to claim Vesalius for this or that nation. When describing him as a "Northerner," in relation to the human hand, it is with Albrecht Dürer in mind; Dürer was, it seems, the first to be keenly aware of the hand as the stamp of artistic style and uniqueness, in a manner unknown and incomprehensible across the Alps in his day and age; cf., for Dürer's curious misunderstanding in this re-spect, E. Panofsky, *Albrecht Dürer,*[356] p. 284. For the role of the hand as a *leitmotif* in the Preface, see Note 79 above. Undoubtedly Vesa-lius might have come across the creative *manus Dei* through his scholastic training. The Middle Ages, after all, had known the hand as the creative organ of the Divinity *par excellence;* see L. Charbonneau-Lassay,[94] chap. xii, pp. 109ff. More or less parallel to Vesalius' endeavors there ran a totally different current of interest in the human hand and its chiromantic signifi-cance: beginning with Johannes Hartlieb's *Die kunst chiromantia (das buch von der hand,* ed. princ., 1470), there have been numerous works in its wake emphasizing that the human hand can reveal the human personality; cf. H. Mier-zecki,[319] pp. 1319–22. For the most fabulous treatment of the human hand see Octavio Scarlatini,[422] pt. *Index* (56 main entries) under such headings as "Manus: anatomica / moralia & mystica / chiromantia / saturnia," etc.

The passage quoted on the piece of paper in the Vesalius woodcut portrait of 1542 (Pl. XIV-18) refers to the disputed question of the num-ber of metacarpal bones of the hand. It was this passage that roused the particular wrath of Jacobus Sylvius, who in his *Calumniarum depul-sio*[463] (1551) quoted from it *in extenso.* Nicolaas Tulp may have known of this dispute through Dr. Paaw's lectures at Leiden. There is, how-ever, no evidence that he himself voiced an opinion in the matter. I have been unable to trace in the relevant documents evidence con-cerning Tulp's supposed only known contro-versy, in which he engaged with C. G. Plem-pius, who, it is said, attacked Dr. Tulp in his book on muscles (Amsterdam, 1630); cf. E. H. M. Thijssen,[468] p. 3 and note 3, where Plem-pius' epigrams are quoted in full. In this argument, incidentally, Vesalius happened to side with Galen, and both happened to be wrong; see Harvey W. Cushing,[115] pp. 66f., 84f., frontispiece, and fig. 56. As Cushing points out, the Vesalius portrait (including the written reference to Book and chapter of the *Fabrica,* duly, though not always correctly, adjusted to new chapter numberings of the later enlarged editions) was recut and used as late as 1752.

[122] For the Casserio portrait, see J. G. de Lint, *Atlas,*[287] fig. 65 on p. 49.

[123] For the Coiter portrait see J. G. de Lint,[287] fig. 62 on p. 48.

[124] But see A. van der Boon,[62] pp. 40f. and C. H. Rogge,[406] esp. p. 99. For the tulip beaker see Note 127 below.

[125] The earliest systematic pharmaceutical handbook known to me is Valerius Cordus, *Dispensatorium,*[107] Nuremberg, 1535. This im-mensely influential practical handbook was not known in Holland before the last decade of the sixteenth century. Until then the *Antidotarium* of Salerno, twelfth century, had been the stand-ard work in the Lowlands; cf. C. H. Rogge,[406] pp. 90ff.

[126] Undoubtedly Tulp was also inspired in this respect by Pieter Paaw, whose *opus magnum* (1615)[350] was graced by engravings of bones (including one folding plate of the human skull) of great merit.

[127] H. Rogge's "Nicolaas Tulp,"[406] pp. 77–125, must still be regarded as the authoritative

biography. See also Johan E. Elias,[137] No. 111, 348, for many factual data, though it is not entirely accurate. A brief but sound article on Tulp over the name of E. D. Baumann will be found in the *Nieuw Nederlandsch Biografisch Woordenboek*,[340] pp. 1250f. The most comprehensive collection of material on Dr. Tulp's life and career has been gathered in the splendid work by E. H. M. Thijssen,[468] to which every student of the history of medicine owes a great measure of gratitude. The director of the Centraal Bureau voor Genealogie in The Hague, W. Ph. Veeren, had the great kindness to point out to me (letter of June 18, 1954) that possibly Tulp adopted his name from a signboard bearing the picture of a tulip, found on his father's house at the west side of the Keizersgracht. For the house "in de Tulp" see also J. van Lennep and J. ter Gauw,[283] p. 381, and Frits Lugt,[293] p. 67. At a later point Dr. Tulp adopted the flower for both his name and his coat of arms: "in azure a green-stemmed golden tulip and in the right hand top-corner a golden star with eight corners. Crest: the star." The particular connection between tulip and *vanitas* is the subject of an investigation on which P. J. Vinken is at present engaged.

The beautiful silver-gilt Tulip beaker in the Collection of Jonkheer Six van Wimmenum (Laren, Noord-Holland) (Pl. XLVI-55) is most likely the work of Joannes Lutma Sr., although his son has also been suggested. See Elias Voet Jr.,[498] No. 33 on p. 21. The beaker was used by Dr. Tulp for a final toast to his anatomical colleagues on October 23, 1652; he left it to the Guild as a sign of affection on retirement; see Monnikhoff's report as cited by E. H. M. Thijssen,[468] p. 15. The beaker was stolen in 1704 but retrieved in the nineteenth century, when it came into the possession of the descendants of the Six-Tulp family once more; see also Mevrouw Duyvené de Wit-Klinkhamer and Others,[131] No. 51 on p. 38. The lizard, shown somewhat less than lifesize, is found in Holland. Jhr. Six drew my attention to a hole on the upper part of the mound of earth, which plainly must have accommodated a second animal; of this no trace is left. I am grateful for his permission to reproduce a contemporary water color from a Catalogue in his possession, and therefore possibly derived from Tulp himself[315] (No. 411), which by its inscription is identified as "Admirael de France. 200 guldens" (Pl. XLVII-56) and which, curiously enough, has precisely the measurements of the tulip of the Beaker. For this kind of illustrated catalogue (which served both dealers and the owners of fashionable gardens), cf. E. H. Krelage,[276] pp. 55f. and 124 (listing nine other contemporary representations of this tulip).

For the orangutan see Tulp's *Observationes*,[477] II, chap. lvi, entitled: "Satyrus Indicus"; *tabula* XIIII, on p. 275; see H. W. Janson,[253] p. 354, note 37 on p. 350, and Plate LIII. Menno Hertzberger, Amsterdam, offered and sold recently a copy of the *Observationes* in which the place of the plate is taken by an excellent drawing that might conceivably be the original design. For the *unicornu marinum* cf. Thijssen,[468] pp. 116ff.

[128] Tea was mentioned from 1559 onward (Giovanni Battista Ramusion). The first tea reached Europe at Amsterdam (1610). Eight years later a gift of tea leaves was made to the anatomical theater at Leiden; this is listed in the *Inventory* of 1620[28] under "Rariteiten," box "D" (p. 66) as "Taeae fructis in China provenientis folia nos delata ex Javae insulae civitate Bantham anno 1618. Haec in aqua decocta eam rubro colore tingunt, quae colata, ac calide potata mirabiliter stomachum omniaque viscera corroborat." Jacobus Bontius (d. 1631) had written an earlier account of the Chinese tea, which, however, lacked the ethnographic description entirely; see M. A. van Andel,[61] pp. xxixf., and C. Louise Thijssen-Schoute,[469] p. 325, note 4 (with further literature). Tulp's account appeared first in the second edition[477a] of the year 1652. After discussing the medicinal properties of "a drink cooked from an herb which the Chinese call 'thee,'" Tulp refers to it as a drink of friendship, "which even princes do not disdain to prepare with their own hands,

but rather consider it a great honor to cook this herb for their friends." He goes on to describe the utmost care with which special cabinets in the innermost parts of Chinese palaces are equipped with funnels, beakers, spoons, and other pure equipment. For this passage in Tulp's own Dutch translation of the original Latin see Thijssen,[468] pp. 118f.

129 See Note 38 above and Appendix III.

130 The first work on midwifery was published by G. Sc. Mercurio.[316] As late as 1677 we hear that medical demonstrations for midwives (by Dr. Fr. Ruysch) were ridiculed as a novelty in the medical comedy; see J. B. F. van Gils,[184] pp. 116f.

131 How busy these fifty-eight (Rogge mentions eighty) physicians must have been in 1635, when in Amsterdam alone 17,193 (out of ab. 150,000) died of the Plague!—Coaches in Amsterdam were disallowed in 1663; cf. Elias,[137] p. 351. On the whole the Dutch physician in the seventeenth century was pedestrian, whereas his Flemish colleague preferred to be equestrian; see J. B. F. van Gils,[184] p. 64.

132 Tulp's portrait was executed on more than ten different occasions by nearly as many artists (Frans Hals, Quellinus, C. van Voort, and others) between *ca.* 1624 and 1660, not counting the engraved portraits that graced the later editions of his book. In one instance (see Chapter XVI and Pl. XLIV-53) we know that Dr. Tulp accepted his portrait in lieu of payment for having treated the sick child of Nicolaes Eliasz. Pickenoy; see E. W. Moes,[323] II, No. 8123, and F. Muller,[329] Nos. 5482–90. As my colleague J. G. van Gelder pointed out to me, a list of Tulp portraits would certainly have to be amplified by drawings not recorded. See Note 136 below.

133 For a complete enumeration of eds. and (Dutch) trs. of the *Observationes* see H. C. Rogge,[406] pp. 94f. I have listed in the Bibliogr.[477-80] the British Museum holdings as well as others that I have been in a position to examine myself. The *Observationes* (not counting the Pharmacopoeia that Tulp inspired) were

Tulp's only published work; he is said to have had another book ready for publication, but he destroyed the manuscript for unknown reasons; its subject was the thesis that each country produces the remedies for its own diseases. For the scarce copy of Tulp's dissertation *De Cholera Humida,* see E. H. M. Thijssen,[468] p. 2, note 1.

134 Two important stages had been reached in the Vesalius *fortuna* when Pieter Paaw wrote: "Principis imo Anatomicorum titulum ipsi [i. e. Vesalio] conferente totius humani generis consensu": (i) Vesalius had permanently come into his undisputed right to be called the great sixteenth-century reformer of anatomy; (ii) Dr. Paaw consciously staked Leiden's claim to enter into the glorious legacy that had hitherto been vested in Padua and Louvain; see M. Roth,[410] pp. 289f. and note 7 on p. 289. Paaw's edition of the *Epitome*[492] appeared twice, Leiden 1616 and Amsterdam 1633, illustrated with 13 engravings after woodcuts of the *Fabrica Epitome;* see Harvey W. Cushing,[115] pp. 141f. For Amsterdam's scientific advance in 1632 see Note 212 below and p. 27.

135 For Barlaeus, Descartes, Sir Thomas Browne as representative of those newly attracted by Amsterdam see Notes 3, 7, 16 above. Kauffmann, in his stimulating article,[267] pleads for Barlaeus as the main agent in bringing Rembrandt into contact with Huygens and other members of the *Muiderkring* (to which Dr. Tulp himself belonged) whereby Rembrandt would have been persuaded to settle in Amsterdam. This argument, naturally, does not preclude the possibility that commissions from others added to the magnetic force of the city—a possibility stressed by the testimony of the burgomaster of Rembrandt's home town, Leiden, J. J. Orlers, who explicitly stated: "Dewijle dat zijne Konst ende arbeyt / de Borgeren ende Innewoonderen van Amsterdamme ten hoochsten behaechde ende aengenaem was / ende dat hy veeltijden versocht werde omme 'tzy Conterfeytselen ofte ander stucken aldaer te maecken / zoo heeft hy goet ghevonden hem [= zich] van Leyden te transporteren naer Amsterdamme..." Bibli-

ogr.,[347] p. 375; also ed. Seymour Slive,[449] pp. 203f., with an English tr. p. 36; also pp. 192f. (with further evidence).

136 See Chr. P. van Eeghen,[134] and for Rembrandt's "Portrait" of Six's mother see *Rembrandt Tentoonstelling*,[393] No. 45. The age of the lady represented, however, as well as questions of style and quality, cast doubts on the identity of Anna Wijmer in this painting as well as upon Rembrandt's authorship.

137 Cf. J. Six,[448] pp. 158–60, with quotations from the *Insigten over de Geneeskunde in vier bouken*, viz. Dr. Tulp's own unpublished translation of his book[478] into "patrium sermonem." For the complete text of the Tulp passage see our Appendix I. For a nice summary, chiefly of J. Six's findings, cf. I. van Esso Bzn.,[144] pp. 125f. Also see P. Hofmann Peerlkamp,[369] pp. 340f. and quotation, Note 138 below.

We need not wonder at a seventeenth-century physician's leaning heavily on Celsus' terminology (and manner of diagnosing) in matters of melancholy; the great Boerhaave (1667–1738) still uses terms such as "atrabilious humor" and "melancholy juice." Dr. Tulp used purging simples which, as the reader of Robert Burton's *Anatomy of Melancholy*[78] (pt. II, sect. iv, Memb. 2, subsect. I–III) will recall, were designed to act either simply or in compound, purging in degrees ranging from gentle to violent, either upward or downward. The seventeenth century might be called the age of the enema. In one year (ab. 1632) 215 enemas were administered to Louis XIII. On his deathbed (1643) he is supposed to have berated his physician with the words: "C'est par votre ignorance l'état où je suis maintenant. . . . Il ne fallait pas me donner tant de remèdes qui m'ont ruiné les entrailles." See Philippe Erlanger,[141a] p. 103. For the sad case of a young lady killed by the enemas administered by the overzealous wife of a pharmacist, see N. Tulp,[477] III, chap. xvi, pp. 206f., *s.t.* "Immoderatus Clystiris usus." The enema, however, lost none of its popularity. In the *examen rigorosum* at the end of Molière's *Malade Imaginaire*[324] the overuse of this method is ridiculed: "Clysterium donare, / postea seignare, / Ensuita purgare." Five years before (1668) there had appeared Reinier de Graaf's classic *De clysteribus*,[193a] pp. 177–214, advertising an improved method of self-application and generally encouraging the use of this treatment as a panacea in almost any disease accompanied by a fever.

The only painter who, in the estimation of contemporaries, might have vied with Rembrandt in fame was Joachim von Sandrart, who in those years (1637–42) was in Amsterdam. Both Rembrandt and Sandrart were close to Barlaeus, Vossius, and Hooft; see F. Schmidt-Degener,[428] p. 13. As pointed out by Six,[448] p. 161, Baldinucci, in his *Vita di Reimbrond Van Rein* (composed in 1686), stressed Rembrandt's undisputed fame as culminating in Amsterdam around the year 1640; see C. Hofstede de Groot,[228] No. 360 on p. 420.

Rembrandt's medical biography has never, so far as I am aware, been seriously investigated. For Rembrandt's weakening of his body by his sedentary life in his young years (before and after 1631) see Constantine Huygens' beautiful and sympathetic report, § 21, ed. C. Hofstede de Groot,[228] No. 18 on pp. 17f. Huygens speaks of his feverish industry — "testari cogor, non vidisse me parem diligentiam aut assiduitatem ullo in hominum genere, studio vel aetate"—of his lack of leisure—"non satis otii esse"—and of his health as undermined by a sedentary mode of life. To this report must be added the rather mysterious inquiry concerning Rembrandt's state of health. The notary Jacob van Zwieten, on request of the honorable Pieter Huygen de Boys, a citizen of Leiden, interrogates Rembrandt at the house of his host, Hendrik Uylenburch the art dealer, at the Breestraat. The tone is that of an *examen rigorosum* solely conducted to establish the fact of the painter's well-being or illness; the impression on van Zwieten is favorable, and it is corroborated by Rembrandt, whose emphatically exuberant reply is quoted *verbatim*: "dat [viz. the impression of vitality, strength, and well-being] is waer, ick ben Godtloff in goede dispositie en wel te pas"—"that is true; I am, thank God, in good shape and healthy," to which the notary adds: "Alles oprecht," which may perhaps be rendered as "[Said] in good faith." This fragmentary document, dated July 26, 1632, does not divulge the purpose of this unique inquiry in the first year of Rembrandt's residence in Amsterdam; see Hofstede de Groot,[228] No. 25, pp. 24f. Even more speculative is the case history recorded in Appendix I below.

For strenuous attempts that Rembrandt made in the years preceding his return to Amsterdam (1628–30) to absorb the (pictorial) language of melancholy, see van Gelder,[176] pp. 22–24 (294–96). For Vasari's report on Piero di Cosimo cf. E. Panofsky,[354a] pp. 33–67. Curiously, Prior Thomas, like Dr. Tulp himself an art lover, was an accomplished calligrapher.—Philip Hofer kindly informs me that in his forthcoming study of Goya's prints he shall be able to give a new interpretation of the decidedly psychosomatic character of the artist's illness of the years from 1792 onwards.

[138] The Theophrastian origin of the association of genius with melancholia (the source of Aristotle, *Problemata* XXX, i) has recently been discussed by Walter Müri,[333] pp. 21f. This information is based on, among other sources, Descartes *(Discours)*; see H.F.V.[483] "Saepius enim laborabat metu quodam et tristitia ab atra bile ortis, quod morbi genus praeclaris ingeniis [sic] non semel adhaeret"; P. Hofmann Peerlkamp,[369] pp. 340f.

[139] Quoted after E. Panofsky and F. Saxl,[364] p. 21, note 2 and *passim*.

[140] Jacob van der Gracht's *Anatomie der wtterlicke deelen*,[194] etc. (i.e. "anatomy of the external parts of the human body . . . suited for painters, sculptors, engravers as well as surgeons"), 1634; also, in part, preserved in manuscript; see Harvey W. Cushing,[115] pp. 137ff. Two years later the first Italian artists' anatomy appeared in print: Jacobus Palma Giovane (1544–1628), *Regole per imperar*,[351] Venice,

1636 (with reissue at Nuremberg, *eodem anno,* or later), with twenty-six engravings of human anatomy for the use of artists and engravers. To my regret I have been unable to examine a copy of this work. In the Wellcome Historical Medical Library in London I came across an artists' anatomy that precedes van der Gracht by almost half a century: Arfe y Villafane's *opus*[15] of the year 1585; here an attempt is made to present artists with the measurements of all living beings and also, characteristically enough, of members of architecture. The book is indebted to Dürer's *Proportionslehre,* but, by contrast with Dürer, it actually operates with skeletons and dissected parts of the human anatomy (Book II). This work is not listed in Julius Schlosser,[425, 426] nor is it in Choulant's[97] list of "Works on Artistic Anatomy" (but see pp. 218–21 *ibidem*).

The postulate for an anatomy for artists existed in Holland some three decades before van der Gracht's *Anatomie*: Carel van Mander[303, 304] advises the young painter that he must look, as it were, through the human body and that by watching the dead being flayed ("met dooden te sien villen") he will learn to understand form and function of muscles; cf. chap. ii, §§ 18f.

[141] "In his own field [in the early 1660's] he [Rembrandt] cites, paraphrases and emends with an acuteness, a tenacity and a factual knowledge, which, from the point of view of method, could be compared to that of the great 17th century philologists"; H. van de Waal,[505] p. 23. See also J.G. van Gelder,[176] p. 403.

[142] For the drama by Jan Zoet cf. Seymour Slive,[449] p. 45 and note 1. The text of Barlaeus' Dialogue runs as follows:

> . . . tota matrona mihi miraculum est, & consummatissimus Superum, si ita fas loqui, labor. Ingenio nihil divinius sublimiusque. ea concipit in quae non penetrant vulgares animae. quicquid demissum ac humile, pedibus calcat, ipsis nubibus contemplatione altior. apophthegmata non fa-

bricat, sed fundit. sententiis responsisque arguta est & faceta. Versus scribit non una lingua, Belgicos, Gallicos, Italicos, & illos elaboratos, ut lucernam oleant, & reconditorum sensuum plenos, ut a secunda etiam tertiaque lectione doctior redeas. Videbam in aedibus variarum artium exquisitissima monimenta, nec enim supellectilem suam emit, ipsa fecit . . . Pingit penicello, & Apellem provocat. Sculpit & Praxitelem lacessit. Texit & net Arachnes aemula. canit in invidiam Sapphus. Testudinem pulsat Orphei instar aut Amphionis. Lemniscos & corollas e fructibus, foliis, floribus, conchis eo artificio concinnat & ordinat, ut dubium sit, an natura arti, an ars naturae concedat. Flores bysso repraesentat, ut vivere jures. Ea accuratione & elegantia scribit, ut praelis dudum sua laus decesserit. Orationi Suada inest & mira venustas, oculos verecundia, incessum modestia, gestus comis gravitas insedit. Animae virtus una est. sed quae reliquas omnes συλλήβδην habet. Graeci δικαιοσύνην καθόλου vocant. [Caspar Barlaeus, *Dialogi aliquot*[31] (dialogue: "De conjugii necessitate. Collocutores Hoofdius, Barlaeus"; the latter is speaking), pp. 22f.]

Professor Henry S. Robinson, at the Institute for Advanced Study, Princeton, kindly pointed out to me that this last sentence is nothing but a slight paraphrase of Aristotle, *Nicomachean Ethics*,[17] V, i, 15ff. (ed. Loeb, p. 529): "Justice then in this sense is perfect Virtue, though with a qualification, namely that it is displayed towards others. This is why Justice is often thought to be the chief of virtues, and more sublime 'or than the evening or than the morning star'; and we have the proverb: 'In Justice is all Virtue found in Sum' [ἐν δὲ δικαιοσύνῃ συλλήβδην πᾶς ἀρετή ἐνί]." Elsewhere Barlaeus collected his more or less amatory poems in praise of Maria Tesselschade Visscher *(Poematvm Pars* II, *Miscell.*[32] II, pp. 428–38 [in

minute *italics*]). Here we learn, among other things, that the wreaths were actually used as decorations in the Muider Castle: "In corollas & lemnicos, opus TESSELAE, suspenso in atrio Satrapae Muydensis." It seems to me quite possible that Barlaeus regarded himself as a second Poliziano celebrating his Alessandra Scala; for striking parallels cf. especially Poliziano's *Greek Epigram*[380a] XXIX, pp. 199ff., where Alessandra's eyes, gait, and gestures are praised. For a detailed account of the relationship between Alessandra and Poliziano cf. James Hutton,[245] pp. 127ff. While Alessandra, in the early 1490's, played the part of "Electra" in Greek, Joost van den Vondel, in 1639, dedicated his "Elektra" to Maria Tesselschade.

143 Cf. Seymour Slive,[449] p. 54 and *passim*. Condivi,[104] chap. lxvii, maintains that Michelangelo held that plebeians should not be admitted to the arts; this argument, far from dead in the Holland of the 1630's, would have militated heavily against the miller's son from Leiden, in spite of Huygens' benevolent efforts to overlook Rembrandt's low origins and undignified artistic schooling. It should be added, however, that Constantine Huygens in his estimate of Rembrandt (*ca.* 1631) compared the "unbearded Dutch youth and miller's son" to Apelles, Protogenes, and Parrhasios (§ 12, ed. C. Hofstede de Groot,[228] No. 18 on p. 16); and in 1667 the poet Jeremias de Decker, in his "Danck-Bewijs Aen den uytnemenden en wijtberoemden Rembrandt van Rhyn,"[119] speaks of the painter as "van onses tijds Apell."

144 See William Ringler.[400] The mere knowledge of the aphorism (which was revived by Polydore Virgil, writing in 1499) does not necessarily indicate its being endorsed or even understood by those who used it. Similarly the Middle Ages quoted the NOSCE TE IPSVM, or even the Greek original in its degenerate form: *gnotos solidos* (and similar bastardized variants of the Greek γνωθί σεαυτόν). A twelfth-century abbot declares that he inscribed the Greek version on the southern porch of the restored monastery of Korvei, and in the Seba-

stian's chapel at Tauberbischofsheim we find the mediaeval representation of a young man with the Greek bastardized words. See W. S. Heckscher,[205] p. 220, to be complemented by K. Preisendanz, "Gnotos solidos,"[385] pp. 92ff., and R. Bischoff,[55] *passim*. Be it added that this aphorism experiences a strong revival in the later Middle Ages; e. g. *Gesta Romanorum, XXX,* where we find the detailed description of a classical *trionfo* in which the conqueror is accompanied by a slave who, as the conqueror beats him, repeats the phrase NOSCE TE IPSVM; ed. Oesterley,[179] pp. 328f.

145 With the subtitle *In a Letter to the Author of Sir Charles Grandison,*[524] London, 1759, soon to be followed by a German tr. which vastly helped to release the *Sturm und Drang* movement in Germany. See Ernst Cassirer,[89] esp. pp. 318ff., who shows that the use of "genius" was "reserved for the productive, formative, creative forces" for the first time by Shaftesbury. Artistic genius presupposes the *l'art pour l'art* concept, which in turn assumes that the work of art produced by a genius cannot and must not serve any useful ends. "Even as late as the seventeenth century, Nicolaus Poussin's statement that the end of art is delectation was quite a revolutionary one." E. Panofsky, "Meaning in the Visual Arts,"[359] p. 45. An important stage has been reached with the assertion that only the artist can judge the work of art; this we first meet with, I believe, in the late sixteenth century when Justus Julius Scaliger maintains: "de Poesi debet judicare Poeta, non ut Lipsius qui voluit judicare de Seneca Tragico, sed perperam," *Scaligerana,*[421] s. v. "poesi," p. 318. See also Note 142 above.

Interestingly enough, the sociological type of artist who may claim the sobriquet "genius" replaces earlier similarly "useless" types of society, the hero, the sage, the saint, the *cortegiano,* the gentleman, the *honnête homme*; for this concept in general, see Herbert Dieckmann,[124] p. 151 and *passim*. Edgar Zilsel has convincingly demonstrated that the modern use of "genius" designating a person extraordinarily

gifted does not come into currency before the eighteenth century; Bibliogr.,[529] esp. pp. 296–99.

146 For Jonathan Richardson's reference to Rembrandt as "vrai génie," cf. Seymour Slive,[449] p. 152. We might cite Vincent van Gogh as typical of this attitude when he based his admiration for Rembrandt and his fellow painters in the seventeenth century on the fact that "they painted things just as they are, apparently without intellectual intervention"; cf. Carl Nordenfalk,[341] p. 136. In 1817 a fictitious Rembrandt was made to speak for "Day-Light," advocating a "bold and direct approach to Nature itself," inveighing against "the IN-DOOR GLOOM of our OLD PICTURES," praising the new approach for "its originality"; see Henry Richter,[397] esp. p. 12. For Shakespeare, revaluation in the light of the concept of creation after nature "without intellectual intervention" seems to occur at a very early point: in the year of the poet's death, when Francis Beaumont wrote the following verse (discovered in 1921):

Heere I would let slippe,
(If I had any in me) schollershippe.
And from all Learning keepe these lines as cleere
As Shakespeare's best are, which our heirs shall heare
Preachers apte to their auditors to showe
How farr sometimes immortal man may goe
By the dimme light of nature.

See Hugo Wolf,[519] p. 81.

147 The later occasion was in 1677; see Edgar Zilsel,[529] p. 146.

148 Houbraken mentions the large family portrait in which Rembrandt insisted on commemorating his dead pet monkey, which canvas, when the portrait group had been rejected, he used as a partition in his studio; see Hofstede de Groot,[229] No. 933a on p. 389. Could it be that the monkey in the lower right-hand corner of the first great group portrait in the North,

Holbein's "Thomas More and His Family" (1526/27), had been projected in the Rembrandt legend? Erasmus, the first owner of Holbein's preparatory sketch (Basel, Museum), referred to the monkey in his *Colloquies*.[140] This monkey was undoubtedly a member of the Morus ménage and probably the pet of Alice, Morus' second wife; see also Otto Benesch,[46] p. 66. Needless to say, Rembrandt was in mores, appearance, and social bearing a veritable Proteus. In the humanistic phase especially (1632–38), he was wavering between the elegance of the cavalier and the dignity of the humanist; see H. Kauffmann,[267] pp. 46ff.

The earliest "long-haired musician" on record may have been a member of the Papal Choir under Innocent VIII (1484–92) who sang in the Sistine Chapel; it was stipulated that he "shall not wear his hair down to the neck"; cf. Edward E. Lowinsky,[292] p. 511. The most outstanding Dutch Baroque *bohémien* of this type was Claude Bernart, carillon player at Deventer (d. 1625). He scandalized the Church Council, which refused to employ him until he had had a proper haircut, and once employed he was a constant cause of offense. He gambled and drank in the "Valck," he engaged in fist fights with Mr. Matthijs the clockmaker, and his battles with his mother-in-law made it necessary for the city officials to intervene. Still worse, rather than play Psalms Bernart improvised on the organ. Yet, with one serious exception, he was not even in danger of losing his employment, because he was simply a first-rate artist whose "sweet song gave profound delight for many years"; see B. van den Sigtenhorst Meyer,[443] p. 92.

149 The tradition of the artist as primarily an imitator is classical: "Neque dubitari potest quin artis pars magna contineatur imitatione," Quintilian; see Gertrud Herzog-Hauser,[222] p. 133 and *passim*. For the problem of imitation in the Holland of the early seventeenth century, cf. R. Hoecker in his "Kommentar" to ed. and tr. of van Mander's *Grondt der Schilder-const*,[303] pp. 396f. G. I. Vossius devoted a whole treatise

to imitation [502a] and discussed its role in painting in his treatise *De Graphice* [502] §27. Franciscus Junius devoted the better part of Book I [262-64] to a thorough commentary on Quintilian and others. He sees in imitation a deep-seated human urge, "the proofe of which point could here most readily be drawne out of that busie eagernesse we do see in almost all young children, that follow the tender imaginations of their rude and unexercised conceits in making of babies and other images out of clay or wax, but that we thinke it better not to trouble our selves too much with the proofe of a thing which is cleare enough in itselfe, seeing every one may sufficiently informe himselfe concerning this point, who will but cast an eye upon the daily pastimes used among little ones" (I, i, § 4, p. 8). As I have indicated on p. 19, much speaks in favor of the assumption that Rembrandt, at the time of the "Anatomy," instructed young people in the imitation of the paintings of others. Also see Note 152 below.

150 "Pictus es ergo, o homo, et pictus a Domino Deo tuo"; St. Ambrosius,[7] VI, viii, 47, col. 276. Needless to say, this simile might be approached from opposite points of departure. In the Middle Ages it was employed to understand God and his operations; in the Renaissance it was used to ennoble the *artifex*; and ultimately it contributed to the concept of the divinely inspired artist. For the mediaeval (scholastic) reminiscences bearing on this point in Federigo Zuccaro's *L'Idea* [532] (1607) see E. Panofsky, *"Idea,"* [352] p. 49, and Ital. tr. Bibliogr.,[353] pp. 63ff.

151 See E. Panofsky, *"Idea,"* [352] notes 86 and 92, Ital. tr.,[353] notes 20f. on p. 116.

152 For the operation of authority in mediaeval art and thought see E. Panofsky,[358] pp. 65ff. and *passim*. The theory of *imitatio* reached new heights in the writings of Rembrandt's contemporaries. G. I. Vossius, in his treatise [502a] devoted to *imitatio* in rhetoric and poetry, saw four chief kinds, ranging from "servilis" via "puerilis" to "virilis" and finally "ingenua"; the latter is the form in which the

model is adapted "jure nostro" (chap. iv, § 2, p. 14). Junius points out that art which had begun poorly could never have progressed "by a bare Imitation." He too speaks of "servile Imitation" as the lowest form, being both "unprofitable and hurtfull"; I, iii, § 2, p. 29. Not only must the highest kind of *imitatio* be selective, but the painter should also observe his own natural limitations: "It is then required that we should not onely bend our naturall desire of Imitation towardes the best things, but that we should likewise study to understand wherein the excellency of the same things doth consist: the which having diligently performed, we shall by the same meanes perceive how necessary it is that we should duly examine our owne abilitie and strength . . ." ". . . there is in us a certaine unablenesse of imitating such things as do not very well agree with our naturall disposition: for every one hath within his own brest a certaine law of nature, the which he may not neglect . . ." *ibidem*, § 7, pp. 36f. The following passage seems to me to express Rembrandt's attitude best of all; it occurs only in the Dutch version[264] (I, iii, § 6, p. 29): "'t Staet yeder een vry den eenen ofte den anderen Konstenaer . . . hooghe te verheffen: wat my belanght, die Konstenaers spannen . . . de kroon . . ., de welcke d'oude Konst . . . naerstighlick oeffenen, om haere Schildereyen door dit middel met het aengenaeme vermaeck van een ongelijcke gelijckheyt [unequal equality] behendighlick te vervullen." Also see Note 171 below.

153 Guido da Vigevano, *Haec est anothomia,*[199] Plates I, fig. ii, and II, fig. vii (for the canopied figure of the "Homo nudus vivus," cf. I, i). As in the tombs of the time, some of Guido's figures must be understood as being prone and upright at the same time. Skeletons and upright corpses (often with the abdominal incision necessary to remove the viscera before readying the body for embalming, autopsying, etc.) had been a more or less familiar sight in ecclesiastical sculpture. In the second half of the fourteenth century we get,

for the first time, skeletons and decaying corpses on tombs (possibly in awareness of the appearance of the human corpse in actual autopsies?) purporting to be portrayals of the deceased; see Rudolf Helm,[216] pp. 67f. For a thirteenth-century "Adam's Tomb," which combines with anatomical understanding an appreciation of the phenomena of decay, see *ibidem*, Plate I, fig. 1, and p. 18. See also Note 112 above and pp. 85ff.

154 The title of the first chapter is: "Le premier chapitre du corps de lomme et de ses parties de quoy la saincte escripture fait mencion." This tr. was made for Charles V of France, and there is no reason why the manuscript of the fourteenth century would already have been illustrated. Another similar woodcut is found in the edition Westminster, 1495 (?)[38] (sign. o o. iij *verso*), in which the woodcut also appears at the head of Book V.

155 Additional influence, at least in Italy, may have come from deathbed scenes, such as the relief by Andrea Verrocchio (Pl. XIX-24), which, in turn, is an imitation of the Roman sarcophagus relief showing the "Death of Meleager." This has been demonstrated by Frida Schottmüller,[431] *passim*. Similarly we might think of the drawing after Pollajuolo in the Wallace Collection representing the "Death of a Nude Giant Attended by Ten Lamenting Figures," a scene that, as E. Panofsky[356] (p. 96) has shown, should be titled "Lamentation of Pallas." Next to such scenes of secular laments we ought to consider Christian representations of the animation of Adam. Here we encounter an important *dramatis persona,* needed for the anatomies and lacking in the secular laments, viz. the figure of the Lord, who appears touching the head of Adam, often shown as a prone figure diagonally placed; cf., for example, the "Genesis Scene" produced in the Carolingian scriptorium of St. Martin at Tours (Codex British Museum, Add. 10546, fol. 5 *verso*) reproduced by Kurt Weitzmann,[511] who has demonstrated that this particular scene is originally a classical motif: Prometheus

animating the first Man; cf. figs. 19 and 22 and pp. 115ff. The use of an animation motif for an anatomical scene would represent what Aby Warburg has called the case of an "energetic inversion"; "aus der *Tötung* wird *Heilung* und aus dem *Schrecken, Sieg*"; see the résumé of Aby Warburg's theory by Fritz Saxl,[420] p. 21.

In summing up we might say with some justification that Renaissance deathbed as well as anatomical table corresponds to the Roman *lectus funebris,* the bystanders to the classical *praeficae* (i.e. the professional mourners), and the male chief mourner or the surgeon-master to the *pollinctor* (who bathes, anoints, and embalms the corpse); and that the *pugillares* (i.e. tablets with the last will and testament of the deceased) may, by some stretch of imagination, be considered the ancestors of the anatomical books still found in Rembrandt's "Anatomy"; see Note 119 above for another possible source of the anatomical book still life. For the *lectus funebris* and its conventional crew see Wolfgang Helbig,[214] pp. 30f. (No. 1192.)

156 J. Playfair McMurrich made the interesting observation that in illustrations of Mundinus' *Anothomia* (which, after all, was of such long-lasting influence on the conduct of academic anatomies) the professor will invariably be shown seated in his cathedra; Bibliogr.,[297] p. 18; cf., for example, the Ketham and Berengario da Carpi woodcuts (Figs. 7 and 5) of 1493 and 1535 respectively. See also Notes 61 and 54 above and the text (pp. 117f.) to Note 225 below.

157 For little St. Simon of Trent (martyred in 1475) cf. the Italian engraving, probably Florentine, of about 1475–85 (see Pl. XX–26; Arthur M. Hind,[224] Plate 74). The tradition of the Jewish torturer goes back in Christian art to the early Middle Ages: in the eleventh century Jewish floggers and tormentors began to take the place of Roman soldiers in the scenes of the Flagellation of Christ. In the Middle Ages Jews, like other underprivileged minorities, were often forced to act as executioners and torturers. Instances are documented for the early and high Middle Ages in the Byzantine Empire, Corfu, Sicily, Spain, and England; see Cecil Roth,[409] p. 102. It is readily seen how from this compulsion the accusation of ritual murders could arise and how innocent persons were thereby drawn into a self-renewed vicious spiral of suspicion, defamation, persecution. For the influence of primitive magic dissections, cannibalism, and plain cruelty as indispensable stages antecedent to surgical advance, cf. Hofschlager,[226] *passim.* It has recently been pointed out that the earliest anatomically correct representation of the human body (in Northern Renaissance art) may well be the "Bad Thief" in the panel by the Master of Flémalle (in the Städelsche Kunstinstitut); see Robert Herrlinger,[221] pp. 283–88.

158 For masses *contra injustos judices* see E. Panofsky,[361] I, p. 271 and note 1.

159 Ed. Hermann Oesterley,[179] XXIX (28), pp. 327f.

The possible relationship between the commissioning of David's Justice Picture and actual events of as early as 1488 (i.e. ten years before the final execution) has been discussed by W.H. James Weale,[509] p. 8. The painting was commissioned a year before, in 1487, and finished in 1498. In general, see Lederle,[282] pp. 42–45, who shows that the Cambyses story was pre-eminently a story of the Lowlands (p. 44), and A. Janssens de Bisthoven and R.A. Parmentier,[254] No. 5, pp. 12–19, Plates XXVI–LI, where the panels are listed *s.t.* "Le Jugement de Cambyse," without reference to the *Gesta Romanorum* (bibliography meager).

160 Cologne, Utrecht, Hasselt, Gouda, and (in Dutch) Zwolle (1484),[180] Hasselt; only one South German and one French incunabulum are known to have been published in this period; see E.P. Goldschmidt,[192] p. 10. Also see Note 161 below.

161 This edition[180] has eight woodcuts of very high quality, of which all but one are full-page blocks (each one containing from five to seven different scenes) illustrating chaps. xvii,

xviii, xx, lxxx, cxxx, cxc; that of chap. xlv is smaller, occupying about one fourth of the page. I am planning to publish these woodcuts later.

[162] The skin, placed on the Judge's seat, is interpreted as signifying Christ's Passion, for Christ offered up not only his skin but also his life for us, "in sede crucis"; ed. Oesterley,[179] p. 328. We have previously noted that the *tabula anatomica* on which the criminal was exposed to the people was placed on the site of the altar; see Note 28 above.

The story occurs elsewhere, i.e. outside the *Gesta,* before the year of completion of Gerard David's painting, 1498, in a number of collections and *exempla* which I quote after Oesterley[179] (p. 717):

> 1477: Jacob Cessolis, *Das buoch menschlicher sitten;*
> 1480: *Dialogus creaturarum;*
> 1480: *Scala celi;*
> 1486: Johannes Herolt, *Promptuarium exemplorum;*
> 1489: Johannes Gallensis, *Communiloquium;*

and in the next two centuries in at least twenty-six collections.

[163] Several possibilities suggest that Rembrandt may have been familiar with David's composition, directly (i.e. through a literal copy, as indicated in our text) or indirectly. As to the latter possibility, there exist Cambyses Justice medallions of the mid-sixteenth century, which, however, go back explicitly to the classical source, as shown by the inscription (in German) on the reverse; for reproductions (not of the flaying scene) see Guido Kisch,[272] pp. 105–15 and fig. 8, and Edward Gans, Guido Kisch,[170] pp. 121–25; *ibidem* also a reproduction of Rubens' Justice Panel in the Metropolitan Museum of Art. Dr. J. Bruyn, Utrecht University, draws my attention to a number of stained-glass windows of the late sixteenth century that treat of the Cambyses Judgment in some detail, of which pieces are preserved in the Rijksmuseum, Amsterdam (acq. 193; ascribed to Dirck Vellert) and in the Westfriesch Museum (Leeuwarden; Cat. No. 37). The possibility of a print cannot be ruled out; Rubens' original painting was finished ten years before Rembrandt's "Anatomy of Dr. Tulp," in 1622 (payments recorded) or perhaps a little earlier. It was installed at that time in the Town Hall at Bruges; it was lost in 1695, but the composition at least seems to be preserved in a copy by Remoldus Eynhoudts (1613–79/80), which may have served as a model for the copyist of the canvas in the Metropolitan Museum. (Pl. XXIII-29.) I am indebted to the kindness of Miss Margaretta M. Salinger (Dept. of Paintings, The Metropolitan Museum of Art) for advice and for permission to use the above information. Rubens visited Holland (The Hague) last in 1631; that his influence on the Dutch North was particularly strong up to then has been shown by J. G. van Gelder,[175] *passim.*

Some kind of representation of the "Judgments of Zeleuci [of Locri] and Cambyses" graced the walls of the anatomical theater at Leiden (1620ff.)—a print, a drawing, a painting, we do not know which; see J. A. J. Barge,[28] No. 16 on p. 44. The Zeleucus story (also found in the *Gesta Romanorum*) glorifies the Just Judge who punishes not only his son but also himself most cruelly; this theme had been used by Holbein, and later it occurs in the City Hall at Amsterdam; see Lederle,[282] pp. 48ff. The Cambyses theme was extremely popular for a long time. There existed, of course, many totally different renderings of it in art. These may be quite independent of David's rendering; among this latter category we find, for example, J. Uytewael's manneristic approach in his *Thronvs Iustitiae*[482] of 1607, which, in an engraving of W. Swanenburgh (Plate VI), shows the inthronization of the son in the foreground while the heroic father is shown against a kind of martyr mast to which his wrists are attached. The (unpaginated) text to *Tabvla Sexta* discusses in detail, in about a page and a half, the historical as well as the emblematic aspects of the

161

case. For other examples—especially the curious rendering of (Ni) Claes van der Heck (d. 1652) for the City Hall of Alkmaar (1616–20), in which the flaying occurs in a tent in the market square (as a background scene)—cf. Karl Simon,[444] pp. 64f. and fig. 10. One of the earliest known works by Rembrandt is a Justice Scene; see *Rembrandt Tentoonstelling*,[394] No. 2.

164 *S.t.* [Charel van Mander, Schilder] *Het Leven*[302] etc.; the date of this, the all-important third book, is *not* 1604, as is commonly stated (probably on the authority of Julius von Schlosser,[425] p. 332), but 1603.

165 Cf. Hans Tietze,[471] pp. 40 and 41, and, for the documentation, Heinrich Alfred Schmid,[427] pp. 205f. See also Hulda Heckscher,[204a] p. 2.

166 "t proportie boeck van Albert Durer, houtsnee,"[128] is listed in Rembrandt's Inventory of July 25, 1656; cf. C. Hofstede de Groot,[228] No. 169 (273), p. 240. Dürer's woodcut of the triumph of Maximilian was published as a folding plate in Willibald Pirckheimer's *Theatrum virtutis*[379a] (Nuremberg, 1606), and, as J.G. van Gelder has shown,[177a] the fame of Lucas van Leyden, antedating even the efforts of Carel van Mander, was still flourishing 1660–71 in the faithful copies of the amateur artist Jan de Bisschop (Episcopius, 1628–71). Systematic research on the tradition that influenced Rembrandt is supposedly of a relatively recent date, beginning, it is asserted, with Eugène Müntz,[327] 1892. C. Hofstede de Groot ("Entlehnungen Rembrandts"),[227] 1894, seems to have been the first (but see below) to have paid attention to the diversity of Rembrandt borrowings, including those from the art of the Northern Renaissance (Dürer, van Heemskerck, Hans Sebald Beham). Rembrandt's debt to this or that motif had been recognized before in individual examples. It seems, however, to have been forgotten that as early as 1854 some of the best and soundest comment on Rembrandt in the nineteenth century was published by Eduard Koloff: "Rembrandt's Leben und Werke nach neuen Actenstücken und Gesichts-

punkten geschildert."[274] We find on p. 508 the following pertinent observations:

Rembrandt repräsentiert ... die holländische Nationaltradition in der Kunst und stammt in gerader Linie von Lucas van Leyden ab. ... Rembrandt hatte die alten niederländischen Meister und ihre nahen Geistesverwandten, die Meister der altdeutschen Schule sehr sorgfältig studiert. Man merkt dies besonders in seinen Kupferstichen. Bei dem *Tod der Maria* schwebte ihm offenbar die Composition desselben Gegenstandes von Martin Schöngauer vor ... [und] Lucas van Leyden, dessen *Ausstellung Christi* auch Rembrandt bei seinem breiten *Ecce homo* zum Vorbilde genommen hat.

For Koloff's importance, see Wilhelm Waetzoldt,[506] pp. 95ff.

A selective résumé of the previous writings on the subject will be found in Jhr. J.L.A.A.M. van Rijckevorsel's *Rembrandt en de Traditie*.[399] (N.B. The "Anatomy of Dr. Tulp" is not discussed.) Also see Wilhelm R. Valentiner,[484] 1905, pt. II, "Anmerkungen zu Rembrandts Kunstbesitz," pp. 64–113.

167 There is, to my knowledge, no evidence that Rembrandt ever interfered with Northern drawings as he did with those by Italian masters; to name only one example of the latter procedure, a drawing by (or after) Gentile Bellini, now in the British Museum (Dept. of Prints and Drawings), cf. Popham-Pouncey,[381] No. 9 on p. 6. Needless to say, Northern drawings must have been scarce as they are now. The inventory of Rembrandt's *inboedel* of the year 1656 lists a great number of Northern Renaissance art works (a.o. the Jan van Eyck "Head of Christ"). We may be fairly certain that Rembrandt's truly astonishing collection was got together from more than a purely aesthetic collector's point of view. After all, in the late sixteenth and early seventeenth centuries the use of engravings by artists was taken for granted. Engravings as working tools belonged

as much to the ordinary equipment of the artist's studio as plaster casts (in Holland: the *anatomie-mannen*) and manikins (the so-called *leemannen* or *ledepoppen*). How dependent artists could become on this kind of apparatus becomes evident when we hear of one seventeenth-century instance of a devoted father's rushing a manikin to England with the advice to young Gerard Terborch to put it to good use ("een laet hem niet stille staen als Hij hijr gedan heeft"); cf. Arpad Weixlgärtner,[512] p. 65 and note 2. Roger de Piles, in his *Abrégé,*[379] has a chapter on the "usefulness and application of prints to the artists" (*ed. princeps,* 1699; for which see ed. 1776, II, ii, p. 368); and Hieronymus Cock published his series of topographic prints, the *Variae variarum regionum typografice adumbrationes,* with the significant subtitle "in publicam pictorum usum," Antwerp, 1558; see Rijckevorsel,[399] p. 2, note 3.

[168] See Otto Benesch,[45] pp. 285–304 (esp. p. 294) and figs. 9 and 10.

[169] See the detailed visual demonstration achieved by eleven comparative pairs of pictures illustrating astonishing agreements in parts and in the whole, found in the catalogue entitled *Herinnering;*[411] Dr. E. Panofsky kindly brought this publication to my notice. The panel formerly attributed to Jan Scorel (Pl. XXVI-33) is now ascribed to Maerten van Heemskerck in A. C. Esmeijer's and Simon H. Levi's *Catalogus,*[142] No. 83.

[170] See Koloff's article[274] dealt with in Note 166 above; also Rijckevorsel,[399] p. 105 and figs. 114f. The head of the Christ of the early "Ecce homo!" derives from Guido Reni; for the late "Ecce homo!" p. 199 and figs. 225f. Mrs. Panofsky draws my attention to the important additional rendering (in turn influenced by Lucas van Leyden's engraving and influential on Rembrandt) of the theme in Callot's engraving (Fig. 16). But note Müntz,[328] Catalogue No. 235 (Vol. II), who points out the relationship suggested here and adds Nicolaes de Bruyn's "Ecce homo!" (1618); for figs. and text, *ibidem,* pp. 107f.

Rembrandt's ownership of Lucas van Leyden's prints in "saubersten Abdrucken" is dealt with by Seymour Slive,[449] note 2 on p. 92. For the iconography of Rembrandt's "Ecce homo!" which, by rights, ought to be called an "Ostentatio Christi," see Erwin Panofsky,[363a] p. 108 and Note 35. Also see Franz Dülberg's[127] detailed discussion of Rembrandt's debt to Lucas van Leyden, pp. 110–15, with further bibliography.

[171] Quintilian, *Institutio,* X, ii, 7; see Note 152 above. On the theory of imitation in the Renaissance see William G. Crane,[110] chap. vi, pp. 80–96. For the quotation from Junius,[263] cf. I, iii, §§ 7 and 8.

[172] E. Panofsky,[354] pp. 193–217. For Vondel's poem,[500] cf. pp. 380 f. and note 1 on p. 34.

[173] See Notes 14, 26, 45, 59 above and Chap. III, *passim.*

[174] See B. W. Th. Nuyens,[343] pp. 23f.; also text to Note 26 above (p. 31), which incidentally shows that anatomists and *Reederijkers* shared their quarters.

[175] J. G. van Gelder[176] offers the engaging hypothesis that the boy Rembrandt may have visited the private collection of the head of his Grammar School, Theodorus Schrevelius (Barlaeus' friend!); p. 1 (273) and note 2.

[176] For Swanenburgh's engraving after J. C. Woudanus' slightly earlier drawing, see Julius S. Held,[215] figs. 15 and 20 and text pp. 246–65 *passim,* with further literature, note 127 on p. 260. For a most thorough investigation of anatomical theaters at Rembrandt's disposal, see pp. 260ff. For van Regteren Altena's restricting arguments see *Rembrandt Tentoonstelling,*[393a] No. 225, p. 164.

It seems to be difficult to determine to what extent in the seventeenth century, as Held suggests, "these symbols had lost their fateful meaning." I believe I have adduced documentation to the opposite effect. Erasmus Francisci, writing in the latter part of the seventeenth century, took it for granted that anatomical theaters were being haunted by the spirits of the dissected criminals, whom he handsomely describes as "die erscheinende Malefiz-Person"; Bibliogr.,[157] chap. lxxiii, pp. 723–80, 974f., and *passim*. Jacobus Balde, S. J.,[22] in his panegyric of Vesalius' "statues" (1643) (by which he means the skeletons set up with artful skill, which he prefers to all the noble statuary that can be admired in Rome), was very much aware of associations between present and hereafter roused by the contemplation of anatomies—"Mutatio quanta!"—and his admiration was kindled because the cadavers under investigation stress the fugitive quality of life. Balde, we might say, saw Vesalius' achievement in the light of Lucian's *Dialogues of the Dead;* cf. W. S. Heckscher,[206] pp. 295ff. For Balde's *Medizinische Satyren,*[23] see Note 191 below.

177 Ep. ad Rom.[53] vi:23. See Note 206 below.

178 In one respect the *theatra anatomica* differed from the privately owned *Kunst- und Wunderkammern:* for the latter one needed letters of introduction, while the former could be seen for an admission fee. Jan Wagenaar[508] (chap. "De St. Antonies of Nieuwe Waag," § 3, p. 56) describes the situation in Amsterdam's permanent anatomical theater as follows: "Deze byde vertrekken [viz. the theater proper and the guild room] zyn, den meesten tyd van 't Jaar voor een ieder te zien, wanneer men slegts twee stuivers voor den opgang betaald." Also see Note 191 below.

179 An anonymous English guide to the anatomical theater at Leiden, printed by Jacobus Voorn[501] in 1683, lists four skins as follows: (i) "the Skin of a Man Tann'd" (p. 4, No. 43); (ii) "The Skin of a Man dressed as Parchment" (p. 5, No. 63); (iii) "the Skin of a childe when first born" (p. 5, No. 97); (iv) "The Skin of a Molacca woman aboue 150 Years old . . ." (p. 7, No. 4). The taxidermist's dream, it seems, was realized at Cassel, where one could see: "Zwo ausgestopfte Menschen-Häute, davon der eine ein Soldat, der so wohl und natürlich gemacht ist, und mit seinen Haaren, Augen, und allem sich so ähnlich scheinet, daß ihn seine Officiers, von denen er

desertirt, nach der Hand gleich erkannt haben"; Z. C. von Uffenbach,[481] November 14, 1709, I, p. 13.

Calewaart's skin is listed among the twenty-seven curiosities of the *Theatrum Anatomicum* of Amsterdam; see E. H. M. Thijssen,[468] p. 21, No. 4: "een huijt van een misdader genaemt Gielis Calewaart van Haarlem gevilt [i. e. flayed] op de Anthonis Waag." "Suster Luijt's" skin, it seems, was particularly holy to the guild members because it reminded them of Amsterdam's first public dissection (1550), on the occasion of which they got their nickname "menschenvilders," "flayers of human beings"; see Monnikhoff[325] (1736) and Thijssen,[468] p. 13.

For the confinement of osteology to the actual *auditorium medicum* of the university of Leiden see J. A. J. Barge,[28] pp. 15f.

Animated skeletons became a fashion through Vesalius' *Fabrica* illustrations; for a "Tödlein-schrank" made of ebony and containing in miniature an ivory replica of Vesalius' skeleton meditating over a skull, see Julius Schlosser,[424] p. 57 and fig. 39 on p. 58. The skeletons arranged to enact the Fall of Man, as we find them in the Leiden theater, were copied in Copenhagen (1643); see Gottfried Richter,[396] p. 46 and fig. 8 b. The Swiss anatomist Caspar Bauhinus,[41] in imitation of the Vesalius tradition, has a weeping (skeleton) gravedigger, a melancholy Death leaning on his scythe, contemplating an hourglass, and equipped with bow and arrow; figures on pp. 1287ff.

180 For the copy of Michelangelo's "Last Judgment" mentioned and for the "Judgment of Cambyses," which are listed in the handwritten inventory of Leiden (1620–28), see Barge,[28] pp. 43f. That Rembrandt was familiar with the art collection in the theater is highly probable; its items were meant to be seen, and they were freshly exhibited and catalogued in the decade just preceding his move away from Leiden to Amsterdam. Nevertheless it is probable that certain symbolical information on the human skin may have reached Rembrandt

simultaneously via the anatomical atlases of the sixteenth century. The influence of Michelangelo's concept has been great; Rubens undoubtedly inserted it in his otherwise David-inspired "Justice Panel"; see Note 163 above. The skin with its miserable human features is, we may say, ubiquitous. For example, Juan de Valverde's *Historia,*[485] 1556 (with many following editions in Spanish, Italian, Latin, Dutch), which excels in thefts from Vesalius, inherits from Michelangelo the "Muscle Man Holding His Skin" (Pl. XXXV-42); cf., for a reproduction, A.W. Meyer and Sheldon K. Wirt, fig. 1 on p. 669. See also Lola L. Szladits,[464] pp. 420–27, with excellent reproductions of skinned muscle men; also W.S. Heckscher,[209] pp. 19f.

It is astonishing to find how long the moral-didactic interpretation of the flayed skin will persist, even in civilized circles. Readers of William Roughead's delightful *Murderer's Companion,*[412] p. 120, will recall that the great Scottish criminal William Burke was publicly anatomized, his carcase thereafter flayed, his hide tanned and sold (Mr. Roughead inherited a piece from his father), and his skeleton, by order of Court, preserved in the Anatomical Museum of Edinburgh University, "where it remained as a memorial of his infamy even unto this day." Burke's crime had been the murder of sixteen persons whose bodies he sold, through the agency of an intermediary, to the anatomy of Dr. Knox in Edinburgh:

> ... Burke's the butcher,
> Hare's the thief,
> Knox the boy that buys the beef ...

Burke met his end—he was executed before 25,000 witnesses, among them Sir Walter Scott—in 1829. The above jingle expresses the *vox populi,* which also shouted, according to the *Times*[289] of February 2, 1829: "Burke him, Burke him," giving rise to a new verb in the English language; see *A New English Dictionary,*[335] *s.v.* "Burke." For a similar German neologism of the seventeenth century see

Note 198 below. Some curious material on the medicinal-therapeutic properties attributed to the human skin, especially for spastic afflictions, will be found in David Murray's *Museums,*[334] pp. 57f.

[181] For Barlaeus' poem in its entirety see pp. 112f. The account of the skinned criminal is found in Erasmus F. Francisci [von Finx],[157] *Der höllische Proteus,* pp. 773f.

[182] This is the so-called "spiegelnde Strafe," for which concept see Wilhelm Wundt,[523] pp. 448f.

The contrapuntal character of such penal amputations led to elaborate catalogues in the Middle Ages, not only in fiction but also in law and moral writings. The following instances may serve as an illustration of what I would call the protoanatomical tradition:

(i) In the *Carmina Burana,*[87] No. 117, stanza 1, p. 192, the punishment of the mendacious tongue assumes suspiciously realistic forms:

> Lingua mendax et dolosa,
> Lingua procax, venenosa,
> Lingua digna detruncari
> Et in igne concremari ...

(ii) The legal status of the punishment of the youth who has willfully and wrongfully abandoned his God-ordained estate, although still fictitious, lies on the surface in Wernherr der Gartenaere's Middle High German epic, *Meier Helmbrecht.*[513] The peasant son, turned highway robber in the guise of a knight errant, is in the end sent home in a horribly dismembered state. Where classical antiquity and the Renaissance might have stressed the tragic fate of the misguided youth, the epic ends with expressions of gratified "I told you so's."

(iii) Among actual legal cases, the well-known antecedents of Shakespeare's Shylock have familiarized the reader with the "pound of flesh" (see Note 177 above and text) as an epic-dramatic motif. We hear, to name only one typical example, of actual amputation of the foot of a debtor who fails to pay his debt within the usual ten days; see, for example,

Anna Toole Sheedy,[438] pp. 102f. For the similar amputations demanded by Old Irish Law (*ca.* 697ff.) see John T. McNeill,[298] etc., p.136.

(iv) *Ca.* 1376 we find a graphic representation of the just and self-inflicted punishment of the sinful Pope who has risen through a pact with Satan to his high office; Codex Munich, Staatsbibliothek, Germ. 5, fol. 196 *verso;* reprod. Hans Fehr,[152] p.105 and fig.131.

(v) It is perhaps astonishing to find that even in theological allegory the principle of the *spiegelnde Strafe* was taken for granted. See Pierre Bersuire, *Dictionarium*[50] (composed in the 1340's), *s.v.* "Amputare" (pt. I, p.162), where we find the following argument:

Amputatio meritoria
damnatoria
afflictatoria, etc.

with the following specifications:

Vnde quidam habent linguam amputatam, in quantum carent recta locutione, quidam aurem, quia carent obedientia & auditione, quidam humerum [sic], quia carent fortitudine & patientia sustentativa, quidam caput, quia carent praedicatione, & spiritali filiorum productione, quidam manus, quia carent omni bona operatione.

(vi) According to a decree passed by the Parliament of Paris (1647), blaspheming of God, the Virgin Mary, or the Saints was punished by cutting off the lips and piercing the tongue; cf. Preserved Smith,[450] p.501.

183 Cf. the careful observations concerning the circumstances of such suspicions in the sixteenth century by M.Roth,[410] "Anhang," section ix, pp.473–85. Nevertheless, besides the documented evidence there is the emotional and rational response with regard to the public anatomies of criminals, which at all times were regarded as the ultimate form of punishment of the criminal; cf. the remarks by Johann Neubig[23] (1833), pt. II, pp.67f., who repeats the assertion that Vesalius had gone on a pilgrimage to Jerusalem to atone for vivisection:

er hatte viele Verfolgungen auszustehen, wozu auch seine Reise nach Jerusalem gehört, um die Sünde abzubüssen, als ob er einen noch nicht ganz Verstorbenen geöffnet hätte, der noch einige Zeichen des Lebens bei der Sektion gegeben habe.

Vesalius died on the way home. This explanation for the reason of his pilgrimage to Jerusalem seems still to be accepted; cf. George Sarton,[419] pp.131–37, and C.Donald O'Malley,[345] pp.138–44.

Vesalius devoted the last chapter of the *Fabrica,*[490] VII, xix, to a discussion of vivisection (applied, of course, to animals)—"De vivorum sectione nonnulla," pp.818–24—and illustrated it, p.882, with the woodcut of a living pig strapped to the anatomical table (Fig.8). Cf. Benjamin Farrington,[150] "The Last Chapter." For such an animal vivisection see also the titlepage of the Giunta ed. of Galen's *opera,*[166] which shows Galen (with a top hat) at work with the great anatomists of Antiquity behind the *tabula;* reprod. on the cover of Charles Singer's ed. of Galen, *On Anatomical Procedures*[163a] (1956). Book XIIII of the fifteen books constituting Realdo Colombo's *De re anatomica*[102] is also devoted to *Viva Sectio;* the fourteenth book is actually the last of the treatise (pp.256–61) inasmuch as Book XV is nothing but a letter or tract appended to the work.

There was conducted in London in 1631 an anatomy that came close to vindictive dissection: we read in Helkiah Crooke's work[112] (by either Thomas or Richard Cotes, the printer of this work) how, not without gratification, he saw dissected "a cruell Wretch, who had murthered the Son of one Master *Scot* a Chyrurgian of good note in this City." He described the wretch's appearance in the greatest detail, concluding that "Almighty God doth sometime set his brand and marke vpon wicked men"; the flavor of just retribution is certainly present (2 unpaginated leaves, after p.1012).

184 See A. W. Meyer and S. K. Wirth,[318] p.683, fig. 7c. Valverde's dead anatomizing

the dead is a clever combination of figures one and two of Book Six of Vesalius' *Fabrica,*[490] pp. 698 and 699.

The tradition of Death who has himself died can be traced back to the early *Danses macabres,* where he is shown as a prone skeleton sadly pointing at the crown that rolls away in the grass; see Guyot Marchant's woodcut[307] (1492) (Fig. 21).

[185] See Ludwig Edelstein,[132] p. 552 and note 13. See also Note 183 above. The dogmatists among the sects of the Greek physician-philosophers favored vivisection, which, as we know, was practiced from the early third century B.C. until the first century A.D. For the late classical and patristic sources cf. Drabkin,[126] note 4 on p. 339; for further bibliography of L. Edelstein's special studies, cf. Drabkin, note 3 on p. 338. Also see, for a quotation from Celsus, Note 204 below. See Pl. XII-15.

[186] See pp. 63f. Cf. H. W. Janson,[253] pp. 361f. and fig. 30. For the association of ceremonial anatomies with the idea of triumph of the anatomist over the cadaver, see pp. 117ff. and Note 230 below.

In Gerard David's "Notabile de judicibus malis" (cf. Note 159 above) the unjust judge's fate, torture by flaying, is hinted at in the first panel (being the "Arrest of the Unjust Judge") by a medallion that shows the flaying of Marsyas; see A. Janssens de Bisthoven and R. A. Parmentier,[254] p. 14 and Plate XXI. In the "Justice Medal," mentioned in Note 163 above, the figures in attendance on the emperor are characterized by their conical hats as Jews.

[187] See Note 186 above and Notes following.

[188] *Cursor mundi,*[113] lines 21, 418ff., III, pp. 1227ff. The Jew's victim is a Christian goldsmith who is saved when Helena decrees that the Jew may take his flesh but not his blood. In view of the mediaeval "spiegelnde Strafen" (cf. Note 182 above) such demands must have appeared perfectly reasonable to a fourteenth-century audience; much less so to one of the late sixteenth and early seventeenth. Then martyrdoms, ritual murders, and justice pieces,

as well as the annual formal anatomies, suggested penal anatomies as a more up-to-date course of action.

[189] See Cecil Roth,[409] pp. 140ff. and esp. 143; also Frank Marcham,[306] quoting Gabriel Harvey's effusion, and M. Steinschneider,[455] No. 1315, on p. 155.

[190] *The Works of Thomas Nashe,*[336] II, pp. 304ff.

[191] Cf. Jakob Balde's *Medizinische Satyren,*[23] I, pp. 118–29. It seems to me that Balde had in mind two fundamentally different kinds of representations: the cabinets of rarities and the anatomical museums, i. e. the *theatra anatomica* outside the anatomical winter season.

(i) The cabinets of rarities are perhaps best represented by Athanasius Kircher's Musaeum in Rome (dismembered, alas, but in some of its parts still in existence), which, in the frontispiece of the catalogue published at Amsterdam, 1678,[271] shows obelisks and a skeleton and which, like so many other *Wunderkammern* of the age, contained practically all the items enumerated by Balde; see Julius von Schlosser,[424] fig. 88 and text *passim.* Readers may be more familiar with Sir Thomas Browne's charming *Musaeum clausum*[70] (originally published in 1684 but composed considerably earlier); his prototype may have been the Tradescant catalogue of the *Museum Tradecantinum*[472] (1656) or the extremely handsome *Museum Wormianum*[521] of Ole Worm, an author who was intimate with Tulp and whose catalogue of his Danish cabinet appeared at Leiden one year after its author's death (1655). Miss Barbara J. Balsiger is working at an analytical bibliography of the several hundred *Kunst- und Wunderkammern* of the sixteenth and seventeenth centuries that are known to us through printed catalogues.

(ii) The other type of museum that Balde had in mind is represented by the musaeal *theatra anatomica.* (See also Note 176 above.) Balde shows himself a careful reader of Vesalius' Preface to the *Fabrica;* undoubtedly he knew the frontispiece, which shows the ceremonial-practical anatomy underneath the animated skeleton; undoubtedly he was aware of the great beauty of the Vesalian figures, whose landscape backgrounds, as has been shown, can be conjoined into one continuous frieze while some of the musclemen strike poses clearly derived from classical statuary.

Representations of such musaeal *theatra* are unknown to me, except those incidental views that mostly stress the purely anatomical aspects and especially the actual anatomical dissections. (Figs. 2, 10; Pls. III-3, III-4, IX-12.) The term *theatrum* derived, I am sure, from the anatomical theaters *qua* museums; in this sense we should understand Federico Cesi, first president of the Accademia dei Lyncei, when he refers to botanical specimens as coming "ex amphitheatro nostro"; see Edward Rosen,[407] pp. 42 f. Oddly enough, the symbiosis of dissection room and museum was not felt to be a hindrance until well into the second half of the seventeenth century, when the first separate anatomical museum was installed at Amsterdam; its founder was Frederik Ruysch (1638–1731), who became professor of anatomy in 1665; his Cabinet, begun ab. 1691 and known as the *Museum anatomicum Ruyschianum,*[415] was sumptuously recorded (1701–16) but soon after dispersed when Ruysch sold his treasures to Czar Peter the Great (1717). For records of one of the most completely equipped collections of this kind, the one at Leiden (1622–28), see J. A. J. Barge,[28] *passim.* B. H. Stricker[459] deals *passim* with the correspondence of the Leiden anatomist and curator of the anatomical collection, Otto van Heurn, and with a Maecenas in Egypt who, among others (letter of October 8, 1621), is asked to supply for the *theatrum* "caput et genitalia hippopotami"; the correspondence contains also a very interesting report on the restoring, exhibiting, and labeling of an Egyptian mummy.

Ruysch's *Thesaurus Anatomicus,*[415] exquisitely illustrated, represents the height of the *theatra anatomica* as museums but at the same time announces a fundamental change, leading to the purely scientific collections of the eighteenth century. The best representative of the old anatomical museum, that of Leiden, which invited as it were the entire visible and tangible world to share in its spiritual and metaphysical experiences, is well recorded in J. A. J. Barge's publication[28] of its first inventory, 1620 (1628).

Balde's poems, although he was a Jesuit living at Munich, were known to his Dutch contemporaries; we can be certain that his praise of Vesalius' "statues" was known in the North. Caspar Barlaeus corroborates this point in a letter that he addressed to Balde (he had received a letter from Munich through the good services of Joachim von Sandrart), dated March 1644: "Restituisti nobis lyram neglectam" and "Sunt qui his in terris de poematum tuorum nova editione cogitant"; see Barlaeus, *Epistolarum liber,*[35] pt. 2, No. 467, pp. 910 ff. For Barlaeus' agreement with Balde's statements on man the God-ordained Microcosm, cf. the former's *Oratio de animae humanae admirandis* (1635): "Et quamquam in corporis humani fabrica totius Vniversi compendium artificiose exhiberi deprehenderim... totique naturae analogas partes, tamen..." [follows a discussion of the soul] (ed. Amsterdam,[34] pp. 98 f.). It is not to be wondered at that the wording, if not the precise idea, should have crossed the Channel, where we meet it in Sir Thomas Browne's *Religio Medici,* Sect. xxxvi: "In our study of anatomy there is a mass of mysterious philosophy, and such as reduced the very heathens to divinity"; to which he adds: "yet... in all the fabric of man... I find... no sign or instrument for the rational soul..." (1642/43, *ed. latina,* Leiden, 1644), ed. Simon Wilkin,[71] p. 378. Browne may have attended lectures by Barlaeus in Amsterdam. The word MICROCOSMOS (often spelt in Greek characters) appears with increasing frequency in the titles of anatomical works. Naturally only a small fraction of them are listed, more or less accidentally, in our Bibliogr.;[112, 155, 239] see also our Fig. 13. F. G. Zorzi's *De harmonia mundi totius* (1525), an important landmark in the microcosm-macrocosm discussion, was "considered important enough to deserve a special controversy by Mersenne"; cf. R. Allers,[5a] p. 397, note 221. The interrelation between macro- and microcosm is also expressed in the anatomical theater in the old University Building of Bologna, the Archiginnasio. It was erected after the designs of Antonio Levanti (architect as well as sculptor) in 1638. Its most prominent feature must have been the ceiling, whose strongly profiled caissons were adorned with large sculptures of the signs of the Zodiac, traditional governors of parts of man's body, surrounding the figure of Apollo. Although the theater was badly damaged in the Second World War, some of the sculptures are not beyond repair, and the whole is about to be restored to its original state (1958). See also Notes 59 and 101 above.

¹⁹² For an attempt to account for Hogarth's curious relapse into the magic and superstition of this kind of atonement ritual see Note 197 below. The attitude is anything but isolated in the eighteenth century; there are many examples of an unexpected triumph of the irrational over the most enlightened minds. I shall cite two:

(i) We learn that spatial voyages, amazingly rationally conceived in Renaissance and Baroque times, were frequently experienced in the eighteenth century as mere "raptures" and "trances"; for an excellent exposition of this problem, see Marjorie H. Nicholson,[339] pp. 201f.

(ii) In the year and month of the publication of the "Four Stages of Cruelty" Frederick II of Prussia (admired, at least temporarily, by Voltaire as an enlightened Prince) granted a thousand thalers to a Frau von Pfuhl to conduct alchemical experiments for him; see Johann Heinrich Gottlob von Justi,[265] p. 435.

¹⁹³ Illuminating is the commentary of John Nichols[231] (1808), p. 204: "... the wretch who has been executed seems to feel the subsequent operation." The wretch, Thomas Nero, had been one of the boys of St. Giles Charity School. The dissection took place in the quarters of the Barber-Surgeons Company (1540 ff.) on Monkwell Street, just inside the old London wall. The building was destroyed by enemy action in 1940; see William Thomson Hill,[223] p. 133. The skeletons left and right are those of two well-known criminals, a boxer and a robber, both executed. The finished prints were published in February 1751, first as engravings and later as woodcuts. The engravings sold for as little as one shilling apiece, ab. one fifth the price that Hogarth ordinarily charged for a "subscription-ticket." Later, when turned into woodcuts, they sold for even less. The reasons were sociological and therefore of great interest to us: the prints were issued cheaply "with the hope of in some degree correcting that barbarous treatment of animals, the very sight of which renders the Streets of our Metropolis so distressing to every feeling mind"; to this Hogarth adds: "If they have had this effect..., I am more proud of being their author, than I should be of having painted Raphael's Cartoons." Every stylistic means at the artist's disposal was summoned to put over this message: "The leading points in these as well as the two preceding Prints, were made as obvious as possible, in the hope that their tendency might be seen by men of the lowest rank. Neither minute accuracy of design, nor fine engraving, were deemed necessary; as the latter would render them too expensive for the persons to whom they were intended to be useful. And the fact is that the passions may be more forcibly expressed by a strong bold stroke, than by the most delicate engraving. To expressing them as I felt them, I have paid the utmost attention; and, as they were addressed to hard hearts, have rather preferred leaving them *hard,* and giving them the effect by a quick touch, to rendering them languid and feeble by fine strokes and soft engraving, which require more care and practice than can often be attained,

except by a man of a very quiet turn of mind
..." Bibliogr.,[232] p. 35. The use of technical
devices to express and evoke emotions through
an appeal to the human eye is badly in need of
investigation; to mind comes an anonymous
seventeenth-century treatise that, to express
revulsion from Cromwell's regime of blood,
was printed in red throughout; *The Bloody
Court*,[10] ... London, 1649.

In 1751 Hogarth published his well-known
print "Paul Before Felix," which, in his own
words, was "designed and etched in the ridiculous manner of Rembrant."

[194] James Townley (1714–78) was the author
of the farce *High Life Below Stairs*. He incurred
the wrath of the trustees of Christ's Hospital
when in 1752, in the presence of the bishop of
Salisbury and aided, it seems, by his friend
Garrick, he had his students perform Terence's
Eunuch. He collaborated with Hogarth on
other occasions; see *Dictionary of National Biography*,[125] LVII, pp. 101f.

[195] A brief note on John Freke will be found
in Bibliogr.[39] with a reproduction of a contemporary portrait bust at advanced age.

[196] For the illustration by Cornelis Troost to
P. de la Croix' *Krispijn Medecijn* (1685), which
shows such a writhing patient in a pose much
resembling that of Thomas Nero, cf. J. B. F.
van Gils,[184] illus. on p. 84.

[197] See Karl von Amira,[8] pp. 134ff., 213,
and 387f. ("das Ausdärmen"), and G. A.
Rost.[408a]

[198] For the problem of possible sensory per-
ceptions after death see Note 222 below.

The story of the condemned peasant is told
by Erasmus Francisci,[157] p. 984: "Denn es
werden solche arme Sünder," comments the
author, "allezeit lieber hören / dass ihr Leich-
nam gantz aneinander bleibe / als dass man
ihn / nach der Hinrichtung / wolle zerstücken
und trennen." The term "rollfincken" does not
occur in Grimm's *Deutsches Wörterbuch*. Werner Rolfink (1599–1673), a native of Hamburg,
was in all likelihood as fine a showman as Dr.
Tulp. He had spent two years at Leiden before

acquiring his doctoral degree at Padua (1625).
He finally settled down in Jena, where he
founded the anatomical theater. From there,
we are told, he would visit Weimar every year
to perform a dissection at the archducal court.
See the article on him in the *Allgemeine Deutsche
Biographie*,[6] XXIX, Leipzig, 1889. To my
great grief I have been unable to find the original passage in which Hugo Grotius' frequently
cited *dictum* occurs; it is quoted after J. G. de
Lint,[288] *Rembrandt*, pp. 39f.

In primitive African societies the dissection
of evildoers and witches proceeds in quest of
pathological deformations of certain organs,
above all the heart, gall, liver, kidneys, and
uterus, which must then be destroyed in order
to destroy the evildoer's magic power, the *evu*
or *likundu;* see Hermann Baumann,[42] p. 79.

[199] Conveniently accessible in ed. and tr.
Evelyn Underhill and Mrs. Theodore Beck,[252]
pp. 268–73; also see Jacopone da Todi, *Le
Laude*,[251] No. xxv.

It is perhaps characteristic of the undertones
of folklore that the sentiment of fairy tales,
manners of speech of the uneducated, and the
vocabulary of satirical cartoons tend to side
with the victim of the anatomies, the criminal:

(i) There exists a Grimm fragment ("Der
Mann vom Galgen") in which an old woman
who has served a hanged criminal's liver to
unexpected and unsuspecting guests is tor-
mented by the victim in the following dialogue: "Where is your hair?—The wind has
blown it away. Where are your eyes?—The
ravens have pecked them. Where is your
liver? — That you have eaten." Grimm,[197]
III, pp. 478ff. See also Note 181 above.

(ii) We can hear the *vox populi* in Henry Miller's odd observation: "In the background
Rembrandt is studying the anatomy of our
Lord Jesus Christ...," *Tropic of Capricorn*,[322]
p. 198.

(iii) Pierre Daninos' *Les Carnets du Major...
Thompson*[117] ..., Paris, 1954, wittily tones
down the idea to a social anatomy, "une séance
vivisalonsection" (illus. by Walter Goetz, p. 93).

200 Cf. Jacques Gamelin,[169] Plate VIII, and V. Robinson,[404] ill. on p. 851. The *Dies Irae,* n.b., according to the *Roman Missal,* is to be sung "in die obitus seu depositionis defuncti."

201 It seems that Petrarch was the first to voice the inner conviction that death was a force that could be viewed stoically; that is, in essence, scientifically. To him death was, rather than a moral or spiritual experience, a tangible menace that deeply affected the *dignitas humana.* He planned a treatise, by way of supplement or complement to the one by Innocent III, entitled *De miseria humana,* which he intended to call *De dignitate humana.* The mediaeval, post-paradisian curse of the "non posse non mori" ceased to exist to him as a real menace. Death, which in the Middle Ages had been a *transitus,* now became a *finis.* St. Cyprian, in reference to death, said: "Non est exitus iste, sed transitus et temporali itinere decurso ad aeterna transgressus"; to him death means "mutari et transformari ad Christi speciem"; *Liber de mortalitate,*[116] chap. xxii, ed. Migne, *P.L.,* IV, col. 597. This treatise was composed in the face of death, during the plague at Carthage, 252–54. Mediaeval man and, for that matter, every good Roman Catholic knows that, whatever his mode of dying, at the trumpet of the Last Judgment he shall rise in what may be called a flawless reissue of his old Adam:

> Restituetur ergo quidquid de corporibus uiuis uel post mortem de cadaueribus periit, et simul cum eo, quod in sepulcris remansit, in spiritalis corporis nouitatem ex animalis corporis uetustate mutatum resurget incorruptione adque immortalitate uestitum . . . erit ergo spiritui subdita caro spiritalis, sed tamen caro, non spiritus . . . [St. Augustine, *De civitate Dei,*[19] XXII, xxi; II, p. 619].

With Petrarch, on the other hand, the awareness of death as a democratic, all-equalizing power that menaces not only the body, but the very integrity and permanence of personality, gains the upper hand for the first time in the Christian era. Cf., for example, his *Triumph of Death,*[371] I, 79ff., in which the dances of death appear to be anticipated, inasmuch as we hear of popes, kings, and emperors that they died and that now, poor and naked, they are found with empty hands.

To express this novelty differently, negatively: we often miss in Petrarch an expression of anxiety concerning the fate of his soul, even where, from a thematic point of view, such a religious or eschatological turn might have been expected as part of the mediaeval mode of experiencing Death; for this complex, see Walter Rehm,[392] pp. 27 and 435, and Charles Trinkaus,[475] esp. pp. 172ff.

It was Petrarch also who perhaps discovered man's wisest attitude toward Death, to treat it as a personal predicament. In 1344 he wrote one of his beautiful metrical epistles (*Metricae,*[372] II, 19, pp. 184ff., addressed to Guillelmo Veronensi, i. e. G. da Pastrenzo), which, as it begins, differs little from the kind of letter we might hope to receive from a good friend: "You ask me what I am up to? I answer, What mankind is doing all along. What I am desirous of? Peace. What I am hoping for? No rest. Where I move? To and fro. What my final goal may be? I am speeding straightaway toward death." Then, in lighter vein, the poet starts to tell how at this point he is engaged in writing his great epic, *Africa,* while at the same time he is building a house. He has discovered a crack in the foundation, and the architect, reprimanded, reassures him by saying that this house will stand to give safe shelter to his descendants and that, in the end, what man builds cannot very well be expected to stand permanently. At these words Petrarch is taken aback. In a soliloquy he reminds himself of the "shaky foundation of his own frail body" — "quin cassa caduci / Fundamenta tui circumspice corporis . . ." (line 35f.). Full of gloom he reflects on the prospect that in one day he shall relinquish both his body and his house. At this a line of Horace's comes to his mind:

"et sepulchri immemor struis domus" (*Carmina,* [238] II, 78, 16f.), and this phrase, as in a flash, makes him desirous to flee the world and live in the forest forever. A mediaeval poet might have ended his poem here. In the final words of his epistle Petrarch reveals the last and, as I think, the deepest secret of modern man in the face of death and its disintegrating and humiliating power:

> And yet, while I am pondering all this, I feel like smiling, smiling at myself and at whatever is mortal in this world.
>
> Tandem omnia librans, / Rideo meque simul mortali quidquid in orbe est.

202 It is almost impossible to imagine Vesalius unaware of a passage such as the following from St. Augustine, *De civitate Dei,* [19] pp. 629 and 628:

> Quia etsi medicorum diligentia nonnulla crudelis, quos anatomicos appellant, laniauit corpora mortuorum [i. e. butchered the bodies of the dead] siue etiam inter manus secantis perscrutantisque morientium adque in carnibus humanis satis inhumane abdita cuncta rimata est, ut quid et quo modo quibus locis curandum esset addisceret; numeros tamen de quibus loquor [previously, St. Augustine had said: Certe enim nihil creatum uidemus in corpore utilitatis causa, quod non habeat etiam decoris locum. Plus autem nobis appareret, si numeros mensurarum, quibus inter se cuncta connexa sunt et coaptata, nossemus], quibus coaptatio, quae ἁρμονία Graece dicitur, tamquam cuiusdam organi, extrinsecus adque intrinsecus totius corporis constat, quid dicam, nemo ualuit inuenire, quos nemo ausus est quaerere? qui si noti esse potuissent, in interioribus quoque uisceribus, quae nullum ostentant decus, ita delectaret pulchritudo rationis, ut omni formae apparenti, quae oculis placet, ipsius mentis, quae oculis utitur, praeferretur arbitrio.

For St. Thomas Aquinas as a disciple of St. Augustine in these matters cf. Edgar de Bruyne, [75] III, 1946, pp. 308 ff. and 280.

203 See the discussion of this topos, "the proper study of mankind is man," and the possibility that one of its earliest instances is found in Vesalius' Preface to the *Fabrica,* [490] in Ludwig Edelstein, [132] pp. 558 to end.

204 ho sspechulatore dj / questa nosstra machina, / nontj contristara 'pchè / collaltrui morte tu ne / dja notitia, ma rallegrati che / il nostro al / tore abbi / a fermo lo intelletto / a ttale e / celletja / dj strume / to. [Leonardo da Vinci, *Quaderni d'Anatomia,* [285] II, Entry [vi], on p. 13.]

There is here, *mutatis mutandis,* an echo perhaps of a well-known passage in Celsus' *De medicina* [92] I, proemium: "It is [so the dogmatists declare] by no means cruel, as most people represent it, by the torture of a few guilty, to search after remedies for the whole innocent race of mankind in all ages."

205 This observation was made by Leonardo Olschki, [344] note 1 on p. 100:

> Keinem anderen Problem der Anatomie und Physiologie wurde im 16. Jahrhundert von Berufenen und Unberufenen so viel Aufmerksamkeit gewidmet als gerade diesem, das in der populärwissenschaftlichen Literatur eine grosse Rolle spielt. Es steht in innigstem Zusammenhang mit metaphysischen Problemen, wie bei Dante, *Purgatorio,* XXV, 37 ff., nach Thomas von Aquin und Albertus Magnus.

206 The *Decretum de peccato originali,* § 1, merits quotation in full:

> Si quis non confitetur, primum hominem Adam, cum mandatum Dei in paradiso fuisset transgressus, statim sanctitatem, et justitiam, in qua constitutus fuerat, amisisse, incurrisseque per offensam praevaricationis hujus modi iram et indignationem Dei, atque ideo mortem, quam antea illi comminatus fuerat Deus [Gen.

iii: 3], et cum morte captivitatem sub ejus potestate, qui mortis deinde habuit imperium, hoc est diaboli [Hebr. ii: 14], totumque Adam, per illam praevaricationis offensam, secundum corpus et animam in deterius commutatum fuisse; anathema sit. [Bibliogr.,[473] pp. 9f.]

For the mediaeval tradition, here revived, two examples may suffice:

(i) Adam corpus animale habuit, non modo ante paradisum, sed et in paradiso (quamvis in interiori homine fuit spirituale) quod amisit peccando, et meruit corporis mortem, qui non peccando meretur in corpus spirituale mutationem. [*Glossa ordinaria in librum Gen.* (ii: 7), ed. Migne, *P. L.,*[185] CXIII, col. 85. The authority cited is St. Augustine.]

(ii) Mors erat arma per quae vincebat diabolus. [*Glossa ordinaria in Epist. ad Hebr.* (ii: 14), ed. Migne, *P. L.,*[185] CXIV, col. 648.]

207 "Natura est que nihil, nisi virtus insita rebus. Et lex qua peragunt proprium cuncta entia cursum"; *De Immenso,* VIII, chap. ix, *Opera latina,*[73] I, pt. 2, p. 310, as cited and translated by Ernst Cassirer,[89] p. 44 and note 4. A similar scientific-organic view might still be encountered in the sixth century A.D.: "Corpus corrumpitur," etc.; see the first motto of our Chapter XIV (Eugippius, *d.* after 533,[146] p. 97).

208 Cf. Giulio Camillo (d. 1544), *L'Idea del Theatro*[81] (1550; posthumously printed), p. 51; these words occur in an astonishing chapter entitled: "La rinouatione delle cose." We find here, indeed, one of the most lucid expositions of Renaissance ideas encountered in the sixteenth century.

209 *Iconologia,*[401] p. 189 (misnumbered 198).

210 See E. Latham,[280] *s. v.* "Patriarch of Ferney."

211 For the controversy Leiden–Amsterdam as well as historical details concerning the founding of Leiden see Note 214. Tulp,[477]

p. 66, speaks of a relative "Casparis Barlaei, summi, nostri seculi, cùm Oratoris, tum Pöetae." The argument is often heard that Dutch writing in the seventeenth century remains essentially parochial; this seems to be true only when we concentrate on the vernacular works of Vondel, Cats, Visscher, *et al.,* and of the *Reederijkers,* to the complete neglect of poets such as Jacobus Revius and of Holland's great neo-Latin writers; for an example of this attitude, read the second of J. Huizinga's otherwise superb lectures on *Holländische Kultur des siebzehnten Jahrhunderts.*[243] Characteristically enough, the last serious attempt to compile, along with the biographies of Netherlandish neo-Latinists, an anthology of their verse was made by P. Hofmann Peerlkamp[369] in 1838 (2nd ed.).

212 A commemorative coin was struck which on its obverse shows the figures of Prudence and Justice flanking Religion with the motto: PRAEVALET HAC TRIGA VIS CONCORS AMSTELODAM; cf. G. van Loon,[290] pp. 202f.

Barlaeus' oration, followed by a noble invocation, the *Praecatio,* appeared in print in the year of its delivery (on Jan. 8, 1632) and soon after also in a Dutch translation. The title changes in the editions.[33] The names given to the new *schola,* which later in the century was to become a full-fledged university, waver among Athenaeum, academia, gymnasium. Barlaeus gave his first lecture on January 13, 1632 at 9 a.m., beginning a course on the history of philosophy down to Aristotle's *Physica;* cf. J. A. Worp,[522] pp. 95 ff.

The poet's vision of Amsterdam that begins the oration is probably one of the earliest descriptions of the psychological impact of a modern metropolis on one of its own inhabitants. See also the passages cited in Note 7 above.

213 Cf. C. H. Rogge,[406] p. 92, note 2.

214 Cf. C. H. Rogge,[406] pp. 99f.

215 For observations of as early as 1497 on the best anatomical season, viz. winter, cf. Appendix II. Supposedly the first scientific

observations on the property of ethereal oils and their use in the preservation of corpses is found in print in Gabriele de Zerbis' *Anatomiae corporis humani*[527] of 1502. The first systematic treatise entirely devoted to a discussion of preservation and embalming methods is found in the Third Book of Pierre Belon's work of 1553.[43] It was my privilege to inspect it in the author's own copiously corrected and annotated copy in the Wellcome Historical Medical Library in London. It should be noted, however, that as early as 1485 keen interest in the preservation of corpses is voiced at the chance discovery of a maiden's intact body found by Lombardic workmen in an ancient Roman sarcophagus some six miles outside Rome; see Christian Hülsen,[242] *passim*.

216 One of the first to question these anatomies was Paracelsus. "Die Welschen [i. e. the French and Italians] zu Montpellier, zu Salerno, zu Paris rühmen sich grosser Anatomie und sehen doch nichts, so viel gehenkte Diebe sie auch beschauen"; quoted after Helm,[216] note 10 on p. 14. — The beautiful and functional (that is, useful) human body as a reflection of God's plan of creation is, of course, a commonplace in the Middle Ages. We may even get a reversal of cause and effect when we hear that it was the fine structure of the body and the composition of the nerves that account for the virtue of fortitude: "Non igitur mentes per accidens habent fortitudinem per bonam corporis et nervorum compositionem τὴν ἀνδρίαν ἐξ εὐθεσίας σώματος καὶ νεύρων." Cf. St. Maximi *Scholia,* chap. xiii, III, ed. Migne, *P. G.,*[312] IV, col. 98. Also cf. St. Augustine's passage referred to in Note 202 above.

217 "To bolster his argument, Huygens cites the report of Trajano Boccalini, an Italian satirist, who said that when a group of doctors dissected the corpse of a nobleman, in order to examine his blood, they discovered that it did in no way differ from that of an ordinary burgher or farmer"; Seymour Slive,[449] p. 14 and note 1.

218 This feeling exists everywhere; cf., for example, the inscription that Moritz Hoffmann (1621–98) had affixed to the entrance of the anatomical theater at Altorf in 1650:

QVISQVIS ES QVI TE IPSVM
NOSSE AMAS
INTVS QVI ET IN CVTE SIS
HVC ADES ET STVDIIS
PRAEPITVS FORTIBVS
DISSECTIONES SPECTA HVMANI
CORPORIS
SIMVLQVE GRATO ANIMO
INCLITAE REIP. NORIMB.
BENEFICIVM AGNOSCE
NON HIC MOMI FENESTRA
SED PARVVM THEATRVM EST...

See Baier,[21] pp. 100f. and note on p. 101; also our Pl. IX-12.

219 *Poematvm Pars II,* 1646 (poematvm miscellanorvm lib. II. epigrammata),[32] p. 537; cf. Julius S. Held,[215] p. 262; cf. p. 99 and Note 23 above. For Barlaeus see above all J. A. Worp,[522] pp. 95 ff., H. de la Fontaine Verwey,[156] pp. 17–20, and, still useful, P. Hofmann Peerlkamp,[369] pp. 340–47. Also J. Prinsen Lzn.,[386] p. 329, and H. Kauffmann,[267] pp. 54 ff. Kauffmann on pp. 60 ff. speculatively discusses material pointing to a relationship between Barlaeus and Rembrandt, possibly from as early as 1627. Kauffmann's article is unfortunately less particularized in the treatment of what its author so well characterizes as the "humanistic period" (1631–36). Dr. Ursula Hoff is at work on an investigation of indications of the change in Rembrandt's work that still dates from the Leiden period.

For the version of Barlaeus' poem as it actually appeared in the first permanent theater of 1639 see E. H. M. Thijssen,[468] p. 18, and B. W. Th. Nuyens,[343] p. 35.

220 *Poematvm Pars II*[32] (elegiarvm lib. III), p. 207. The poem is addressed to Constantine Huygens. For similar sentiments cf. the Inaugural Speech of Professor Willem van der Straten, Utrecht, March 17, 1636: "Hoe aan-

genaam, nuttig en nodig het is zichzelf te leeren kennen door de anatomie" ("how pleasant, useful, and necessary it is to get to know oneself through Anatomy"); Bibliogr.,[12] pp. 2f.

221 *Poematvm Pars II*[32] (elegiarvm lib. III), p. 249.

222 Of Dr. Tulp's first five ceremonial anatomies all but one (April 1, 1634) date in the second half of January.

The reader unfamiliar with the concept of the "Criminal God" will find it elucidated, *s. h. t.* and with further bibliography, by Edgar Wind.[516] The tradition according to which public anatomies were conducted as part of crime's punishment by society is very ancient indeed. The idea existed in classical antiquity; it was favored by, among others, Democritus and Parmenides, who held that "after death the human body is still capable of sensation"; see Ludwig Edelstein,[133] p. 241. For similar beliefs in primitive society see Reinhard Hofschlager,[226] p. 78. On the other hand there is, to my knowledge, no evidence that the corpse of a respectable person who had died in a hospital was ever used in public anatomies. For the statutes of the University of Florence providing for the delivery of criminals, preferably alien, cf. J. Playfair McMurrich,[297] p. 48. For the use of cadavers of criminals in the time of Shakespeare see Ronald McKerrow,[336] IV, p. 122. For the problem as a whole see M. Roth,[410] p. 16; also Alexander Benedictus, Appendix II and Note 58 above.

Related to the problem of sensory perception after death—the *conditio sine qua non* of penal anatomies—was that of a revival after death. It was still commonly thought in the seventeenth century that animals could die and come back to life; the migration of birds was explained in this manner, and one could indeed point to St. Paul's word: "Thou fool, that which thou sowest is not quickened, except it die." Also see Note 59 and p. 105 above.

223 See C. Hofstede de Groot,[228] pp. 23f. (No. 24, January, 1632) and p. 113. For addi-

tional material pertaining to the two criminals in Rembrandt's anatomies see I. H. van Eeghen,[135] pp. 34–36. Except for insignificant divergences, the passages in the two authoritative versions (Gemeentelijke Archieven Amsterdam)[305a, aaa] are identical.

224 The situation culminated in a petition on the part of the University of Leiden, which, founded in 1575, had proudly assumed the title of *presidium libertatis;* cf. van Gelder,[177] p. 401. Leiden's charter plainly stipulated that it should be the only university in the Province of Holland. Amsterdam's counter-petition was admitted by the Supreme Council of the States General and granted December 22, 1631; see *Amsterdam University,*[9a] where this dispute is set forth (p. 1). For greater detail see I. H. Eeghen,[136] pp. 75f. I shall here merely point out that an abortive attempt had been made, 1617–18, to initiate in Amsterdam a school in which "professors" taught in the Dutch language; cf. Anon.,[11] pp. 69f.

225 I am deeply grateful to Mr. Philip Hofer, who has provided me with a photograph and permitted me to publish this woodcut (Fig. 21) from the copy in his possession.

226 The type of broad-rimmed hat was relatively modern (from *ca.* 1620 onward); cf. Friethjof van Thienen,[467] p. 62. Note, however, that the crown of this hat has been lowered (Rembrandt's own pentimento) so as to heighten the shell niche behind and above Dr. Tulp's head. Incidentally, the custom whereby the *professor cathedraticus* is the only one to keep his head covered is still observed at Inauguration Speeches at the University of Utrecht and, I assume, at the other Universities of Holland. For unknown reasons Dr. Pieter Paaw seems to have preferred to anatomize without a hat; at least two representations show him so at work while, as curiously, everyone else is hatted. (Fig. 2 and Pl. III-3 and 4.)

227 Cf. M. Bratschkova,[63] p. 63 and fig. 47, Catalogue XVII, p. 128, Nos. 981–85, and W. S. Heckscher,[211] pp. 22–26; also Note 228 below.

228 For the Holbein panel see Note 165 above.

Another important link exists between the ideas of shell-foiled portrait bust and Death. "We may perhaps surmise that as the shell is the chosen vehicle of Aphrodite across the seas . . . so the sepulchral shell [in the Roman sarcophagi], like the other marine emblems which so often appear on Roman tombstones, may be the vehicle of the soul's transit to the other world"; Eugenie Strong,[460] p. 149. (Pl. XL-48.) Similarly, W. Déonna,[121] esp. pp. 410 and 414.

What does William Hogarth mean when he shows, in a decidedly unfavorable sense, the "Lawyer" ("Law's the Wisdom of all Ages") consulted by Hudibras and both represents him as *cathedraticus* and puts him beneath a pecten shell? (Pl. XXXVIII-46.) The text (Pt. III, Canto iii)[79] makes no explicit reference to this: "To this brave Man, the Knight repairs / For Council in his *Law-Affairs;* / And found him mounted *in his Pew,* / With *Books,* and *Money* plac'd, for shew, etc." Undoubtedly Hogarth here uses the paraphernalia of inspired wisdom to mock at their usurpation by shrewd legal quacks. The idea of inversion of the shell and cathedra symbols was, in fact, not new, and I consider it possible that Hogarth was aware of Jan Steen's impressive "Christ at the Age of Twelve in the Temple," in which the High Priest, whose nonwisdom is the iconographic *crux* of the theme, is shown in the same manner. (Pl. XXXVII-44.) The motif was introduced by Hogarth at a later point in his illustration and is not as yet found in the illustrated *ed. princ.* of the year 1726.[79] In one or two rare instances the intentional inversion, which urges us to interpret the inhabitant of the shell-foil niche *in malo,* is encountered in the fifteenth century; thus in Fra Angelico's "St. Lawrence Before Decius," Capella di Niccolò V in the Vatican, where Decius appears seated against a shell-capped niche.

For *Reederijkers* plays featuring *Rhetoricam sub concha* see George Kernodle,[268] p. 118 and fig. 45. The shell niche belonged to the vocabulary of Rembrandt's Maecenas at Amsterdam and was liberally used to emphasize the two chief forms of its application: in Art and in Law, of which the following two illustrations will suffice:

(i) The idealized design (1630) of the planned *schouwburg* of Amsterdam (erected 1637) showed as a decorative centerpiece a throne raised by three steps and behind it a shell niche flanked by two niches—left and right—accommodating the figures of Hercules and Mercury, the entire structure topped by an architrave with the inscription: MENTEM MORTALIA TANGUNT (cf. the contemp. engraving of W. van der Laegh, Gemeente Museum at Amsterdam, which will be published by Katharine D. H. Fremantle);[159]

(ii) Dr. K. Fremantle also informs me that the general layout of the stage with its niches (so curiously anticipated in Rembrandt's painting) is next employed by van Campen for the public Court of Justice ("de Vierschaar") of the Town Hall of Amsterdam. The reader is referred to the end of my third chapter, where an attempt is made to see Rembrandt's "Anatomy of Dr. Tulp"—and indeed every other ceremonial anatomy that took place in Amsterdam—as a drama that moved from the *Vierschaar* to the anatomical table.

For "Esther Putting on Her Royal Apparel" see *Rembrandt Tentoonstelling,*[393a] No. 21 (illustrated), in which the Ottawa painting is officially listed as "Young Woman at Her Toilet"; she is tentatively identified as either Bathsheba or as the shepherdess Bocena. Curiously enough—and this seems to strengthen the argument for my renaming—Aert de Gelder (1645–1727), Rembrandt's last and most faithful disciple (1661 ff.), apparently returned to Rembrandt's early Esther motif in one of his most impressive paintings; cf. *Rembrandt als Leermeester,*[394] No. 58 (illus.).

229 This amounts to a tautology; for the equation canopy = shell = canopy see M. Bratschkova,[63] pp. 18 f. Professor Dario Covi furnished me with the exact wording of Filippino Lippi's inscriptions. Julius Schlosser,[423] pp. 17f., has shown that the antecedents of St. Thomas' triumph must be sought in representations of the ninth and tenth centuries. See also Note 230 below.

230 Colet's tomb under the motto ISTVC RECEDIT GLORIA CARNIS consisted of a "depicta ad vivum effigies"; having been destroyed in the Great Fire, it is preserved, among others, in an engraving by Daniel King found in [Sir] William Dugdale's *History*,[130] Plate 64; I am indebted to an article by F. Grossmann,[198] pp. 206 ff. and figs. 54a, c, d (the last one for the portrait bust of Ficino).

We happen to know that Colet, who died of the sweating disease—a kind of influenza peculiar at the time to inhabitants of the British Isles—was dissected to ascertain the exact cause of death, but "anatomia nihil indicauit noui"; thus Erasmus of Rotterdam in a letter to Jodocus Jonas,[141] from Anderlecht, June 13, 1521, p. 519, lines 374–86.

The triumph over death in and through death goes back ultimately to the very ancient (seventh-century and ff.) representations of the Crucifixus over the skull and crossbones of Adam. For Christ crucified in triumph, as it were, above the open coffin containing the skeleton of Adam, cf. Herrad of Landsperg's large "Crucifixion" (Fig. 21). First the Liturgy ("Offices of the Dead") and later secular literature (Dances of Death) evolved the image of the apostle (philosopher or author) as an authority enthroned to the right and lecturing upon (and at the same time at) a prone cadaver —a significant configuration that has its place in the formal and conceptual family tree of Rembrandt's "Anatomy." Two examples will help to illustrate this evolution:

(i) Offices of the Dead in a Book of Hours from Mâcon,[286] Mâcon, Collection Jehan Siraudin, fol. 91 *recto,* Plate VIII (Pl. XLIII-52), shows St. Paul using a *comput digitale*-like gesture of speech as he stands on a socle above a tomb on whose lid there lies a corpse (*ca.* 1480);

(ii) Guyot Marchant appears seated to the right as he holds forth on the prone cadaver of Death himself, whose crown has rolled off his skull; woodcut illustration[307] (Fig. 21); see Notes 186ff. and p. 117 above.

For Barlaeus' lines see also Kauffmann,[267] p. 54. For the idea of the triumph of the anatomist over his victim on a level of personal and professional vindictiveness, see p. 100 above.

The most original variation on the manner in which Rembrandt had formulated the theme of the master anatomist showing his skill is found as early as 1679 in the frontispiece of Olaf Rudbeck's *Atlantica,*[413] which shows the slightly maniacal author, in the pose of Dr. Tulp, as he anatomizes the map of Scandinavia in quest of Atlantis (Pl. XIII-17). The connection was first observed by Eric von Rosen.[408]

231 Tulp's motto was quite generally described in the seventeenth century as suitable for officials both secular and religious; see for example Philippo Picinelli,[377] V, chap. xx, § 307, p. 378. A possible contributing source may be a book written by Tulp's friend the bailiff of Muider Castle, Pieter Cornelisz. Hooft, *Emblemata amatoria,*[236] Emblem XII. (Pl. XLV-54.) In early Christian times burning torches ("cerei ardentes") were carried at funerals, even in daylight, to symbolize Christ's victory over death. The Middle Ages add the image of the self-sacrificing candle as pointing at Christ's mortality; thus Honorius of Autun, Durandus, and others. The Renaissance creates the specific concept of Christ as the true medicine against death and sees in Him the true physician (cf. Ingvar Bergström,[51a] esp. pp. 6f.). Andrea Mantegna showed in his last work (1506) a "Saint Sebastian" (Venice, Ca' d'Oro, Galleria Franchetti) with a smoldering candle in the corner. The inscription wound around the body of the candle, NIL NISI DIVINVM STABILE EST CAETERA FVMVS, reveals that Mantegna wished the dying light to be interpreted as a commentary on the vicarious

suffering of the saint. More generally the image occurs in mediaeval writing as that of the candle that "turns to ashes as it produces light," "zeiner aschen wirt / enmitten dô sî licht birt"; Hartmann von Ouwe, *Der arme Heinrich,*[204] 11, 97 ff. We find it earlier yet in Carolingian literature, where we encounter the following dialogue: "Pippinus: How is man situated? Albinus: Like a lamp in the wind"; Alcuin,[5] col. 975. In Tulp's own age the conceit was spread everywhere by the emblematists; see Mario Praz,[384] p. 82. In the year 1638 alone two independent emblem books appeared whose theme was man's life under the aspect of a burning light; see Rosemary Freeman,[158] p. 122. As early as 1672, however, the motto was deprived of its metaphysical character; J. de Bisschop, under a portrait of Dr. Tulp, changed it to: ". . . inserviendo sanitati et Patriae"; see F.W.H. Hollstein,[235] II, No. 5 on p. 44.

[232] For the Gallo-Roman and Romano-Teutonic tombstones found in Northern France and on the Lower Rhine and for their significant role in the genesis of the modern portrait, see E. Panofsky,[357] who confronts Jan van Eyck's "Tymotheos" (Plate 28 opposite p. 80) with the tombstone of C. Vetienius (Cologne, Mus. St. Germain, between 10 and 35 A.D.; Plate 29, e); both portrait busts should be compared with the portrait of Dr. Tulp by Eliasz. (Pl. XLIV-53). J. A. Emmens,[138] p. 135, has suggested that the words LEAL SOUVENIR should be paraphrased: "behold a faithful rendition of myself which shall survive beyond my death." Also see the Introduction.

[233] It seems significant that Rembrandt managed to escape the emblematic fashion where few others among his colleagues would have done so: He inscribed Burchard Grossmann Jr.'s *album amicorum* June 18, 1634: "Een vroom gemoet / Acht eer voor goet / ..." "a devout mind prefers honor to possessions," followed by his name and accompanied by the portrait-like sketch of a rabbinical head; cf. C. Hofstede de Groot,[228] No. 33 on p. 32 and H. F. Wijnman,[515] pp. 100 f. with reproductions of Rembrandt's and Uylenburgh's entries as well as Rembrandt's sketch (figs. 2a, b, and c). The instances where Rembrandt posed an emblematic riddle are few and far between.

Appendix I

Nicolai Tvlpii / Amstelodamensis / Observationum Medicarvm / Libri Tres. / Cum aeneis figuris. / Amstelredam / Elzevier. / 1641.
Book I, chap. xviii, pp. 37–39

Imaginary Softening of the Bones

Even as it is not given to everyone to cure melancholiacs, it is hard to uproot covertly from their minds the false fancies stamped thereon by the black bile; of which farfetched fancies a signal example that once came to light occurred when the physician Philodotus, by means of a leaden headgear, restored to a certain melancholiac the head that he imagined had been cut off a good while before. With this example in mind Cornelius Celsus argues in his Book III, chapter xviii [of *De Medicina libri octo*] that such delusions should be more generally humored than combated, and that the minds of such persons should be beguiled from their follies to better things by no overt means.

A distinguished Painter, for some time harassed with black bile, was under the delusion that all the bones of his body had softened to such a flexibility that they might easily buckle like wax if he put the slightest weight on them. Being rooted and grounded in this notion,

p. 38] he kept to his bed for a whole winter; for if he were to get out of it something disastrous would assuredly come to pass, and that with even more certainty than the decomposition of his bones that he had feared hitherto—nay, rather the total collapse of his body.

Once I had comprehended this dread, I did not want to antagonize him; I wanted to take roundabout rather than direct measures to undermine the fancy that he had conjured up. Granting, then, that this species of softening was no new story to the medical profession—that, indeed, it had been observed long ago by the celebrated Fernelius (Book II, *De abditis rerum caussis*)—I said that, just as softened wax is rehardened, so the art of medicine can work upon the bones, provided that the patients show themselves compliant. Within three days there would return to his own bones their former rigidity, and before the sixth day, if he paid heed to what was told him, he would be able to walk wherever he wanted.

What hope of recovered health these assurances inspired, it is hard to convey, and like-wise how amenable they made him to medications designed to cope with the black bile. This having been duly eliminated from his body, I was vindicated and easily proved reliable in prescribing that he get up from the bed in which he had lain for a whole winter—with the restriction, however, that he was merely to stand on his feet and not move an inch; if he did otherwise, the consequences would be his own fault; and on the sixth day I would myself give him leave to walk anywhere

p. 39] if he properly deferred to my knowledge.

These admonitions were the more binding upon him in proportion to his dread of a recurrence of his trouble. As it abated I kept on unobtrusively with the cathartic medications. But with the approach of the second three-day period I made an outright demonstration of the truth of my promise by suffering him not only to walk about his bedroom, but also to show himself in public and to perform all the functions of a healthy person.

So rejoiced was he at this liberation that he could not find enough to say in praise of the mentor of his health. By turns he marveled at the prowess of medicine and execrated his own distrust because he had so persisted in withholding the faith with which he had finally accepted advice so beneficial.

This patient perceived the restoration of strength to his bones, the return of normal functioning to his joints, the freeing of his stride, and some other matters; but how that foolish delusion of one whole winter had been cunningly extirpated—that he neither perceived nor suspected, though he was a man in other respects anything but dull-witted, and in his own art accomplished and second to hardly any.

*   *   *

Imaginaria ossium mollities

p. 37:] VElut non cujusvis est, melancholicis mederi, sic difficulter quoque eradicantur clanculum, ex ipsorum animis imagines, ab atrâ bile, falsò impressae: cujus tamen ingeniosi inventi, nobile specimen, olim editurus, Philodotus medicus, restituit, plumbeo pileo, cuidam melancholico caput, quod putaverat sibi, jam diu, amputatum. Quo respiciens Cornelius Celsus, suadet lib. III, cap. XVIII. insaniae huic saepiùs assentiendum, quàm repugnandum: & non evidenter, ab his, quae stultè dicuntur, ad meliora, mentem ipsorum abducendam.

Insignis Pictor, infestatus aliquandiu, ab atrâ bile, imaginabatur sibi falsò, cuncta corporis ossa, adeò mollia, ac flexibilia sibi esse, ut instar sequacis cerae, facillimè in se complica-rentur; si vel minimùm illis inniteretur. Quâ opinione menti penitiùs impressâ,

180

p. 38:] continuit se integram hiemem in lecto: veritus inde si surgeret, aliquid sinistri. & certò certiùs eventuram, quam hactenùs metuerat, deformem ossium suorum, vel potiùs totius corporis conglobationem.

Quo metu intellecto, nolui ipsi adversari: neque palàm, sed clam surreptum ire, quam conceperat imaginationem. Asserens propterea, mollitiem hanc non latere medicos: quin potiùs iam diu animadversam ab Incluto Fernelio lib. II. de abd. rer. causs. & sicuti cera emollitur, ac induratur: sic plurimùm in ossibus etiam posse artem medicam, modò morigeros se praebeant aegri. Ipsius autem ossibus, intra triduum, restitutum iri pristinum stabilimentum. Et ante diem sextum, potentiam quocunque ambulandi; dummodò fuerit dicto audiens.

Quae promissa, dici vix potest, quantam excitaverint spem recuperandae sanitatis: & quam morigerum reddiderint ipsum, in admittendis remediis, atrae bili destinatis. Quâ convenienter ex corpore depulsâ, exsolvimus & nos facilè fidem nostram: jubentes ipsum surgere, ex cubili: in quo integram hiemem decubuerat. Verùm cum eâ lege, ut duntaxat insisteret pedibus; neque procederet vel latum unguem. Secùs si faceret, penes se culpam futuram. Sexto verò die, me veniam ipsi daturum, quocunque deambulandi.
p. 39:] Modò rite obtemperaret arti.

Quae certè monita eò fuêre rigidiora, quò minùs expediit ipsi dolum hunc resciscere. Qui quò magis lateret, continuavimus tectè, in medicamentis catharticis. Sed appropinquante jam secundo triduo; ostendimus coram promissi veritatem. Factâ non tantùm veniâ, ambulandi per conclave, sed etiam in publicum prodeundi, & obeundi jugiter, qualiacunque, sani hominis, munia.

Quâ libertate tantoperè gavisus fuit; ut ignoraverit quibus encomiis extolleret sanitatis suae Praesidem. Admiratus hinc artis potentiam; illinc detestatus suam diffidentiam. Quod tam diu denegasset fidem: à quâ tam salutare recepisset consilium.

Vidit quidem hic aeger robur ossibus suis restitutum: vidit rediviva cruruum officia: vidit expeditum incessum: vidit alia: sed stultam hanc, totius hiemis imaginationem clanculùm sibi eripi, nec vidit, nec sensit, homo caeteroquin minimè stupidus, sed in arte suâ abundè sagax, & vix ulli secundus.

Appendix II

A

Historia corporis humani, by Alexander Benedictus, physician of Verona, Book I, Chapter i: Of the uses of public anatomies, the selection of a cadaver, and the arrangement of an adequate theater.

a ii] It has come down to us that the very kings, solicitous of the general welfare, took criminals out of prison and dissected them alive, in order that they might probe the secrets of nature and nature's internal cunning while consciousness was still present—the location, color, shape, size, arrangement, development, and deterioration of the organs, many of which undergo changes in the dead—and that they might

verso] make accurate rather than reverential observations. . . . But this practice our religion forbids, inasmuch as it is of the utmost cruelty and charged with abominations of the torturer, and to die in the despair of such torments means the pitiful loss of hope of a future life. Be these usages applied by the barbarians and foreigners that devised them, who take pleasure in those evil doings and culpabilities. But let us more mercifully spare the living and investigate the inmost secrets of nature in the corpses of criminals. . . . Only humble and unknown persons, then, and those from distant regions may rightly be claimed for dissection, that there shall be no outrage to neighbors or relatives. Those are chosen who have been strangled by hanging and who are middle-aged, neither lean nor fat, and of rather large frame, that their components may be of more generous size and more distinctly visible to the onlookers. In addition severe winter cold is needed, lest the cadavers putrefy too soon. Furthermore a properly adapted theater should be located in a spacious and well-ventilated place, with ranks of seats like those of an amphitheater, as at Rome and at Verona; and it should be large enough to accommodate all the spectators comfortably, that the barber-surgeons who do the dissecting may not be

fol. 7 *recto,* sign. a iii *recto*] jostled by the crowd. Only those who have great skill must continue to dissect. The seating arrangement is to be according to rank. There must be some one man in charge who oversees and arranges everything. Warders are to be provided for regulation of the unruly incoming rabble. Two reliable stewards are appointed who out of the admissions fees supply the necessary [here follows a list of surgical instruments].

The cadaver should be placed at the center of the theater on a fairly high bench in a well-lighted place convenient for the dissectors. The time of reconvening should be announced at the end of each session, that the work may be entirely completed before decomposition sets in. . . .

Venetiis. .M.IIID. Kalendis aug. Alexandri Benedicti Veronensis physici historiae corporis humani. Liber primus. De utilitate anatomices: & de cadauere eligendo: deque temporario theatro constituendo. Cap. primum.

a ii] NOcentes homines ex carcere acceptos uiuos resecasse reges ipsos publicae saluti consulentes traditum est: ut spiritu etiam remanente naturae archana: & quid natura magna solertia intra se agit: perquirerent: membrorum posituram: colorem: figuram: magnitudinem: ordinem: processum: recessumque: ex quibus multa in defunctis mutantur: distincteque /

verso] magis quam pie annotarent: [ut illatis uulneribus: quid integrum: quid corruptum sit intelligeretur.] At id relligio nostra uetat: quoniam truculentissimum est nel [uel] carnifici hororis plenum: ne morituri inter tantos cruciatus desperationae [sic]: futurae uitae spem misere ammittant. Haec barbari externique ritus: qui excogitarunt faciant. qui ea piacula & onera [?] adamant. At nos clementius uiuis parcentes noxiorum cadaueribus intima: atque naturae archana indagabimus: . . . Ad resectionem igitur ignobiles / ignotos: ex longinquis regionibus sine uicinitatis iniuria: propinquorumque nota iure dumtaxat peti possunt: suspendioque strangulati deliguntur: mediocris aetatis: non gracilis: non obesi corporis: staturae maioris: ut uberior materia: euidentiorque sit spectantibus. Adhoc pergelida hyems requiritur: ne cadauera protinus putrefiant: Loco praeterea amplo perflatili: temporarium theatrum constituendum est circumcauatis sedilibus: quale romae ac ueronae cernitur: tantae magnitudinis: ut spectantium numero satisfaciat: Ne uulnerum magistri qui resectores sunt a mul /

a iii] titudine perturbentur: hi sollertes esse debent / quique saepius resecauerint / sedendi ordo pro dignitate distribuendus est / ob id praefectus unus esse debet: qui omnia intueatur / ac disponat / custodes dandi sunt / qui ingredientem importunam plebem arceant / Quaestores duo fidi deliguntur / qui ex collatis pecuniis necessaria comparant [Ad id nouaculis opus est cultellis: uncis: terebris / modiolis chenicia graeci uocant / spongiis / quibus sanguis in secando rapiatur / recisoriis / ac catinis / Funalia praeterea per nocte parata esse debet.] Cadauer uero in medio theatro editiore scamno collocandum est / loco claro resectoribus apto. tempus adeundi statuendum est / dum conuentus dimittitur / ut antequam materia putrefiat opus penitus absoluatur: [Primumque de humani corporis forma figuraque dignitate pauca percurremus = the end of chap. i].

J. J. Orlers, [347] pp. 208–10

p. 208:] Description of the Anatomical Place of the City of Leiden

Description of the Anatomy:

Inasmuch as a doctor of Medicine and a student in that Faculty, as well as a surgeon, is not a little interested in a thorough knowledge of man's body . . . /
p. 209:] it has pleased the Lord Curators and the Burgomasters of this Academy—and this happened in the year 1592 [sic]—to order by decree the fitting up of a suitable place in the Falijde-Begijnen Church after the manner of the ancient Roman *theatra*, that is playhouses, so that therein, at appointed terms, the Anatomy might be performed and demonstrated . . . [in a place (which Orlers, p. 208, illustrates with an engraving similar to our Pl. XXXIII-40)] wherein a large number of people can watch and behold whatever there will be anatomized and dissected.

Further Account of the Anatomical Place:

In order to acquaint the curious reader with all this in a proper manner, I shall give a close account and description of the particulars of this place, and I shall begin with its arrangement. Apart from the circular place in the middle, where the anatomizing is done, the *theatrum* is divided into six circles or galleries which rise obliquely and which each, properly placed one above the other (the higher one without having its field of vision obstructed by the one below), enable one to see with ease and unhampered what dissecting is being done below. In the circle that lies at the bottom, there has been placed a rotating table upon which the body destined to be anatomized is to be placed. This is covered with a white linen sheet and draped with a black cloth. At this table only the professor who performs the dissection has his place, where he stands [for the standing anatomist at Leiden cf. Fig. 2 and Pls. III-3, 4] so that he may perform free and unhampered that which he has set himself to do. In the first circle, immediately around the (anatomical) table—this being the most convenient place to behold and observe whatever is being dissected—the professors are seated and certain other persons of rank and dignity; in the two following circles, which are provided with separate boxes, there stand the surgeons and all the students of Medicine; in the subsequent circles all the other students as well as whoever else has the desire and inclination to follow and observe the performance.

Exhibits on View in the Anatomical Place:

All around those ranks there are separately placed in careful arrangement seven frames, that is skeletons, of persons male and female who have been put together with utmost skill by means of copper wires. Some of these hold sundry banners in their hands whereto have been affixed various devices and mottoes in the Latin tongue bearing upon the brittleness and fleeting quality of Man's body. But in the center, in front of the (anatomical) table, there have been placed the bones of a man and a woman, underneath a tree, in order to depict that through the lapse of our first parents death has come /

p. 210:] to mankind. . . . Besides all these [viz. skeletons of man and beasts] (we encounter) a piece of human skin which by way of lesson has been tanned and prepared. . . .

At What Times the Anatomy Is Generally Carried Out:

Almost every year in the month of either December or January, at the season of frost and severe cold, a body—be it that of a man or of a woman—is being anatomized or dissected under the eyes and in the presence of the *rector magnificus,* the assessors, the professors, doctors, surgeons, and students of Medicine, as well as many persons of every rank of Society who are desirous of knowledge of the human frame and instruction regarding it. All of which—certain hours of the day having been appointed and set aside to this purpose by the professor who does the dissecting—is carried out and performed with great dignity. . . . And this has been done, year in year out, by the adroit, learned hands of the Most Learned and Most Eloquent Dr. Pieter Pauw, . . . *ordinarius* and *anathomicus* of the Leiden Academy, whom I shall here mention to his honor inasmuch as at this place he has, to his great praise and glory, anatomized several bodies of men, women, and sundry beasts to the unspeakably great profit and advance of those that have attended, understood, and perceived this properly.

p. 208:] Beschrijvinghe vande *Anathomie*-Plaetse der Stadt *Leyden*.

Beschrijvinge vande Anathomie:

NAerdien dat een *Doctor* inde Medicijnen / ende een Student inde selvige faculteyt / ende een *Chyrurgus,* niet weynich gheleghen is / aende volcomen kennisse des menschen Lichaems . . .

p. 209:] soo hebben de *H. Heeren Curateurs* ende *Burgermeesteren* deser *Hoghe Schole* . . . te weten inden Jaere 1592. inde Falide-Bagijnen Kercke een bequaeme plaetse gheordonneert ende doen maecken / op de wijse vande oude Romeynsche *Theatra* ofte Schouplaetsen / om in de selvige tot behoorlicke tijden / de *Anathomie* te doen oeffenen ende wijsen / [wesende de voornoemde plaetse van forme als het voorgestelde Figuercken uytwijst.] Waerinne een groote menichte van Menschen gemackelicken mogen sien ende aen-schouwen / 'tgene aldaer geanathomiseert ende ghesneden werdt.

Naerder verhael vande Anathomie plaetse:

Omme den begeerigen Leser ten vollen te moghen te vreden stellen / soo sal ick de Beschrijvinghe van dese plaetse wat naerder ondersoecken ende beschrijven / beginnende mette verdeelinghe der selver. Het *Theatrum,* is beneffens de ronde Plaetse int midden daer men anathomiseert / verdeelt in ses schuyns opgaende Circulen ofte ronde ommegangen / de eene boven de andere behoorlicken verheven zijnde / op dat altijdt de bovenste / sonder dat hy vande onderste verhindert werde / tgene ghesneden werdt / ghemackelijck ende onbekommerlyck sien kan: Inde benedenste rondicheyt is gemaeckt een omdraeyende Tafel / waer op het lichaem 'twelck men anathomiseren sal geleydt werdt / met een wit linnen ende met een swert laecken kleedt ghedeckt wesende: aen welcken Tafel de *Professor* die de Snijdinge doet alleen sijne plaetse heeft ende staet / op dat hy vry ende onverhindert verrichten mach tghene hy aldaer te doen heeft. Daer aen inden eersten Circkel rondtomme de Taefel / wesende de bequaemste plaetse omme wel ende perfect te mogen sien tghene datter ghesneden wert / sitten de *Heeren Professoren,* ende eenige andere van State ende aensien / inde eerst daer aen volghende twee Circkels / de welcke met sloten afghesondert ende gescheyden zijn / staen de Chyrurgijns ende alle de Studenten de welcke inde Medicinen studeren / ende inde verdere Circkelen de andere Studenten / ofte andere lust ende begheerte hebbende om sulcx te aenschouwen ende te sien.

Wat inde Anathomie plaetse te sien is:

Rondtom opte voorgaende ommegangen zijn gestelt / met goede order tot verscheyden plaetsen / seven riffen ofte gheraemten van Mans ende Vrouwen persoonen seer bequame-licken met koper-draden aenden anderen ghehechtet wesende / vande welcke sommighe eenige wimpelkens inde handen hebben / waer inne in Latijnsche Tale eenighe devisen ende spreucken de broscheydt ende nieticheydt vande menschelicke lichamen betreffende / ghestelt zijn. Maer in het midden opte Tafel zijn gestelt een Mans ende Vrouwen gebeenten onder een Boom / uytbeeldende dat door de sonde van onse eerste Voor-ouderen / de doot over alle menschen

p. 210:] gecomen is... Boven desen alle [Gedierten, *scil.*] [hangt hier] ... een stuck van een Menschen Vel / dat tot leer ghetout ende bereydet is: ...

Tijde wanneer datmen gemeenlijck snijdt:

Meest alle Jaeren inde maend van December oft Januarius / ten tijde wanneer dat het vriest ende seer kout is / soo werdt alhier een lichaem 'tzy van Man ofte van Vrouwe gheanathomiseert ofte ghesneden / ten aensien ende inde teghenwoordicheyt vande *Magnific. Dom. Rector, Assesseuren, Professoren, Doctoren, Chyrurgijns,* ende Studenten inde Medicinen / mitsgaders vele verscheyden andere Persoonen / die lust totte kennisse der Menschelicker lichaemen / ende de onderwijsinge vande selve hebben. Het welcke op sekere uyren vanden dage / daer toe vanden *Professor* die de snijdinghe doet gheordonneert ende bestemt wesende / met grooter aensienlickheydt uytgherecht ende gedaen werdt /

ende nu vele jaren aenden anderen ghedaen is / door de kloecke ende verstandighe handen vanden Hooch-gheleerden ende Wel-spreeckenden Heere / *D. Pieter Pauw,* eerste *Professor* ende *Doctor* inde Medicinen / *Botanicus,* ende *Anathomicus* vande *Leydtsche Academie,* alhier ter eeren ghenoemt / de welcke alhier ter plaetsen met grooten loff ende eere vele ende verscheyden lichaemen van Mannen / Vrouwen / ende verscheyden andere Ghedierten geanathomiseert heeft / tot grooten onuytsprekelicken nut ende profijt vande gene die sulcx terecht gesien / verstaen / ende waerghenomen hebben. . . .

Appendix III

Data from the City Archives of Amsterdam

In this Appendix will be found material from the Amsterdam Archives (Gemeentelijke Archieven) pertaining to Rembrandt's "Anatomy of Dr. Tulp"; this material has been placed in section A. Under B are added a few data concerning Rembrandt's "Anatomy of Dr. Deyman." Miss I. H. van Eeghen of the Amsterdam Archives has been most generous in giving advice and contributing information (especially from MS. 245[305aaaa]), for which I wish to express my sincere thanks. Of course, the responsibility for conclusions drawn from the material rests solely with me.

A. Rembrandt's "Anatomy of Dr. Tulp"

The numbers given below are those of the roll call sheet (see Pl. XLVIII-57 and diagram below). The seventeenth-century spelling of names (following each number in italics) is highly arbitrary. Given names, often patronymic, are relatively stable. Family names, on the other hand, will frequently be dropped or changed to completely new forms, which, like the name of Nicolaas Tulp, may be derived from the name of a family-owned house. Dr. van Eeghen agrees that on palaeographic grounds the script of the roll call sheet dates from the seventeenth century. Although it must be considered a palimpsest not by Rembrandt's own hand, there is no reason why its identification of individuals should not be trusted.

The two main sources of the time concerning the annual guild events (the "Anatomij-Boek," MS. 294[305a] and MS. 243[305aa]) confirm my main point, viz. that only a minority— two—of the seven guild members appearing in Rembrandt's painting were in the administration of the guild in the guild year (running from September to September) 1631–32. The misconception according to which Dr. Tulp appears in Rembrandt's painting attended by the "foremen of the guild" dates back to as early as the year 1693; see C. Hofstede de Groot,[228] No. 369 on p. 429. Since only two of those represented in the painting belonged among the foremen of the year 1631–32, we are impelled to conclude that it was not the guild but Dr. Tulp himself and those portrayed with him that commissioned the painting individually and at their private cost. A second point of importance becomes clear: none of the guild members held the degree of doctor of medicine; they were, therefore, in no sense "colleagues" or, as has also been said, "students" of Dr. Tulp. The guild consisted of a body of ordinary members out of whose midst there were annually chosen six foremen. Four of this number were known as "overluyden" in charge of administration, a fifth was specified as "bosmeester," i.e. treasurer (see *Woordenboek*,[520a] III, col. 1930, *s.v.* "busmeester"), the sixth served as "proefmeester" in charge of examinations of the guild "knegten" apprenticed to individual members. The function of "bosmeester" ceases in 1654; that of "proefmeester" in 1704. In the listing below I have given, on the basis of information received from Dr. van Eeghen, the dates of membership acquired. The listing is preceded by a diagram that shows the numbers of the roll call sheet in the relative position of the eight faces that appear in the painting. The cadaver bears no number.

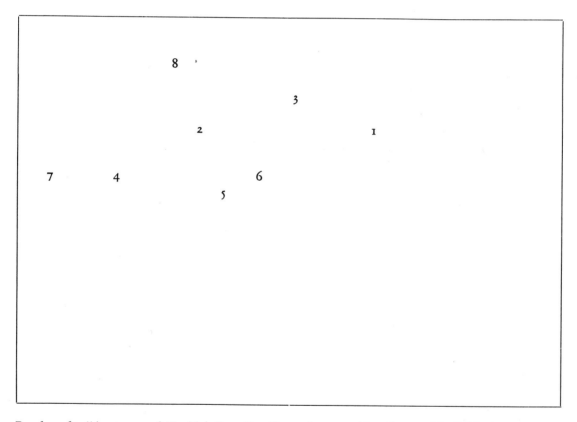

Rembrandt, "Anatomy of Dr. Tulp"; roll call numbers marking faces of individuals portrayed.

1. *D Nicl Tulp*. See Note 38, pp.74–76 and this study *passim*. Docents of Anatomy *(prae-lectores)* attached to the Amsterdam Guild were:

    1) Dr. Maarten Jansz. Koster (Aedituus), burgomaster, died 1599.
    2) Dr. Sebastian Egbertsz., burgomaster, 1599–1621.

3) Dr. Joan Fonteyn, 1621–28.
4) Dr. Nicolaas Pietersz. Tulp, burgomaster, 1628–53.
5) Dr. Joan Deyman, 1653–66.
6) Prof. Frederik Ruysch, 1666–1731.
7) Prof. Willem Röell, 1727–55.
8) Prof. Pieter Camper, 1755–61.
9) Prof. Folkert Snip, 1762–71.
10) Prof. Andreas Bonn, 1771–98.

Cf. J. W. R. Tilanus,[471a] pp. 28 f.

2. *Jacob Blok*. Jacob Dielofsen Block acquired guild membership March 21, 1623. Mentioned as a member 1637 and February 24, 1640. According to MS. 229, [305aaa] fol. 3 *verso*, Gisbertus Jacobi Block (a son?) was granted the degree of doctor of medicine at Angers (Maine-et-Loire), July 10, 1647. For other relatives of individuals represented in the painting, see Nos. 3, 6, and 7. Block Sr. is listed as one of the "overluyden" on two occasions (1639 and 1640).

3. *Hartman Hartman*. Acquired membership August 9, 1615. His name occurs repeatedly in the "Anatomij-Boek":[305a] 1639, February 24, 1640, January 8, 1645. A son, Hartmannus Hartmann, Junior, was inscribed as *studiosus medicinae* (No. 391) at Leiden November 16, 1651. On January 24, 1653, H. H., "Chirurgus Amstelraedamensis," defended his thesis "De carbunculo" before the medical faculty *ibidem* and was granted the degree (source of information: Dr. G. I. Lieftinck, Conservator MSS., Leiden University Library).

4. *Adriaan Slabraen*. Adriaen Cornelisz. Slabberan acquired membership January 1, 1625. He was, according to MS. 243,[305aa] fol. 10 *verso,* an "overman" in the guild year 1631–32. Also see No. 5, Jacob de Witt.

5. *Jacob de Witt*. Dr. van Eeghen assumes that he is identical with Jacob Jansz. Cruys, who acquired membership in 1611. He occurs as a member (Jacob Jansz. de Wit) in 1631 and 1632. He was one of the "overluyden" in the guild year 1631–32, according to the "Anatomij-Boek," MS. 294,[305a] and MS. 243[305aa] fol. 10 *verso.* He and No. 4, Adriaan Slabraen, are the only ones appearing in Rembrandt's painting who were foremen of the guild in the crucial guild year 1631–32.

6. *Mathys Kalkoen* [partly illegible]. According to Dr. van Eeghen the Mathys Evertsz. who acquired membership October 2, 1615 should be the same, since no other "Mathys" is found listed. His son, Gysbrecht Mathysz. Calcoen, became guild master November 15, 1645. Dr. van Eeghen reminds me that he is said to appear in 1656 in Rembrandt's "Anatomy of Dr. Deyman" holding the cranium (see Pl. XII-16); see also section B of this Appendix.

7. *Jacob Koolvelt.* Jacop Jansz. Coolevelt acquired membership August 20, 1620. Hendrik Claesz. Coolevelt (a relative?) is listed in MS. 243,[305aa] fol. 10 *verso,* as one of the "overluyden" for the year 1631–32.

8. *Fran[s] van Loenen.* Dr. van Eeghen is sure that he is identical with the Frans Jacobsz. who acquired membership February 7, 1620. Just as there is no other Mathys (No. 6), there is no other Frans in the lists of guild members. He was, again according to Dr. van Eeghen, probably the son-in-law of one Antonij Jansz. Testament who, in 1631–32, was "overman" (cf. No. 5 above). Frans van Loenen, despite all previous claims to the contrary, was a member of the Amsterdam Guild.

[9.] "*Adriaen Adriaenson,* anders genaemt het Kint." The name of the anatomical object appears thus (with slight variations in the spelling) in two contemporary documents of the guild: the "Anatomij-Boek," MS. 294[305a] and MS. 229[305aa]: "Adriaan adriaansz anders genaamt het Kint. was kokermaaker geboren tot leijden in hollant int 28 Jaar is voor sijn moetwil met de koorde gestraft an. 1632 den 31 Januarij bij die vant gilt ontleet." For further data cf. I. H. van Eeghen[135] and this study, *passim.*

B. Rembrandt's "Anatomy of Dr. Deyman"

In the following the passages of the "Anatomij-Boek," MS. 294,[305a] referring to the lesson conducted by Dr. Deyman that Rembrandt commemorated are excerpted and in part translated.

Den 28 Januarij A° 1656 is met de coorde gestraft Joris fonteijn van diest, die ons van de EE. Heeren van de gerechte tot ons subjectum Anatomicum is vergundt. ende 29 dito heeft de heer Prelector – Dr. Johan Deijman sijn eerste demonstratie daer over gedaen op de hal jn de ordinari snij plaets en heeft daer over drie lessen gedaen, heeft de ene dach. door d'ander opgebracht jnt geheel de somme van f 187/6
Als Proefmeesters waren –
   Abraham de hondecoeter
   Dirck vis.
Overluijden.
   Klaes Janson fruijt.
   Daniel florianus
   Laurens de langhe
   Augustus Maijer.
De 2 februari op woensdach des avonts de clocke 9 uren is t' lichaem op het suijder kerckhof met een redelijke statie jn d'aerde geset.
Vereert aan de Docter voor sijn gedane lessen 6 silverde lepels bedragende f 31/19 stuijvers.

191

On January 28, 1656 there was punished with the rope Joris Fonteijn of Diest [a village in the Province of Gelderland; cf. A. J. van der Aa[1] III, 1841, p. 329], who by the Worshipful Lords of the Lawcourt was granted us as anatomical object.

On the 29th Dr. Johan Deyman made his first demonstration on him [i. e. the first he conducted as praelector of the guild] in the theater of the Anatomy, three lessons altogether. The sum total of the sessions amounts to 187 guilders and 6 stuyvers. ...

[N.B. The following entry is in the same hand but in different ink] Wednesday, February 2, at 9 o'clock in the evening the body was interred with fitting dignity in the South Churchyard.

Presented to the Doctor in recompense for his lessons: six silver spoons to the value of 31 guilders and 19 stuyvers.

Bibliography

Note: This bibliography is not (where avoidable) drawn from other bibliographies. Of the classics, ancient and modern, it was thought unnecessary to give full titles; and where subtitles, etc. seemed superfluous short titles have generally been used.

1. Aa, A. J. van der, *Biographisch Woordenboek der Nederlanden . . .*, Haarlem, 1852–78, in 12 vols.
2. *Affiche*, Printed Announcement of a Public Anatomy at Leipzig, March 10, 1646. Zwickau (Saxony), Städtisches Museum. *See also* Clemen, Otto, 99, and Bogdanus, Martinus, 58.
3. Aitken, P. Henderson, *A Catalogue of the Manuscripts of the Hunterian Museum in the University of Glasgow*, Glasgow, 1908, No. 364, pp. 290f.
4. Alanus ab Insulis (1128–1202), *Liber in distinctionibus dictionum theologicalium*, ed. Migne, *P. L.*, CCX, cols. 685–1012.
5. Alcuin (*ca.* 735–804), "Disputatio juvenis . . ., "*Didascalia*, ed Migne, *P. L.*, CI, cols. 975–80.
   Alexander Benedictus. *See* Benedictus Alexander, 44.
5a. Allers, Rudolf, "Microcosmus. From Anaximandros to Paracelsus," *Traditio*, II, 1944, pp. 319–407.
6. *Allgemeine Deutsche Biographie*, Leipzig, 1875–1910.
7. Ambrosius, *Saint* (339–97), *Hexaemeron libri sex*, ed. Migne, *P. L.*, XIV, cols. 123–272.
8. Amira, Karl von, *Die germanischen Todesstrafen. Untersuchungen zur Recht- und Religionsgeschichte* (Abhandlungen der Bayerischen Akademie der Wissenschaften, philosophisch-philologische

8. Amira, Karl von *(Cont.)* und historische Klasse XXXI, 3), Munich, 1922, pp. 134ff.
   Amman, Jost (1539–91). *See* Schopper(us), H., 430.
9a. Amsterdam, *Amsterdammer Courant*, March 23, 1720. *See also* Thijssen, E. H. M., 468.
9b. *Amsterdam University. History and General Information*, Amsterdam, *s. a.*
   Andel, M. A. van. *See* Bontius, Jacobus, 61.
10. Anon., *The Bloody Court; or, the Fatall Tribunall*, London (Horton), (1649).
11. Anon., "Coster's Academie, Voorloopster van het Athenaeum Illustre," *Amstelodamum*, XIX, 1932, pp. 69f.
12. Anon., "Het klinisch onderwijs te Utrecht tot 1650," *Sol Iustitiae*, XI, 21, Utrecht, 1956, pp. 2f.
13. Anon., *Theatrum Honoris in quo Nostri Apelles, Saeculi seu, Pictorum, qui patrum nostrorum memoria vixerunt celebriorum praecipue quos belgium, tulit, verae ad vivum expressae imagines in aes incisae exhibentur*, Amsterdam (apud Ioannem Iansonium), 1618.
14. Anon., *Campi clysteriorum*, n.p., *s. a.*
15. Arfe y Villafane, Juan de (1535–95), *De varia commensuracion para la esculptura y architectura*, in 3 pts., Seville, 1585.
16. Argellata, Petrus de (d. 1423). *See* Rudloff, Ernst von, 414.

17. Aristotle (384–22 B.C.), *Nichomachean Ethics* (Loeb Classical Library).

18. Artelt, Walter, "Das Buch im Anatomiebild und das Anatomiebuch im Bild," *Deutsche Medizinische Wochenschrift*, LXXVII, 52, Dec. 26, 1952, pp. 1637–40.

19. Augustine, *Saint* (354–430), *De civitate Dei*, ed. J. E. C. Welldon, London, 1926.

20. Bacon, Francis, *Viscount of St. Albans* (1561–1626), *The Charge of . . . touching Duells, upon an information in the Star-Chamber against Priest and Wright . . .*, [London], 1614 (35 pp.).

21. Baier, Iohannes Iacobus (1664–?), *Biographiae professorum medicinae qui in Academia Altorfina vnquam vixervnt*, Nuremberg and Altorf, 1728.

21a. Bakhuizen van den Brink, J. N., *De Romeinsche Catacomben en haar Fresco's*, The Hague, 1933.

22. Balde, Jacobus, S. J. (1604–68), "Vesalii anatomici praestantissimi laus," *Medicinae gloria per Satyras XXII asserta* (No. XII), *(ed. princeps)*, Munich, 1643.

23. ———, ed. & tr. Johannes Neubig, *s.t. Jakob Baldes medizinische Satyren . . .* (in two pts.), Munich, 1833.

24. Baldinucci, Filippo (d. 1696), "*Vita di Reimbrond Van Rein*" (1686). *See also* Hofstede de Groot, C., 228.

25. Balsiger, Barbara Jeanne, *An Analytical Census of Early Printed Catalogues of Kunst- und Wunderkammern* (M. A. thesis), State University of Iowa, 1955.

26. Banister (Banester), John (1533–1610), Manuscript of Anatomical Tables, Glasgow University, Hunterian Museum Library, No. V. 1.1. (1581), size: $14^7/_8 \times 11^1/_4''$. *See also* Young, John, 525.

27. ———, *The Historie of Man, sucked from the sappe of the most approued Anatomistes . . .*, London, 1578. *See also* Aitken, P. Henderson, 3.

28. Barge, J. A. J., *De oudste Inventaris der oudste Academische Anatomie in Nederland*, Leiden-Amsterdam, 1934.

29. Barlaeus, Casper (van Baerle) (1584–1648), "Amstelodamvm," *Hollandiae Encomiae*, ed. *Poematvm editio nova . . .*, Leiden, 1631.

30. ———, *Marie de Medicis entrant dans Amsterdam: ou Histoire de la Reception faicte . . . par les Bovrgmaistres & Bourgeoisie de la Ville d'Amsterdam . . .*, Amsterdam, 1638.

31. ———, "De conjugii necessitate . . .," *Dialogi aliquot nuptiales . . .*, Amsterdam, 1643.

32. ———, ("Poemata"), ed. *Poematvm Miscellaneorvm / Elegiarvm libri . . .*, Amsterdam, 1645–46, in 2 vols.

33. ———, "Mercator sapiens, sive Oratio de conjugendis Mercaturae et Philosophiae Studiis, Illustris Amstelodamensium Gymnasii Inaugurationem" (January 9, 1632), *Orationes variae*, Amsterdam, ed. 1652, pp. 1–28.

34. ———, "Oratio de animae humanae admirandis (1635)," *Orationum liber*, Amsterdam, ed. 1643, pp. 96–125.

35. ———, *Epistolarum liber*, ed. Amsterdam, 1667 in 2 pts.

36. Bartholomaeus *Anglicus* (d. *ca.* 1260), *De proprietatibus rerum*, ed. Lyons, 1482 (without illustrations).

37. ———, [tr. completed *ante*: 1380, by: Jehan Corbichon] *Cy commence vng tresexcellent liure nomme le proprietaire des choses translate de latin en francoys a la requeste de trescrestien et trespuissant roy charles quint de ce nom [1364–80] a donc regnant en france paisiblement lecquel traicte moult amplement de plusieurs notables matiers comme on pourra apperceuoir par les prologues qui sensyuent.* (colophon:) Lyon, Nov. 12, 1482 (first illustrated).

38. ———, *De proprietatibus rerum . . . By Wyken* [sic] *de Worde . . . at prayer and desyre of Roger Thorney*, Westminster, 1495 (?).

39. Bartholomew's, St. (London), *St. Bartholomew's Hospital Journal*, LIX, 1955, p. 241 (unsigned article on Dr. Freke).

40. Bartisch, Georg (1535–1607?), *"Stein-schneidebuch." See also* Holländer, E., 234.

41. Bauhinus, Caspar (1560–1624), *Theatrvm Anatomicvm . . .*, Frankfort, 1605.

Baumann, E.D. *See Nieuw Nederlandsch Biografisch Woordenboek,* 340.

42. Baumann, Hermann, "Likundu. Die Sektion der Zauberkraft," *Zeitschrift für Ethnologie,* LX, Berlin, 1928.

43. Belon, Pierre (Petrus Bellonius) (1517?–64), [*De admirabili operum antiquorvm et rerum suscipiendarum praestantia Liber primus.*] *De medicato funere, seu cadauere condito . . . Liber secundus. De medicamentis nonnullis, servandi cadaueris vim obtinentibus. Liber tertius,* Paris, 1553.

Benedetti, Giacopone de'. *See* Jacopone da Todi, 251.

44. Benedictus, Alexander (*ca.* 1460/70–1525) (*Anatomice sive de*) *Historia corporis humani . . .* (in five books), ed. Venice, 1502 (*ed. princeps,* 1497); Paris, H. Stephanus, 1514.

45. Benesch, Otto, "Rembrandt and the Gothic Tradition," *Gazette des Beaux-Arts,* 86th year—series 6, XXVI, 1944, pp. 285–304.

46. –––, *The Art of the Renaissance in Northern Europe,* Cambridge, 1947.

47. –––, *The Drawings of Rembrandt . . .,* I, London [1954].

48. Benivieni, Antonio (Antonius Benivenius) (*ca.* 1450–1506), *De abditis nonnullis ac mirandis morborum et sanationum causis* (ed. Girolamo Benivieni), Florence, Ph. Giuntae, 1507.

49. Berchorius, Petrus (Pierre Bersuire) (fl. 1340; d. 1362), *Metamorphosis Ouidiana Moraliter a Magistro Thoma vvaleys Anglico de prof. pred. sub sanctissimo patre dominico: explanata* (Paris), (1515). *See also* Henkel, M.D., 217.

50. –––, *Dictionarium seu Repertorium morale . . . partes tres* (composed ab. 1340), ed. Venice, 1583, in 2 vols.

51. Berengarius, Jacobus, *Carpensis* (Berengario da Carpi) (*ca.* 1470–1530), *Anatomia Carpi. Isagog(a)e breues perlucide ac uberime in anatomiam humani Corporis . . .,* ed. Bologna, Dec. 30, 1522; Venice, 1535. *See also* Singer C., and C. Rabin, 447.

51a. Bergström, Ingvar, "Medicina, fons et scrinium . . .," *Konsthistorisk Tidskrift* XXVI, 1–2, 1957, pp. 1–20.

52. Bestermann, Theodore, *The Beginnings of Systematic Bibliography,* London, 1936².

53. Bible, *Vulgatae editionis,* Douay version. *See also Glossa ordinaria,* 185.

54. Bieber, Margarete, *Laocoon . . .,* New York, 1942.

55. Bischoff, R. "Das griechische Element in der abendländischen Bildung des Mittelalters," *Byzantinische Zeitschrift,* XLIV, 1/2, 1951, pp. 27–55.

56. Bleeker, G.J., "Nox revelatrix," *Pro regno . . .* (. . . Bijdrage . . . G. van der Zeeuw . . .), Nijkerk, 1950, pp. 47–59.
Bloody Court, The. See Anon., 10.

57. Bode, Wilhelm von, *Adriaen Brouwer . . .,* Berlin, 1924.

58. Bogdanus, Martinus B. (1631–*post* 1679), [Broadside] "ILLVSTRISSIMI . . .," Berne, December 18, 1660. *See also Affiche,* 2.

59. Bontemantel, Hans (1613–88), *De Regeeringe van Amsterdam. Soo in 't civiel als crimineel en militaire* (1653–72), pt. I (ed. G.W. Kernkamp, Werken uitgegeven door het Historisch Genootschap, series 3, No. 7), The Hague, 1897.

60. Bontius, Jacobus (1592–1631), *De medicina Indorum . . .,* Leiden, 1642.

61. –––, ed. and tr. M.A. van Andel, *s.t. Bontius Tropische Geneeskunde* (Introduction) (Opuscula Selecta Neerlandicorum de Arte Medica X), Amsterdam, 1931, pp. viii–xli.

62. Boon, A. van der, Cz., *Geschiedenis der Ontdekkingen in de Ontleedkunde van den*

62. Boon, A. van der *(Cont.)*
Mensch, gedaan in de Noordelijke Neder-
landen, tot aan het begin van de negentiende
eeuw, Utrecht, 1851.

62a. Boulenger [Bulengerus], Julius Caesar,
S.J. (1558–1628), *De pictvra, plastice,*
statvaria libri dvo . . ., Lyon, 1627.

Bovio, *brothers abbate* Guido and Giulio.
See Brom, Gisbert, 68.

Brack, B(W)enceslaus. *See Vocabularium*
rerum, 497.

63. Bratschkova (Bruchkova), Maria, "Die
Muschel in der antiken Kunst," *Bulletin*
de l'Institut Archéologique Bulgare, XII,
1938 (1939), pp. 1–131.

64. Bredius, A. (and others), *Amsterdam in de*
Zeventiende Euw, III, The Hague,
1901–4.

65. ———, *The Paintings of Rembrandt,* Vienna,
1936.

66. Brendel, Otto, "Symbolik der Kugel.
Archäologischer Beitrag zur Geschichte
der älteren griechischen Philosophie,"
Mitteilungen des deutschen archaeologischen
Instituts. Roemische Abteilung, LI, 1936,
pp. 1–95.

67. British Museum, *Catalogue* (of the Reading
Room).

Broadside. *See also Affiche,* 2.

68. Brom, Gisbert, "Een Italiaansche Reis-
beschrijving der Nederlanden (1677–
78)," *Bijdragen en Mededeelingen van het*
Historisch Genootschap, XXXVI, 1915,
pp. 81–230.

69. Brouwer Ancher, A. J. M., *De Gilden,* The
Hague, 1895.

70. Browne, *Sir* Thomas (1605–82), "Musaeum clausum, or Bibliotheca Abscon-
dita: containing some Remarkable Books,
Antiquities, Pictures, and Rarities of
several kinds, Scarce or never seen by
Any Man Now Living" (publ. 1684),
Miscellany Tracts, XIII, ed. Simon Wilkin, Vol. IV, London, 1885, pp. 239–50.

71. ———, *Religio Medici* (1642–43), Lat. ed.
Leiden, 1644; ed. Simon Wilkin, II,
London, 1883.

72. Brun(s)fels, Otto (1488–1534), *Herbarum*
vivae ei coneb ad naturae imitationem, summa
cum diligentia et artificio effigate, . . . (ed.
princeps), Strassburg, 1530 (colophon).

73. Bruno, Giordano (1550–1600), *De immenso,*
ed. *opera latina,* Naples, 1879–91.

74. Brunschwig, Hieronymus (1450–1512),
(Cirurgia) Dis ist das buoch der Cirurgia
Hantwirckung der wundartzney, Augsburg,
Joh. Schönsperger, 1497.

75. Bruyne, Edgar de, *Etudes d'Esthétique mé-*
diévale, Bruges, 1946, 3 vols.

76. Burdach, Konrad, "Faust und die Sorge,"
Deutsche Vierteljahrsschrift für Literatur-
wissenschaft und Geistesgeschichte, I, i, 1923,
pp. 1–60.

77. Burger (Bürger-Théophile Thoré), W.,
Les musées de la Hollande. Amsterdam et
La Haye. Études sur l'École Hollandaise,
Paris-Brussels, 1858.

78. Burton, Robert (1577–1640), *The Anatomy*
of Melancholy: What it is . . ., Oxford,
1624^2.

79. Butler, Samuel (1612–80), *Hudibras. In*
Three Parts . . . Adorn'd with a new Set of
Cuts Design'd and Engrav'd by Mr. Ho-
garth, London, 1726. *See also* Hogarth,
W. (1822), 232.

80. Cabanès, *Docteur, Mœurs intimes du Passé*
(quatrième série), Paris, *s.a.*

80a. ———, *Remèdes d'Autrefois,* 2 vols., Paris,
1905 and 1913.

81. Camillo, Giulio (1479–1544), *L'Idea del*
Theatro dell'eccellen. M.G.C., Florence,
1550.

82. Canano, Giovanni Battista (1515–58), *Mus-*
culorum humani corporis picturata dissectio
per J.B.C. . . . nunc primum in lucem edita
[with engravings by Augostino de' Musi
after G. Grassi, da Carpi], lib. I [no
more published], Ferrara, F. Rossi,
1543 [or earlier].

83. ———, facsimile copy (late 18th century), *sub eodem titulo,* London, The Wellcome Historical Medical Museum, MS. 755 (purchased 1922) (41763) (20 fols., 19 ½ × 14 cm., pen and ink illustrations).

84. ———, *Musculorum, etc.,* facsimile ed. annotated by Harvey Cushing and Edward Streeter (Monumenta Medica, IV), Florence, 1925.

85. Cardanus, Hieronymus (Gerolamo Cardano) (1501?–76), "Item de geniturae LXVII. insignes casibus & fortuna, . . . [= Vesalius' horoscope]," *Libelli duo . . .,* ed. Nuremberg, Apud I. Petreium, 1543. *See also* Cushing, Harvey W., 115.

86. ———, *De Subtilitate libri XXI . . .,* Lyon, 1580².

87. *Carmina Burana* (saec. XIIIf.), ed. Alfons Hilka and Otto Schumann, I, Heidelberg, 1930.

88. Carpi, da. *See* Berengarius, Jacobus, *Carpensis,* 51; Fulvio, Andrea, 161.
Cartesius. *See* Descartes, René, 122 and 123.

89. Cassirer, Ernst, *The Philosophy of Enlightenment,* Princeton, 1951.

90. Castiglione, Arturo, *A History of Medicine* (tr. E. B. Krumbhaar), New York, 1941.

91. ———, "The Origin and Development of the Anatomical Theater to the End of the Renaissance," *Ciba Symposia,* III, ii, 1941, pp. 826–44.

92. Celsus, Aulus Cornelius (14 B.C.–37 A.D.), *Medicinae libri VIII,* ed. Venice, 1528; Hagenau, 1528; Leiden, 1592.

93. ———, *De re medica liber octavus. Eius priora quatuor capita commentariis illustrata a P. Paaw,* Leiden, 1616.

94. Charbonneau-Lassay, L., *La Mystérieuse Emblématique de Jésus-Christ. Bestiaire du Christ . . .,* s.l. [Belgium], (1940).

95. Chasseneu[x], Barthelemy (de) (1480–1541), *Catalogus gloriae mundi laudes, honores, excellentias, ac praeeminentias omnium fere statuum, plurimarumque rerum illius continens, ed. princeps,* Lyons, 1529 (ed. *ibid.* 1546 and 1586).

96. Chomentovskaja, O., "Le Comput digital," *Gazette des Beaux-Arts,* 6 sér., XX, ii, Oct. 1938, pp. 157–72.

97. Choulant, (Johann) Ludwig, *History and Bibliography of Anatomical Illustration . . .,* tr. and ed. Mortimer Frank, New York, 1945.

98. Cicero, Marcus Tullius (106–43 B.C.), *Tusculanae Disputationes* (with the commentary of Philippus Beroaldus), ed. Venice, 1471 and 1499.

99. Clemen, Otto, "Einladung zu einer Anatomia publica in Leipzig 1646," *Sudhoffs Archiv für Geschichte der Medizin und der Naturwissenschaften,* XXXVI, Wiesbaden, 1943, pp. 103–5.

100. Cohen, Gustave, *Écrivains français en Hollande dans la première moitié du XVIIe siècle,* Paris, 1920.

101. Colbert, *Inventarium seu collectarium in parte cyrurgiali seu medicine, compilatum et completum a. 1363 per Guidonem de Gailhiaco,* MS. Paris, Bibliothèque Nationale, français 396.

102. Columbus, Matthaeus Realdus (Colombo, Realdo) (1494–1559/60), *De re anatomica libri XV, ed. princeps,* Venice, 1559.

103. Columna, Franciscus (Colonna, Francesco) (1433–1527), *Hypnerotomachia Poliphili . . .,* Venice, 1499.

104. Condivi, Ascanio (b. *ca.* 1520), *Vita di M. Angelo Buonarroti,* Rome, 1553 (ed. Quellenschriften für Kunstgeschichte V, Vienna, 1888).

105. Constantinus Africanus (d. 1087). *See* Panofsky, E., and F. Saxl, 364.

106. Copernicus, Nicolaus (1473–1543), *De revolutionibus orbium coelestium libri VI,* Nuremberg, Joh. Petreius, 1543.

107. Cordus, Valerius (1515–44), *Dispensatorium pharmacorum omnium . . .,* Nuremberg, 1535 (ed. Venice, 1556, etc.).
Cotes, Thomas and Richard. *See* Crooke, H., 112.

108. Coulton, G. G., *Art and Reformation,* Oxford, 1928.

109. Courboin, François, *Histoire illustrée de la Gravure en France*, 4 pts., Paris, 1923–28. Plates: 4 vols., Paris, 1923–26.

110. Crane, William G., *Wit and Rhetoric . . .*, New York, 1937.

111. Crescentius, Petrus de (b. 1230–*ca.* 1316), *Liber ruralium commodorum, ed. princeps*, Augsburg, 1471 (Strasbourg, 1486).

112. Crooke, Helkiah (1576–1635), *ΜΙΚΡΟΚΟΣΜΟΓΡΑΦΙΑ. A Description of the Body of Man . . .*, London, Thos. and Richard Crooke, 1631².

113. *Cursor Mundi* (*ca.* 1300), ed. B. Morris, London, 1892.

114. Curtius, Ernst Robert, *Europäische Literatur und lateinisches Mittelalter*, Bern, 1948.

115. Cushing, Harvey W., *A Bio-Bibliography of Andreas Vesalius*, New York, 1943. *See also* Canano, G.B., 84.

116. Cyprian, *Saint*, Thascius Caecilius (*ca.* 200/210–58), *Liber de mortalitate*, ed. Migne, *P.L.*, IV, cols. 581–602; ed., comment., and tr. M.L. Hannan, Washington, 1933.

117. Daninos, Pierre, *Les Carnets du Major W. Marmaduke Thompson*, Paris, 1954. *Danse macabre. See* Marchant, G., 307.

118. Dante Alighieri (1265–1321), (*Divine Comedy*), *Lo 'nferno e 'l Paradiso, di D.A., Commento di Christophoro Landino fiorentino sopra la comedia di D.A. poeta fiorentino* (with 19 engravings after designs by Botticelli), Florence, Nicholo di Lorenzo della Magna, Aug. 30, 1481.

119. Decker, Jeremias de (1609–66), *Lof der Geldsucht ofte Vervolg der Rijmoeffeningen*, II, Amsterdam, 1668.

120. Deguileville, Guillaume de (fl. XIV *c.*), *Songe du pèlerinage de vie humaine*, MS. Brussels, Bibliothèque Royale, 10176–78 (*ca.* 1395).

121. Déonna, W., "Aphrodite à la Coquille," *Revue Archéologique*, 5me sér. VI, 1917, pp. 392–416.

122. Descartes, René (1596–1650), *Les Traitez de l'homme et de la formation du fœtus . . .*, in 3 pts., Amsterdam, 1680.

123. ———, *Lettres*, ed. *Œuvres de Descartes*, I, Paris, 1897.

124. Dieckmann, Herbert, "Diderot's Conception of Genius," *Journal of the History of Ideas*, II, 2, 1941, pp. 151–82.

125. *Dictionary of National Biography*, London, 1885–1900.
Dionysius *Areopagita* (*ca.* 500 A.D.). *See* Maximus, *Saint*, 312.

126. Drabkin, I.E., "On Medical Education in Greece and Rome," *Bulletin of the History of Medicine*, XV, 4, 1944, pp. 333–51.

127. Dülberg, Franz, "Rembrandt und Lucas van Leyden," *Jaarboekje voor Geschiedenis en Oudheidkunde van Leiden en Rijnland*, III, 1906.

128. Dürer, Albrecht (1471–1528), ["Proportionslehre"], *Beschryvinghe van Albrecht Durer van de Menschelijcke Proportion . . . tot Nurenbergh gedruckt . . . 1527. Ende nu in onse Nederlandtsche sprake overgheset . . .*, Arnhem, 1622.

129. Dufflaeus, Cornelius Kilianus (d. 1607), *Etymologicum . . . Dictionarium Teutonico-Latinum . . .*, Utrecht, 1777.

130. Dugdale, [*Sir*] William (1605–86), *The History of St. Paul's Cathedral in London . . .*, London, 1658.
Du Jon, François, the Younger. *See* Junius, Franciscus, 262, 263, 264.
Du Laurens, André. *See* Laurentius, Andreas, 281.

131. Duyvené de Wit-Klinkhamer [Mevrouw], Th. M., and others, *Vier Eeuwen Nederlands Zilver* (Exhibition Cat. Gemeentemuseum), The Hague (July–September), 1952.

132. Edelstein, Ludwig, "Andreas Vesalius, The Humanist," *Bulletin of the History of Medicine*, XIV, v, 1943, pp. 547–61.

133. ———, "The Development of Greek Anatomy," *Bulletin of the Institute of the*

133. Edelstein, Ludwig *(Cont.)*
History of Medicine, III, 4, 1935, pp. 235–48.

134. Eeghen, Chr. F. van, "De schilder de Rijck en de vrouw van Govert Flinck als patiënten van dr. Nicolaes Tulp," *Oud Holland*, LX ("Archiefsprokke-lingen"), 1943, pp. 94f.

135. Eeghen, I. H. van, "De anatomische lessen van Rembrandt," *Amstelodamum*, XXXV, 1948, pp. 34–36.

136. ———, "Het Athenaeum en de Universi-teit van Amsterdam," *Amstelodamum*, XXXIX, 1952, pp. 72–77.

136a. ———, *Inventarissen der Archieven van de Gilden en van het Brouwerscollege* (Archief der Gemeente), Amsterdam, 1951.

137. Elias, Johan E., *De Vroedschap van Amster-dam 1578–1795*, I, Haarlem, 1903.

138. Emmens, J. A., "'Ay, Rembrant, maal *Cornelis* stem,'" *Nederlands Kunsthisto-risch Jaarboek* [1956], pp. 133–65.

139. Erasmus, Desiderius (Gerhard Gerhards) (1469–1536), *ΜΩΡΙΑΣ ΕΓΚΩ-ΜΙΟΝ. Stultitiae Laus . . .* (cum com-mentariis Gerardi Listrii [*ed. princeps*, Basel, 1519], et fig. J. Holbenii), ed. C. Patin, Basel, 1676 (illus. with etchings by "C. M." after Holbein).

140. ———, *Colloquiorum familiarum opus, postrema Auctoris manu . . . recognitum . . .*, Frankfort, 1555.

141. ———, (Letters, ed. H. M. Allen) *Opus Epistolarum . . .*, IV, Oxford, 1922.

141a. Erlanger, Philippe, *Louis XIII*, Paris, 1946.

142. Esmeijer, A. C., and Simon H. Levie, *Catalogus Jan van Scorel* (Centraal Mu-seum), Utrecht, 1955.

143. Essen, C. C. van, *La Découverte du Laocoon* (Mededeelingen der koninklijke Neder-landse Akademie van Wetenschappen, Afd. Letterkunde. Nieuwe Reeks, Deel 18, No. 12), Amsterdam, 1955, pp. 291–305.

144. Esso Bzn., I. van, "Over waanvoorstel-lingen bij beroemde personen," *Amste-lodamum*, XXXVII, 1950, pp. 125f.

Estienne, Charles. *See* Stephanus, Carolus, 456.

145. Euclid (fl. *ca.* 300 B.C.), *Elementa, ed. princeps*, Venice, Erhart Ratdolt, 1482.

146. Eugippius (d. after 533), *Excerpta ex operibus S. Augustini,* ed. and comment. Pius Knoell (Corpus Scriptorum Eccle-siasticorum Latinorum I, pt. i), Vienna, 1885.

147. Eustachius, Bartolomaeus (1520–74), *Opvscvla Anatomica . . .*, Venice, 1564 (preceded by [nine] "tabulae & figurae Anatomicae ad haec opuscula pertinen-tes," pp. 1–24).

148. ———, *Tabulae anatomicae . . . quas e tene-bris tandem vindicatas . . . Praefatione, Notisque illustravit . . .* (J. M. Lancisius), *ed. princeps*, Rome (*Imprimatur* 1714).

149. Fabricius ab Aquapendente, Hieronymus (1533–1619), *De venarum ostiolis . . .*, ed., tr., and notes by K. J. Franklin, Spring-field, Ill., Baltimore, 1933.

149a. Faller, A., *Die Entwicklung der makrosko-pisch-anatomischen Präparierkunst von Ga-len bis zur Neuzeit*, Basel, 1948.

150. Farrington, Benjamin, "The Last Chapter of the *De Fabrica* of Vesalius entitled Some Observations on the Dissection of Living Animals, Translated from the Latin," *Trans. of the Royal Society of South Africa* (Cape Town), XX, 1931, pp. 1–14.

151. ———, "The Preface of Andreas Vesalius to De Fabrica Corporis Humani, 1543," *Proceedings of the Royal Society of Medicine*, XXV, ii, London, 1932, pp. 1357–66.

152. Fehr, Hans, *Das Recht im Bilde*, Erlenbach-Zürich, 1923.

153. Fernel(ius), Jean (1497–1558), *De abditis rerum causis libri II* (also known as *Dialogi*), *ed. princeps*, Paris, Christian Wechel, 1548.

154. Feyfer, F. M. G. de, "Die Schriften des Andreas Vesalius . . .," *Janus,* XIX (Leiden), 1914, pp. 1–73.

Feyrabend, Sigismund. *See* Schopperus, H., 430.

155. Fludd, Robert (1574–1637), *Anatomiae amphitheatrum effigie triplici, more et conditione varia, designatum . . .,* 2 pts., Frankfort, 1623.

156. Fontaine Verwey, H. de la, "Descartes en Amsterdam," *Amstelodamum,* XXXVII, 1950, pp. 17–21.

157. Francisci, Erasmus F. (von Finx) (1627–94), *Der höllische Proteus oder merkwürdige Begebenheiten von Gespenstern . . .,* Nuremberg, *ed. princeps,* 1708 [not 1689 as on the handwritten title of copy in the Library of the University of Michigan].

158. Freeman, Rosemary, *English Emblem Books,* London, 1948.

159. Fremantle, Katharine D. H., *The Royal Palace* [i.e. City Hall] *at Amsterdam* (Ph. D. thesis, London University), 1956 [forthcoming in book form].

160. Fuchs, Leonhard (1501–66), *De historia stirpium New Kreüterbuch . . .,* Basel, Michael Isengrin, 1542.

161. Fulvio, Andrea (fl. 1510–43), *Illvstrivm imagines (colophon:) Imperatorum: & illustrium Virorum ac Mulierum uultus ex antiquis numismatibus expressi: emendatum correptumque opus per A. F.,* Rome, I. Mazochius, 1517 (wood engravings by Ugo da Carpi (*ca.* 1450–1525)).

162. Gabriel, A. L., "The Preparatory Teaching in the Parisian Colleges During the XIVth Century," *Revue de l'Université d'Ottawa,* Oct.–Dec. 1951, pp. 5–39.

163. Galen, Claudius (*ca.* 129–99 A.D.), *De anatomicis administrationibus libri novem, Joanne Guintero Andernaco Medico interprete* [and tr.], Paris, 1531.
(a) ed. and tr. *s.t. Galen on Anatomical Procedures . . .* (Publications of the Wellcome Historical Medical Museum, N. S. No. 7), Oxford University Press, 1956.

163. Galen, Claudius *(Cont.)*
(b) ed. *Omnia quae extant in Latinum sermonem conuersa,* Basel, 1562.

164. ———, *De libris propriis liber* (1525).

165. ———, *De ordine librorum suorum liber* (1525).

166. ———, *Omnia opera,* Venice, 1541–42. *See also* Guenther, Johannes, 200.

167. Gallonius, Antonius (1550?–1605), *Trattato de gli Instrvmenti di martirio, e delle varie maniere di martoriare vsate da' Gentili contro Christiani . . .,* Rome, 1591.

168. ———, *De S.S. martyrum cruciatibus . . .,* Rome, 1594.

169. Gamelin, Jacques (1738–1802), *Nouveau recueil d'ostéologie et de myologie, dessiné d'après nature,* 2 pts., Toulouse, 1779.

170. Gans, Edward, and Guido Kisch, "The Cambyses Justice Medal," *Art Bulletin,* XXIX, ii, 1947, pp. 121–25.

171. Garzoni, Tomaso (1549–89), *La piazza universale di tutte le professioni del mondo, e nobili et ignobili,* Venice, 1586.

172. ———, *La Piazza Universale: Das ist Allgemeiner Schauplatz . . . Professionen . . .,* Frankfort, 1659. *See also* Schopperus, 430.

173. Geerts, A. M. F. B., *Vondel als Classicus bij de Humanisten in de Leer* (Diss. Utrecht), Tongerloo (Antwerp), 1932.

174. Gelder, H. Enno van, *Rembrandt,* Amsterdam, *s.a.*

175. Gelder, J. G. van, "Rubens in Holland in de zeventiende eeuw," *Nederlandsch Kunsthistorisch Jaarboek,* 1950–51 (1951), pp. 103–50.

176. ———, "Rembrandt's Vroegste Ontwikkeling," *Mededeelingen der Koninklijke Nederlandsche Akademie van Wetenschappen* (Afd. Letterkunde. N. R., deel 16, No. 5), Amsterdam, 1953, pp. 1–26 (273–98).

177. ———, "Rembrandt en de zeventiende Eeuw," *De Gids,* CXIX, vi, 1956, pp. 397–413.

177a. ———, "Verloren werken van Lucas van Leyden," *Miscellanea D. Roggen,* Antwerp, 1957, pp. 91–100.

178. Gerstenberg, Kurt, "Das Bücherstilleben in der Plastik," *Deutschland–Italien. Beiträge zu den Kulturbeziehungen zwischen Norden und Süden. Festschrift für Wilhelm Waetzold zu seinem 60. Geburtstage . . .,* Berlin, 1941, pp. 135–59.

Gesner, Conrad (1516–65). *See* Galen, ed. 1562, 163b.

179. *Gesta Romanorum* (ca. 1320), ed. Hermann Oesterley, Berlin, 1872.

180. ———, [*s.t.:*] *HIer beginnen ter eren gods ende totter menschen leringhe ende salicheyt seer notabile hystorien ghetogen vten gesten ofte croniken der romeynen . . . (colophon:)* Zwolle, 1484 (illus. with seven full-page woodcuts of approx. five scenes each and one smaller cut).

181. Geyl, Dr. [sic], "Kleine Bijdragen tot de Geschiedenis van de Schilderijen van 't Amsterdamsche Chirurgijnsgild, o.a. van de Anatomische Les van Rembrandt," *Oud Holland,* XXIV, 1906, pp. 38–40.

182. Giedion, Siegfried, *Mechanization Takes Command,* New York, 1948.

183. Gilbert, William (1544–1603), *De Magnete, Magnetisqve corporibvs, et de Magno magnete Tellure; Physiologia noua, plurimis & argumentis, & experimentis demonstrata,* London, 1600.

184. Gils, Johan Baptist Franciscus van, *De Dokter in de oude Nederlandsche Toneelliteratuur* (Diss. Leiden), Haarlem, 1917.

185. *Glossa ordinaria* (O. and N.T.), ed. optima, s.t. *Glossa ordinaria, cum expositione litterali et necnon additionibus et relicis,* Basel, Froben, 1506–8.

ed. Migne, *P.L.,* CXIII, CXIV.

186. Goethe, Johann Wolfgang von (1749–1832), *Faust,* pts. I and II.

Gogh, Vincent van. *See* Nordenfalk, Carl, 341.

187. Goldschmidt, Adolph, "Willem Buytewech," *Jahrbuch der preussischen Kunstsammlungen,* XXIII, 1902, pp. 100–17.

188. Goldschmidt, Edgar, *Entwicklung und Bibliographie der pathologisch-anatomischen Abbildung,* Leipzig, 1925.

189. ———, "Les scènes anatomiques vues par les artistes au cours des siècles," *Rivista di storia delle Scienze mediche e naturali,* XLIII, ii, 1932 (reprint).

190. ———, "Zur Geschichte der pathologischen Anatomie," *Schweizerische medizinische Wochenschrift,* LXXIV, xxxiii, 1944, pp. 892f.

191. ———, "Autopsie und Sektion im Bild," *Schweizerische Zeitschrift für Pathologie und Bakteriologie,* XI, 1948 (reprint).

192. Goldschmidt, E.Ph., *Mediaeval Texts and Their First Appearance in Print,* London, 1943.

193. ———, *The Printed Book of the Renaissance . . .,* Cambridge, 1950.

193a. Graaf, Regnerus (Reinier) de (1641–73), *De virorum organis generationi inservientibus, de clijsteribus . . .,* Leiden and Rotterdam, 1668.

194. Gracht, Jacob van der (1593–1652), *Anatomie der wtterlicke deelen van het Menschelick Lichaem . . . Bequaem voor Schilders, Beelt-Houwers, Plaet snyders, als oock Chirurgiens . . .,* The Hague, 1634.

195. ———, *Den tweeden druk . . .,* Rotterdam, 1660.

Graesse, Johann Georg Theodor. *See* Jacobus de Voragine, 249.

196. Gregory the Great, *Saint* (540–604), *Moralia in Job* (compl. 595). *See also* Robertson, D.W., Jr., 403.

197. Grimm, Ludwig Karl Jacob (1785–1863), *Anmerkungen zu den Kinder- und Hausmärchen . . .,* ed. Johannes Bolte & Georg Polívka, Leipzig, 1918.

198. Grossmann, F., "Holbein, Torrigiano and Some Portraits of Dean Colet . . .," *Journal of the Warburg and Courtauld Institutes,* XIII, 1950, pp. 202–36.

199. Guido da Vigevano (*ca.* 1280–after 1345), "Haec est anothomia Philippi Septimi . . . designata per figuras per Guidonem, medicum suprascripti regis," *Liber notabilium a libris Galieni extractum,* pt. III, MS. Chantilly, Musée Condé, 334 (fols. 257–73), ed.
(a) Ernest Wickersheim, "L'Anatomie' de Guido de Vigevano, médecin de la reine Jeanne de Bourgogne (1345)," *Archiv für Geschichte der Medizin,* VII, i, Leipzig, 1913, pp. 1–25;
(b) Ernest Wickersheim. *See* Mundinus (1926), 332.

200. Guinterus, Johannes (Winther), *of Andernach* (1505–74), *Institutionum anatomicarum secundum Galeni sententiam ad candidatos medicinae libri quatuor . . .,* ed. *princeps,* Basel, 1536.

201. revised and augmented ed. Andreas Vesalius, Venice, 1538.
Guy de Chauliac (Guido de Cailhiaco) (fl. 1363). *See* Colbert, 101.

202. Haarlem, Frans Halsmuseum, Catalogue, 1955.

203. Hall, H. van, *Repertorium voor de Geschiedenis der Nederlandsche Schilder- en Graveerkunst . . .,* The Hague, 1936, 1949, in 2 vols.

204. Hartmann von Ouwe (*ca.* 1170–*ca.* 1210), *Der arme Heinrich,* ed. Basel, 1885.

204a. Heckscher, Hulda, *Der kleine Meyer von Basel auf Holbeins "Darmstädter" Madonna,* Hamburg, 1956.

205. Heckscher, William S., "Relics of Pagan Antiquity in Mediaeval Settings," *Journal of the Warburg Institute,* I, iii, 1938, pp. 204–20.

206. ———, "'Was This the Face . . .?'" *Journal of the Warburg Institute,* I, iv, 1938, pp. 295–97.

207. ———, (reviewing Fussell's *Farming Books*), *Renaissance News,* IV, iv, 1951, pp. 55f.

208. ———, "Renaissance Emblems. Observations Suggested by Some Emblem-

208. Heckscher, William S. *(Cont.)* Books in the Princeton University Library," *The Princeton University Library Chronicle,* XV, ii, 1954, pp. 55–68.

209. ———, *Art and Literature,* New York, 1954.

210. ———, *SIXTVS IIII AENEAS INSIGNES STATVAS ROMANO POPVLO RESTITVENDAS CENSVIT,* The Hague, 1955.

211. ———, "The *Anadyomene* in the Mediaeval Tradition . . .," *Het Nederlands Kunsthistorisch Jaarboek,* VII, 1956, pp. 1–38.

212. Heinrichs, Heinrich, *Die Überwindung der Autorität Galens durch die Denker der Renaissancezeit* (Renaissance und Philosophie XII), Bonn, 1914, pp. 1–79.

213. Heischkel, Edith, *Die Medizingeschichtschreibung von ihren Anfängen bis zum Beginn des 16. Jahrhunderts* (Abhandlungen zur Geschichte der Medizin und Naturwissenschaften, Heft 28), Berlin, 1938.

214. Helbig, Wolfgang, *Führer durch die öffentlichen Sammlungen klassischer Altertümer in Rom,* II, Leipzig, 1913[3].

215. Held, Julius S., "Rembrandt's 'Polish Rider,'" *Art Bulletin,* XXVI, iv, 1944, pp. 246–65.

216. Helm, Rudolf, *Skelett- und Todesdarstellungen bis zum Auftreten der Totentänze,* Strassburg, 1928.

217. Henkel, M. D., *De houtsneden van Mansion's Ovide Moralisé Bruges 1484 . . .,* Amsterdam, 1922. *See also* Ovid, *Metamorphoses,* 348.

218. Herder, T. den, *Oude Gebouwen van Amsterdam* (Heemkennis Amsterdam), Amsterdam, 1949.

219. Herrad of Landsperg (Abbess of Hohenburg) (fl. *ca.* 1167–95), *Hortus deliciarum,* ed. A. Straub and G. Keller, Strasbourg, 1879–89; ed. Joseph Walter, Strasbourg-Paris, 1952.

220. Herrlinger, Robert, "Die Anatomie des Jost Amman . . .," *Sudhoffs Archiv . . .,*

220. Herrlinger, Robert *(Cont.)*
XXXVIII, i, Wiesbaden, Feb. 1953,
pp. 29–38.

221. ———, "Zur Frage der ersten anatomisch richtigen Darstellung . . .," *Centaurus,* II, iv, 1953, pp. 283–88.

222. Herzog-Hauser, Gertrud, "Zum Problem der imitatio in der lateinischen Literatur," *Wiener Studien,* LXVI, 1949, Vienna, 1950, pp. 133ff.

223. Hill, William Thomson, *Buried London. Mithras to the Middle Ages,* London, 1955.

224. Hind, Arthur M., *Early Italian Engraving . . .,* II, London, 1938.

225. Hippocrates (460?–377? B.C.), *Aphorismorum selectiones septem. Ex Franc. Rabelaisi recognitiones . . .,* Lyons, 1543.

Hoecker, R. *See* Mander, Carel van, 304.

226. Hofschlager, Reinhard, "Der Ursprung des Kaiserschnittes (II)," *Sudhoffs Archiv . . .,* XXXVII, i, Wiesbaden, Feb. 1953, pp. 77–92.

227. Hofstede de Groot, C., "Entlehnungen Rembrandts," *Jahrbuch der preussischen Kunstsammlungen,* XV, 1894, pp. 175–81.

228. ———, *Die Urkunden über Rembrandt . . .* (Quellenstudien zur holländischen Kunstgeschichte III), The Hague, 1906.

229. ———, *Beschreibendes und kritisches Verzeichnis der Werke der hervorragendsten holländischen Maler des siebzehnten Jahrhunderts,* VI, Esslingen-Paris, 1915.

230. Hogarth, William (1697–1764), *Four Stages of Cruelty,* London (Feb. 1), 1751 (four poems, presumably by the Rev. James Townley (1714–78)).

231. *The Genuine Works of William Hogarth . . .,* I, London (ed. John Nichols), 1808.

232. ———, *The Works of William Hogarth from the Original Plates . . .,* London (ed. James Heath), 1822. *See also* Butler, Samuel, 79.

233. Holinshed, Raphael (d. *ca.* 1580), *The Chronicles . . .* (1578). *See also* Nashe, Thomas, ed. McKerrow, 336.

234. Holländer, Eugen, *Die Medizin in der klassischen Malerei . . .,* Stuttgart, 1923[3].

235. Hollstein, F.W.H., *Dutch and Flemish Etchings, Engravings and Woodcuts,* Amsterdam, *s.a.*

236. Hooft, Pieter Cornelisz. (1581–1649), *Emblemata amatoria . . .,* Amsterdam, 1611.

237. Hoogewerff, G.J., *Verbeelding en Voorstelling. De Ontwikkeling van het Kunstzinnig Inzicht,* Amsterdam-Antwerp, 1948.

238. Horace, Quintus H. Flaccus (65–8 B.C.), *Carmina* (Loeb Classical Library).

239. Horne, Joannis van (1621–70), *MIKPOΚΟΣΜΟΣ seu Brevis Manductio ad Historiam Corporis Humani . . .,* Leiden, 1665[3].

240. Houbraken, Arnold (1660–1719), *De groote Schouburgh der Nederlantsche Konstschilders en Schilderessen . . . zynde een Vervolg op het Schilderboek van K.v. Mander,* II, Amsterdam, 1719.

241. Houghton, Walter E., Jr., "The History of Trades . . .," *Journal of the History of Ideas,* II, i, 1941, pp. 33ff.

242. Hülsen, Christian, "Die Auffindung der römischen Leiche vom Jahre 1485," *Mittheilungen des Instituts für österreichische Geschichtsforschung,* IV, 1883, pp. 433–99.

243. Huizinga, J., *Holländische Kultur des siebzehnten Jahrhunderts,* Jena, 1932.

244. ———, *Erasmus of Rotterdam,* New York, 1952.

245. Hutton, James, *The Greek Anthology in Italy to the Year 1800* (Cornell Studies in English XXIII), Ithaca, New York, 1935.

245a. Huygens, Constantijn (1596–1687), *Ghebruik, en Onghebruik van 't Orghel, In de Kerken der Vereenighde Nederlanden . . .,* Amsterdam, 1660.

246. ———, [Autobiography, *sine titulo*], Dutch tr. and ed. A.H. Kan, Rotterdam-Antwerp, 1946. *See also* Hofstede de Groot, C. (1906), 228.

247. Isidorus Hispalensis (of Seville) (*ca.* 560–636), *Originum sive Etymologiarum libri XX,* ed. Oxford, Clarendon Press, 1911 in 2 pts.

248. s' Jacob, Henriette, *Idealism and Realism. A Study of Sepulchral Symbolism,* Leiden, 1954.

249. Jacobus, *de Voragine, Archbishop of Genoa* (Jacopo da Voragine) (1226–98) *(Legenda sanctorum) Legenda Aurea,* Dresden and Leipzig (ed. J. G. Th. Graesse), 1846.

250. Jacobus, . . . *Sermones aurei ac pulcherrimi varijs scripturarum doctrinis referti de tempore per totum annum . . . feliciter incipiunt,* Cologne, 1478 (?).

251. Jacopone da Todi (Benedetti, Giacopone de', *da Todi*) (1228–1306), *Le Laude* (1490). *Ristampa integrale della prima edizione . . .,* Florence (ed. Giovanni Papini), (1923).

252. ed. and tr. Evelyn Underhill and Mrs. Theodore Beck, *s. t. Jacopone da Todi, Poet and Mystic—1228–1306 . . .,* London, Toronto, etc., 1919.

253. Janson, H. W., *Apes and Ape Lore in the Middle Ages and the Renaissance* (Studies of the Warburg Institute XX), London, 1952.

254. Janssens de Bisthoven, A., and R. A. Parmentier, *Le Musée Communal de Bruges* (Les Primitifs Flamands, Fascicules 1 à 4), Antwerp, 1951.

255. Jantzen, Hans, "Rembrandt, Tulp und Vesal," *Kunst und Künstler,* XXIV, 1926, pp. 313f.

Jazari (al-Jazari), Ismā'il ibn al-Razzāz (fl. first decade XIIIth c.), *Theory and Practice Useful in the Craft of Ingenious Contrivances. See also* Weitzmann, Kurt, 510.

256. Jöcher, Christian Gottlieb (1694–1758), *Compendiöses Gelehrten-Lexicon . . .,* ed. Leipzig, 1733 and 1756, in 2 vols.

257. ———, *Allgemeines Gelehrten-Lexicon, Darinne die Gelehrten aller Stände . . . vom*

257. Jöcher, Christian *(Cont.)* *Anfang der Welt bis auf ietzige Zeit,* in 4 pts., Leipzig, 1750–51.

258. ———, *Fortsetzung und Ergänzungen . . . von Johann Christoph Adelung,* in 2 pts., Leipzig and Delmenhorst, 1784–1810 (to letter "K").

John of Scythopolis. *See* Maximus Confessor, *Saint,* 312.

259. Jones, Ernest, *Sigmund Freud . . .,* I, London, 1954.

260. Jordan, Albrecht, "Bemerkungen zu einigen Bildern Rembrandt's," *Repertorium für Kunstwissenschaft,* VII, 1884, pp. 185ff.

261. Judson, J. R., *Gerrit van Honthorst. A Discussion of His Position in Dutch Art* (Diss. Utrecht), The Hague, 1956.

262. Junius, Franciscus F[rancisci] F[ilius] (François du Jon, *the Younger*) (1589 or 1591?–1677), *De Pictvra Vetervm Libri Tres (ed. princeps),* Amsterdam, 1637.

263. ———, *The Painting of the Ancients, in three Bookes: Declaring by Historicall Observations and Examples, the Beginning, Progresse, and Consvmmation of that Most Noble Art. And how those ancient Artificers attained to their still so much admired Excellencie. Written first . . . in Latine . . ., and now Englished . . .,* London, 1638.

264. ———, *De Schilder-Konst der Oude, Begrepen in drie Boecken,* Middelburg, 1641.

264a. ———, *Etymologicum Anglicanum* (ex autographo ed. Edward Lye), Oxford, 1743.

265. Justi, Johann Heinrich Gottlob von (1717–71), *Chymische Schriften . . .,* II, Stettin, etc., 1751.

266. Kalff, G., "Bijdrage tot de Geschiedenis van het Amsterdamsche Toneel in de 17de eeuw," *Oud-Holland,* XIII, 1895, pp. 1–33.

267. Kauffmann, Hans, "Rembrandt und die Humanisten vom Muiderkring," *Jahrbuch der preussischen Kunstsammlungen,* XLI, 1920, pp. 46–81.

268. Kernodle, George, *From Art to Theater...*, Chicago (1943).

269. Ketham, Joannes de (fl. 1460) (editor of:) Mundinus, "Quodlibetum anatomicum," *Fasciculo di Medicina (Fasciculus medicinae), ed. princeps,* Venice, 1491; ed. Venice, J. and G. de Gregoriis (Feb. 5), 1493.

270. (ed. and tr. Charles Singer, *s.t. The Fasciculo...*), in 2 vols., Florence, 1925; ed. 1551.

271. Kircher, Athanasius, S. J. (1602–80), *Romani Collegi Societatus Jesu Musaeum celeberrimum, cujus magnum Antiquariae rei, Statuarum imaginum, picturarumque partem... luci votisque exponit Georgius de Sepibus Valesius, Authoris in machinis concinnandis Executor,* Amsterdam, 1678.

272. Kisch, Guido, *Recht und Gerechtigkeit in der Medaillenkunst* (Abh. der Heidelberger Akademie der Wissenschaften, Philos.-Histor. Klasse I), Heidelberg, 1954. *See also* Gans, Edward, 170.

272a. Knipping, John B., and P. J. Meertens, *Van de Dene tot Luiken. Bloemlezing uit de Noord- en Zuid-Nederlandse Emblemata-Literatuur der 16de en 17de Eeuw,* Zwolle, 1956.

273. Kömstedt, Rudolf, *Vormittelalterliche Malerei...,* Augsburg, 1929.

274. Koloff, Eduard, "Rembrandt's Leben und Werke, nach neuen Actenstücken und Gesichtspunkten geschildert," *Raumers Historisches Taschenbuch,* 3rd series, V, 1854, pp. 401–587.

275. *Koran* (Latin tr. *s.t. Machumetis Sarracenorum Principis vita ac doctrina... Alcoranum dicitur, ex Arabica lingua...*), ed. *princeps,* Basel, 1543 (in 3 vols.).

276. Krelage, E. H., *Bloemenspeculatie in Nederland. De Tulpomanie van 1636–'37...* (Patria. Vaderlandsche Cultuurgeschiedenis ... XXX), Amsterdam, 1942.

277. Kris, Ernst, and Otto Kurz, *Die Legende vom Künstler...,* Vienna, 1934.

278. Kronfeld, Adolf, "Die Entwicklung des Anatomiebildes seit 1632...," *Beiträge zur Geschichte der Medizin,* II, Vienna, 1912, pp. 5–29.

279. Kurz, Otto, "Medical Illustrations. 2. The Ketham Group," *Journal of the Warburg and Courtauld Institutes,* V, 1942, pp. 138–41. *See also* Schlosser-Magnino, Julius, 426; and Kris, Ernst, 277.

   Landino, Cristoforo (1424–1504). *See* Dante Alighieri, 118.

280. Latham, Edward, *A Dictionary of Names, Nicknames and Surnames of Persons, Places and Things,* London, 1904.

281. Laurentius, Andreas (Du Laurens, André) (1558–1609), *Historia anatomica humani corporis et singularum eius partium multis controversiis et observationibus novis illustrata, ed. princeps,* Paris, 1589; ed. Frankfort 1599 and 1600. *See also* Artelt, Walter, 18.

282. Lederle (geb. Grieger), Ursula, *Gerechtigkeitsdarstellungen in deutschen und niederländischen Rathäusern* (Diss. Heidelberg), Philippsburg, 1937.

   Leiden, *A Catalogue* (1683). *See* Voorn, Jacobus, 501.

   ———, *Inventaris der Anatomie, begonnen Anno 1620. See* Barge, J. A. J., 28.

283. Lennep, J. van, and J. ter Gauw, *De Uithangtekens...,* Amsterdam, 1868.

284. Leonardo da Vinci (1452–1519), *Codice Atlantico,* ed. and tr. Edward McCurdy, *s.t. The Notebooks of Leonardo da Vinci...,* New York, *s.a.*

285. ———, *Quaderni d'Anatomia,* ed. C.L. Vangensten, Fonahn, Hopstock, Oslo, 1911ff.; ed. and tr. Edward McCurdy, *The Notebooks...,* New York, *s.a.*

286. Leroquais, Abbé V. de, *Un Livre d'Heures ms. à l'usage de Mâcon...,* Mâcon, 1935.

287. Lint, J. G. de, *Atlas of the History of Medicine I. Anatomy,* London, 1926.

288. ———, *Rembrandt* (series: Great Painters and Their Works as Seen by a Doctor, No. I), The Hague [1930].

205

289. (London) *Times, The,* Feb. 2, 1829.

290. Loon, Gerard van (1683–1758), *Beschrijving der Nederlandsche Historipenningen...,* II, The Hague, 1726.

291. Lowinsky, Edward E., "The Concept of Physical and Musical Space in the Renaissance," *Papers of the American Musicological Society, Annual Meeting,* 1941 [separatum].

292. ———, "Music in the Culture of the Renaissance," *Journal of the History of Ideas,* XV, iv, 1954, pp. 509–53.

293. Lugt, Frits, *Mit Rembrandt in Amsterdam...,* Berlin, 1920.

294. Luiken, Jan (1649–1712), and Casper (1672–1708), *Het Menselyk Bedryf. Vertoond, in. 100. Verbeeldingen: van: Ambachten, Konsten, Hanteeringen en Bedryven; met Versen...,* Amsterdam, 1694. *See also* Schopperus, 430; and Knipping and Meertens, 272a.

295. Lupton, J. H., *A Life of John Colet, D. D., Dean of St. Paul's...,* London, 1887.

296. Luther, Martin (1483–1546), (Commentary on:) *Jesajah,* ed. *Kritische Gesamtausgabe,* XXV, Weimar, 1902. *See also Koran,* 275.

297. McMurrich, J. Playfair, *Leonardo da Vinci the Anatomist...,* Baltimore, 1930.

298. McNeill, John T., *et al., Mediaeval Handbooks of Penance...,* New York, 1938.

299. Macquoid, Percy, and Ralph Edwards, *The Dictionary of English Furniture,* London, 1924, in 2 vols.

300. Major, Ralph H., "Antonio ... Benivieni," *Bulletin of the Institute of the History of Medicine,* III, x, 1935, pp. 739–49.

301. Mak, J. J., *De Rederijkers,* Amsterdam, 1944.

302. Mander, Carel van [den] (1548–1606), *(Schilder-Boeck) Het Leven Der oude Antijcke doorluchtighe Schilders ... Desghelijcx oock der vermaerde Nederlanders ende Hoogduytschen,* Alkmaar, 1603 (1604).

303. ———, *Den Grondt der Edel vry Schilderconst: Waer in haer ghestalt, aerdt ende*

303. Mander, Carel van *(Cont.)* *wesen, de leerlustighe Jeught in verscheyden Deelen in Rijm-dicht wort voor ghedraghen* [Alkmaar, 1603].

304. ———, *Das Lehrgedicht des Karel van Mander. Text, Übersetzung und Kommentar ... von R. Hoecker* (Quellenstudien zur holländischen Kunstgeschichte VIII), The Hague, 1916.

MANUSCRIPTS

305a. Amsterdam, Gemeentelijk Archief, 294, "Anatomij-Boek" (no original foliation). *See also* Thijssen, E. H. M., 468.

305aa. ———, 243, "De Naamen van de gekoosene Overluyden Beginnende van den Jaare 1596" (1596–1794; relevant parts compiled 1658).

305aaa. ———, 229, *sine titulo* (notes of the Amsterdam Guild of Surgeons dealing with anatomies from the beginning until 1645).

305aaaa. ———, 245, *sine titulo* (no foliation; in chronological sequence).

305b. Brussels, Bibliothèque Royale, 10176–78. *See also* Deguileville, Guillaume de, 120.

305c. Chantilly, Musée Condé, 569. *See also* Guido da Vigevano, 199.

305d. Copenhagen, Thott, 399. *See also* Ovid *(Ouidius moralizatus),* 349.

305e. Glasgow, The University of, Hunterian Library, V. 1. 1. (1581). *See also* Banister, John, 26.

305f. Glasgow, The University of, Hunterian Library, MS. 9 (Flemish, second half fifteenth century). *See also* Streeter, E. C., and Charles Singer, 458.

305ff. Leiden, University Library MS. 29. *See also* Barge, J. A. J., 28.

305g. London, The Wellcome Historical Medical Library, No. 755. *See also* Canano, G. B., 82.

305h. Mâcon, Coll. Jehan Siraudin, Book of Hours. *See also* Leroquais, Abbé V. de, 286.

305i. Munich, Staatsbibliothek. *See also Carmina Burana*, 87.

305j. Oxford, Bodleian Library, Ashmole, 399 (XIII/XIV centuries).

305k. Oxford, Bodleian Library, Douce, 45 (XV *c.*).

305l. Oxford, Corpus Christi College, CXXXII (III) (XVII *c.*), fol. 63–69.

305m. Paris, Bibliothèque Nationale, français, 396. *See also* Colbert, 101.

305n. Vatican, Med. graec. I (Dioscurides). *See also* Kömstedt, R., 273.

306. Marcham, Frank, *The Prototype of Shylock* (a pamphlet), Harrow Weald, Middlesex, 1927.

307. Marchant, Guyot, *printer* (pt. I:), *Miroer tressalutaire La nouuelle danse macabre des hommes. Icy est la nouuelle danse macabre des hommes dicte Miroer Salutaire de toutes gens pour pluseurs beaux dicts en latin et francoys lesquelx y sont contenus et si est de grant recreacion pour pluseurs ystoirs et enseignemens monitoirs a bien viure et mourir. Ainsi imprimee pour tous ceulx et celles qui la vouldront auoir et desirent faire leur salut* (pt. II:), . . . *femmes* . . . *(colophon:)* Paris, 1492.

308. Marci, Iacobus (collegit & edidit), *Deliciae Batavicae Variae Elegantesque picturae omnes Belgij antiquitates, & quicquid praeterea in eo visitur, representantes, quas ad album studiosorum conficiendum deservire possunt,* Amsterdam, Ioannes Ianssonius, 1618.

309. Martianus Capella (fl. 450), *De nuptiis Philologie et Mercurii,* Vicenza, Henricus de Sancto Ursio (Dec. 16), 1499.

310. Marx, Friedrich, "Digitis computans" (Festschrift C.F.W. Müller zum 70 . . .), *Jahrbücher für klassische Philologie,* XXVII (Supplementband), Leipzig, 1902, pp. 195–201.

311. Maximilian I (d. 1519), *Weiss Kunig* (last redaction 1514), ed. Vienna, 1775.

312. Maximus Confessor, *Saint* (*ca.* 580–662) (and John of Scythopolis), *Scholia in librum de Coelesti Hierarchia,* ed. Migne, *P.G.,* IV, cols. 29–114.

313. Medici, Lorenzo de' (1449–92), *Canti Carnascialeschi, Opere,* II, ed. Attilio Simione, Bari, 1914.

314. Melanchthon, Philipp (1497–1560), "Philip Melanchthon's Observations on the Human Body," *A Poem Written in Latin . . . on the Flyleaf of a Copy of the First Edition of Vesalius' De humani corporis fabrica, 1543. In the Army Medical Library, Cleveland, Ohio,* facsimile ed., and tr. (Dorothy M. Schullian), privately printed for Elmer Belt, as *A Christmas Greeting,* Los Angeles, 1949.

315. Mensing, Ant. W.M., *Manuscrits–Dessins, etc. provenant de la Collection-Six . . ., Vente* (Oct. 1928), Amsterdam.

316. Mercurio, Geronimo Scipione (1568–1651?), *La comare o riccoglitrice, divisa in tre libri,* Venice, 1601[2] (illuminated).

317. Mersenne, Marin (1588–1648), "Harmoniae theoreticae, practicae, & instrumentalis, libri quatuor," *Cogitata physico-mathematica,* Paris, 1644, pp. 261–370.

318. Meyer, A.W., and Sheldon K. Wirth, "The Amuscan Illustrations," *Bulletin of the History of Medicine,* XIV, v, 1943, pp. 667–87.

319. Mierzecki, H., "Symbolism and Pathognomy of the Hand," *Ciba Symposia,* IV, i, 1942, pp. 1319–22.

320. Migne, J.-P. (ed.), *P.G. (= Patrologiae cursus completus, series graeca).*

321. ———, *P.L. (= Patrologiae cursus completus, series latina).*

322. Miller, Henry, *Tropic of Capricorn,* Paris, 1952.

323. Moes, E.W., *Iconographia Batavia,* 2 vols., Amsterdam, 1905.

Molhuysen, P.C. *See Nieuw Nederlandsch Biografisch Woordenboek,* 340.

324. Molière, Poquelin de, Jean-Baptiste (1622–73), *Le Malade Imaginaire* (first presented Dec. 10, 1673).

Mondino. *See* Mundinus, 331.

325. Monnikhoff, Joh. (1707–87), *Privilegien, Willekeuren en Ordonnantien betreffende het Collegium Chirurgicum Amstelraedamense,* Amsterdam, 1736.

326. Mortet, V., and P. Deschamps, *Recueil de textes relatifs à l'histoire de l'architecture,* II, Paris, 1929.

327. Müntz, Eugène, "Rembrandt et l'art italien," *Gazette des Beaux-Arts,* I, 1892, pp. 196–211.

328. Müntz, Ludwig, *A Critical Catalogue of Rembrandt's Etchings...,* London (1952), in 2 vols.

329. Muller, F., *Beschrijvende catalogus van 7000 portretten van Nederlanders...,* Amsterdam, 1853.

330. Muller Fz., S. (revised by J.W. Smit), *De Universiteitsgebouwen te Utrecht,* Groningen (1956²).

331. Mundinus (Mondino, Raimondo, *dei Luzzi,* of Bologna) (*ca.* 1275–1326), *Anothomia* (completed 1316), *editiones principes duo:* Bologna/Pavia, 1478.

332. ———, ed. Ernest Wickersheimer, *Anatomies de Mondino dei Luzzi et de Guido de Vigevano,* Paris, 1926. *See also* Ketham, Joannes de, 269.

333. Müri, Walter, "Melancholie und schwarze Galle," *Museum Helveticum,* X, i, 1953, pp. 21–38.

334. Murray, David, *Museums. Their History and Their Use...,* I, Glasgow, 1904.

335. Murray, Sir James A.H., *A New English Dictionary on Historical Principles...,* Oxford, 1888–1928.

336. Nashe, Thomas (1567–1600), *The Vnfortunate Traueller* (completed June 27, 1593), ed. Ronald B. McKerrow, *The Works of*

336. Nashe, Thomas *(Cont.)* *Thomas Nashe* (Vols. II and IV), London, 1904.

New English Dictionary, A. See Murray, Sir James, 335.

337. *New York Times, The,* Sept. 9, 1952.

Nichols, John. *See* Hogarth, William, 231.

338. Nicolaus, *de Lyra* (*ca.* 1270–1349), *Explicit Postilla preclarissimi ... super bibilia. tam vetus quam nouum testamentum ...* (in 2 vols.), Nuremberg, 1481.

339. Nicolson, Marjorie H., *Voyages to the Moon,* New York, 1948.

340. *Nieuw Nederlandsch Biografisch Woordenboek* (ed. P.C. Molhuysen, P.J. Blok, K.H. Kossmann), Leiden, 1911–37, in 10 vols.

341. Nordenfalk, Carl, "Van Gogh and Literature," *Journal of the Warburg and Courtauld Institutes,* X, 1947, pp. 132–47.

342. ———, "The Beginning of Book Decoration," *Essays in Honor of Georg Swarzenski,* Chicago–Berlin, 1952.

343. Nuyens, B.W.Th., *Het Ontleedkundig Onderwijs en de geschilderde Anatomische Lessen van het Chirurgijns Gilde te Amsterdam, in de Jaren 1550 tot 1798* (Jaarverslag Koninklijk Oudheidkundig Genootschap), Amsterdam, 1928, pp. 45–90.

344. Olschki, Leonardo, *Geschichte der neusprachlichen wissenschaftlichen Literatur,* II, Leipzig, Florence, etc., 1922.

345. O'Malley, C. Donald, "Andreas Vesalius' Pilgrimage," *Isis,* XLV, 1954, pp. 138–44.

346. ———, and J.B. de C.M. Saunder, "Vesalius as a Clinician," *Bulletin of the History of Medicine,* XIV, v, 1943, pp. 594–644.

Ordinances of the Chirurgs of Amsterdam. *See* Monnikhoff, Joh., 325; Nuyens, B.W.Th., 343.

347. Orlers, J.J. (1570–1646), *Beschrijvinge der Stadt Leyden...,* Leiden, 1641² (*ed. princeps* 1614).

348. Ovidius Naso, Publius (43 B.C.–17 A.D.), *Metamorphoses . . .*, Bruges, May 1484.

349. ———, *Ouidius moralizatus*, MS. Copenhagen, Thott 399, *ca.* 1480. *See also* Berchorius, Petrus, 49.

350. Paaw, Pieter (Petrus Pavius) (1567–1617), *. . . De humani corporis ossibvs*, Leiden, 1615. *See also* Celsus, A.C., 93; Vesalius, Andreas, *Epitome*, 492.

351. Palma, *il Giovane*, Jacobus (1544–1628), *Regole per imparar a disegnar i corpi humani . . ., ed. princeps,* Venice, Marco Sadeler (and Nuremberg?), 1636.

352. Panofsky, Erwin, *"Idea." Ein Beitrag zur Begriffsgeschichte der älteren Kunsttheorie* (Studien der Bibliothek Warburg V), Leipzig–Berlin, 1924.

353. Italian ed. in tr., *s.t.: Idea. Contributo alla Storia dell'Estetica,* Florence, 1952.

354. ———, "Der gefesselte Eros (zur Genealogie von Rembrandts Danae)," *Oud Holland*, L, 1933, pp. 193–217.

354a. ———, *Studies in Iconology. Humanistic Themes in the Art of the Renaissance,* New York, 1939.

355. ———, *The Codex Huygens and Leonardo da Vinci's Art Theory . . .* (Studies of the Warburg Institute XIII), London, 1940.

356. ———, *Albrecht Dürer,* Princeton, 1945.

357. ———, "Who Is Jan van Eyck's 'Tymotheos'?" *Journal of the Warburg and Courtauld Institutes,* XII, 1949, pp. 80–90.

358. ———, *Gothic Architecture and Scholasticism* (Wimmer Lectures, 1948), Latrobe (Pennsylvania), 1951.

359. ———, "Meaning in the Visual Arts," *Magazine of Art,* XLIV, 2, Feb. 1951, pp. 45–50.

360. ———, "Artist, Scientist, Genius: Notes on the 'Renaissance-Dämmerung,'" *The Renaissance . . .* (The Metropolitan Museum of Art 1952), New York, 1953, pp. 77–93.

361. ———, *Early Netherlandish Painting . . .,* Cambridge (Mass.), 1953, in 2 vols.

362. ———, *Meaning in the Visual Arts. Papers in and on Art History,* Garden City, N.Y., 1955.

363. ———, "Galileo as a Critic of the Arts. Aesthetic Attitude and Scientific Thought," *Isis,* XLVII, i, No. 147, 1956, pp. 3–15.

363a. ———, "Jean Hey's 'Ecce Homo.' Speculations About Its Author, Its Donor, and Its Iconography" (Musées Royaux des Beaux-Arts), *Bulletin,* V, 3–4, 1956, pp. 94–138.

364. ———, and Fritz Saxl, *Dürers "Melencolia. I." Eine quellen- und typengeschichtliche Untersuchung* (Studien der Bibliothek Warburg II), Leipzig-Berlin, 1923.

365. ———, "Classical Mythology in Mediaeval Art," *Metropolitan Museum Studies,* IV, ii, March 1933, pp. 228–80.

366. Paracelsus, Aureolus Philippus Theophrastus, Bombastus ab Hohenheim (1493–1541), (a) *Der grossenn Wundartzney das Erst Buoch . . .;* (b) *Der ander Theil der Grossen Wundartzney . . ., ed. princeps,* Augsburg, 1536; ed. Karl Sudhoff, *Sämtliche Werke,* X, Munich and Berlin, 1928.

367. ———, *Prognostication auff XXIIII. jar zukünfftig . . .,* Augsburg, 1536.

368. ———, *Opus Chyrurgicum. Des Weitberumten . . . Wund und Artzney Buch . . .,* Frankfort, 1565.

369. Peerlkamp, P. Hofmann, *Liber de Vita Doctrina et Facultate Nederlandorum Qui Carmina Latina Composuerunt. Editio Altera Emendata et Aucta,* Haarlem, 1838.

370. Peregrinus, Petrus, *Maricurtensis* (Pierre de Maricourt) (fl. 1269), *Petri Peregrini Maricvrtensis de Magnete, seu Rota perpetui motus, libellus* (with commentary of Achilles P. Gassarus (1505–77) and with

370. Peregrinus, Petrus (*Cont.*)
four woodcut illus.), Augsburg, 1558
(BM C. 54. bb. 6. = copy of John Dee,
1562 with six MS. diagrams *in margine*).
Pers, D. P. *See* Ripa, Cesare, 402.

371. Petrarch (Francesco Petrarca), (1304–74),
Trionfi. Sonetti, etc., Venice, Apr. 22,
1490.

372. ———, *Metricae,* ed. O. Rosetti, Florence,
1829.

373. ———, *De vita solitaria,* ed. A. Altamura,
Naples, 1943.

374. ———, *Invectiva contra medicum,* ed. P. G.
Ricci, Rome, 1950.

375. Peutinger, Konrad (1465–1547), *Inscriptiones vetustae Romanae, et eorum fragmenta in Augusta Vindelicorum et eius dioecesi . . . donuo revisae* (first illus. ed.),
Mayence, 1520.

376. Pevsner, Nikolaus, *Academies of Art, Past
and Present,* Cambridge, 1940.
P. G. ed. *See* Migne, J.-P., 320.

377. Picinelli, Philippo (1604–*ca.* 67), *Mundus
symbolicus, in emblematum universitate formatus . . .,* tr. August Erath, Cologne,
1687.

378. Pickering, Charles, *Chronological History of
Plants . . .,* Boston, 1879.

378a. Pigler, Andreas, "Portraying the Dead
. . .," *Acta historiae artium Academiae
Scientiarium Hungariae,* IV, 1–2, Budapest, 1956, pp. 1–75.

379. Piles, Roger de (1635–1709), *Abrégé de la
vie des peintres,* Paris, 1715 (*ed. princeps,*
1699).

379a. Pirckheimer, Wilibald (1470–1513), *Theatrum virtutis et honoris . . .,* Nuremberg,
1606.
P. L. ed. *See* Migne, J.-P., 321.

380. Plempius (Vopiscus), Fortunatus (1601–
71), *Ophthalmographia, sive tractatio de
oculi fabrica, actione, et usu praeter vulgatas
hactenus philosophorum ac medicorum opiniones,* Amsterdam, 1632.

380a. Poliziano, Angelo (1454–94), *Epigrammata Graeca,* ed. Isidoro del Lungo,
Prose Volgari . . ., Florence, 1867.

381. Popham, A. E., and Philip Pouncey, *Italian
Drawings in the Department of Prints and
Drawings in the British Museum . . .,* London, 1950, in 2 vols.

382. Power, d'Arcy, "Notes on Early Portraits
of John Banister . . .," *Proceedings of the
Royal Society of Medicine,* VI, Section of
the History of Medicine, London, 1913,
pp. 18–36.

383. Poynter, F. N. L., *A Catalogue of Incunabula
in the Wellcome Historical Medical Library*
(Publications of the Wellcome Historical Medical Museum V), Oxford University Press, 1954.

384. Praz, Mario, *Studies in Seventeenth-Century
Imagery* (Studies of the Warburg Institute), London, 1939–47, in 2 vols.

385. Preisendanz, K., "'gnotos solidos,'" *Neue
Heidelberger Jahrbücher,* Neue Folge,
1939, pp. 92ff.

386. Prinsen Lzn., J., *Handboek tot de Nederlandsche letterkundige Geschiedenis,* The
Hague, 1920.
Quintilian, *Institutio oratoria. See* Herzog-Hauser, G., 222.

387. Rabelais, François (1490?–1553), *Gargantua. See also* Hippocrates, 225.

388. Ramus, Petrus (Pierre de la Ramée) (1515–
72), *Dialecticae institutiones, ad celeberrimam et illustrissimam Lutetiae Parisiorum
Academiam,* Paris, Jac. Bogardus, 1543.

389. Read, Alexander, *The Manuuall of the Anatomy or dissection of the body of Man . . .,*
London, 1638.

390. Regteren Altena, Johan Quirin van,
*Jacques de Gheyn. An Introduction to the
Study of His Drawings* (Diss. Utrecht),
Amsterdam, 1935.

391. ———, *Rembrandt en Amsterdam. Woorden
gesproken ter herdenking van Rembrandt in
de Westerkerk te Amsterdam . . . 16 Juli
1956 . . .,* Amsterdam [1956].

392. Rehm, Walter, "Zur Gestaltung des Todesgedankens bei Petrarca und Johann von Saaz," *Deutsche Vierteljahrsschrift*, V, iii, 1927.

393. *Rembrandt Tentoonstelling ter Herdenking van de Geboorte van Rembrandt op 15 Juli 1606* (Rijksmuseum, Amsterdam), 1956. (a) paintings; (b) drawings; (c) prints.

394. *Rembrandt als Leermeester* (Exhibition Cat., Stedelijk Museum de Lakenhal), Leiden (June–Sept.), 1956.

395. Reresby, *Sir John* (1634–89), *The Travels and Memoirs of* . . ., London, 1657.

396. Richter, Gottfried, *Das anatomische Theater* (Abhandlungen zur Geschichte der Medizin und der Naturwissenschaften. Heft 16), Berlin, 1936.

397. Richter, Henry, *Day-Light: A Recent Discovery in the Art of Painting with Hints on the Philosophy of the Fine Arts, and on that of the Human Mind, as First Dissected by Emanuel Kant*, London, 1817.

398. Riegl, Alois, *Das holländische Gruppenporträt* . . ., Vienna, 1931², in 2 vols.

399. Rijckevorsel, *Jhr.*, J. L. A. A. M. van, *Rembrandt en de traditie* . . ., Rotterdam, 1932. (296 figs.)

400. Ringler, William, "*Poeta Nascitur non Fit:* Some Notes on the History of the Aphorism," *Journal of the History of Ideas*, II, i, 1941, pp. 497–504.

401. Ripa, *Cavaliere*, Cesare, *Perugino* (ca. 1560– ante 1625), *Iconologia overo Descrittione di diverse Imagini cauate dall' antichità* . . ., Rome, 1603 (first illus. ed.).

402. ———, *Iconologia, of uytbeeldingen des Verstands* . . . (tr. Pers, Dirck Pietersz. (1579–1650)), Amsterdam, 1644.

403. Robertson, D.W., Jr., "St. Foy Among Thorns," *Modern Language Notes,* May, 1952, pp. 295–99.

404. Robinson, Victor, "Anatomical Dissection in the 18th Century," *Ciba Symposia*, III, ii, 1941, pp. 845–53.

405. Roeder, Helen, *Saints and Their Attributes* . . ., London, 1955.

406. Rogge, H.C., "Nicolaas Tulp," *De Gids,* Amsterdam, 1880, pp. 77–125.

407. Rosen, Edward, *The Naming of the Telescope*, New York (1947).

408. Rosen, Eric von, "Olof Rudbeck och Rembrandt. En tafla af den senare förebilden till atlasplanschen i Atlantica?" *Svenska Dagbladet,* Sept. 30, 1917, p. 3 (illus.).

408a. Rost, G.A., "Schinden als Todesstrafe," *Der Hautarzt,* VII, 11, 1956, pp. 513–16.

409. Roth, Cecil, *A History of the Jews in England,* Oxford, 1941.

410. Roth, M., *Andreas Vesalius Bruxellensis,* Berlin, 1892.

411. Rotterdam, Museum Boymans, *Herinnering* (a Catalogue compiled by A.P.A. Vorenkamp on the occasion of the Kersttentoonstelling 1947–48), Rotterdam.

412. Roughead, William, *Murderer's Companion,* ed. New York, 1941.

413. Rudbeck, Olof (1630–1702), *Atlantica* (*Atland eller Manheim, Atlantica sive Manheim, vera Japheti posterorum sedes et patria, ed. princeps,* Upsala, 1675ff.); facsimile ed. Axel Nelson, Upsala, 1937–39.

414. Rudloff, Ernst von, *Über das Konservieren von Leichen im Mittelalter. Ein Beitrag zur Geschichte der Anatomie und des Bestattungswesens* (Diss.), Freiburg, 1921.

Rudolf von Ems, *World Chronicle. See* Sudhoff, K., 462.

415. Ruysch, Frederik (1638–1731), *Thesaurus Anatomicus Primus, etc.* . . ., *Het Eerste Anatomisch Cabinet, etc.* . . ., Amsterdam, in 10(11) pts., 1701–15 (–16) (with numerous folding plates).

415a. Salerno, Luigi, "Seventeenth-Century English Literature on Painting," *Journal of the Warburg and Courtauld Institutes,* XIV, 1951, pp. 234–58.

416. Salzman, L.F., *English Industries of the Middle Ages,* London, 1923.

Sandrart, Joachim von (1606–88). *See* Hofstede de Groot, C. (1906), 228.

417. Sarton, George, *Introduction to the History of Science*, III, in 2 pts., Baltimore, 1947.

418. ———, *Galen of Pergamon* (Logan Clendening Lectures on the History and Philosophy of Medicine. Third Series), Lawrence (Kansas), 1954.

419. ———, "The Death and Burial of Vesalius, and, Incidentally, of Cicero," *Isis*, XLV, 1954, pp. 131–37.

420. Saxl, Fritz, "Die Ausdrucksgebärden in der bildenden Kunst," *Bericht über den XII. Kongress der deutschen Gesellschaft für Psychologie in Hamburg vom 12.–16. April 1931* . . . (ed. Gustav Kafka), Jena, 1932, pp. 13–25. *See also* Panofsky E., 364, 365.

421. Scaliger, Justus Julius (1540–1609), *Scaligerana* . . . (*ed. princeps,* Groningen, 1669), ed. Cologne, 1695.

422. Scarlatini, Octavius (?–1699), [*Homo Symbolicus*] *Homo et ejus Partes Figuratus & Symbolicus, Anatomicus, Rationalis, Moralis, Mysticus, Politicus & Legalis, Collectus et Explicatus cum Figuris, Symbolis, Anatomiis, Factis, Emblematibus, Moralibus, Mysticis, Proverbiis, Hieroglyphicis, Prodigiis, Simulacris, Statuis, Historiis, Ritibus, Observationibus, Moribus, Numismatibus, Dedicationibus, Signaturis, Significationibus Literarum, Epithetis, Fabulis, Miris, Physiognomicis, & Somniis; Reflexionibus et Declarationibus tamen ex Sacris, quàm profanis Auctoribus desumptis,* . . ., *Opus utile Praedicatoribus, Oratoribus, Poetis, Anatomicis, Philosophis, Academicis, Sculptoribus, Pictoribus, Emblematum, ac Inscriptionum Inventoribus,* &c., in 2 pts. (tr. from the Italian [*ed. princeps,* Bologna, 1680; according to Praz,[384] II, p. 150, = 1684] by Mathias Honcamp), Augsburg and Dillingen, 1695.

422a. Schendel, A. van, "De schimmen van de Staalmeesters. Een röntgenologisch onderzoek," *Oud-Holland,* LXXI, 1956, pp. 1–22.

423. Schlosser, Julius von, *Beiträge zur Kunstgeschichte aus den Schriftquellen des frühen Mittelalters* (Sitzungsberichte der K. Akademie der Wissenschaften in Wien, Philos.-Histor. Classe, CXXIII), Vienna, 1891.

424. ———, *Die Kunst- und Wunderkammern der Spätrenaissance* . . ., Leipzig, 1908.

425. ———, *Die Kunstliteratur. Ein Handbuch zur Quellenkunde der neueren Kunstgeschichte,* Vienna, 1924.

426. ——— (= Julius Schlosser-Magnino and Otto Kurz), *La Letteratura Artistica* . . ., Florence–Vienna [1956²].

427. Schmid, Heinrich Alfred, *Hans Holbein der Jüngere* . . ., Textband. Erster Halbband, Basel, 1948.

428. Schmidt-Degener, P., *Rembrandt und der holländische Barock* (Studien der Bibliothek Warburg IX), Leipzig-Berlin, 1928. *See also* Vondel, Joost van den, 499.

429. Schopenhauer, Arthur, "Transcendente Spekulation über die anscheinende Absichtlichkeit im Schicksale des Einzelnen," ed. Paul Deussen, *Arthur Schopenhauers sämtliche Werke,* IV, Munich, 1913.

430. Schopper(us), Hartmann (1542–95, or later), *ΠΑΝΟΠΑΙΑ omnium illiberalium mecanicarvm avt sedentariarum artium genera continens* . . ., *ed. princeps,* Frankfort, 1568 (with illustrations by Jost Amman). *See also* Garzoni, T., 172; Luiken, J. and C., 294.

431. Schottmüller, Frida, "Zwei Grabmäler der Renaissance und ihre antiken Vorbilder," *Repertorium für Kunstwissenschaft,* XXV, vi, 1902, pp. 401–8.

432. Schrade, Hubert, "Rembrandts 'Anatomie des Dr. Tulp,'" *Das Werk des Künstlers. Kunstgeschichtliche Zweimonatsschrift,* I, Stuttgart, 1939/40, pp. 60–100.

433. Schullian, Dorothy M., "Old Volumes Shake Their Vellum Heads," *Bulletin of*

433. Schullian, Dorothy M. *(Cont.)* the Medical Library Association, XXXIII, iv, 1945, pp. 413–48. *See also* Melanchthon, Philipp, 314.

434. ———, "The Newly Discovered Catacomb Fresco," *Journal of the History of Medicine and Allied Sciences,* XI (July 1956), p. 354.

435. Seznec, Jean, *The Survival of the Pagan Gods . . .,* New York, 1953.

436. Shakespeare, William (1564–1616), *Merchant of Venice,* entered Stationer's Register July 22, 1598.

437. ———, *The Tempest . . .,* fol. ed., London, 1623.

438. Sheedy, Anna Toole, *Bartolus on Social Conditions in the Fourteenth Century* (Diss. Columbia University), New York, 1942.

439. Sherrington, *Sir* Charles S., *The Endeavour of Jean Fernel . . .,* Cambridge, 1946.

440. Sigerist, Henry E., "Sebastian-Apollo," *Archiv für Geschichte der Medizin,* XIX, iv (Oct.), 1927, pp. 301–17.

441. ———, "The Historical Aspect of Art and Medicine," *Bulletin of the History of Medicine,* IV, iv (Apr.), 1936, pp. 271–96.

442. ———, "Albanus Torinus and the German Edition of the *Epitome* of Vesalius," *Bulletin of the History of Medicine,* XIV, 1943, pp. 662–66.

443. Sigtenhorst Meyer, B. van den, *Jan P. Sweelinck en zijn instrumentale Muziek . . .,* The Hague, 1934.

444. Simon, Karl, *Abendländische Gerechtigkeitsbilder,* Frankfort, 1948.

445. Simon, Max, *Sieben Bücher Anatomie des Galen . . .,* II, Leipzig, 1906.

446. Singer, Charles Joseph, *The Evolution of Anatomy . . .,* London, 1925. *See also* Galen, *On Anatomical Procedure,* 163a; Ketham, Joannes de, 270; Streeter, E. C., and C. Singer, 458; Vesalius, Andreas, *Tabulae sex,* 493.

447. ———, and C. Rabin, *A Prelude to Modern Science. Being a Discussion of the History, Sources and Circumstances of the 'Tabulae Anatomicae Sex' of Vesalius* (Publications of the Wellcome Historical Medical Museum, N. S. I), Cambridge, 1946.

448. Six, *Jhr.* J., "Iets over Rembrandt," *Oud Holland,* XI, 1893, pp. 154–61. *See also* Tulp, Nicolaas, 478.

449. Slive, Seymour, *Rembrandt and His Critics, 1630–1730,* The Hague, 1953.

449a. Smith College Museum of Art, *Abraham Bosse . . .,* Northampton, 1956 (Exhibition Catalogue).

450. Smith, Preserved, *A History of Modern Culture I, The Great Renewal 1543–1687,* New York, 1930.

451. Smith, R. W. James, *English-Speaking Students of Medicine at the University of Leyden,* London, 1932.

452. *Speculum humanae salvationis,* ed. J. Lutz and P. Perdrizet, Leipzig, 1907, in 2 vols.

453. Spielmann, M. H., *The Iconography of Andreas Vesalius . . .* (Wellcome Historical Medical Museum. Research Studies in Medical History No. 3), London, 1925.

454. Stadtmüller, Franz, "Der Niederdeutsche Andreas Vesalius als Anatom in seinen Beziehungen zu Italien," *Concordia Decennalis. Deutsche Italienforschungen . . . zum 10jährigen Bestehen des Deutsch-Italienischen Kulturinstituts Petrarcahaus,* Cologne, 1941, pp. 201–10.

455. Steinschneider, Moritz, *Jüdische Ärzte* [Frankfort, *ca.* 1914 = a series of loose sheets, Wellcome Historical Medical Library].

456. Stephanus, Carolus (Charles Estienne) (1504–64), (a) *De dissectione partium corporis humani libri tres . . .,* ed. *princeps,* Paris, 1545; (b) (author's tr. *s.t.*) *La dissection des parties du corps humain diuisee en trois liures, faictz par Charles Estienne . . .,* Paris, 1546.

Sterk, J. F. M. *See* Vondel, J. van den, 500.

457. Steudel, Johannes, "Der vorvesalische Beitrag zur anatomischen Nomenklatur," *Sudhoffs Archiv . . .*, XXXVI, Wiesbaden, 1943, pp. 1–42.
Streeter, E. C. *See* Canano, G. B., 84.

458. ———, and Charles Singer, "Fifteenth Century Miniatures of Extramural Dissections," *Essays on the History of Medicine Presented to Karl Sudhoff,* Oxford University Press, London and Zürich, pp. 207–10. *See also* Manuscript, 305f.

459. Stricker, B. H., "De Correspondentie: Van Heurn – Le Leu de Wilhem," *Oudheidkundige Mededeelingen uit het Rijksmuseum van Oudheden te Leiden,* nieuwe reeks, XXIX, 1948, pp. 43–54.

460. Strong, Eugenie, "A Note on Two Roman Sepulchral Reliefs," *The Journal of Roman Studies,* IV, 1914, p. 149.

461. Strzygowski, Josef, "Zur Komposition von Rembrandts Anatomie des Doktor Tulp," *Allgemeine Zeitung,* Beilage 14, Munich, Jan. 18, 1902, pp. 110f.

462. Sudhoff, Karl, "Weitere Beiträge zur Geschichte der Medizin im Mittelalter," *Archiv für Geschichte der Medizin,* VII, vi, Leipzig, 1914, pp. 303–34.

463. Sylvius, Jacobus (Jacques du Bois) (1478–1555), *Vaesani cuiusdam in Hippocratis Galenisque rem anatomicam depulsio,* Paris, 1551.

464. Szladits, Lola L., "The Influence of Michelangelo on Some Anatomical Illustrations," *Journal of the History of Medicine and Allied Sciences,* IX, iv, 1954, pp. 420–27.

465. *Tabula exemplorum* (ca. 1277), ed. J. Th. Welter, Paris–Toulouse, 1926.

466. Thieme, U., and F. Becker, *Allgemeines Lexikon der bildenden Künste,* Leipzig, 1907–50.

467. Thienen, Friethjof van, *Das Kostüm der Blütezeit Hollands . . .,* Berlin, 1930.

468. Thijssen, E. H. M., *Nicolaas Tulp. Als geneeskundige geschetst. Eene Bijdrage tot de geschiedenis der geneeskunde in de 17de eeuw*

468. Thijssen, E. H. M. *(Cont.)* (Diss.), Amsterdam, 1881. *See also* Manuscript, Amsterdam, 305a.

469. Thijssen-Schoute, C. Louise, *Nederlands Cartesianisme* (Avec Sommaire et Table des Matières en Français) (Verhandelingen der Koninklijke Nederlandse Akademie van Wetenschappen, Afd. Letterkunde, Nieuwe Reeks, Deel LX), Amsterdam, 1954.

470. Thomas de Aquino, *Saint* (1225?–74), *Summa Theologiae,* ed. Paris, 1644.
Thoré, Théophile. *See* Burger, W., 77.

470a. Thurnheer, Yvonne, "Die Stadtärzte und ihr Amt im alten Bern," *Berner Beiträge zur Geschichte der Medizin und der Naturwissenschaften,* IV, 1944, pp. 68ff.

471. Tietze, Hans, *Genuine and False. Copies—Imitations—Forgeries,* London, 1948.

471a. [Tilanus, J. W. R.,] *Beschrijving der Schilderijen afkomstig van het Chirurgijns-Gild te Amsterdam . . .,* Amsterdam, 1865.

471b. Timmers, J. J. M., *Symboliek en Iconographie der Christelijke Kunst,* Roermond-Maaseik, 1947.
Townley, The Rev. James (1714–78). *See* Hogarth, William, 230.

472. Tradescant, John, Jr. (1608–62), *Museum Tradescantium; or, A Collection of Rarities Preserved at South-Lambeth near London,* London, 1656 (1652).

473. Trent, Council of, "Decretum de peccato originali," *Canones et Decreta sacrosancti oecumeni Concilii Tridentini . . . Sessio Quinta. Celebrata die XVII. mensis Junii MDXLVI,* ed. Turin, 1890.

474. Triaire, Paul, *Les Leçons d'Anatomie et les Peintres Hollandais aux XVIe et XVIIe siècles,* Paris, 1887.

475. Trinkaus, Charles, "Petrarch's Views on the Individual and His Society," *Osiris,* XI, 1954, pp. 168–98.

476. Troescher, Georg, *Kunst- und Künstlerwanderungen in Mitteleuropa 800–1800,* I, Baden-Baden, 1953.

477. Tulpius, Nicolaus Petreus (Claes Pieterszoon) (1593–1674), [Nicolai Tvlpii Amstelredamensis,] *Observationvm Medicarvm. Libri Tres.* [later: quatuor] *Cum aeneis figuris, ed. princeps,* Amsterdam, Lvdovicvs Elzevirivs, 1641.

Further ed. and tr.:

(a) *N. Tulpii . . . Observationes medicae. Editio nova, libro quarto auctior, et sparsim . . . emendatior,* Amsterdam, 1652.

(b) *Editio nova . . .,* Amsterdam, 1672.

(c) [*dtto.*] . . ., Amsterdam, 1685.

(d) *Editio quinta, cui brevis . . . authoris vitae narratio est praefixa . . .,* Leiden, 1716.

478. (e) [author's own tr. in unpubl. MS., *s.t.*] *Insigten over de Geneeskunde in vier bouken.* But *see also* Six, *Jhr. J.,* 448; Thijssen, E. H. M., 468.

479. (f) *De drie Boecken der Medicijnsche Aenmerkingen, in 't Latijn beschreven van den Heere Nicolaes Tulp,* Amsterdam, 1650.

480. (g) *Observations chirurgiques tirées des Observations médicinales de N. Tulpius . . .,* Paris, 1708.

481. Uffenbach, Zacharias Conrad von (1683–1734), *. . . Merkwürdige Reisen durch Niedersachsen Holland und Engelland,* Frankfort and Leipzig, etc., 1753–54, in 3 vols.

Underhill, E., and Mrs. Th. Beck, ed. and tr. *See* Jacopone da Todi, 252.

482. Uytewael, Ioachim (*ca.* 1566–1638), and Willem Swanenburgh, *Thronvs Ivstitiae. Hoc est de optimo judice tractatus . . .,* Amsterdam, 1607.

483. V., H.F., "De dichter die dacht dat hij van glas was," *Amstelodamum,* XXXVII, 1950, p. 60.

484. Valentiner, Wilhelm R., *Rembrandt und seine Umgebung,* Strasbourg, 1905.

485. Valverde de (H)amusco, Juan de (fl. 2nd half XVI c.), *Historia de la composicion del cuerpo humano, ed. princeps,* Rome, A. Salamanca & A. Lafreri, 1556 (and 1560).

486. Varro, Marcus Terentius (116–27 B.C.), *Disciplinarum libri novem.*

487. Vasari, Giorgio (1511–74), *Le vite de' più eccellenti pittori scultori ed architettori scritte da G. V. Pittore Aretino . . .,* ed. G. Milanesi, Florence, 1878–82.

488. Verwey, H. de la Fontaine, "Caspar van Baerle 12 Februari 1584–14 Januari 1648," *Amstelodamum,* XXXV, 1948, pp. 17–20.

489. Vesalius, Andreas (1514/15–1564), *De Humani corporis fabrica, Libri septem, ed. princeps,* Basel, Joannes Oporinus, 1543.

490. ed. Basel, 1555. *See also* Farrington, Benjamin (for tr. of "Preface" and last chap.), 150, 151.

491. ———, *Epitome,* Basel, 1543; facsimile ed. L. R. Lind, *s.t. The Epitome of Andreas Vesalius . . .* (Historical Library, Yale Medical Library XXI), New York, 1949.

492. ed. Pieter Paaw, *s.t. Andreae Vesalii . . . Epitome Anatomica. Opus redivivum . . .,* Leiden, 1616; Amsterdam, 1633.

493. ———, *(Tabulae anatomicae sex)* (Colophon-cartellino:) "Imprimebat: Venice, . . . sumptibus Ioannis Stephani Calcarensis . . ., [Apr.], 1538"; facsimile ed., *see* Singer, C., and C. Rabin, 447. *See also* Farrington, Benjamin, 150, 151; Guinterus, Johannes, 201; Paaw, Pieter, 350.

494. Veth, Jan, "Rembrandt's Aankomst in Amsterdam," *De XXe Eeuw,* XII, vii, 1906, pp. 3–15.

495. Vitruvius Pollio, Marcus (fl. 10 A.D.), *De architectura,* ed. Venice, Jo. Tacuinus, 1511.

496. Vives, Juan Luis (1492–1540), *De veritate Fidei Christianae contra Ethnicos, Judaeos Agarenos sive Mohametanos, ac perverse Christianos, libri quinque,* Basel, 1543.

497. *Vocabularium rerum* [per B(W)enceslaus Brack, of Costnitz, fl. second half 15th c.] [Latin-German], Augsburg, G. Zainer, 1473–74.

497a. Vocht, Henry de, *History of the Foundation and Rise of the Collegium Trilingue Lovaniense 1517–1550*, I–IV, Louvain, 1951–55.

498. Voet Jr., Elias, *Merken van Amsterdamsche Goud- en Zilversmeden,* The Hague, 1912.

499. Vondel, Joost van den (1587–1679), *Den Gulden Winckel der Konstlievende Nederlanders . . .,* Amsterdam, 1613; facsimile ed. in *De Werken van Vondel,* I, Amsterdam, 1927, pp. 265–426.

500. ———, *De Werken van Vondel,* III (Geschiedkundige bewerking door J. F. M. Sterck), Amsterdam, 1929. *See also* Schmidt-Degener, F., 428.

501. (Voorn, Jacobus, *printer*), *A Catalogue Of all the cheifest Rarities In the Publick Theater and Anatomie-Hall Of the University of Leiden . . . sic erimus cuncti postquam nos auferet orcus,* Leiden, 1683 (a pamphlet of ten unnumbered pages) (*ed. princeps* 1669 ?); the British Museum *Catalogue* [67] lists 20 editions of the seventeenth and eighteenth centuries).

Vorenkamp, A. P. A. *See* Rotterdam, Museum Boymans . . ., 411.

502. Vossius, Gerardus Ioannes (1577–1649), "De Graphice, sive arte pingendi," *De quattuor artibus popularibus . . . libri tres,* Amsterdam, 1650, I, chap. v (§§ 1–60), pp. 61–92.

502a. ———, *De Imitatione, cum Oratoria, tum praecipue Poetica; deque Recitatione Veterum Liber,* Amsterdam, 1647.

502b. ———, *Opusculi varii argumenti, Opera,* IV, Amsterdam, 1698.

503. Waal, H. van de, *Drie eeuwen vaderlandsche geschieduitbeelding,* The Hague, 1952.

504. ———, "De Staalmeesters en hun legende," *Oud-Holland,* LXXI, ii, 1956, pp. 61–107.

505. ———, "The Iconological Background of Rembrandt's Civilis," *Konsthistorisk Tidskrift,* XXV, 1956, pp. 11–25.

506. Waetzoldt, Wilhelm, *Deutsche Kunsthistoriker,* II, Leipzig, 1924.

507. Wagenaar, Jan (1709–73), *Amsterdam in zyne Opkomst, Aanwas, Geschiedenissen, Voorregten, Koophandel, Gebouwen, Kerkenstaat, Schoolen, Schutterye, Gildenen, Regeeringe . . .,* Amsterdam, 1760, 1765, 1767.

508. ———, *Wagenaar's Beschryving van Amsterdam gevolgd, in eene geregelde Aanwyzing van de Sieraaden der Publieke Gebouwen dier Stad, zeer dienstig voor Alle Liefhebbers der Bouw-, Beeldhouw- en Schilderkunst en inzonderheid voor Vreemdelingen, die de merkwaardigste Byzonderheden en Konstsieraaden der Stads-Gebouwen, in een geregelde orde, willen bezigtigen,* Amsterdam, 1790.

509. Weale, W. H. James, *Gerard David . . .,* London, 1895.

510. Weitzmann, Kurt, "The Greek Sources of Islamic Scientific Illustrations," *Archaeologia Orientalia in Memoriam Ernst Herzfeld,* New York, 1952, pp. 244–66.

511. ———, "Die Illustration der Septuaginta," *Münchner Jahrbuch der bildenden Kunst,* Dritte Folge, III/IV, 1952/53, pp. 96–120.

512. Weixlgärtner, Arpad, "Von der Gliederpuppe," *Årstryck* (Göteborgs Konstmuseum), Göteborg, 1954, pp. 37–71.

513. Wernherr der Gartenaere (XIII c.), *Meier Helmbrecht,* ed. Leipzig (Reclam), 1878.

Wickersheim, Ernest. *See* Mundinus, 332; Guido da Vigevano, 199.

514. Wijbrands, C. N., *Het Amsterdamsche Tooneel van 1617–1772 . . .,* Utrecht, 1873.

515. Wijnman, H. F., "Rembrandt en Hendrick Uylenburgh te Amsterdam," *Amstelodamum* ("Rembrandtnummer"), XLIII, 1956, pp. 94–103.

516. Wind, Edgar, "The Criminal God . . .," *Journal of the Warburg Institute,* I, iii, 1938, pp. 243–48.

516a. Winkler, Friedrich, *Der Krakauer Behaim-Codex . . .,* Berlin, 1941.

517. Wither, George (1588–1667), *A Collection of Emblemes . . .,* London, 1635 (1634).

518. Wittkower, Rudolf, *The Artist & the Liberal Arts. An Inaugural Lecture. Delivered at University College London* (Jan. 30, 1950), London, 1952.

519. Wolf, Hugo, "Shakespeare und die Antike," *Antike und Abendland,* I, ix, 1946.

520. Wolf-Heidegger, Gerhard, "Vesals Basler Skeletpräparat aus dem Jahre 1543," *Verhandlungen der Naturforschenden Gesellschaft in Basel,* LV, 1944, pp. 211–34.

520a. *Woordenboek der Nederlandsche Taal,* I– [XVII], The Hague, etc., 1864–[1955, article "TRA"].

521. Worm, Ole (Olao) (1588–1654), *Museum Wormianum seu Historia Rerum Rariorum tam Naturalium, quam Artificialium, tam Domesticarum, quam exoticarum, quae Hafnia Danorum* [= Copenhagen] *in aedibus Authoris servantur . . .,* Leiden, 1655.

522. Worp, J.A., "Caspar van Baerle," *Oud-Holland,* V, 1887, pp. 93–125.
    Wtewael, Joachim. *See* Uytewael, Joachim, 482.

523. Wundt, Wilhelm, *Völkerpsychologie . . .,* IX, Leipzig, 1918.

524. [Young, Edward (1681–1765)], *Conjectures on Original Composition. In a Letter to the Author of Sir Charles Grandison, editiones principes* (2), London, 1759.

525. Young, John, and (continued by:) P. Henderson Aitken, *A Catalogue of the Manuscripts in the Library of the Hunterian Museum in the University of Glasgow,* Glasgow, 1908.

526. Zedler, Johann Heinrich (1706–63), *publisher* [authors: J.A. von Frankenstein, P.D. Longolius, and others], *Grosses vollständiges Universal-Lexicon aller Wissenschaften und Künste welche bishero durch menschlichen Verstand und Witz erfunden und verbessert worden . . .,* in 64 vols., Halle and Leipzig, 1732–[50].

527. Zerbis, Gabriele (Gerbi) de, *di Verona* (d. 1506), *Liber anathomie corporis humani et singulorum membrorum illius, . . .,* Venice, 1502.

528. Zeri, Federico, *La Galleria Spada in Roma. Catalogo dei dipinti,* Rome, [1954].

529. Zilsel, Edgar, *Die Entstehung des Geniebegriffes . . .,* Tübingen, 1926.

530. ———, "Copernicus and Mechanics," *Journal of the History of Ideas,* I, Jan. 1940, pp. 113–18.

531. ———, "The Origins of William Gilbert's Scientific Method," *Journal of the History of Ideas,* II, i, Jan. 1941, pp. 1–32.

532. Zuccaro, Federigo (1543–1609), *L'Idea de' Pittori, Scultori ed Architetti, diuisa in due libri,* Turin, 1607. *See also* Panofsky, E., "*Idea,*" 352, 353.

PLATES

Gratitude is expressed to the private owners and to the officers of museums and other institutions named in the captions of the plates who have graciously permitted the reproduction of works of art in their custody. Acknowledgment is also made to the following photographic agencies: Alinari (Pls. XXXIV–41, XL–48, XL–49); van Dijk (Pls. XLVI–55a, XLVII–56); Dingjan (Pls. I–1a, V–7, XLVIII–57, XLVIII–58); Frequin (Pls. VII–9, VIII–10, XII–16, XXV–32, XXVI–33, XLIV–53); Ver-Vrais (Pl. XXXIX–47).

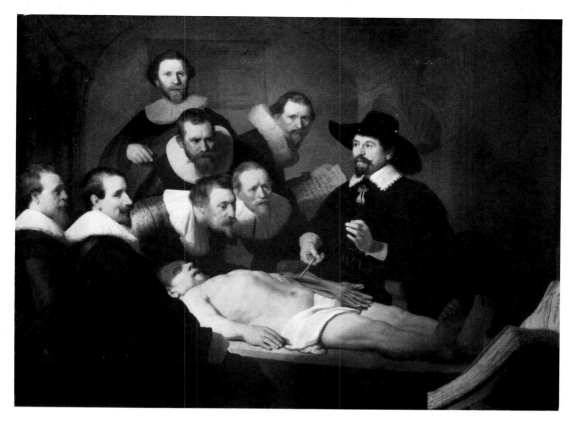

Pl. I–1a. Rembrandt Harmensz. van Rijn (1606–69), "The Annual Anatomy of Dr. Nicolaas Tulp. 1632," The Hague, Koninklijk Kabinet van Schilderijen, Mauritshuis (signed and dated 1632). (Dimensions: 162.5 × *ca*. 216.5 cm.)

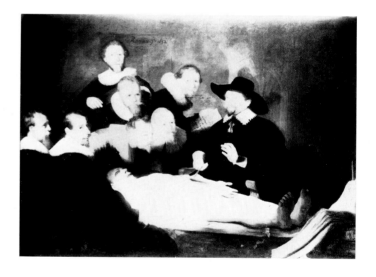

Pl. I–1b. Rembrandt van Rijn, "Anatomy of Dr. Nicolaas Tulp." Infrared photograph.

Pl. I–1c. Rembrandt van Rijn, "Anatomy of Dr. Nicolaas Tulp" (Guildmembers Numbers 7 and 8 omitted). Retouched photograph.

Pl. II–2a.   Salomon Saverij (d. 1653), "Entry into Amsterdam of the Queen Dowager of France." Engraving, folding plate, after Jan Martsen de Jonge (d. 1647) illustrating Barlaeus[30] (August 1638).

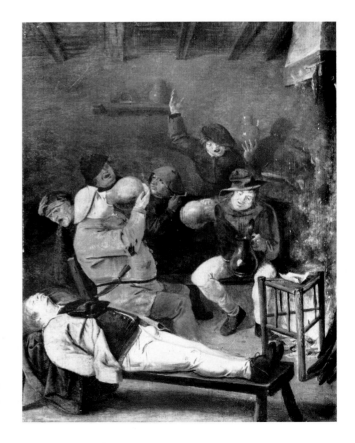

Pl. II–2b.   Adriaen Brouwer (ca. 1605–38), "Drunken Peasants in an Inn," Rotterdam, Museum Boymans (ante 1632).

Pl. III–3. Willem Buytewech (ca. 1591–1624), "An Anatomical Demonstration at Leiden." Drawing, light-brown washes, Rotterdam, Museum Boymans (ca. 1616).

Pl. III–4. "The Anatomical Theater, Leiden, as a *Kunst- und Wunderkammer*." Engraving by Willem Swanenburgh (1581–1612) after J.C. Woudanus (van't Woudt) (1570–1615). Leiden, Akademisch Historisch Museum (1616).

VERA ANATOMIÆ LUGDUNO-BATAVÆ CUM SCELETIS ET RELIQVIS QVÆ IBI EXTANT DELINEATIO.

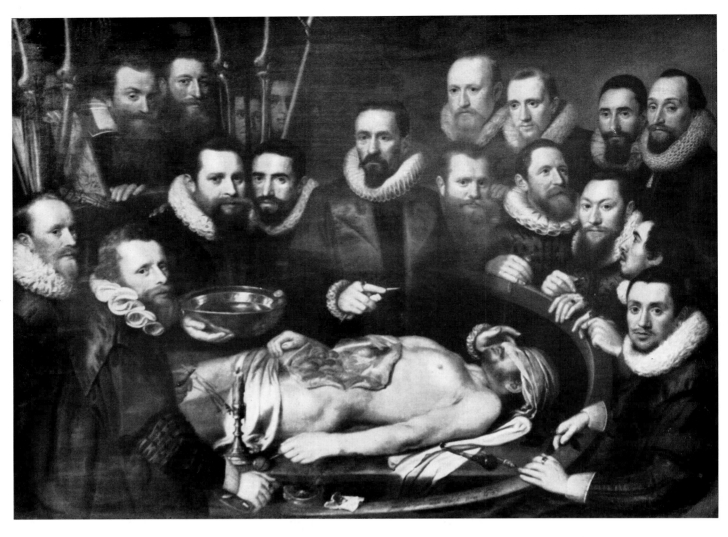

Pl. IV–6. Michiel Jansz. van Miereveld (1567–1641), executed by Pieter Michielsz. van Miereveld *(filius)* (1595?–1623), "Anatomy of Dr. W. van der Meer," Delft, Oude- en Nieuwe Gasthuis. Inscription: "Michaël à Miereveld delineavit: filius vero ejus Petrus praescripto Patris pinxit Delph. Batav. 1617."

Pl. IV–5. Aert Pietersz. *(ca.* 1550–1612), "Anatomy of Dr. Sebastian Egbertsz.," Amsterdam, Rijksmuseum (1603).

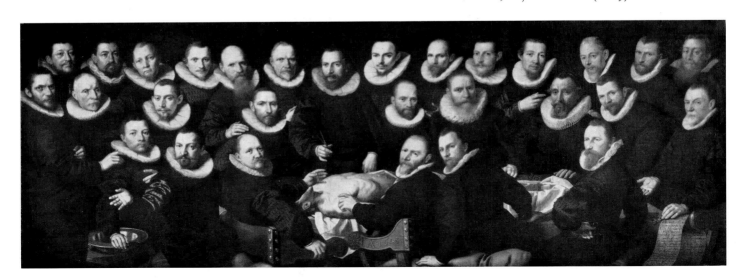

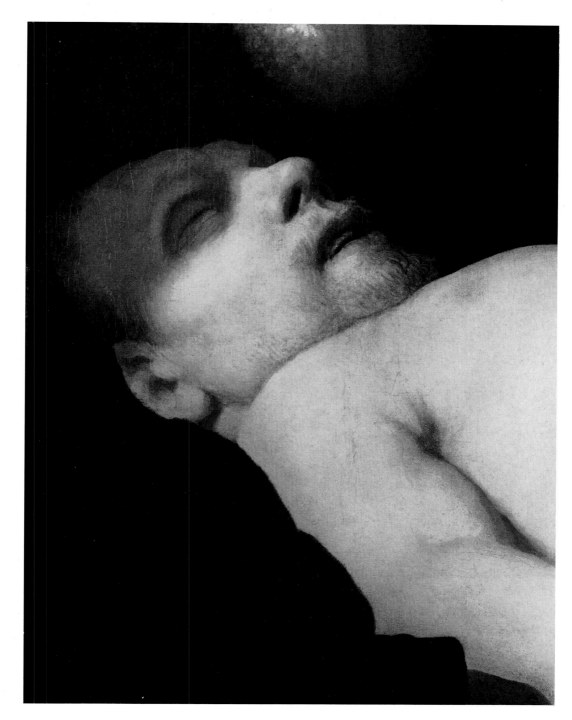

Pl. V–7.   Rembrandt van Rijn, "Anatomy of Dr. Nicolaas
Tulp (the Head of Aris Kindt)." Detail of Pl. I–1a.

Pl. VI–8. "Didactic Anatomy." Miniature illustrating Guy de Chauliac, *Inventarium*, Paris, Bibliothèque Nationale, Manuscript français 396,[305m] fol. 6 *verso* (early 15th century).

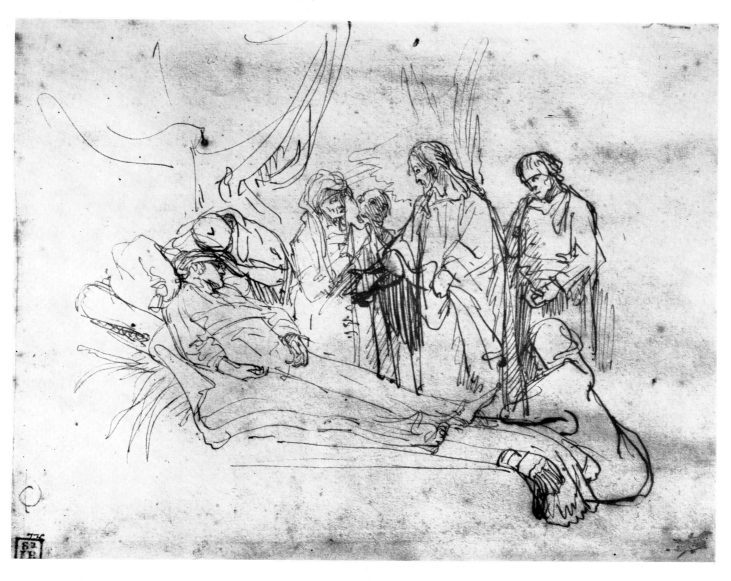

Pl. VII–9. Rembrandt van Rijn, "Raising of the Daughter of Jairus." Drawing, pen and bistre, Rotterdam, Museum Boymans, formerly Coll. F. Koenigs (*ca.* 1632/33).

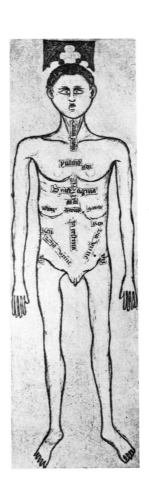

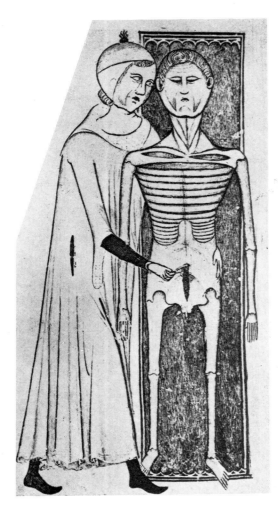

Pl. VIII–11. Guido da Vigevano (ca. 1280–after 1345) (or copy after), "Anothomia per figuras designata." First two figures of Manuscript Chantilly, Musée Condé, 334,[199] fol. 257 (ca. 1345).

Pl. VIII–10. Nicolaes Eliasz. Pickenoy (1591–ca. 1656), "Anatomy of Dr. Joan Fonteyn." Fragment, Amsterdam, Rijksmuseum (1625).

A dextris spectantur
ad Tabulatum Conclavis
parandis sceletis destinati.

1. Sceleton humanum.
2. Tab Musculor subcutane
3. Tab Venae Cavae per Corpus
disseminatae.
4. Tab partium seri evacuatio
ni et seminis ejaculationi dicata
5. Tab Viscerum Vitalium et
Naturalium.
6. Tab Viscerum Equi vivi
dissecti, cujus sceleton in Bibliotheca asservatur.
7. Sceleton Canis Venatici.
8. Scel Lupi et Cap Apri.
9. Sceleton Cervi.
10. Scel. Lyncis.
11. Scel. Vulpis.
12. Scel. Cati sylvestris.
13. Scel. Leporis.
14. Scel. Accipitris.
Post dorsum Anatomici.
15. Scel. recens nati Inf
16. Scel. Vituli bicipitis.
17. Scel. monstrosi foetus
humani sine Cerebro et
Calvaria nati.
18. Sceleton Talpae.

A Sinistris ad Tabula
tum Conclavis rebus
aquis purgandis parati

1. Statua Corporis huma
ni membratim composite
2. Tab Nervorum Cerebri
prolongati et Vasorum
Lymphaticorum.
3. Tab Venar et Arteriar
conjunctarum.
4. Tab partiū Conceptioni
vacantium.
5. Tab Venae Portae et Vasor
pulmonalium.
6. Sceleton Ursi.
7. Sceleta Catulorum.
8. Scel. Sciurorum.
9. Scel Martis sylvestri
10. Scel Erinacei terres
tri
11. Scel. Carpŷ
12. Scel. Ciconiae senioris
Viperinum rostro exhibens
13. Scel. Arietis.
14. Scel. Aquilae.
15. Scel. Taxi.
16. Scel. Testudinis mari,,
nae majoris.
17. Scel. Testudinis pa,,
lustris vulgaris.
18. Scel. Ciconiae junio
ris Caeciliae ossa rostro tenentis

Non ego sum Veterum, non assecla, juro, Novorum
sive Vetus verum, deligo, sive novum.
Idq, docens monstro hic cunctis queis publica Virtus
Corporis humani est sanguinis integritas.

Nec curo partes illaesas, totus in illo, ut
Certa salus populo, gloria sitq, DEO.
Sanguis cum vivat vitali seminis aura,
Ex ejus flamma viscera quaeq, probo M.H.D.

Pl. IX–12. "Anatomical Demonstration of Dr. Moritz Hoffmann Celebrating the Opening of the Anatomical Theater at
Altorf." Etching (dated 1650).

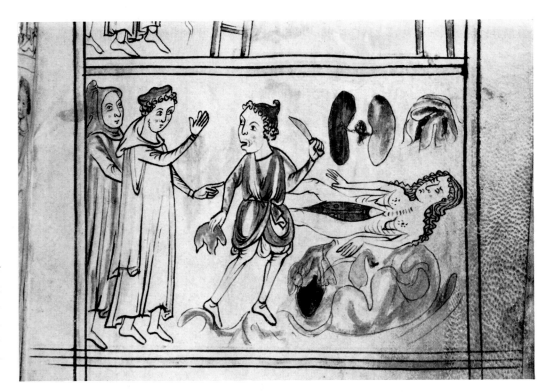

Pl. X–13b. "Knights Attending the Ceremonial Anatomy of a Female." Miniature, Glasgow, Hunterian Library, Manuscript 9,[305f] fol. 22 *recto* (late 15th century).

Pl. X–13a. "Post-Mortem of a Noble Lady." Figure Six of a continuous series of illustrations, Oxford, Bodleian Library, Manuscript Ashmole 399,[305i] fol. 34 *recto* (13th century).

Pl. XI–14. "The Visceral Lecture Delivered by Barber-Surgeon Master John Banister Aged 48." Miniature in oils (mounted on two facing leaves), Glasgow, Hunterian Library, Manuscript V.1.1.[305e] (dated 1581).

Pl. XII–15. "Public Anatomy (?)." Fresco, Rome, catacomb off the Via Latina (Via Dino Compagni). Discovered April 1956; Commissione Pontificale di Archeologia Sacra, Rome. (4th century A.D.) *(ca.* 200 × 150 cm.)

Pl. XII–16. Rembrandt van Rijn, "Anatomy of Dr. Joan Deyman." Fragment since 1723. Amsterdam, Rijksmuseum (signed and dated 1656). (100 × 134 cm.)

Pl. XIII–17.   Dionysius Padtbrugge (b. Amsterdam 1629;
Sweden 1672 and 1676), "Olaf Rudbeck Flanked by Ancient
Authorities Anatomizes the Map of Scandinavia in Search
of Atlantis." Frontispiece of Rudbeck, *Atlantica*,[413]
(1675 ff.).

Pl. XIV–18.   Ascribed to Joannes Stephan, *van Calcar* (1499–*ca.* 1546), "Andreas Vesalius as Anatomist of Arm and Hand." Woodcut illustrating Vesalius, *Fabrica,*[490] (dated 1542).

Pl. XV–19. Leandro da Ponte (Bassano) (1557–1622), "The Anatomist Bontius Leo (originally Andreas Vesalius?)," Schwerin, Gemäldegalerie.

Pl. XVI–20. "Anatomical Theater at Padua (1594)."
Design attributed to Fra Paolo (Pietro Sarpi, 1552–1623).
Photograph of present state, restored.

Pl. XVII–21. "The Anatomist Giulio Casserio (1561–1616)."
Engraving.

Pl. XVIII–22. "Entombment of Christ," Châlons-sur-Marne, Notre Dame de l'Épine (late 15th century).

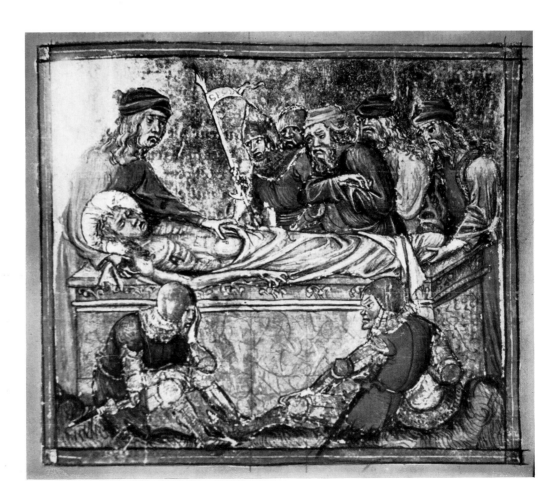

Pl. XVIII–23. "Entombment of Christ." Miniature illustrating Guillaume de Deguileville, *Songe du pèlerinage,*[120] Manuscript Brussels, Bibliothèque Royale, fol. 282 *recto* (Bruges, *ca.* 1395).

Pl. XIX–24. Ascribed to Andrea del Verrocchio (1436–1488), "The Deathbed of Francesca Pitti Tornabuoni." Right half of a marble relief, Florence, Bargello (*ca.* 1477).

Pl. XIX–25. "The Death of Meleager." Drawing after Roman Sarcophagus (right half), Veste Coburg, HZ II (Codex Coburgiensis) (early 16th century).

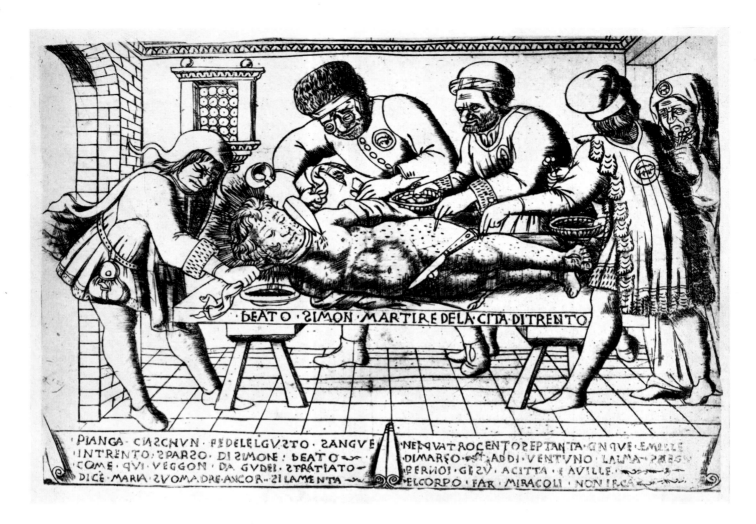

Pl. XX–26. "Martyrdom of Little St. Simon of Trent."
Italian engraving (Florence [?], *ca.* 1475–85).

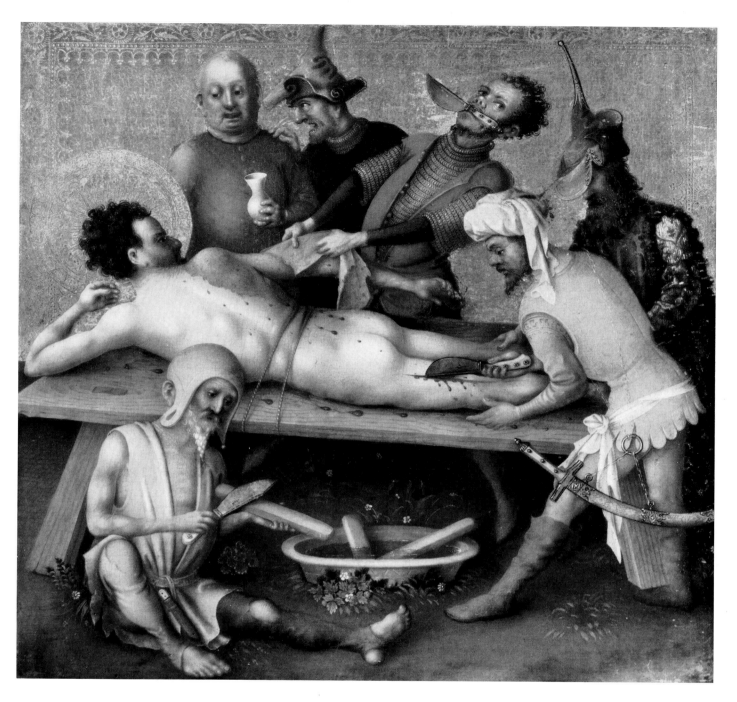

Pl. XXI–27.   Stefan Lochner (d. 1451), "Martyrdom of St. Bartholomew," Frankfort o. M., Städelsches Kunstinstitut *(ca.* 1430).

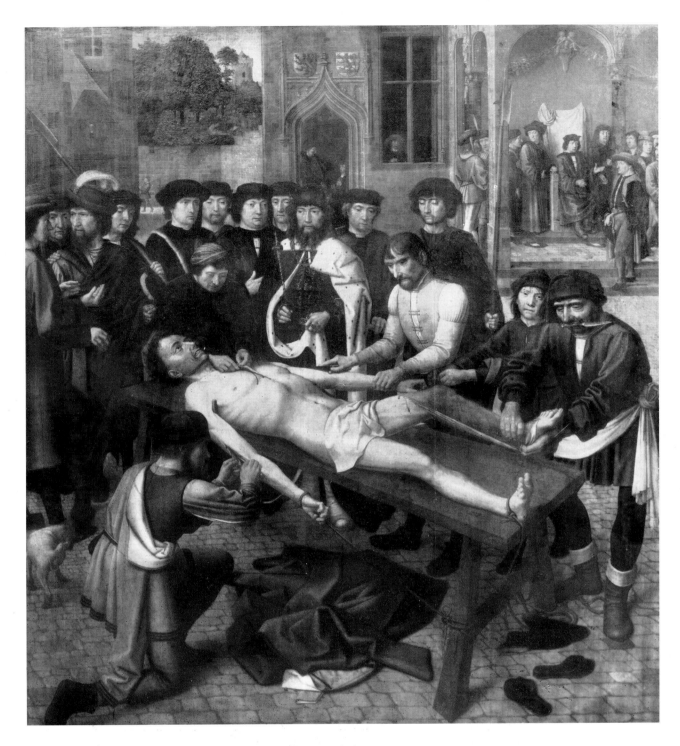

Pl. XXII–28. Gerard David (d. 1523), "Flaying of the Unjust Judge." Second of two Justice panels, Bruges, Musée Communal, formerly City Hall (dated 1498).

Pl. XXIII–29. Remoldus (Rombout) Eynhoudts (1613–1679/80), "Inthronization of the Son of Sisamnes on His Father's Skin," New York, Metropolitan Museum of Art. Copy after P. P. Rubens (1577–1640). (Original formerly at Bruges, City Hall; lost 1695.)

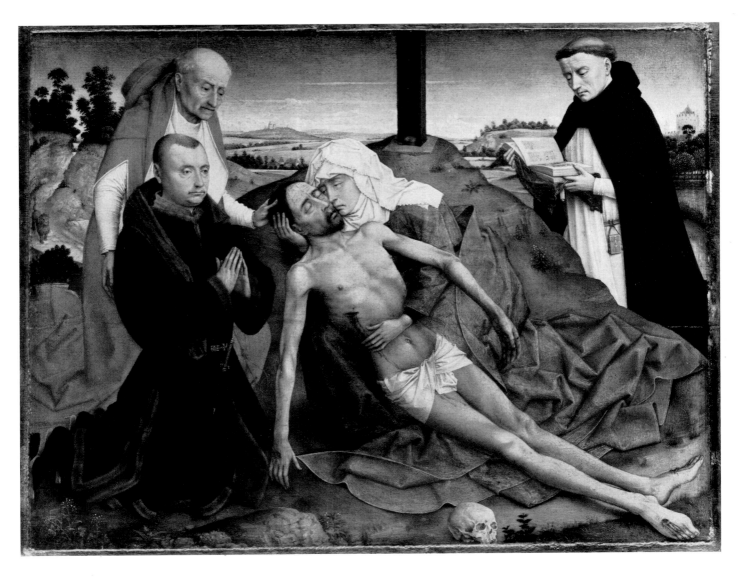

Pl. XXIV–30. Rogier van der Weyden (1399–1464),
"Pietà," London, National Gallery, formerly Coll. Earl
of Powis *(ca.* 1450).

Pl. XXV–31. Rembrandt van Rijn, "Pietà." Drawing, pen and ink and washes, Lake Constance, Wessenberg-Galerie, Brandes Collection.

Pl. XXV–32. Rembrandt van Rijn, "Family Group," Brunswick, Herzog Anton Ulrich-Museum (ca. 1668).

Pl. XXVI–33.   Maerten van Heemskerck (1498–1574),
"Family Group," Cassel, Staatliche Kunstsammlungen
(*ante* 1532).

Pl. XXVII–34. Rembrandt van Rijn, "Ecce homo!"
Etching (dated 1635–36) (L. Müntz,[328] II, No. 204/IV).

Pl. XXVIII–35. Lucas van Leyden (1494–1533), "Ecce homo!" Engraving (B. 71) (dated 1510).

Pl. XXIX–36. Rembrandt van Rijn, "Ecce homo!"
Drypoint (signed and dated—from State IV on—1655)
(L. Müntz,[328] II, No. 235/I).

Pl. XXX–37.   Rembrandt van Rijn, "Ecce homo!" Drypoint (1655) (L. Müntz,[323] II, No. 235/VII).

Pl. XXXI–38.   Rembrandt van Rijn, "Danae," Leningrad, Eremitage (signed and dated 1636). (185 × 203 cm.)

Pl. XXXII–39. Tiziano Vecelli (1477–1576), "Danae,"
Madrid, Prado (No. 425) *(ca.* 1553). (129 × 186 cm.)

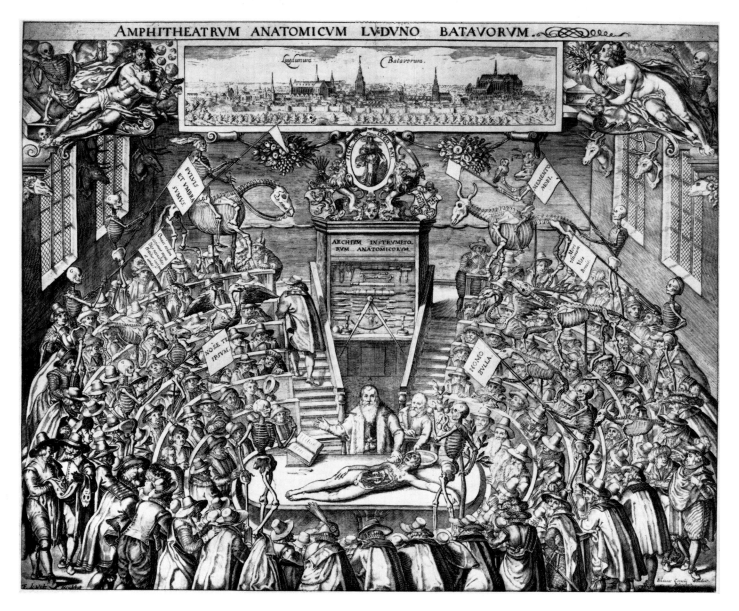

Pl. XXXIII–40. "Anatomy of Dr. Paaw at Leiden."
Engraving by F. de Wit *(fl.* 1650) after J. C. Woudanus
(van 't Woudt) (1570–1615).

Pl. XXXIV-41. Michelangelo Buonarroti (1475–1564),
"The Last Judgment (detail: St. Bartholomew Among the
Elect)." Fresco, Vatican, Sistine Chapel (*ca.* 1540/41).

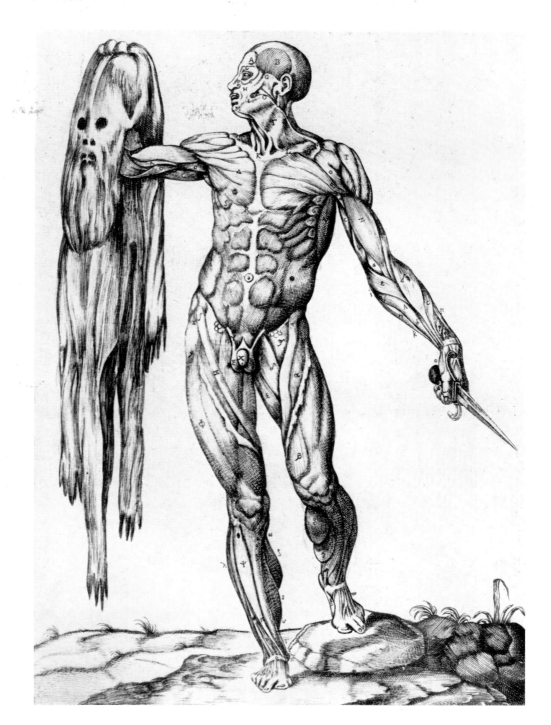

Pl. XXXV–42. Gasparo Becerra *(ca.* 1520–70), "Muscle Man Holding His Own Skin." Engraving illustrating Valverde, *Historia,*[485] Tav. I, Lib. II, p. 64 (1560).

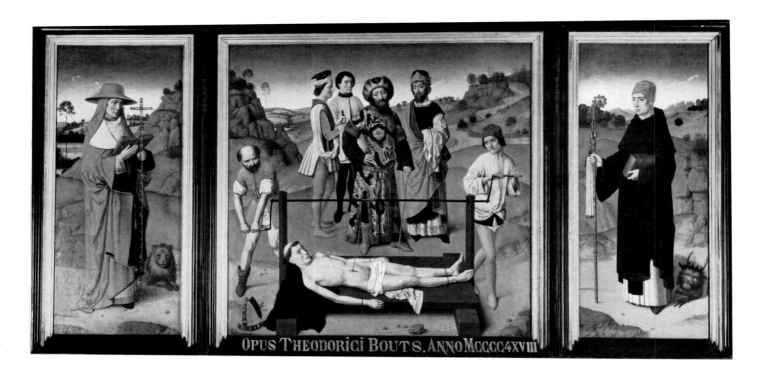

Pl. XXXVI–43a. Dirk Bouts *(ca.* 1410–75), "Martyrdom of
St. Erasmus." Triptych, Louvain, St. Peter's Church.

Pl. XXXVI–43b. Erasmus Master, "Martyrdom of St. Erasmus." German engraving, Nuremberg, Germanisches Na-
tional-Museum (Inv. K 194, Kapsel 96) (mid-15th century)
(Lehr III, No. 84).

Pl. XXXVII–44. Jan Steen (1626–79), "Christ at the Age of Twelve in the Temple," Basel, Kunstmuseum, Öffentliche Kunstsammlung (Inv. No. 906).

Pl. XXXVIII–45. "Four Philosophers Dressed in the Himation Standing in Front of Shell-Topped Niches." Asiatic sarcophagus of the arcade type (front), fragment, Bari, S. Nicola (3d century A.D.).

Pl. XXXVIII–46. William Hogarth (1697–1764), "The Lawyer Consulted by Hudibras." Engraving illustrating Samuel Butler, *Hudibras,*[79] III, Canto iii (1726).

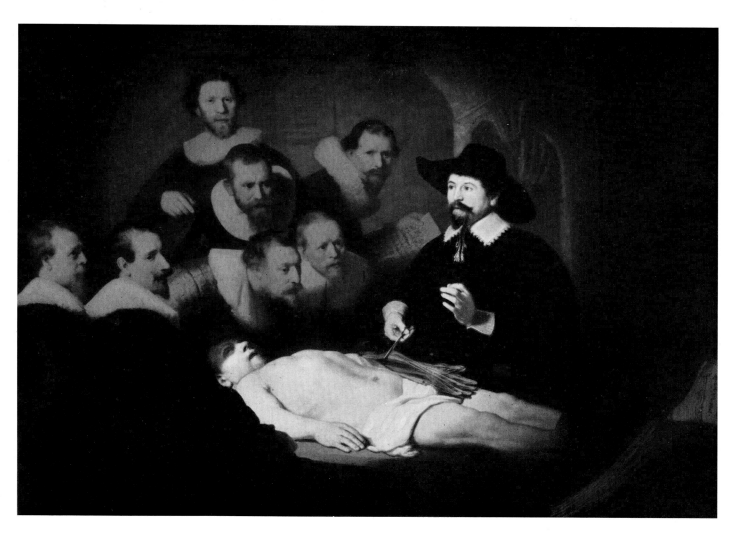

Pl. XXXIX–47. Rembrandt van Rijn, "Anatomy of Dr. Nicolaas Tulp." Retouched photograph (Dr. Tulp and Aris Kindt emphasized).

Pl. XL–48.   "Sepulchral   Shell-Foil Monument of a
Lady with the Cortège of Neptune." Roman sarcophagus
(front), Siena, Museo dell'Opera (Istituto Archeologico
Germanico, Rome) (No. 136) (4th century A.D.).

Pl. XL–49.   Filippino Lippi (1457–1504), "Triumph of
St. Thomas Aquinas." Fresco, Rome, S. Maria-sopra-Mi-
nerva (Caraffa Chapel) (1489).

Pl. XLI–50. Andrea da Fiesole (1465–1526), "Marsilio
Ficino." Marble bust, Florence, Cathedral *(ca.* 1521).

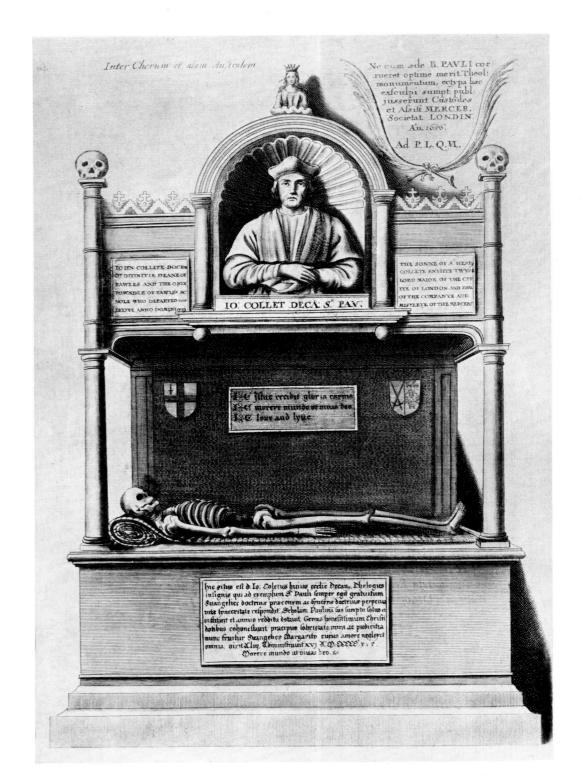

Pl. XLII–51. "Tomb Memorial of Dr. John Colet," London, St. Paul's Cathedral (destroyed 1666). Engraving by Daniel King (d. 1664), after the monument ascribed to Pietro Torrigiano (1492–1528), illustrating William Dugdale, *The History*,[130] (1658). (Engraving dated September 1641.)

Pl. XLIII–52. "Offices of the Dead." Miniature from
Livre d'Heures, Manuscript Coll. Jehan Siraudin, Mâcon,[305h] fol. 91 *recto (ca.* 1480).

ALIIS INSERVIENDO
CONSVMOR

Pl. XLIV–53. Nicolaes Eliasz. Pickenoy (1591–*ca.* 1656),
"Nicolaus Tulpius," Amsterdam, Coll. The Six Foundation, Six House (dated 1634).

Dienende teer ick uyt. SERVIENDO CONSUMOR

Pour servir ie meurs.

Pl. XLV–54. "Serviendo Consumor." Engraving illustrating P. C. Hooft, *Emblemata amatoria*,[236] XII, p. 35
(1611).

Pl. XLVI–55a. Janus Lutma, Sr. (1584–1669) (or Jr.?), "Goblet Shaped as a Tulip." Silver gilt, Coll. Jhr Ir Six van Wimmenum, Laren (formerly Dr. Tulp and Guild of Barber-Surgeons, Amsterdam). (Date mark "x" = 1652.) (Total height 31 cm.)

Pl. XLVI–55b. "The Goblet." Detail of Pl. XLVI–55a (1652).

Pl. XLVII–56. "Admirael de France. 200 guldens."
Dutch watercolor of Tulip Book, Manuscript, fol. 47, Coll.
Jhr Ir Six van Wimmenum, Laren (first half 17th century).

Pl. XLVIII–57. Rembrandt van Rijn, "Anatomy of Dr. Nicolaas Tulp (The Pseudo-Roll Call)." Detail of Pl. I–1a.

Pl. XLVIII–58. Rembrandt van Rijn, "Anatomy of Dr. Nicolaas Tulp (Dissected Arm and Hand)." Detail of Pl. I–1a.

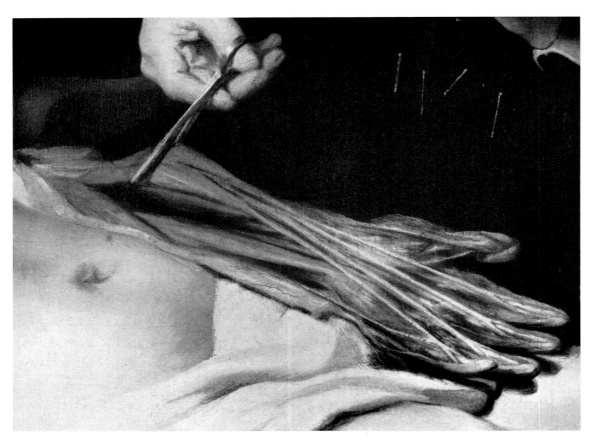

INDEX

Index entries cover primarily the main text and refer to the notes only where they introduce matter not in the text. The bibliography is not indexed. Abbreviations: n., nn. = Note(s), pp. 123–78; Fig(s). = Figure(s), pp. 12–121; Pl(s). = Plate(s), pp. 221 ff.

Horace, 63, n. 201
Houbraken, A., n. 148
Howard, Charles, 61
Howard, Th., Earl of Arundel, n. 3
"Hudibras." See: Hogarth, "Hudibras"
humanists
    aversion to book illustration, 62
    portrait of humanist, 119, Pl. XLI–50
    See also: Vesalius as humanist
Huygens, C., 6, 21f., nn. 21, 137, 143,
    220

Ignatius of Loyola, 45
    post-mortem of, n. 55
Ignorance, 57f.
illustrations, anatomical, pirated, n. 109.
        See also: anatomical illustrations
"Illustre School." See: Amsterdam,
    Athenaeum
imitatio, 81, 82, 92–95, 97
    four kinds, n. 152
    theory of, 83
    Vesalii, 73f.
    See also: *exempla*
incisor. See: barber-surgeon
ingenium. See: artist as imitator; gen-
    ius
initials, 50, 67, 100, Figs. 8, 18
Innocent III, n. 201
Innocent VIII, n. 148
instruments
    anatomical, 43f., Fig. 6
    of martyrdom, Fig. 15
intaglio workers, n. 97
"Invention of the True Cross," 100f.
Isidore of Seville, n. 92

Jacopone da Todi, 105f.
Janson, H.W., 51, 100
Jantzen, H., 67
Jena, anatomical theater, 105
Jerome, St., Fig. 20
Jesus, Society of, 53
Jews, as tormentors, n. 157. See also:
    anti-Semitism
John the Baptist, 118
Joyce, James, 121
"Judgment of Cambyses," in Leiden's
    anatomical theater, 90. See also:
    David, "Notabile"
Junius, F., 3f., 6f., 16f., 19, 23, 39f.,
    65, 83, 94, 97, nn. 149, 152
jurisprudence and anatomy, n. 23
Justice Pictures, as prototypes of the
    anatomies, 88–90

Kalkoen, M., No. 6 in Rembrandt's
    "Anatomy," 190
Kassel. See: Cassel
Kauffmann, H., n. 135
Kerner, Justinus, 29
Kernodle, G., nn. 31, 59
Ketham, J. de, 46–49, 70, 117, Fig. 7
    influences Hogarth, 103, cf. Figs. 7,
        19
    influences Rembrandt's "Anatomy,"
        46, 92
Kindt, Aris, object of Rembrandt's
    "Anatomy," 36, 71, 115, 120f.,
    191; for details: Pls. V–7, XLVIII–
    58
King, D., Pl. XLII–51
Kint, het. See: Kindt, Aris
Kircher, A., n. 191
"Know Thyself," 98, 112–14, nn. 144,
    218
    as aim of anatomy, 14, Fig. 1b
    through anatomy, 111–15, nn. 218,
        220
Knox, Dr., n. 180
Koenigs, F., Collection, Pl. VII–9
Koloff, E., n. 166
Konink, Ph. de, "Sleeping Venus,"
    n. 41
Koolvelt, J., No. 7 in Rembrandt's
    "Anatomy," 18, 40, 191, nn. 1, 48
Korvei, monastery, n. 144
Koster, M. J., 189
Kunst- und Wunderkammern, nn. 97, 191
    (i). See also: anatomical museums;
    anatomical theater, as museum

Lactantius, 56
Laegh, W. v.d., "Theater at Amster-
    dam," n. 228
"Lamentation of Christ," as prototype
    of the anatomies, 86f., Pl. XVIII–
    23
Landino, C., 63
Laocoon group, 51
Laren (N.H.). See: Six, Jhr.
Lastman, P., teaches Rembrandt, 19
laude, 105f.
Laurentius, A., 70
LeBlon, M., 92
lectus funebris, classical, prototype of
    Renaissance anatomical table,
    n. 155
Leeuwarden, Westfriesch Museum,
    n. 163
Legenda aurea, 87f.

legends, saints', and anatomy, 87f.
Leiden
    Akademisch Historisch Museum, Pl.
        III–4
    Amsterdam-Leiden controversy, 115,
        n. 211
    anatomical museum, nn. 163, 191
    anatomical theater, 31, 184–87, nn.
        28, 45, 128, Fig. 2, Pls. III–3,
        4, XXXIII–40
    known to Rembrandt, 97f.
    as *Kunst- und Wunderkammer*, 97f.
    as museum, 90
    auditorium medicum, 98
    Falijde-Begijnen Church, 31, 184
    Rijksprentenkabinet, Fig. 2,
        Pl. XXXIII–40
    University, 26, 76
Leningrad, Eremitage, 67, n. 8, Pl.
    XXXI–38
"Leo, Bontius," Pl. XV–19
Leonardo da Vinci, 42, 45, 50, 64, 80,
    108, n. 101
    as "pittore anatomista," 60f.
Levanti, A., n. 191
lex talionis, 100ff.
Leyden, L. v.
    "Ecce homo!" 93f., Pl. XXVIII–35
    fame in 17th century, n. 166
    Rembrandt uses a composition by,
        93f., cf. Pls. XXVIII–35, XXIX–
        36, XXX–37
Leyden (city of). See: Leiden
liberal arts. See: arts, mechanical and
    liberal
light, 36–38
likundu. See: folklore and anatomy
Lippi, Filippino, "Triumph of St.
    Thomas," 119, Pl. XL–49
liver, 49, Pl. X–13a
    investigation of, 23
    as seat of anger, 29
lizard, 74f., Pl. XLVI–55a
Lochner, S., "Martyrdom of St. Bar-
    tholomew," 87f., Pl. XXI–27
Loenen, F. v., No. 8 in Rembrandt's
    "Anatomy," 18, 40, 191, nn. 1, 48
Loevestein, Castle, 95
London
    anatomical theater, Fig. 19, Pl. XI–
        14. See also: London, St. Bar-
        tholomew's
    British Museum
        Department of Manuscripts, Cod.
            Add. 10546, n. 155